Encyclopaedia on Tagore and Contemporary Thinkers

Encyclopaedia on Tagore and Contemporary Thinkers

(Vol. 1)

Avinash Kumar Jha

KUNAL BOOKS

New Delhi-110002 , India

KUNAL BOOKS
4596/1A, First Floor,
11, Daryaganj, New Delhi-110002
Phones: 011-30125412, 9811043697
E-mail: *Kunalbooks@gmail.com*

Encyclopaedia on Tagore and Contemporary Thinkers

First Published 2011

ISBN - 978-93-80752-13-6

Published in India by Prem Singh Bisht for Kunal Books, and printed at **Asian Offset Press**, Delhi.

PREFACE

Rabindranath Tagore also known as Gurudev, was a Bengali poet, philosopher, religious thinker and intellectual leader, artist, playwright, composer, educationalist and novelist whose works reshaped Bengali literature and music in the late nineteenth and early twentieth centuries. A celebrated cultural icon in India, he became Asia's first Nobel laureate when he won the 1913 Nobel Prize in Literature. He is regarded as a towering cultural figure in all Bengali-speaking regions.

Tagore was not only a creative genius; he was a great man and friend to many. For instance, he was also a good friend from childhood to the great Indian Physicist, Bose. He was educated and quite knowledgeable of Western culture, especially Western poetry and Science. This made him a remarkable person, one of the first of our planet to combine East and West, and ancient and modern knowledge. Tagore had a good grasp of modern - post-Newtonian - physics, and was well able to hold his own in a debate with Einstein in 1930 on the newly emerging principles of quantum mechanics and chaos. His meetings and tape recorded conversations with his contemporaries such Albert Einstein and H.G. Wells, stand as cultural landmarks, and show the brilliance of this great man. Although Tagore is a superb representative of his country - India - the man who wrote its national anthem - his life and works go far beyond his country. He is truly a man of the whole Earth, a product of the best of both traditional Indian, and modern Western cultures. The School of Wisdom is proud to have him as part of its heritage.

In India, Rabindranath Tagore has transcended, as often happens in the Indian paradigm, the simple position of a writer-philosopher. Especially among bodies, he is revered as a Guru. Since great thinkers, who are often religious in their purview, are seen as gurus and close to Bhagavan (God) by Hindus, Rabindranath Tagore is especially revered. Hindus believe that by listening to the words of such wise and enlightened men, people are brought closer to Bhagavan. For this reason, he is affectionately known as Gurudeb (or Gurudev in Hindi), which means, literally, Teacher-God.

During his lifetime, Rabindranath Tagore was a towering and epochal figure of legendary proportions not only within the bounds of his native Bengal, or his beloved India, but to a considerable extent, throughout the world. As a multifaceted genius and renaissance-man par excellence, he not only carried the literature and arts of Bengal, virtually single-handedly, to dizzying heights of creativity, but, by his inspiring words, his lyrically unequalled songs, his unstinting support for the cause of India's freedom during a long and turbulent phase of her history, he lifted Indian culture and the Indian psyche to an unprecedented level of revitalization.

Contents

1

Introduction

Rabindranath Tagore, the creator of our National Anthem "Jana Gana Mana" which inspired millions of Indians to fight for Independence, still rekindles in us the same spirit of daring, of joining the great cause of freedom. Into the old, renowned and highly respected family, Rabindranath was born, between half past two and three early in the morning on Monday, May 7, 1861, in the Jorasanko mansion in Calcutta. He was his parents' fourteenth and last child. Although his mother died when he was very young, the life of his nationalist father inspired him greatly. He expressed the sentiments of his countrymen through poems, songs, essays, speeches and plays since the tender age.

Only for a very little while did Tagore receive regular schooling outside his home. He attended the Oriental Seminary and later the Bengal Academy for a few days. But their uncongenial atmosphere wearied him; he turned his back on schools for ever. In 1874 - his thirteenth year - he studied at St.Xavier's High School for a while; but he was never a regular pupil of any institution whatever. Educating himself under private tutors only, he became proficient in Bengali, Sanskrit, English, History, Mathematics and Science.

He began to write when he was just eight and his work appeared in print before he was 15. He was greatly inspired by Bankim Chandra Chatterjee's Bangadarshan. Rabindranath was sent to England to become a barrister. Instead he found solace in studying French and German to read some of the poets of these languages in original. His compelling interest in literature developed him into a versatile artist.

POET OF THE PEOPLE

Calamities in his personal life made a permanent impact on his sensitive mind. He lost his beloved wife in 1902 and the same year he lost his second daughter and, very soon, one of his sons. But he overcame his sufferings quickly and let his feelings show the way through poetry to bring hope and solace to other people. Tagore's fertile poetry assumed many forms but he was the master of short poems which could be set to music and sung by villagers and the boatmen on the Ganga.

In his verses he expressed his desire to amalgamate himself with the humanity at large by communicating with it in its own language. While helping to manage his family estate, young Rabindranath came into deep contact with the labourers. He understood the needs and difficulties of the peasants. This exposure gave a new turn to his thinking. He conceived that the problem of India was social rather than civil or political. The earliest glimpses of his deep love for humanity is 'Kadi O Kamal' where he expresses his desire "not to leave the beautiful world" and preferred to live among the ordinary people.

'Katha O Kahani' consists of a number of poems which bear eloquent testimony to the poet's sympathy for the oppressed. Through *Gitanjali*, Tagore warns people not to look down upon any one as inferior. There are references to the plight of the struggling humanity in Patraput, Senjuti and Prantik. The partition of Bengal in 1905 shook him to the roots. Tagore marched through the streets of Calcutta reciting his poem "Rakhi" with Tilak and Aurobindo for a holy mass dip in the Ganga and tied rakhi to the people as a symbol of the unbreakable unity of Bengal.

The orator in the poet was roused. The partition found him in the vortex of political turmoil in the country. By this time Tagore had attained popularity as a poet in Bengal. But it was *Gitanjali*, written between 1907-1910, that brought him world fame. In 1913, the Nobel Prize came his way as the acknowledgement of his being a world poet when the English version of *Gitanjali* translated by the poet himself, reached all over. He was the first Asian to attain this distinction and it was the first time when a poet who wrote in an entirely "foreign" language was awarded by the Royal Swedish Academy.

A NATIONALIST TO THE CORE

The fundamental tenet of Tagore's political philosophy was self-reliance. It is by taking his stand on this principle that he first made a place for the Bengali language in political discourses. He had to face much criticism to establish that the country's affairs must be discussed in its own languages only. The revolutionary idea of the mother tongue as the medium of instruction was his brain child. Rabindranath was the intellectual leader of the Swadeshi Movement. As early as in 1904, the poet drew up a complete scheme for the reorganisation of villages with the revival of cottage industries to help remove poverty.

His idea of national regeneration through a comprehensive scheme of rural reconstruction is his signal contribution to constructive politics. His well-known work Swadeshi Samaj was published in 1904. To arouse patriotic feelings among the youth, he wrote and composed many songs. They had been tuned in the baul style. One of his most popular numbers "Ekla Chalo Re" was composed during this period. Tagore composed the National Anthem "Jana Gana Mana" in 1912 and sang it first at his residence in the presence of Gandhiji, Tilak, Pandit Madan Mohan Malviya, Lajpat Rai and others. In 1920, Gandhiji started non-cooperation movement.

It was Rabindranath who first conceived the idea of using only Indian goods and discard the foreign ones. Many of his other ideas concerning social uplift were translated into practice by Gandhiji. He asked national leaders to concentrate on the inferior rural India as the villages alone held the key to the country"s progress. He visualised this years before it was accepted as a national policy by the country's leaders. Tagore was an ardent votary of internationalism. To put his idea of universal humanity into practice, he started a university, Vishva Bharati, on December 23, 1921 - a unique centre of learning where one could train oneself as a citizen of the world. A number of scholars from Britain and Harvard came to join Tagore.

Since his childhood, Tagore was very much influenced by the baul - the folk devotional songs of Bengal. The feeling behind these mystic songs had led him to compose his poems at the tender age of 13. The 1886 Congress session in Calcutta, began with a song which Tagore had himself composed. Irr 1896 he set it to music and sang Bankim Chandra's "Vande Matram" which was to be the rallying point of patriotic fervour. He also introduced a new note in Indian music.

His songs gave expression to the moods of the flowing moments of life.He solemnised the union between the lyric and the melody. His music captured the hearts of millions in the form of Rabindra Sangeet. He composed more than two thousand poems. In the last decade of his life, Tagore suddenly took to painting. About 3,000 pieces of his art are still preserved in his home and at Shanti Niketan. Tagore's mind was ever alert and he kept his interests and his amazing talents alive till the very end.

The end came on August 7, 1941 in the same old Jorasanko house where he had first opened his eyes eighty years and three months ago. His death marked the end of an era. Tagore would always be remembered for his poems, short stories, plays, novels and music. In all these spheres, he occupies the highest place in Bengali literature. But, above all, he was a prince among patriots. India is proud to have its national anthem composed by the great poet of this century. Vast changes have occurred in the world in the seventy years since Tagore's death in 1941.

Many of these changes have been profound in their impact. On the positive side, there has been an unimaginable rise in incomes in Asia, particularly in China and India. Economic growth has been fast and sustained also in the West, accompanied by a surge in foreign trade after the adoption of GATT and WTO treaties. Western Europe reconstructed rapidly after the Second World War, and has now become a peaceful, borderless, and prosperous union. The world as a whole has become a 'flat earth' due to technological advances in communications and transport.

On the negative side, hundreds of millions still live in extreme poverty in Africa and in pockets of Asia and Latin America. Economic growth has hardly reached them, and their development indicators of literacy, life expectancy and child mortality remain very low. Disparities among nations, and within nations, continue to be great. The spread of democracy and human rights have been uneven. Environmental degradation, climate change, and international terrorism have emerged as major concerns. The current economic recession and financial crises around the world, and the continuing problems of religious polarisation, militarism and hostilities, have led the leading countries to review the architecture of the world order.

We may be at the threshold of a new world order which will govern the next hundred years. It may be appropriate at this time to look back at some of the Modern Greats of the past century and re-examine their messages of wisdom for their relevance today. This chapter will attempt to do so with Rabindranath Tagore (1861-1941) who was a leading spokesman for compassionate humanism and culture in India and the world. Tagore lived in the age of science, as we also do. He was proud of the age of science as we also are. But we cannot say our lives are universally more secure or healthy in these times of advanced science and technology than that of our ancestors in the preceding age.

That leads us to ask why this insecurity, why all this terror, why our so-called modern society has led to progressively less harmony between the individual and the society. Even while Tagore greatly appreciated the benefits of science, and made use of science for rural reform which we shall discuss below, he understood that it is not enough by itself, and that our hopes and aspirations must be founded on a Universalist and democratic framework. That brings us to his thoughts on humanism, education and culture, nationalism and internationalism, and their great relevance today.

HUMANISM, NATIONALISM, INTERNATIONALISM

"All human beings are born free and equal in dignity and rights. They are endowed with reason and conscience and should act towards each other in a spirit of brotherhood." *Article 1, Universal Declaration of Human Rights, United Nations*, 1948.

Long before the League of Nations and the United Nations, Tagore was an internationalist who critiqued the narrowly defined concepts of nationalism and patriotism. He wanted all human beings to be treated equally regardless of the country or nation to which they belonged. He also did not want barriers between people even within the same nation-the barriers of caste, race, and religion. Tagore lived and worked during a period of crucial social and political transformation in India. He responded to its intense moments in memorable words.

A product of the nineteenth century, he was profoundly influenced by its liberal humanistic thought and its hope and optimism. He contributed substantially to the making of a modern India. By his own admission his formative influences were from a confluence of three movements which were active in the India of his time: the protestant religious movement of Rammohan Roy (1772-1833), the literary movement of Bankim Chandra Chatterjee (1838-94), and the national movement.

'It [the national movement] was not fully political but it began to give voice to the mind of our people trying to assert their own personality', he wrote. The 'national movement' revived the Indian pride in its past achievement in philosophy and religion, art and architecture, music and poetry. Pride in his own cultural traditions did not however blind Tagore to the moral and social degradation of his country which he directly experienced. Even in his eulogies of India he was remarkably free from the rhetoric of patriotism. He responded to European literature with a keen mind and great enthusiasm.

The first forty years of his life was conspicuous by his fond attraction for the Romantic and the Victorian poets, and Shakespeare, matched equally by his passionate love for Sanskrit literature in general and for the classical Sanskrit writer Kalidasa in particular. This catholicity of taste slowly evolved into his deep and pervasive sense of the 'universal' in thought and culture. Like all the leading intellectuals of his time, Swami Vivekananda (1863-1902) and Mahatma Gandhi (1869-1948) in particular, Tagore also was obliged to address the question of the relation between India and the West.

Like his compatriots he began by believing in an essential dichotomy between the two cultures and, for a certain period of time, he talked of a spiritual East and the materialistic West. But there was an evolution in his understanding when he discovered for himself spirituality in Western civilisation too. He located this spirituality in the West's dynamism and experimentation and its continuous pursuit of truth. Equally, he observed and critiqued the West's arrogant display of power but believed that it clashed with her 'inner ideal'.

This criticism led to his controversial lectures on *Nationalism* in 1916 where he argued that the West's tremendous success in science and technology had led to dehumanisation and an increasing greed for power. Despite such scathing criticisms, Tagore remained a pioneer of the intellectual union of East and West. There again he put his faith in people and not in governments. He believed that despite the West's ruthless politics, there was no absence of martyrs in the West who sacrificed their lives for the wrongs done by their governments.

That is how he sought to turn our minds towards the ideal of the spiritual unity of man. He wrote, 'In India what is needed more than anything else is the broad mind which, only because it is conscious of its own vigorous individuality, is not afraid of accepting truth from all sources'. It is not uncommon for a person to believe in the equality of all men, and yet to regard his or her own country in an exclusionist sense. However, Tagore's strong faith in man led him to an inclusive approach. He was able to shake off all shackles of traditional Hinduism, and arrive at a non-parochial and inclusive concept of India.

This was in a sense a rediscovery of the concept first presented by Rammohan Roy in 1823, but Tagore established it, rooted it in Indian history, and propagated it throughout the country. The history of India had a special message for Tagore. He saw it not so much as a synthesis, as is generally said, but as a 'mixture of ideas' and an 'interpenetration of opposites'. To him it was not the history of Aryans and non-Aryans, not the history of Hindus, or a history of Hindus and Muslims taken together. He did not see the coming of the British as an accidental intrusion.

His essays written during 1898 and 1904 convey an intuitive sense of history. He distanced himself as much from the colonialist historiography as he did from a Hindu nationalist view of the past. His country's social civilisation, he wrote, was founded on 'an adjustment of races, to acknowledge real differences between them, and yet to seek some basis of unity ...' His inclusive nationalism and non-parochial interpretation of India's history became a powerful agent of ideas for the freedom movement that Gandhi and Nehru led between the two world wars.

The idea of India expressed so eloquently by Nehru in 1947, was quite in conformity with Tagore's idea of India, which the Indian nation has cherished ever since. To quote from Nehru's famous speech on August 14, 1947:

"...what shall be our endeavour? To bring freedom and opportunity to the common man, to the peasants and workers of India; to fight and end poverty and ignorance and disease; to build up a prosperous, democratic and progressive nation, and to create social, economic and political institutions which will ensure justice and fullness of life to every man and woman... All of us, to whatever religion we may belong, are equally the children of India with equal rights, privileges and obligations. We cannot encourage communalism or narrow-mindedness, for no nation can be great whose people are narrow in thought or in action."

Several factors contributed to Tagore's inclusive approach, which was so strongly championed by Nehru. First, his father was a leading reformer of the Hindu society and religion, adopting the monotheistic Vedic variant introduced by Rammohan Roy at the beginning of the nineteenth century. Thus Tagore grew up in a household in which the spirit of scrutiny, creativity, and reforms dominated.

Second, his exposure beginning in 1892, to the great poverty and indignities suffered by the Muslim peasantry in his family's agricultural estates, as well as his friendship with Christians like Sister Nivedita, Brahmabandhab Upadhyaya, Rewachand, also some years later Charles Andrews and William Pearson, convinced him that they rightfully belong to the same brotherhood of man. He wrote, 'On us today is thrown the responsibility of building up a greater India in which Hindu and Muslim and Christian will find their place'.

This reasoning found expression in his well-known poem in 1911, beginning with the lines,

He mor chitta, punya tirthe jagore dhire

ei bharater maha-manaber sagoro-tire.

'On the sacred shores of the ocean of humanity of this India,
Awaken, my heart!'

Tagore's song 'jana gana mana adhinayaka' (1911) invoking the same goal of a larger humanity was chosen as our national anthem by Gandhi and Nehru, and remains a symbol of modern India's legacy of universal humanity. The Constitution of India upholds that legacy.

EDUCATION

"To accept the truth of our own age it will be necessary to establish a new education on the basis, not of nationalism, but of a wider relationship of humanity".

When first formulating his ideas for a new Indian education, Tagore was clearly responding to the 'cultural dislocation' of a colonised country. His mind was filled with what he wrote in his essay *Tapoban* in 1909 (in English translation 'The Message of the Forest', 1919): 'The forest, unlike the desert or rock or sea, is living; it gives shelter and nourishment to life. In such surroundings the ancient forest-dwellers of India realised the spirit of harmony with the universe and emphasized in their minds the monistic aspects of truth. They sought the realisation of their soul through union with all'.

He wrote poetically of how 'the voice in the Vedic tongue' guided him to the idea of a Brahmacharya Ashram or a hermitage when starting his school in Santiniketan. But he was soon to decide that a Brahmacharya Ashram was not his notion of a new and modern education. He valued some of its features such as following a life of simplicity for the students and teachers of the school alike. He also greatly valued the need for a forest, or a *Tapoban*- like place, which, in his plan for the Santiniketan School, was to be a quiet rural environment surrounded by nature and away from the confines of a city. He knew that was the closest he could get to establish an intimate community of teachers and students as in the hermitages of the past.

But his ideal school had to be much more than that, especially with regard to opening up the students' minds to a relationship with the world. Almost as soon as the Brahmacharya Ashram began to function he spoke out his disapproval of the institution in the following words, 'I have no desire to magically resurrect some ancient dead thing. It is not my business to bring back the past. I want to work for something which though implicit is yet strongly current, that which is not dead and which is natural to India.

The projects we start fail because we blindly try to get along without acknowledging it ... to say that it is possible to resurrect India's past but not possible to integrate another country's historical time with India's, and to attempt to implement this, is vain and leads to destruction, not to new life'. He opened up his Santiniketan School to those who believed in East and West alike, in peace and goodwill, without distinction of caste and creed and away from nationalist politics.

Tagore was a strong critic of the British Empire but he did not want that to get in the way of his mission to break out of the isolation that colonial rule and militant nationalism imposed. He argued that the lessons of the First World War proved that 'tomorrow's history' must begin with a chapter on 'internationalism' and that education must be in harmony with the times. In his 1919 essay *A Centre of Indian Culture*, he raised the crucial question of what must be the religious teaching given at such a centre? He pointed out how 'India' or 'national' tended to be identified with 'Hindu' which he argued was limited to only one historical aspect of India.

He deplored the fact that India was divided by religious and social barriers and asked, 'Can there be no wide meeting place where all sects may gather together and forget their differences'? This fundamental question became even more urgent with the bitter lessons of the First World War when he began to proceed gradually to transform Santiniketan into a world university to which scholars from the East and West would be invited to meet and study each other's cultures. He named this university 'Visva-Bharati' and chose an excerpt from a Vedic text as its motto when inaugurating the institution in 1921:

Yatra visvam bhavati ekanidam

'where the whole world forms its one single nest'

In the midst of an unprecedented political unrest and excitement, and against the whole force of the popular sentiment for the Non-cooperation Movement, he stated his views with passion in two essays, 'Satyer Abahan' (1921, The Call of Truth) and 'Sikshar Milan' (1921, The Union of Cultures).

Those essays stated his goal of bringing the West on terms of equality to the India of his aspiration -- which for him had to be an India of multiple cultures, an India where the impoverished village is given education and dignity of life, an India building its strength and nationhood by uniting castes and communities under an enlightened leadership. He recognized that the colonial education system was out of touch with Indian life. This was why he pressed for an education to first understand this weakness, and then endeavour to bridge the gap by working for village reorganisation as an essential part of a 'new' education based on self-reliance and human dignity.

He wanted this education to combine local or indigenous knowledge with modern scientific know-how from which both sections of Indian society could learn and make progress. Visva-Bharati's 'mission of rural construction', he wrote, was to 'retard' the process of 'racial suicide'. He held firmly that organizing the villages would be the right way to spread 'national consciousnesses. He argued that 'national unity' could become a reality only when the masses get a gut feeling about it, and that could happen if the educated classes and the masses unite in a common programme of work. Such was the 'sacrifice' needed, he wrote, to make the country 'our own'.

He criticized the Indian National Congress for looking to our alien government to do the work that had to be done 'by us' for the country that was 'our own'. He knew squarely we were faced with two stupendous problems: first, the poverty of our intellectual life and, second, the poverty of our material life. The Santiniketan-Sriniketan institution or Visva-Bharati – a world university in rural Bengal – became his life-long activity to build a centre of cultures which would not only be a centre of intellectual life in India but also a centre of her economic life.

He wrote, 'Our education should be in full touch with our complete life, economic, intellectual, aesthetic, social, and spiritual; and our educational institutions should be the very heart of our society. It must cultivate land, breed cattle, weave cloth, and produce the necessities of life, calling science to its aid, and uniting teachers and students in productive activities on cooperative principles whose motive force is not the greed of profit'. At the start this programme was limited to three villages in the south-west of Santiniketan where his school for urban boys and girls was established in 1901.

With the problems of over three hundred million people staring him at the face, Tagore could only have hoped that his efforts would touch the hearts of his village neighbours at Santiniketan and would help them reassert themselves in a bolder social order. 'I alone cannot take responsibility for the whole of India', he wrote. 'But even if two or three villages can be freed from the shackles of helplessness and ignorance, an ideal for the whole of India would be established. These two or three villages must be liberated fully; all must have education; there must be joy in these villages with songs and readings as in the past'.

These ideas of a new education were founded upon an urge and an instinct to create a new type of humanity whose scientific-technological progress and economic development would grow through dialogue and respect for values. That was the persistent basis of Tagore's debate on India and the world in his powerful and spirited writings on education, culture, science, nationalism, internationalism. These give meaning to his stand against colonialism, discrimination and dehumanisation. They give coherence to his faith in the relationship between human beings and their environment. All of his arguments were drawn directly from his life experience of the social and natural environment in which he lived a hundred fifty years ago, and we still do today. His 1919 essay *City and Village* says it all.

NATIONAL POLICY, SOCIETY AND VALUES

India's history after Independence is a complex story with far-reaching ramifications across all aspects of its society. But the two most prominent features of its personality in the early years were its foreign policy and its approach to economic development. Nehru's famous foreign policy of 'non-alignment' sought to avoid taking sides in the Cold War. This gave India freedom to choose, and to reason things out before making commitments on the basis of short-term expediency alone. India had also hoped to bring about greater harmony and moderation in world affairs, and to project an image that suited the reemergence of a compassionate and wise civilisation. This was very much in line with Tagore's philosophy and understanding of history.

If Nehru or Krishna Menon sounded too high-minded at times, it was an echo of what Tagore's audiences must have felt during his lectures on nationalism in USA and Japan in

1916. India's approach to economic development began with planning. At its simplest, planning is simply a tool for understanding the possibilities and prospects of the economy. It was seen as a useful way of organizing statistics on the economy, about which the new leaders had little organized knowledge. But the government also adopted a highly interventionist policy, characterised by extensive controls at all levels (this regime of controls became popularly known as the "Control Raj").

Along with that, the government adopted an 'inward-looking' or insular policy behind high tariff barriers and quotas. It was only after 1991, that India started to moderate or reverse these policies. The extensive controls and state ownership that accompanied insular policies, especially during the 1960s and 1970s, would certainly have been deplored by Tagore. They would not have appealed to his sense of freedom nor survived his penchant for reasoning. This is apparent from his observations on the Soviet Union in 1930, although he did appreciate Soviet achievements in the field of education.

A market-oriented outlook, in contrast to the "Control Raj", is also expected from a man of his background. Since the early days of his ancestor Nilmoni (d.1793), the fortunes of the Tagores were linked to trade-related businesses with the British. Tagore's grandfather, Dwarkanath Tagore (1794-1846), was a hugely successful entrepreneur and the first independent merchant of the British Raj. As an internationalist, Tagore surely would have preferred open trade policies. For example, he always opposed boycotts of foreign goods whenever such proposals came up, whether from Gandhi or from others. He would have also opposed barriers to cultural integration.

He would have welcomed globalisation among different cultures and languages, and he would have been wary of protecting national cultures by excluding foreign cultures. Gandhi's advocacy of the household spinning wheel, or *Charka*, did not make sense to him at all, as he felt it would not be economic. This was later confirmed to be so by Amartya Sen in his Ph.D. thesis. Once again, Tagore's position revealed his instinctive distrust of *ad hoc* exhortations for political gain. Because of that instinct and because of his strong feelings about secularism, he also would have been concerned about the *ad hoc* introduction of parochial personal laws which vitiate the Indian Constitution.

He would have questioned the Directives on special treatments for Scheduled Castes and Other Backward Classes, which enhance discrimination among Hindus, and also among Hindus and non-Hindus. These policies were meant to be short-term expedients, but they have become permanent anomalies in Indian political and social life. Tagore was an early environmentalist with a strong sense of aesthetics, who adored wide-open spaces and the riverine areas of Bengal. He disliked smoke-stacked industry and other ugly and noisy aspects of urban life. He felt that mechanisation and assembly-line production would strip away freedom and dignity from human beings; this was the theme of his powerful play, *Rakta Karabi* (1923).

Throughout his life he was a passionate champion of women's rights and empowerment, like Rammohan Roy and Iswar Chandra Vidyasagar (1820-91) before him. The first story he ever wrote, *Bhikharini,* was all about the misfortunes and abuses that a mother and her daughter had to suffer. He was only 16 at the time when he wrote this. His school in Santiniketan was coeducational, which was a major break from accepted social norms. And the characters of women protagonists he developed in one novel after another were an early expression of the empowerment of women we see in our national life today. The poverty that Tagore encountered in the country-side in Bengal in late nineteenth century could not have been less dire than the poverty of the serfs in Czarist Russia, which had so moved Chekov and Tolstoy.

His approach to dealing with poverty was through the spread of basic education with the goal of self-reliance, the application of science and technology to agriculture, the provision of cooperative credit, and the setting up of cottage industries. Most important of all in Tagore's scheme of things was to establish a relationship with the village based on a genuine attempt to understand its problems, whether in every instance successful or not. Some important results were obtained from the Sriniketan experiment. Health work in the villages reduced the number of deaths from epidemic over a period of time.

Rotation of crops helped the growth of agricultural productivity. A large number of villagers obtained employment in the industries department, albeit assisted by the requirements of the Second World War. The long term effect of the Sriniketan enterprise was seen in the full flowering of the rural development strategies in post-independent India through the government's Block Development Schemes, its Community Project and its Cottage Industries movement. The things that would have most disappointed Tagore about the developments after Independence are first, the failure to provide basic education and health care to the underprivileged.

Tagore would have accepted the lead of the government in this area, as in China, Vietnam and other countries which have rapidly reached high literacy levels. The elimination of social backwardness and poverty would have been very high on his agenda were he alive today. The second area which would have disturbed him greatly would have been the rise of sectarianism and the politics behind animosities toward, and occasional hostilities against, religious minorities. Thirdly, he would not have endorsed modes of political dissent which bypass the Constitution and lead to anarchy.

Methods of opposition which may arguably have been acceptable under the colonial rule of Britain would not have been acceptable to him under the democratic framework after Independence. Like Tagore we also live in the age of science and internationalism. Today we call it globalisation, and our education is still similar to Western-style colonialist education. Given how troubled our world is becoming, there is a growing awareness of the need to reconcile the values of 'universal' and 'diversity', a conviction that Tagore pioneered not only in thought but also in his life of action.

There was not a great deal he or any one individual could do to bring change to an unequal and unjust world. But he was never indifferent to the need, and he tried hard to make a difference with whatever constructive work was possible for him. We can try to make that his legacy in our individual lives.

2

Poetry and Philosophy

More and more mankind will discover that we have to turn to poetry to interpret life for us, to console us, to sustain us. Without poetry, our science will appear incomplete, and most of what now passes with us for religion and philosophy will be replaced by poetry. . . . The day will come when we shall wonder at ourselves for having trusted to them, for having taken them seriously; and the more we perceive their hollowness, the more we shall prize "the breath and finer spirit of knowledge" offered to us by poetry. Rabindranath is essentially a poet and not a philosopher, though it is possible for us to gather his philosophical views from his poetry.

There are critics who consider Rabindranath's poetry not to be first-rate, because it is full of metaphysics and mysticism. His departure from the conventions of poetic form adds to the difficulties and helps to make the suspicion gather in weight and become well-nigh certain. Let us here consider how far the criticism is just, and incidentally notice Rabindranath's views about the relation of poetry to philosophy, and topics of a kindred nature. The question to be decided at the outset relates to the aim of art, especially poetic art. In The Cycle of Spring, Rabindranath says: "We [poets] set men free from their desires." In these words he lays his finger on the true function of art as the pathway to freedom.

The artist helps us to forget the bonds with the world, and reveals to us the invisible connections by which we are bound up with eternity. True art withdraw our thoughts from the mere machinery of life, and lift our souls above the meanness of it. It releases the self from the restless activities of the world, and takes us out "of the noisy sickroom of ourselves." It disengages the mind from its imprisonment in the web of customary associations and routine ideas. The secret of all art lies in self-forgetfulness. The poet or the artist sets free the poet or the artist in us.

And this he can do only if his artistic creation is born of self-forgetful joy. The true artist lifts himself above all worldly passions and desires, into the spiritual mood where he waits for the light. He turns away from all other objects, identifies himself with the particular subject he wishes to interpret, merges his consciousness in it, and loses himself. He calls out to the object whose beauty he wishes to be revealed:

... Be thou, Spirit fierce,

My spirit! be thou me, impetuous one.

When this forgetfulness of self and identification with the not-self occurs, when the life within the artist becomes one with the life without him, art takes its birth. It is because art is born of this joy that it produces joy. When we say that the function or aim of art is to produce enjoyment, it is not to be understood that either the artist, or the creator, or the enjoying man starts with any conscious purpose to delight or the deliberate design to enjoy. Artistic creation and enjoyment are both spontaneous and unconscious. The artist does not create his work with any specific motive of pleasing the audience or delighting the world.

What is felt deeply in the soul of the artist finds outward shape in the work of art? Out of the fulness of the heart the mouth speaketh. "The road of excess leads to the palace of wisdom," says William Blake. Art has its origin, according to

Rabindranath, "in the region of the superfluous." The surplus energy seeks its outlet in art. Art is the daughter of joy. It is due to play, the expression of the superfluous energies of man. Man speaks with his voice when he has a purpose to gain; but when he has none such, he sings. He walks with his feet when he has an end to reach, but when he has none such, he dances.

Man writes with his hand, and works with it when he has an axe to grind, but when he has none such, he paints with it. But if all our time and energies are taken up by war and trade, science and industry, then we cannot afford to waste our precious time and energies in painting and chiselling, singing and dancing! Our society will have no place for those idlers, we mean the artists! But art is born of idle-ness, and not busy-ness. In art we do not seek for the fulfilment of our physical or intellectual needs. We only feel and enjoy, but do not analyse or measure.

Repetition of facts that can be turned to use and advantage, such as "the sun is round, water is liquid, fire is hot, would be intolerable. But a description of the beauty of the sunrise," which has absolutely no economic or utilitarian value, will have "its eternal interest . . . because there, it is not the fact of the sunrise, but its relation to ourselves, which is the object of perennial interest." Art deals with the world of personality. Art is the expression of personality. But it may be argued that all activity is self-expression, and so, to say that art is self-expression does not go far. But we have to remember that everywhere else, activity is a means to something else, while in beauty we have no ulterior aim.

We want to know a thing that we may use it. In art, self-expression has no other end. It is its own object. Self-expression occurs because it cannot but occur. It is not to satisfy any physical or economic needs. "When our heart is fully awakened in love, or in other great emotions, our personality is in its flood-tide." Poetry is not work, but an outburst or an effluence as

Browning puts it. It is the expression of the excess where the whole soul comes out. As art is born of the joy of self-forgetfulness it fulfils the aim of delighting, or producing joy, and thus helps the soul to leap free of its fetters and attain peace with itself and the world.

It lifts us up into a mood where everything actual becomes practically nothing. It helps the soul to enter its own natural home, and claim its citizenship in that kingdom of freedom and beauty where all are sovereigns and none subjects. At the same time it affects the greater life of which it is a part; for it brings the infinite into the common life. It thus adorns life and gladdens existence. Art is not didactic. It is to delight and not to instruct. It is to stimulate us unconsciously to noble ends and not to teach lessons. Philosophy may argue and instruct; religion may exhort and command; but art only delights and pleases.

Instruction and edification may be the results of art, but its aim is only to delight. While it shines by its own light, the light may produce other effects. As a species of art, the aim of poetry is to please and not profit. The popular notion that Indian thought is not in sympathy with this conception of the aim of art is a mistake. "The rhetoricians in old India had no hesitation in saying, that enjoyment is the soul of literature, the enjoyment which is disinterested." When delight, the aim of art, is confused with pleasure interpreted in the vulgar hedonistic sense, then Indian thought enters its emphatic protest. When art caters to our craze for r.ensation, it is criticised and condemned.

The ascetic note in India is the expression of the revolt against, not the spiritual aim of art, but the hedonistic degradation of that aim. The aesthetic emotion is a spiritual experience and not a mere subjective feeling. When art ceases to be a means of attaining spiritual freedom, and becomes merely the occasion for the amusement of the vulgar, it has forfeited its true nature as art. Though it is not the aim of poetry as a species of art to tell us of a philosophy, still it cannot fulfil its purpose unless it embodies a philosophic vision. It must offer an interpretation of life; give us a fuller view of reality. Poetry would not delight and give joy if it did not reveal the eternal through its form.

Poetry aims, in the language of Hegel, "to present in forms for the imagination features of the ultimate ideal of the harmonised universe." Aristotle has said that poetry is the most philosophic of all writing, as its object is truth. The true poet is he who sees the whole in every part and makes his poetry expresses his whole vision. " The chief office of poetry is not merely to give amusement, not merely to be the expression of feelings good or bad of mankind, or to increase our knowledge of human nature, and of human life, but that, if it includes this mission, it also includes a mission far higher, the revelation, namely, of ideal truth, the revelation of that world of which this world is but the shadow or the drossy copy, the revelation of the eternal, the unchanging and the typical which underlies the unsubstantial and the ever-dissolving phenomena of earth's empire of matter and time."

Poetry should give us a vision of the whole. We may well say that one of the decisive tests to help us to find out whether a particular work is poetry or not is this, whether it gives us a wholeness of vision or reads only the surface appearances. Instead, therefore, of saying that philosophy and poetry are incompatible, we should say that poetry to be poetry must be essentially philosophical, in the sense here explained. For it is only a mind that is at rest, a soul at peace with itself that can produce good poetry? A disturbed soul or a worried mind cannot be a great poet. It is the rhythm of life that expresses itself in the rhythm of poetry.

There will be melody in the tongue only if there is melody in the heart. The harmony of the soul is attained when the mind is not seized with doubts. It is only then that the soul sinks into a kind of passivity, surrenders itself to the spontaneity of creation, and finds its joy therein. The human soul to rise into poetic rapture should become attuned with the soul of things beyond. The inner and the outer self must melt into one sweet harmony. "This world, whose soul seems to be aching for expression in its endless rhythm of lines and colours, music and movements, hints and whispers, and all the suggestion of the inexpressible, finds its harmony in the ceaseless longing of the human heart to make the Person manifest in its own creations."

It is the universal joy that takes shape in the song of the poet. Poetry is the echo in the human heart of the melody of the universe. A soul ill at ease with the world, which thinks that the world is given up for lost, as God is confined to His heaven, cannot be a great poet. The pessimist who sees an irreconcilable breach between the higher and the lower, the transcendentalist who looks upon the ideal as something beyond time and the world-process, and the world-negating ascetic who longs to fly from this life into nothingness, these cannot be great poets, as they are at war with the world. Pessimistic poetry is a contradiction in terms; for he who finds nothing valuable in this world cannot be a poet. The true poet finds his happiness in the world or not at all.

The poet must have love of nature and of creation. Rabindranath thus describes the relation of the artist soul to the world soul: "The world asks the inner man, ' Friend, have you seen me? Do you love me? Not as one who provides you with foods and fruits, not as one whose laws you have found out, but as one who is personal, individual? ' The artist's answer is, ' Yes, I have seen you, I have loved and known you, not that I have any need of you, not that I have taken you and used your laws for my own purposes of power. I know the forces that act and drive and lead to power, but it is not that. I see you, where you are what I am.'

"Disinterested love for the universe, as it is only a revelation of one's own soul, is the true artist's attitude to the world. A poet who wishes to see beauty everywhere must love the earth. The soul must be at home in the world and feel no strangeness in it. It must cry out, "Is not this earth also His who made heaven?" The true poet hears harmony in the babel of sounds called nature, sees good in the heart of evil, and views eternity in time. The disturbances of the soul and the antinomies of the world do not make him think that God is either non-existent, or, if existent, has gone stark mad, but only strengthen his world-view in its wholeness. Of course he would feel ugliness and evil like pain.

"When they had struck thee and thou wert pained, it pierced me to the quick." 'But in all true poetry as in all true philosophy, the end must be reconciliation. The poet may display his art in describing the tragic contrasts of the world, but he is convinced that the end of it all is peace and atonement, and not discord and despair. This does not mean that the fifth scene of the fifth act should be one of marriage or benediction. Nor does it mean that he should view the world as a pure paradise without any conflicts and contrasts.

The poet should face the world with its ugliness and misery, horror and imperfection, but in the end let us feel that the world we live in is good enough. He may describe the tumult of the soul, but only to conclude that underneath it there is a settled peace. Pure and ennobling are the effects of great tragedies which describe the agonies of soul and the groanings of spirit. A tragedy which leaves on the mind an impression of disgust and dissatisfaction is a failure as a work of art. The ultimate feeling in true art should be one of triumph and satisfaction.

The tragedy is an illustration of the law of the universal in the particular, and exhibits the realisation of the whole in the sorrows of the individuals. Any other course would be to give up the rationality of the beauty of the universe. The dull world may have discords and contradictions, but the world of poetry which is nature idealised cannot contain them. Roughly speaking, only partial views, which are the monopoly of science and prose, can consider contradiction the end of things. To them the world may appear an interrogation, but to the philosopher and the poet it cannot be so. Their task is to show that conflict and confusion is not the last thing.

They make a perfect round of the broken arcs of the earth. The beauty and order of the world are recreated alike in the vision of the poet and the mind of the philosopher. The philosopher argues that all discord is harmony not understood; the poet shows us the soul of goodness in things evil. The eternal harmony of the world is heard in the song of the poet. "My poet, is it thy delight to see thy creation through my eyes and to stand at the portals of my ears silently to listen to thine own eternal harmony?"

On this view the naturalistic conception of poetry stands self-condemned. As art is distinct from nature, so is naturalistic poetry distinct from true poetry. The former requires mere observation, while the latter demands meditation on the material observed. While in the former our mind is in a relatively passive condition, in the latter it is in an active state, reflecting on the data observed. As philosophy is not common sense but a criticism thereof, even so poetry is not life but a criticism of it.

As philosophy does not catalogue facts but reduces them to law and order, even so poetry does not copy facts but interprets them. Philosophy, by revealing the deeper meanings of things, criticises the superficial appearances, and the poet sets against the ugly show of things their inner spiritual beauty. Philosophy according to the idealist tradition is a construction of experience. The immediate facts of the world, which constitute the starting-point of the philosophic inquiry, are taken up into a synthesis where their immediacy and externality are broken down.

Even so the imagination of the poet plays with the facts of the world and makes them express the spirit of the whole. Poetry is not therefore an unimaginative copying of life and matter. The aim of the poet is to reveal the life within things, the soul within matter. The philosopher tells us that mechanism is not the ultimate category of the universe, while the poet sees the life in things which pass for dead. As truth is no mere correspondence to fact, so poetry is no mere imitation of the facts of nature or the flow of mind. Both are creative reconstructions. Both are mirrors of life, not of life at its surface, but of life at its deepest and the best side.

If poetry consists in putting down exactly what we see without wavering, as some of our modern poets do when they sing of the kerosene tin and the telegraph wire, it is not true poetry. Beauty is truth, as Keats observed, and not naturalism. Poetry is creation, not copying. It is vision, not imitation. It is picture, not photograph. Indian thought never cared for nature divorced from spirit. Nature thus viewed is an illusive phenomenon. It is real as revealing the divine essence or spirit. Art is the effort of the human mind to grasp the spiritual meaning and inner beauty of the facts of nature.

Things of the world are not beautiful by themselves; but as containing suggestions of things above, they are beautiful. But when poetry attempts to photograph things it ceases to be poetry, and becomes prose or science, or something else. Poetry must attach greater importance to the inner informing spirit than to the outward semblance. Fidelity, not to nature but to the soul in it, is the principle of true poetry. So while it is right to say that poetry should be the expression of feeling, it should not be the expression of subjective or individual feeling. It should be the utterance of the universal mind or the general will.

As every natural fact is presented to us in the light of its ideal aim, so every subjective feeling should be given out as an illustration of the poet's whole experience. In poetry not merely a particular emotion, but the poet's whole perception should be released. Every feeling should be given out as an item of the poet's whole vision, which is the inspiration of the poet's work. Rabindranath writes: "Poetry is not a mere matter of feeling or expression; it is the creation of form. Ideas take on shape by some hidden subtle skill at work within the poet. This creative power is the origin of poetry. Sensations, feelings, or language are only its raw material."

True poetry will be a compound of emotion and reflection. Mere feeling or emotion will have no voice or utterance. It would be speechless as subjectivism in philosophy is. Without restraint of feeling by thought there would be no realisation, and so no poetry. "The creation of beauty is not the work of unbridled imagination. Passion when it is given its full sway becomes a destructive force like fire gone out of hand." This is Wordsworth's meaning when he says that poetry is emotion remembered in tranquillity. The simplicity of the poetic garb sometimes misleads us into thinking that poetry is only the expression of a surface feeling; but spontaneity and simplicity are in inverse proportion to the training and thought involved.

"That training is the most intricate which leads to the utter simplicity of a tune." Poetry is not to be put down for a relaxation of our powers or a detention of our faculties. It involves much strenuous exertion and critical reflection. When the powers of man are at the highest, we feel as if they were at the lowest. It is similar to the optical illusion where both motion and motionlessness seem one. The artist lives a more intense life than the common folk; for only of intensity is insight born.

The transcendental view, which makes poetry, as distinct from prose, deals with ideals which have no reality in life, is at the opposite extreme to the naturalistic view, and is equally abstract and unreal. The classical poet, who "as a swimmer without the impediments of garments cleaves the water with greater ease," constructs a dream world or a fairy land, neglecting the pain and suffering inherent in life, is at the opposite pole to the realistic poet, who pictures the world as it strikes the retina of his eye, and gives us a photograph of the world at its surface. To say that poetry is unrelated to life is as incorrect as to say that poetry is a mere imitation of life. To the poet, earth is his home and heaven his hope.

A true philosophy tells us that the distinctions between the actual and the ideal, nature and art, life and criticism, and observation and reflection are relative. The two become opposed when we draw a hard-and-fast line of distinction between the surface view of things, which we call the natural, and the deeper one which penetrates the veil, which we call the philosophical. But art is merely nature deeply felt and meditated upon. "The art itself is nature." The naturalistic and the transcendental views of poetry, which consider that poetry should deal with surface facts or abstract ideals, correspond to the two extreme positions in philosophy, represented by naturalistic realism and transcendental idealism. These have for their counterparts in ethics, hedonism in the utilitarian sense, and rationalism in the ascetic sense.

All these are one sided. True philosophy teaches us that the whole consists of ideals permeating actualities. The real is the rational. A divorce between the two is unreal and untrue to fact. Poetry should embody elements of actual experience, but set them in the light of the genuine ideal. In this we presume that the final truth of nature and man is the same, and this is the conclusion of sober philosophy. The earliest Upanishads of India with the latest systems of modern Critical Idealism assert that the principle which works in the human imagination as the ideal of man, and the end towards which nature moves by force of its immanent idea, are identical.

What true poetry does is to shadow forth the identity of the whole, man and nature. Goethe's lines, as translated by Carlyle, bring out the true spirit of the poet:

As all Nature's myriad changes still one changeless Power proclaim,

So through Thought's wide kingdom ranges one vast Meaning, e'er the same:

This is Truth Eternal Reason that in beauty takes its dress,

And serene, through time and season, stands complete in righteousness.

The poets who lack this spirit are not of the right type, whatever their writings may achieve. The abiding judgment of man will put them down for counterfeit coin. Rabindranath is of opinion that both realism and idealism in their extreme forms are wrong. To him realism, which would have art reproduce nature in all the coarse reality of its surface appearance, is as false a conception of poetry as idealism, which would not deign to walk the streets, but would fain fly in the medium of an ideal unrelated to fact. He adopts the true view, which is a higher union of the two, limiting both and fulfilling both.

Art is concerned neither with the actual and the imperfect, nor with the ideal and the hazy, but with the natural transfigured by the ideal immanent in it. "I believe in an ideal life. I believe that, in a little flower, there is a living power hidden in beauty which is more potent than a Maxim gun. I believe that in the bird's notes Nature expresses herself with a force which is greater than that revealed in the deafening roar of the cannonade. I believe that there is an ideal hovering over the earth, an ideal of that Paradise which is not the mere outcome of imagination, but the ultimate reality towards which all things are moving. I believe that this vision of Paradise is to be seen in the sunlight, and the green of the earth, in the flowing streams, in the beauty of springtime and the repose of a winter morning. Everywhere in this earth the spirit of Paradise is awake and sending forth its voice. . . ."

So deep is Rabindranath's love of nature that to him every aspect of nature becomes a symbol of beauty. He does not love nature for its own sake, but because he views it as an attribute of the divine; not for the abundance of joy that it brings into life, but for the intimations it gives of a higher spiritual life. To him even a blade of grass or an atom of dust brings a message from the unknown.

To him every flower is a symbol of worship, every garland a *Gitanjali*, every forest a temple, and every hilltop God's dwelling - place. The sound of the running water, the rustle of the leaves, and the song of the bird are so many hymns of praise to the great God. He has faith in the soul of the universe. He cannot be a great poet who has no faith in it. It is a philosophy of divine immanence that should be at the basis of true and great poetry. The East has faith in this universal soul. To the Indian poet this universal Presence is not a mere matter of philosophical speculation, but is as real as the sunlight or the earth under his feet.

To him "in Art the person in us is sending its answers to the Supreme Person, who reveals Himself to us in a world of endless beauty across the lightless world of facts." The actual hides the ideal; the natural the spiritual; and what art does is to reveal the hidden spiritual ideal. The destiny of nature is to become spirit. The function of the artist or the poet is to exalt the natural towards its destined spiritual perfection. The poet releases the spirit imprisoned in matter. When the poet, oppressed by the idealism which fills his body and soul, touches matter it loses its materiality.

What is common loses its commonness, what is earthy loses its earthiness and what is finite and imperfect its finiteness and imperfection. The poet's mind, dominated by an overpowering sense of the spiritual, penetrates through the veil of their earthly covering into the life of things. The Greek view that there are certain objects which are beautiful and others ugly, and the artist has only to take note of them, loses its force. The Greek framed his images of gods from perfect human models which he looked upon as beautiful. But the Hindu does not care for the human models, but simply surrenders himself to the spontaneity of the spiritual vision.

"The artist," says Sukracharya "should attain to the images of the gods by means of spiritual contemplation only. The spiritual vision is the best and truest standard for him. He should depend upon it, and not at all upon the visible objects perceived by external senses. ... It is far better to present the figure of a god, though it is not beautiful, than to reproduce a remarkably handsome human figure." To Rabindranath, as to Indian thought in general, beauty is subjective.

Anything may be made the vehicle for it. Even the grotesque is not useless. "In Art, man reveals himself and not his objects." We should have the spiritual harmony, and then the whole world will burst into music. Everything depends on us. "It is like our touch upon the harpstring: if it is too feeble, then we are merely aware of the touch, but if it is strong, then our touch comes back to us in tunes and our consciousness is intensified." So the harp-string is neither the one nor the other. Everything depends on our touch, whether it is feeble or strong; in other words, whether we are full of spiritual fire or not.

Or we may put it the other way, and say that the soul with the fire in it is like some stringed instrument, and any object which strikes it produces sound. "The one effort of man's personality is to transform everything with which he has any true concern into the human. And art is like the spread of vegetation, to show how far man has reclaimed the desert for his own." The things of the world are rescued from the flux of time and the relativity of space, and viewed under the light that never was on sea or land. To the eye of the genuine poet the spiritual aspects are as simple and natural and as real as the sea or the sunlight to the naked eye.

In true poetry the real is idealised, and the ideal realised, and we have quite a genuine but a higher kind of real object. As Tennyson puts it, poetry is truer than fact. So the greatest poetry must embody an ideal vision or a true philosophy. Without this philosophic vision no great poetry can exist. Poetry may charm us by its wit, surprise us by its skill, thrill us by its richness, amuse us by its variety, lull us into sleep by its rhythm, and satisfy our craving for extraordinary incident; but let it lack the vision, it sinks to the level of verse and ceases to be poetry.

Poetry is creative while prose is narrative; poetry is an end in itself while prose is a means to an end. A genuine poet has the creative vision which makes beauty. The peace of the soul will work out in terms of visible beauty, and the poet by swift image and noble phrase puts forth his ideal. If the creation is present, it is poetry whether it is in verse or not. Rules of prosody are for the poet and not the poet for them. Rules are his servants and not his masters. Technique is only a means to an end. Those who observe technique and make rhyming lines without any creative idea or spiritual vision are versifiers and not poets.

Their products are verses and not poems. Verses can be turned out with a certain number of feet, but not poetry, which requires the artistic vision and inspiration. Technique will not make for vitality. It may even be said that an art which follows rules is an art without beauty. It is like religion without faith, morality without heroism. There are people who imagine that it matters not what the poet says, provided he says it well. But this is to separate matter and form, which we cannot in justice do. To Rabindranath the vision and the form in which it is bodied forth are inseparable. The soul and the body are one; the outward is the expression of the inward.

"It is meritorious," writes Carlyle, "to insist on forms. Religion and all else naturally clothes itself in forms. All substances clothe themselves in forms; but there are suitable true forms, and then there are untrue, unsuitable. As the briefest definition one might say, Forms which grow round a substance, if we rightly understand that, will correspond to the real Nature and purport of it, will be true, good ; forms which are consciously put round a substance, bad." Similarly S. T. Coleridge observes: "The form is mechanic when on any given material we impress a predetermined form, not necessarily arising out of the properties of the material as when to a mass of wet clay we give whatever shape we wish it to retain when hardened.

The organic form, on the other hand, is innate; it shapes as it develops itself from within, and the fulness of its development is one and the same with the perfection of its outward form. Such as the life is, such is the form." Form and substance are of a piece; they are made for each other. As water makes its channel, so the substance creates its form. In poetry the spirit becomes incarnate and the body becomes instinct with spirit. The essential point is the creative vision, and if art should be the expression of it, it will do. Art should be the expression of life and should be informed by it. In the absence of the vision, poetry becomes merely an academic affectation or pedantic word - display.

There are critics who think that Rabindranath is not a great poet because he disregards poetic form. But form is only the vehicle for the vision, the means for self-realisation. The end of art is not the realisation of form, but that of spirit. Art is more the expression of thought than the revelation of form. India never worshipped form for its own sake. Indian theory of art agrees with Hegel in thinking that "the outward shape by which the content is made perceptible is merely there for the sake of mind and spirit."

The artist tries to represent not the form but the ideal. He tries to materialise the idea, show us the subtle soul. The idolatry of form to be met with in the West is due to confusion about the object of art. The aim of art is self-expression; and this it realises by the arts, sculpture and painting, music and poetry. Beauty happens to be the main element of this expression, and so it is thought that the production of beauty is the aim of art, "whereas beauty in art has been the mere instrument and not its complete and ultimate significance."

It is this conception of beauty as the end of art that makes some people imagine that manner is more important than matter. A poetic genius like Rabindranath need not be bound by forms. He is a law unto himself, makes his own rules and breaks through the ordinary conventions. Feeling that convention is the curse of poetry, realising that rhymes have a restricting effect on the free flight of the poetic spirit, Rabindranath employs the rhythmical prose which is turned to such good account in *The Song of Solomon* and *Whitman's Leaves of Grass*. How well the soul of Rabindranath's poetry has shaped its body may be seen by taking any of his poems at random.

We have music and melody in his poems as well as sweetness and light. What, after all, is the good of poetry where the freedom of spirit is lost in the desert sands of dead forms? It does not come into the group of poetry at all, unless the breath of life blows over the desert sands and makes them blossom into fruits and flowers. If poetry is so closely related to philosophy, to what is their traditional opposition due? A false idea of 'philosophy is responsible for it.

A philosopher is supposed to be one who merely feeds his intellect at the expense of the whole man. His heart and moral nature are left starving. We have a representative of this type in the *Pundit of The Cycle of Spring*, who, while talking glibly of renunciation and worldly wisdom, is most selfish, and wants to dole out by bits his learning to the king in "exchange for the rich province of Kanchanpur," while the poet with true detachment " never accepts reward " for preaching love and charity.

The Pundit, who, like "the newer people of the modern age," is "more eager to amass than to realise," cannot see deeper than the surfaces of things, and his outlook is sordid, materialist, and utilitarian. To him If bamboos were made only into flutes,

They would droop and die with very shame. They hold their heads high in the sky, because they are variously useful. He is sorry that the "numerous stars in the midnight sky which hang in the air for no purpose," do not come down to earth for street lighting, and thus help the ratepayer. The Pundit has before him the ideal of usefulness, while the poet has that of enjoyment. One bows down before machinery, while the other worships personality.

One has the practical, worldly, business point of view, while the other has the childlike, unworldly point of view. The poet is for dreams and not business. To him who is an infant in worldly affairs things appear in their spiritual significance. It is clear that mere intellect will not make a great poet any more than an honest trader or a good governor. The philosophical ideal, we have already seen, cannot be reached by intellectual categories. To catch sight of the philosophical ideal we require meditation and mystic insight.

Intellect revelling in distinctions and opposites can give us, in the words of Bradley, an unearthly ballet of bloodless categories which is no substitute for the concrete riches of life. For the synthetic vision and the reconciling view we have to transcend intellect by means of intuition. "Full many an hour have I spent in the strife of the good and the evil, but now it is the pleasure of my playmate of the empty days to draw my heart on to him." An intellectualist plays with words, concepts, and categories, but misses the truth and reality. Mysticism is the key which would open the door to the shrine where the "invisible king" is.

"The dust of the dead words cling to thee, \ washes thy soul with silence." So if the term Philosopher is taken in the sense of an intellectual metaphysician paying homage to the logical intellect and not an intuitive seer, then poetry has nothing to do with philosophy. In the story of "The Victory," Rabindranath gives us a description of the genuine poet as distinguished from the counterfeit. The intellectual poet Pundarik is contrasted with the true poet Shekhar, the poet of King Narayan. The king received Pundarik with honour and said, "Poet, I offer you welcome." Pundarik proudly replied, "Sire, I ask for war." But "Shekhar, the court poet of the king, did not know how the battle of the muse was to be waged."

Here is the contrast between the arrogance of the word-builder and the humility of the true poet. "With a trembling heart Shekhar entered the arena in the morning. . . . With his head held high and chest expanded, he (Pundarik) began in his thundering voice to recite the praise of King Narayan. . . . The skill with which he gave varied meanings to the name Narayan, and wove each letter of it through the web of his verses in all manner of combinations, took away the breath of his amazed hearers." Such is the way the world judges poets. The effect of the performance on the audience was one of astonishment at the intellectual profundity of the phrase maker and the versifier.

But Shekhar produced just the opposite effect. When he began he was full of feeling ready to burst out. "His face was pale, his bashfulness was almost that of a woman, his slight youthful figure, delicate in its outline, seemed like a tensely strung vina ready to break out in music at the least touch." And when Shekhar finished what was the effect? "Tears filled the eyes of the hearers, and the stone walls shook with cries of victory." Such is the effect of true art. When true music is heard, rafters ring, serpents sing, the very stones melt, and the whole world dances, as some Indian poets would have it. Pundarik stands for stupendous learning, and in the conceit of his knowledge he asks: "What is there superior to words?"

To him "the Word was in the beginning, and the Word was God." But what did Shekhar prove? "Next day Shekhar began his song. It was of that day when the pipings of love's flute startled for the first time the hushed air of the vrinda forest. The shepherd women did not know who the player was or whence the music came. Sometimes it seemed to come from the heart of the south wind, and sometimes from the straying clouds of the hill-tops. It came with a message of tryst from the land of the sunrise, and it floated from the verge of sunset with its sigh of sorrow.

The stars seemed to be the stops of the instrument that flooded the dreams of the night with melody. The music seemed, to burst all at once from all sides, from fields and groves, from the shady lanes and lonely roads, from the melting blue of the sky, from the shimmering green of the grass. They neither knew its meaning nor could they find words to give utterance to the desire of their hearts. Tears filled their eyes, and their life seemed to long for a death that would be its consummation." The true poet forgets himself in his poetry." Shekhar forgot his audience, forgot the trial of his strength with a rival. He stood alone amid his thoughts that rustled and quivered round him like leaves in a summer breeze, and sang the Song of the Flute."

He attains that exaltation and freedom where the individual becomes free from self-consciousness. The trappings of the world fall away and he sees things as they are, and sings his inspired poetry. He feels the whole world to be a harmony and all nature music. He is not a man of words but full of feeling. When Shekhar took his seat "his hearers trembled with the sadness of an indefinable delight, immense and vague, and they forgot to applaud him." In other words, they were filled with freedom and careless joy. Pundarik challenged his rival to define who was the lover and who was the beloved, and "then he began to analyse the roots of those names.

Each letter of those names he divided from its fellow, and then pursued them with a relentless logic till they fell to the dust in confusion, to be caught up again and restored to a meaning never before imagined by the subtlest of word mongers." Who were the men to appreciate this wonderful gymnastics? "The pundits were in ecstasy." A thin, stiff, and straight vision was what the intellectualist conjured up. "The atmosphere was completely cleared of all illusion of music, and the vision of the world around seemed to be changed from its freshness of tender green to the solidity of a high road levelled and made hard with crushed stones."

But the king declared that Pundarik had the victory. Shekhar returned home and threw his writings into the fire, for they were "mere words and childish rhymes." At night " he spread upon his bed the white flowers that he loved, the jasmines, and opened wide his windows," and drank a poisonous juice. Then Ajita appeared on the scene, "and it seemed to him that the image made of a shadow that he had ever kept throned in the secret shrine of his heart had come into the outer world in his last moments to gaze upon his face." "The princess whispered into his ear: The king has not done you justice. It was you who won at the combat, my poet, and I have come to crown you with the crown of victory.

'As he was singing, joy, the secret of the universe, was being laid bare. Pundarik beats down his hearers by mere words, dumbfounds them by his intellectual subtleties, and makes them believe that giving names to things and calling relations categories is to explain them. In his arrogance he feels that the secret of the universe is to be found in his waistcoat pocket. He thinks that he has a key which would unlock the doors of all problems in heaven and earth, and a good many in neither. Everything from the stars of heaven to the shells of earth had a fixed place in his scheme of the universe. But the pity of it is that intellectual legerdemain does not constitute truth and poetry.

Poetry is a cry of the spirit and it has nothing to do with pretences born and bred of books, as these are useless to the spirit. The people along with the king who applauded him did so because they were "deluded into the certainty that they had witnessed, that day, the last shred of the curtains of Truth torn to pieces by a prodigy of intellect. But they forgot to ask if there was any truth behind it after all." Victory was beaming from the breast of Pundarik and found response in the king's heart. And the people caught the suggestion from the king and were hypnotised into admiration of Pundarik. They neither considered nor questioned but carried away by the tide, threw their hats up, cheered him and jumped for joy.

No wonder Pundarik triumphed. Such is the way reputations are built in this world. Thus Rabindranath points out that intellectual poetry is a contradiction in terms. So if by philosopher we mean an intellectual juggler, then philosophy has nothing to do with poetry. But if by philosopher we mean the intuitive seer who has risen above his small self, a man who has attained true freedom of consciousness, and then he is one with the poet who hears the whispers of the soul and gives voice to them. Such were the ancient Rishis who broke away from the fetters and revealed their souls in the Upanishads. And such is Rabindranath.

It is often urged that poetry and philosophy are opposed because poetry deals with life, becoming, movement, while philosophy deals with stillness, rest, and immutability. Philosophy is represented as being thin, lifeless, and unsubstantial, while poetry is regarded as rich, warm, and glowing. But we have seen that this description of philosophy is unjust and one-sided. While a few systems conclude that being alone is real and not becoming, the attempt of philosophy is to gather in a whole both being and becoming.

Modern systems of concrete idealism present us with such reconciling wholes. Neither philosophy nor poetry deals with things as they appear, but concerns it with things as they really are. Both poetry and philosophy are criticisms of life at first sight or interpretations thereof. Both protest against "the sloth which takes things as they are, and the poorness of spirit which is satisfied with first appearances." And so this charge that philosophy deals with abstractions while poetry deals with life is unfounded. The poet worships God as the spirit of beauty, while the philosopher pays his homage to God as the ideal of truth. Philosophy is the temple of truth, while poetry is the shrine of beauty. The two are not opposed, as truth is beauty and beauty truth.

Reality is absolute, though there are many ways of realising it. Philosophy tells us how a synoptic vision which binds together all terms and relations in a concrete spiritual whole is the Real. Poetry individualises this vision of philosophy. Rabindranath, as is obvious from the chapters dealing with his philosophy, is a reflective thinker, but in him reason and reflection are subordinated to imagination and emotion. His philosophical views are caught up in his spiritual vision and held captive in his poetic creations. The spirit of his poetry is the spirit of his life. The abstract and intellectual categories become suffused with the glow and warmth of things seen and realised.

The example of Rabindranath Tagore, if examples were needed, would give the lie direct to the cry, which evens the street urchin of the present day raises, that mysticism is incompatible with good poetry. To these critics it matters little if Dante and Goethe and many of the classical poets of religious Asia held the opposite view, and asserted and practised the doctrine that all true poetry is mystic. The authors of the Upanishads were poet-philosophers. Most of the great Persian poets were Sufi or mystic philosophers, who had for their aim the attainment of a state of spiritual perfection where the soul will be absorbed in holy contemplation to the exclusion of the pleasures of the world. Eternity is in the looks and eyes of these poets.

Philosophy and religion are counted among the creative forces which moulded Asiatic art and poetry. Mr. Havell observes: "Indian art is not concerned with the conscious striving after beauty as a thing worthy to be sought after for its own sake; its main endeavour is always directed towards the realisation of an idea, reaching through the finite to the infinite, convinced always that, through the constant effort to express the spiritual origin of earthly beauty, the human mind will take in more and more of the perfect beauty of divinity."

The same point is thus described by Mr. Laurence Binyon: " Not the glory of the naked human form, to Western art the noblest and most expressive of symbols; not the proud and conscious assertion of human personality; but, instead of these, all thoughts that lead us out from ourselves into the universal life, hints of the infinite, whispers from secret sources, mountains, waters, mists, flowering trees, whatever tells of powers and presences mightier than ourselves; these are the themes dwelt upon, cherished and preferred." It is the aim of Indian art to relate the seen and the unseen, the material and the spiritual, through imagination.

The "building of man's true world ... is the function of Art. Man is true, where he feels his infinity, where he is divine, and the divine is the creator in him." Browning, speaking of the subjective poet, observes that he " is impelled to embody the thing he perceives, not so much with reference to the many below, as to the one above him . . . not what man sees, but what God sees it is toward these that he struggles." We cannot therefore say that because Rabindranath's poetry is mystic it is not good poetry. It is undoubtedly mystic, and on that account he should hold a permanent place in the firmament of world-poets.

While both philosophy and poetry aim at the same end, their starting-points are different. They approach reality from different angles. While philosophy aims at grasping the synthesis which gathers together all aspects of the universe, poetry aims at catching the vision which sees the things of beauty of the world as a whole. Philosophy is an attempt to conceive the world as a whole by means of thought. It aims at a theory of the universe; and if this theory is held with a certain intensity and depth of feeling, if it captures the whole consciousness instead of being merely intellectually assented to, then the philosophic vision becomes creative and poetic.

Thought suffused with feeling and the other elements of consciousness becomes exalted into contemplation. The soul in this mood acquires imaginative vision with its spontaneity and creativity. It is then called mystic. But so long as the theory remains a mere intellectual creed, the difference between philosophy and poetry is kept up. The philosopher has his hand firm on the distinctions which are reconciled in the thought synthesis, and his reconciliation remains abstract and conceptual. The poet does not reason, but intuits. He does not make guesses at truth, but feels the truth as deeply real, and fierce with meaning. He lives life, and distils his doctrines from life.

The living unity of life is given in poetry in all its immediacy and concreteness, while it is only argued about in philosophical dissertations. The hard distinctions of philosophy melt into a sweet harmony in the flow of poetry. But the true philosopher with the true poet follows the intuitive method. Both are characterised by self-forgetfulness and spontaneity. The vision creative and the poetic impulse burst out like a volcanic force. Plato's description of the poet as one, who is bereft of reason but filled with divinity, holds good of the philosopher also. Our conclusion is that a poet is nothing if he is not a philosopher. A true poet will be a philosopher, and a true philosopher a poet.

Philosophy tells us that the world is rational; poetry tells us that it is beautiful. Philosophy reconciles the world to our reason; poetry to our feelings. Disorder and irrationality, philosophy cannot tolerate; ugliness and disgust with nature and society, poetry cannot accept. The greatest tragedies are tragic only at first sight; the poet finds in them a world of good-ness. He shows us how sorrow "is not sorrow but delight." The world is after all lovable. Poetry attunes our soul to the world and makes us feel that the world is a place worth living in.

This he does, not by concepts and arguments, but by music and fancy. Poetry pleases by an immediate appeal to imagination, and convinces not the intellect but the soul. The vision which the philosopher sees, the poet recreates. He realises it in his work. In poetry, philosophy lives. It puts on flesh and blood. It gives us not the philosophic idea, but the idea as lived or the life of the idea. For the spread of philosophy and true knowledge, nothing is so good a medium as poetry. It spreads truth more quietly. Truth slides into the mind unconsciously, effortlessly, easily.

Wordsworth says: "That which comes from the heart goes to the heart." Poetry is not intended to be a statement of truth, but only an expression of experience. It expresses what is held within the heart. By flooding the soul with emotions, by steeping the spirit in a bath of joy or delight, poetry puts the reader en rapport with the mind of the poet, induces him to sympathise with his temper, and breathe the atmosphere which floats before his eyes, and in which the poet lives, moves, and has his being. Poetry is a flower to be smelt, a sweet to be tasted or "drunk in every limb," and not taught. It does not cram the mind with facts and theories, but gives it a direction.

It does not teach, but touches the heart, warms the emotions, and moulds the whole mind. As an instrument of propagating knowledge, it is better than philosophy; for while a philosophic conclusion may commend itself to the intellect, it may quite possibly be regarded as incapable of satisfying the other sides of human life, though a true philosophic conclusion would satisfy not merely the intellect, but life as a whole. Philosophy may satisfy man the knower, but he is "not fully himself." In poetry we need have no such fear; for the appeal is to the whole personality of man. The "world which takes its form in the mould of man's perception still remains only as the partial world of his senses and mind. It is like a guest and not like a kinsman.

It becomes completely our own when it comes within the range of our emotions": Poetry "brings to us ideas, vitalised by feelings, ready to be made into the life-stuff of our nature." We have the assurance that the poet has lived what he is giving voice to, for he speaks straight out of life. "Consciously or unconsciously, I may have done many things that were untrue, but I have never uttered anything false in my poetry, that is the sanctuary where the deepest truths of my life emerge."

The work of the poet bears the impress of his life and individuality, and what is a part of one man's life can surely enter others' lives. The poet speaks as man to other men. Poetry appeals to the mind as a whole, for it is the expression of mind's free and unrestrained work. Besides, all true poetry forces acceptance of the poet's message, as he expresses it with such a passion and feeling, force and fulness, that to read it is to be convinced of it. The appeal of the artist compels into acquiescence those who cannot grasp the reasoning of philosophy.

If the truth of the world cannot be hammered into a man's head by the engines of argument and proof, the beauty of the poet's verse may yet win a way to the heart, and succeed where reasoning has failed. In the presence of its fancy and fragrance, music and sound, man feels helpless and his critical faculty sinks into silence. Poetry rouses the imagination and lets logic slumber and reason rest. The soul thinks, feels, and enjoys with the poet. Poetry attunes the soul to the life of truth, and the reader sees truth with the eye of the mind, and hears it with the ears of the soul.

By its music and melody, poetry induces consent, disarms criticism, and overpowers the soul. It has in it the power to coerce, or rather charm, the unwilling mind into homage. We do not ask for proof in poetry, for poetry is its own proof, "truth is its own testimony." If Rabindranath has touched Indian hearts, it is because he is first and foremost a poet and not a philosopher. But in all his works he has in view the great ideal of ancient Hindu art, viz. "to make the central ideas of Hindu religion and philosophy intelligible to all Hinduism, to satisfy the unlettered but not unlearned Hindu peasant as well as the intellectual Brahmin."

The highly abstruse notions of Hindu philosophy and religion are set free in his songs from their academic isolation and become a part of the common life of men. Rabindranath is following the tradition of the great Indian Rishis who spoke what they felt in the lyric songs of the Upanishads and their other creations. The devotional and poetic literature of India is embodied in poetry and music. By means of the epic poetry of India, the *Ramayana* and the *Mahabharata*, the priest and the peasant, the prince and the workman have become acquainted with the essentials of Hindu religion and philosophy, thought out by the sages of India.

Art has penetrated so deeply into the national life of India that the Indian peasant-folk, though illiterate in the sense of unlettered, can challenge comparison in point of culture with their corresponding classes anywhere in the world. Mr. Yeats observes in his Introduction to the *Gitanjali*: " A tradition, where poetry and religion are the same thing, has passed through the centuries, gathering from learned and unlearned metaphor and emotion, and carried back again to the multitude the thought of the scholar and the noble." By making truth live in forms of beauty the poet forces his ideas into the life of man.

Truth enters into man's nature through the gate of emotion. While it is true that poetry is not didactic and does not teach, still it thrills the reality and burns its ideas into the emotional nature of man. True to the saying of Plutarch, that poetry should initiate us into philosophy, Rabindranath's writings are waking many to the possibilities of spiritual life. His songs have become national songs, replete with words that breathe and thoughts that burn. His words please the ear, his ideas sink into the heart. His poetry is at the same time a light that fills the mind, a song that stirs the blood, and a hymn that moves the heart. The voice of Rabindranath, vibrating with the passion of genius, and glorifying his entire race, instils into the sinking heart of India faith in her, faith in her future, and faith in the world.

3

The Philosophy of Rabindranath Tagore

"The condemnation which a great man lays upon the world is to force it to explain him." Rabindranath Tagore has not failed to force the world to come with its magazine articles and monographs to expound his views. The worldwide interest and popularity of his writings are due as much to the lofty idealism of his thoughts as to the literary grace and beauty of his writings. Rabindranath's teaching, with its vital faith in the redeeming power of the spiritual forces and their up-building energy, has a particular value at the present moment, when the civilised world is passing through the crucible of a ghastly war which, whether or not it purges the nations of their pride and hate, lust for gold and greed of land, at least proclaims, in no uncertain tones, the utter bankruptcy of materialism.

To be great is not merely to be talked about, it is also to be misunderstood, and Rabindranath has not escaped this fate. The many attempts made to explain him contradict each other, for "from the words of the poet men take what meanings please them." There are two views regarding his philosophy of life. If we believe one side, he is a Vedantin, a thinker who draws his inspiration from the Upanishads. If we believe the other, he is an advocate of theism more or less like, if not identical with, Christianity. Rabindranath inclines to the former view.

"To me the verses of the Upanishads and the teachings of Buddha have ever been things of the spirit, and therefore endowed with boundless vital growth; and I have used them, both in my own life and in my preaching, as being instinct with individual meaning for me, as for others, and awaiting for their confirmation my own special testimony, which must have its value because of its individuality." J Rabindranath's philosophy by life is viewed by this school as nothing but the ancient wisdom of India restated to meet the needs of modern times. His writings are a commentary on the Upanishads by an individual of this generation on whom the present age has had its influence.

The soul of ancient India is mirrored in them. His idealism is a true child of India's own past and his philosophy is thoroughly Indian both in origin and development. In Dr. Coomaraswami's words, "the work of Rabindranath is essentially Indian in sentiment and form." The other view holds that Rabindranath Tagore, like other regenerators of Hinduism, has freely borrowed from Christianity and Western teaching, and has woven these alien elements into the woof of his own faith. If he does not confess his indebtedness to the West, it is, in the words of the Spectator s reviewer, a case of "local patriotism," "ingratitude," and " insincerity."

"We have Mr. Tagore employing his remarkable literary talents in teaching borrowed Ethics to Europe as a thing characteristically Indian." "There is a fatal flaw of insincerity in its most seemingly elevated utterances." These critics believe that the morals and philosophy underlying Rabindranath's thought are essentially Christian. They identify the Vedanta philosophy with a doctrine that makes the absolute an abstract beyond, the world an illusion, contemplation the way of escape, and extinction of soul the end of man. Obviously Rabindranath is not all this. He gives us a "human" God, dismisses with contempt the concept of the world - illusion, praises action overmuch and promises fulness of life to the religious soul.

These are essentially the features of the Christian religion, and what is Rabindranath Tagore if not a typical Christian of the type spiritual India would produce in larger numbers in years to come? The Rev. Mr. Saunders remarks: "The God of *Gitanjali* is no impersonal, imperturbable absolute of Hindu philosophy, but in fact, whether He be explicitly Christ or not, He is at least a Christ-like God, and the experience of His suppliant and lover is one with the deep core of all Christian experience." J The Rev. Mr. Urquhart observes: "He opened his soul to the ideas of the West and he has drawn from Chrisiianity, especially, ideas the influence of which upon his whole trend of thought has not always been acknowledged.

The Eastern dress which he has given to these ideas has often concealed both from his own eyes and those of his readers their true origin, and although truth is one and inhabits no particular clime, absence of indication here has sometimes led to consequences prejudicial to the development of truth itself. The ideas of Rabindranath, like those of so many thinkers of modern India, have often been quite wrongly assigned to Indian sources."

Mr. Edward J. Thompson, who calls it " nonsense " to say that *Gitanjali* represents "true Hinduism," observes: "The man who henceforward must rank among the great religious poets of the world does not call himself a Christian: but in him we get a glimpse of what the Christianity of India will be like, and we see that it is something better than the Christianity which came to it." There is no use dogmatising at the very outset, for that would be to attack the central question at issue.

An impartial exposition of Rabindranath's views would set at rest all doubts and disputes. We do not find any systematic exposition of his philosophy of life in any of his writings. Even Sadhana is a book of sermons, or mystic hymns, or perhaps meditations. It is a sigh of the soul rather than a reasoned account of metaphysics; an atmosphere rather than a system of philosophy. But we feel that the atmosphere is charged with a particular vision of reality. In his writings we have the reaction of his soul to the environment, his attitude in the face of life.

His personality is completely revealed in his poems, which are the unconscious expression of his soul, the outpourings of his devotional heart, and the revelation of his poetic consciousness. His writings must and do contain suggestions of his intellectual creed. Though poetry is not philosophy, it is possible for us to derive from Rabindranath's works his philosophical views. Human consciousness is the starting-point of all philosophic inquiry. The contradictions of human life provoke the quest for truth. Man is a finite- infinite being. He combines in himself spirit and nature. He is earth's child but heaven's heir. "At one pole of my being I am one with stocks and stones .... but at the other pole of my being I am separate from all."

As a link in the natural chain of events, man is subject to the law of necessity; as a member of the spiritual realm of ends, he is free. It is this contradiction, which we come across in science, art, and morality, that demands a solution. The individual aspires after perfect truth, perfect beauty, and perfect goodness. But in the finite world he can only approximate to, but never completely possess, them. We can see the ideals as through a mist. Intellectually we aspire after an ideal of truth which is complete, harmonious, and all-comprehensive.

The world of isolated facts is at best finite and conditioned. Intellect, with its separatist tendencies and dissecting habits, finds itself unable to grasp the whole. On the moral side, we feel the break between ideal aspirations and actual facts. There is a struggle between the infinite within, which makes the soul yearn for an ideal, and the lower finite, which is the heritage from the past evolution. "O Great Beyond, O the keen call of thy flute! I forget, I ever forget, that the gates are shut everywhere in the house where I dwell alone."

There is a tension between the higher and the lower. The two elements have not attained a harmony. The higher self presents us with a moral imperative which we recognize to be right, but our actual lower self contests its higher birth and pays homage to the delights of sense. This conflict is described in *Gitanjali*, 28.

Obstinate are the trammels, but my heart aches when I try to break them.

Freedom is all I want, but to hope for it I feel ashamed.

I am certain that priceless wealth is in thee, and that thou art my best friend, but I have not the heart to sweep away the tinsel that fills my room.

The shroud that covers me is a shroud of dust and death; I hate it, yet hug it in love.

My debts are large, my failures great, my shame secret and heavy; yet when I come to ask for my good, I quake in fear lest my prayer be granted.

Even if we identify ourselves with the higher and fight the lower, it sometimes happens that we feel worsted. The natural forces seem too much for the moral. In this distress the finite individual asks: Is the moral ideal a dream, and am I a fool to fight for it against the tremendous odds of nature? Have I a fighting chance of victory, or is the enterprise foredoomed to failure? Is the struggle between good and evil presided over by a higher Being on whom I could depend, or is it a great hazard where the result can be anything? As a rational being he craves for a working probability.

So long as nothing definite is known, the finite soul, struck by the galling injustice and evil of the world, wrings his hands in despair and cries out to Heaven: What must I do to be saved? Wretched man that I am who shall deliver me from the body of this death? The contradictions of finite life clearly establish that the finite individual is not the ultimate in the world but only an incomplete something requiring supplementation. The need for a philosophy which would reconcile the opposing elements of life, self and not-self, is felt to be urgent.

If what our intellect reveals to us is true, if the world is a chance congeries of individuals attempting without success to fight and conquer nature, the best thing for the wise man would be to withdraw from the universe and contemplate the noble ideals in his cloister, leaving the world to rack and ruin. Mr. Bertrand Russell represents this tendency very forcibly in his brilliant article on "The Free Man's Worship": "That man is the product of causes which had no prevision of the end they were achieving; that his origin, his growth, his hopes and fears, his loves and his beliefs are but the outcome of accidental collocations of atoms; that no fire, no heroism, no intensity of thought and feeling can preserve an individual life beyond the grave; that all the labours of the ages, all the devotion, all the inspiration, all the noonday brightness of human genius, are destined to extinction in the vast depth of the solar system, and that the whole temple of Man's achievement must inevitably be buried beneath the debris of a universe in ruins, all these things, if not quite beyond dispute, are yet so nearly certain that no philosophy which rejects them can hope to stand." "Blind to good and evil, reckless of destruction, omnipotent matter rolls on its relentless way."

Spiritual tempers recognise the high worth of human aspirations and require of men a contemplation of the ideals sacred to humanity. The way to escape from the sway of fate lies in giving up the ties binding man to the external world. We are exhorted by Mr. Russell "to abandon the struggle for private happiness, to expel all eagerness of temporary desire, to burn with passion for eternal things. This is emancipation; this is Free Man's Worship." The pessimists of all ages demand an extirpation of desires and an attainment of inner freedom.

The world is full of contradictions and human life is a great discord. The external world appears to be so awry that it drives man into the deepest solitudes of the soul. A sort of other worldly mysticism which treats with contempt both nature and man develops. The Absolute is said to be quite different from the world, just the opposite of the finite. The characteristics we are acquainted with in the finite universe can only be denied of it. It alone is real and the world is unreal. Such an intellectualist philosophy will make the Absolute an abstract beyond, the world an unreality, contemplation the way of escape, and extinction of soul the end of man. But the Absolute will then be left in a perilous state, having nothing to do with the universe.

This view is a confession of the defeat or discomfiture of man and can never satisfy his real needs. In this conflict of forces, self and not-self, right and might, there are thinkers who ask us to take up sides with might and wicked-ness. Nietzsche demands worship of force. The God of earth is a God of might and vengeance and not a God of right and conscience. This view is so patently absurd that we need not waste words over it. A different view, meant especially to emphasise the religious needs of man, prevails in the West. According to it self and not-self are opposed. "The West seems to take a pride in thinking that it is subduing nature, as if we are living in a hostile world where we have to wrest everything we want from an unwilling and alien arrangement of things."

The world of nature is regarded as a refractory force hard in resisting and slows in giving in. Man in his battlings with matter presided over by Satan requires the help of God. God along with mankind struggles to overcome the forces of evil and darkness. All such theistic conceptions generally end in making God a finite being. Leibnitz, in his famous Theodicy, makes God a limited one. He says the existing world is the best of all possible worlds.

Evidently all worlds were not possible to God; He selected the best possible, and it has turned out to be not quite a good one. Mill holds to a limited God in his Essay on Religion. Doctors James, Schiller, and Rashdall postulate a finite and personal God. These thinkers hold to a religious Asia and scientific Europe can be traced ultimately to this difference in view regarding man and environment. He writes: "The scientific movement arises from a peculiar attitude of the mind to the world found amongst certain peoples of the globe, and without this attitude science will always appear a curiosity or an irrelevance.

The attitude may be shortly described as due to a sense of the detachment of man from the world as something alien and external, to a sense of the supremacy of his aims over the process of the outer nature. In the East man seems to feel no sense of alienation; he seems to feel himself as much a part of the universe as a plant is inseparable from its environment. So much is this the case that man's life is felt to be part of the very current of the stream of the vaster life of the world pluralistic conception of the universe and find themselves unable to account for the unity of the world process.

No religion can finally rest in a God who is engaged in a conflict with evil in which He requires the help of man. We can never be sure of the outcome of the struggle. It is quite possible that a God who is limited by the resisting evil may have, like man, defeat for His end; only, if man fails with the help of God, great is his fall indeed. The defeat is more fearful when God has not deserted the side on which man is. A suffering God, a deity with a crown of thorns, cannot satisfy the religious soul. He is one among many, subject to the limitations of man. There is a great gulf fixed between humanity presided over by God and nature led by His opposite.

So long as one principle has not universal sway, so long the basis of pessimism is sound and safe. How can man, without the joy of hope and confidence in victory, bear up against the pressure of alien force? The fear of what the unknown and the unknowable energy might do fills his life with doubt and misery, weakness and distraction. Only a universal principle can deliver human life from despair. The Absolute is nothing short of the universe in its totality. It is the whole of perfection in which the opposition of good and evil is overcome. But the theist's God is identified with a part of the universe, the good, while the evil is left in its own independence. God is the virtue of the virtuous, and there is another opposing Him, the wickedness of the wicked.

The God of theism is only an aspect of the Absolute, an appearance of a deeper reality. Modern theism, aware of this difficulty, lays stress on Divine immanence, thus watering down the personal God into the Absolute whole. The views here referred to "read the world wrong" and do not give us a philosophic synthesis of God, world and self, for in a true synthesis we cannot have absolute divisions between man and nature. We need a principle, superior to them all, which would assign to each, self and not-self, its appropriate value, and give harmony to their mutual relations; a principle of synthesis which would comprehend both elements and transform their apparent antagonism into an organic relationship.

A closer scrutiny reveals to us the kinship of nature and spirit, not -self and self. The fact that we are able to interpret nature, know it, appreciate it, fight and conquer it, shows that it is akin to human consciousness: "We could have no communication whatever with our surroundings if they were absolutely foreign to us." Man is "reaping success every day, and that shows there is a rational connection between him and nature, for we never can make anything our own except that which is truly related to us."

If we separate man from nature "it is like dividing the bud and the blossom into two separate categories, and putting their grace to the credit of two different and antithetical principles."

"The Indian mind never has any hesitation in acknowledging its kinship with nature, its unbroken relation with all." In India where civilisation developed in forests near to nature, there was no thought of an antagonism between man and nature, no idea of forcibly wresting treasures from nature. Human consciousness, animal life, and inanimate nature are different grades of the same energy, stages of the same development.

Self and not-self into which the universe has been dichotomised are no rivals, but are the different expressions of the same Absolute, different modes of its existence. Nature is not antagonistic to spirit; not-self is there for the purpose of being used up by the spirit. It is fuel for the flame of the spirit. The Taittiriya Upanishad calls matter *annam* or food. The human will convert its environment into food. Objective nature is capable of being determined in accordance with the subject's wishes. The past progress of the Universe clearly establishes the success which has attended man's attempt to utilise the environment for the ends of life and spirit. The not-self is a means for the manifestation of spiritual power. Only through nature can spirit realise itself.

"The earth, water and light, fruits and flowers, to her were not merely physical phenomena to be turned to use and then left aside. They were necessary to her in the attainment of the ideal of perfection, as every note is necessary to the completeness of the symphony." If we adopt the right attitude to nature, we feel the pulse of spirit throbbing through it. A true seer sees in natural facts spiritual significance. The poetic temper hears the voice of spirit crying aloud in nature.

"The man, whose acquaintance with the world does not lead him deeper than science leads him, will never understand what it is that the man with the spiritual vision finds in these natural phenomena. The water does not merely cleanse his limbs, but it purifies his heart; for it touches his soul. The earth does not merely hold his body, but it gladdens his mind; for its contact is more than a physical contact, it is a living presence. When a man does not realise his kinship with the world, he lives in a prison-house whose walls are alien to him. When he meets the eternal spirit in all objects, then is he emancipated, for then he discovers the fullest significance of the world into which he is born; then he finds himself in perfect truth, and his harmony with the All is established."

The eye of an artist is needed to perceive the spiritual beauty of the things of nature. Only .his eye can penetrate through the confusing chaos of shadows and appearances, and see the cosmos within. Rabindranath has the eye which pierces into the secret of which the natural fact is the sign and prophecy. He is a poet of nature in whose hands the crudest stuff of existence acquires a poetic colouring. The spiritual phases of nature leap up to his God-filled eyes, kindle devotion in his heart, and set song on his lips. To his soul touched by God the physisal world of science appears in all its sweetness and simplicity as to a child. It is a "fairy universe where the stars talk and the sky stoops down to amuse him, and all nature come to his window with trays of bright toys."

To him "the touch of an infinite mystery passes over the trivial and the familiar, making it break out into ineffable music." "The trees, the stars, and the blue hills " ache " with a meaning which can never be uttered in words." A breath of divine passion passes over the whole world, making it pure and perfect. He feels "a thrill passing through the air with the notes of the far-away song floating from the other shore." He can never escape the divine presence, twist and turn as he will. The deep shadows of the rainy July and the stormy night suggest God's presence. He is a mystic soul who can hear the voice of God in the tempest and see His hand in the stilling of the wave.

It is no wonder that Rabindranath advocates life in nature and in the open as the best means of spiritual progress, for in nature the religious eye will see the infinite lying stretched in silent smiling repose. Rabindranath sings not of the cloister or the retreat, but of the open highway and the King's Post Office. He revels in the open air and is not afraid to stand under the golden canopy. According to him the best way to derive divine inspiration is to lose oneself in the contemplation of nature. In silence and in solitude we have to enjoy the presence of the divine in nature never escape the divine presence, twist and turn as he will. The deep shadows of the rainy July and the stormy night suggest God's presence. He is a mystic soul who can hear the voice of God in the tempest and see His hand in the stilling of the wave.

It is no wonder that Rabindranath advocates life in nature and in the open as the best means of spiritual progress, for in nature the religious eye will see the infinite lying stretched in silent smiling repose. Rabindranath sings not of the cloister or the retreat, but of the open highway and the King's Post Office. He revels in the open air and is not afraid to stand under the golden canopy. According to him the best way to derive divine inspiration is to lose oneself in the contemplation of nature. In silence and in solitude we have to enjoy the presence of the divine in nature. I woke and found his letter with the morning. When the night grows still and stars come out one by one I will spread it on my lap and stay silent.

The rustling leaves will read it aloud to me, the rushing stream will chant it, and the seven wise stars will sing it to me from the sky. He does not lay stress on religious instruction in the Bolpur School, but believes that religious feeling and piety will work their way into the life of the students if the environment is pure and noble. "We do not want nowadays temples of worship and outward rites and ceremonies. What we really want is an Asram. We want a place where the beauty of nature and the noblest pursuits of man are in a sweet harmony. Our temple of worship is there where outward nature and human soul meet in union."

Recognising the influence of environment upon temperament, the ancient teachers chose the forest shades or the banks of holy rivers as the sites for their Asrams. When we are filled with the sense of the divinity that surrounds us, then we feel impelled to give ourselves up to reverie or meditation on God. To-day the summer has come at my window with its sighs and murmurs; and the bees are plying their minstrelsy at the court of their flowering grove. Now it is time to sit quiet, face to face with thee, and to sing dedication of life in this silent and overflowing leisure.

Again:

In the busy moments of the noontide work I am with the crowd, but on this dark lonely day it is only for thee that I hope.If thou showest me not thy face, if thou leavest me wholly aside, I know not how I am to pass these long rainy hours.

In moments of such exaltation when we silently adore the living presence that reveals itself through the grandeur of nature, which makes it heard in the soul through the contemplation of the world of immanent divinity, a great peace steals over us. The infinite then murmurs its secret into our ears, and tells the story of the soul and the legend of the earth. To commune with the unutterable, we should get away from the noisy world of action, escape from the machinery of life which kills the soul. Dull mechanical work degrades and brutalises the individual, while a life of nature elevates and purifies the soul. Rabindranath beautifully depicts how an enthusiastic surrender to the spontaneity of natural scenery leads a man to his goal. I laid myself down by the water and stretched my tired limbs on the grass. My companions laughed at me in scorn.

They held their heads high and hurried on; they never looked back rested; they vanished in the distant blue haze. They crossed many meadows and hills, and passed through strange, far-away countries. All honour to you, heroic host of the interminable path! Mockery and reproach pricked me to rise, but found no response in me. I gave myself up for lost in the depth of a glad humiliation in the shadow of a dim delight. At last, when I woke from my slumber and opened my eyes, I saw thee standing by me, flooding my sleep with thy smile. We then lie exposed to all the winds of heaven that blow. We feel a presence, all love and peace. The load slips off our heart, and the soul is lifted above life, petty, vexatious, and harassing, and slides into a perfect harmony. The divine light floods the soul, the divine music ravishes it, and the soul expresses its joy by humming the hymn of the universe. So running "upon the dusty path of the despised" takes us nearer to God.

In The Post Office, the child Amal, rid of the prejudices of the sophisticated Madhav, wistfully yearns to get away from the clank of crowds, the noise and glare of the town, into countryside with its hills and dales. Even though his continuance in the world is said to depend on his keeping indoors, the cage bird longs to be a free bird and enjoy the freedom of the woodland. For as it is put in *The Cycle of Spring*: "This outer world has been made with a lavish expenditure of sun and moon and stars. Let us enjoy it, and then we can save God's face for indulging in such extravagance."

Rabindranath's conception of nature is antagonistic to the view which makes nature opposed to the self and its aspirations. He has a positive view of the relation of spirit to nature. The two are aspects of the Absolute. Nature and society are revelations of the divine spirit. The same light dwells in the world outside and the world within. This ultimate oneness of things is what the Hindu is required to remember every moment of his life. "The text of our everyday meditation is the Gayatri, a verse which is considered to be the epitome of all the Vedas. By its help we try to realise the essential unity of the world with the conscious soul of man; we learn to perceive the unity held together by the one Eternal Spirit, whose power creates the earth, the sky, and the stars, and at the same time irradiates our minds with the light of a consciousness that moves and exists in unbroken continuity with the outer world."

The song of the soul and the music of the spheres are but the expressions of the divine harmony. The same stream of life that runs through my veins night an'd day runs through the world and dances in rhythmic measures. The same spirit dwells in the most distant sun and in the darkest depths of the soul. Nature is not a hostile power harassing man at every turn; the universe is not foreign to us. When in the morning I looked upon the light I felt in a moment that I was no stranger in this world.

Rabindranath's conception of the unity of the world gives us the assurance that the ideals of Science and Morality are real, and sustains us on the path of right untempered by the grim realities of pain and crime. It makes us realise how the spiritual forces of the world co-operate with us in our endeavours. If the distinction of man and world, self and not-self, were the last thing, then "there would have been absolute misery and unmitigated evil in this world. Then from untruth we never could reach truth, and from sin we never could hope to attain purity of heart; then all opposites would ever remain opposites, and we could never find a medium through which our differences could ever tend to meet."

Then our life would become a hideous tragedy of waste and wrong, fear and weakness. But progress in the realms of Science, Art, and Morality shows that self and not-self are only relatively opposed. It is the business of man to break down the opposition, and make both express the one spirit. This view restores the balance between nature and spirit, and makes life worth living. "It were well to die if there be Gods, and sad to live if there be none."

If there is the all-embracing spirit, the glooms and shadows of life lose their edge and bitterness. Then we feel that we are not battling with an unknown antagonist on a doubtful issue, but that we are trying to realise progressively a victory that is guaranteed to us. Perfect confidence takes the place of blank despair. The confused and shadowy world of experience becomes quite clear and transparent. Doubt is vanquished; the contradictions of life cease. "All that is harsh and dissonant melts into one sweet harmony."

The creation of the universe is only the realisation of the Absolute, the revelation of its freedom. "God finds himself by creating." It is the creative joy that gives birth to the universe, which is not only separate from God but also united to Him. God is the basis of the whole universe. It is the self-sundering of the Eternal which calls into existence the universe of men and things. But this must have "duality for its realisation." The whole breaks up its individuality into the two aspects of self and not-self, Iswara and Maya, Purusha and Prakriti. "When the singer has his inspiration he makes himself into two; he has within him his other self as the hearer and the outside audience is merely an extension of this other self of his. The lover seeks his own other self in his beloved. It is the joy that creates this separation, in order to realise through obstacles the union."

The not-self or Prakriti or Maya is generally conceived of as the passive and the self as the active principle. It is their mutual supplementation that promotes the unity of the universe. The Eternal One realises itself by the action and interaction of the two principles. The principle of negativity impels the Eternal One to realise itself in the world. It is the woman "in the heart of creation." "She who is ever returning to God his own outflowing of sweetness; she is the ever fresh beauty and youth in nature; she dances in the bubbling streams and sings in the morning light; she with heaving waves suckles the thirsty earth; in her the Eternal One breaks in two in a joy that no longer may contain itself, and overflows in the pain of love."

The first existent out of the Absolute is Iswara with the not-self over against him. Iswara is the personal God who represents the ideal of goodness to the finite minds. He is the father, creator or governor of the universe. The not-self is the negative reflection of the affirmative Iswara. The whole universe develops in, through, and by means of, the interaction between these two. Whatever being is born, the unmoving or the moving, know thou, O best of the Bharathas, that to be owing to the union of Kshetra and Kshetragnya (matter and spirit, finite and infinite).

Between the poles of the conscious and the unconscious, there has the mind made a swing: Thereon hang all beings and all worlds, and that swing never ceases its sway. Millions of beings are there: the sun and the moon in their courses are there: Millions of ages pass, and the swing goes on. All swing! the sky and the earth and the air and the water; and the Lord Himself taking form: And the sight of this has made Kabir a servant. The universe is the eternal sacrifice of the supreme. The *Bhagavad Gita* says: "The whole world rests on sacrifice. It is the law of the universe."

He is sacrificing himself that nature and humanity may live. This self-sundering of the whole in which the world is contained is but the expression of his joy and the law of the universe. It is " the joy that makes the earth flow over in the riotous excess of the grass, the joy that sets the twin brothers, life and death, dancing over the wide world, the joy that sweeps in with the tempest, shaking and waking all life with laughter, the joy that sits still with its tears on the open red lotus of pain, and the joy that throws everything it has upon the dust, and knows not a word." The outburst of joy is needed for the realisation of the concrete richness of the world. The universe is new-born continually, as a result of this joy.

This frail vessel thou emptiest again and again, and fillest it ever with fresh life.

This lesson that "the old is ever new" is the central theme of *The Cycle of Spring*. The Absolute realises through separation and union. The child finds its mother when it leaves her womb. When I am parted from you, thrown out from your household,

I am free to see your face. This separation is needed to make the eternal concrete. You did not know yourself when you dwelt alone. I came and you woke. Thou settest a barrier in thine own being and then callest thy severed self in myriad notes. This thy self- separation has taken body in me.

The great pageant of thee and me has overspread the sky. With the tune of thee and me all the air is vibrant, and all ages pass with the hiding and seeking of thee and me. It is the pang of separation that spreads throughout the world and gives birth to shapes innumerable in the infinite sky. But the separation of the two is not the last word. The universe is not merely a going forth from God, but is also a coming towards Him. The union of the two is complete, but in the universe it is being made. The finite represents to us the tension of the self to become the infinite.

The universe is the struggle of the finite to reach the infinite. It is a play of hide and seeks between the two, God and man. All objects of the world are finite-infinite, but the tension between the two is at its highest in the human consciousness. Man approximates to the ideal but never qua man reaches it. The world is the process of becoming infinite, but not the consummation. Should man completely realise the infinite, and should the world reach its goal of becoming the infinite, then there will be no universe and necessarily no Absolute.

O thou lord of all heavens, where would be thy love if I were not? Though God is everything, everything is not God. While the whole universe is regarded by Rabindranath as the expression of God, still different things express God in different degrees. He thus admits the conception of degrees of reality. "The revealment of the infinite in the finite, which is the motive of all creation, is not seen in its perfection in the starry heavens, in the beauty of the flowers. It is in the soul of man." Man, the animal with the upward look, is a higher revealment than the mere animal, and the animal is higher than the worm, which is higher than the clod. "To all things else you give; from me you ask." Subject to this reservation we can say that the objects of the universe are parts of God aspiring to be the whole. God is the infinite ideal of perfection.

Man has yet to become what he is. On account of his finiteness he does not realise his aim. The content of his ideal passes beyond his existence. It has a reach beyond his grasp. He strives towards it, but it eludes his effort. He sees it as a vision beheld in dreaming, something ardently longed for. The finite universe of persons and things represents to us the passage from the imperfect to the perfect. We see the road, the end is not yet. Through the world, the opportunities it affords, "they are coming, the pilgrims, one and all coming to their true inheritance of the world." The world is but the progress of pilgrims in their quest for the infinite. Every object in it cries out, "I want thee, only thee," and struggles to attain immortal life.

Man cannot reach the ideal so long as fragments of finiteness stick to him, so long as his intellect, emotion, and will are bound in the realm of finite nature. The finite intellect reduces the universe to the opposites of self and not-self, organism and environment, and leaves us there without revealing to us the final unity in which these relative opposites rest. The ultimate unity breaks itself into the two factors of subject and object, man and nature. Intellect reads the manifestations, but misses the unity in which the two are gathered together. It exults in the strife of the opposites which is the play of the universe. The whole in which these distinctions are, not abolished, but overcome, the unity which is the final or the ultimate explanation of the things, is not grasped by it.

What it does is to break up the world-poem and discover in it "the law of its rhythms, the measurement of its expansion and contraction, movement and use, the pursuit of its evolution of forms and character." These are no doubt "true achievements of the mind," but Rabindranath says, "We cannot stop there." Our thought cannot finally rest in them. We are in the rands of opposites still. The Upanishad says: "You will have fear so long as there is dualism." The universe of intellect " is like a railway station; but the station platform is not our home."

The world of intellect, with its distinctions of good and evil, truth and error, self and not-self, beauty and ugliness, is only a stage on the pathway to reality. The intellectual vision is full of hard- and - fast lines of distinction. It makes the opposites absolute, and the system becomes full of contradictions; but if we pierce behind it we shall find that the rigid distinctions of intellect are fluid, and mingle in a wondrous whole. "This screen that thou hast raised is painted with innumerable figures with the brush of the night and the day. Behind it thy seat is woven in wondrous mysteries of curves, casting away all barren lines of straightness."

Beyond the two, beyond the finite and the infinite, we have the Absolute, which the finite intellect cannot grasp. Our mind cannot reach it. Our soul looks into the dim unknown to catch sight of it, but cannot find it where we come across motor cars and aeroplanes. Our vision is external, and God is not there; our vision is turned inside, and God is not there. If I say that He is within me, the universe is ashamed: If I say that He is without me, it is falsehood.

We shall not see Him until we see Him everywhere, in and out, in darkness and in light. In the drama of Job it is put in the mouth of Zophar: "Canst thou by searching find out God canst thou find out the Almighty unto perfection? It is high as heaven; what canst thou do deeper than Sheol; what canst thou know? "The intuitive insight by which we can see God, the intellect cannot give. The Absolute is the highest unity from which all being proceeds; but it is so exalted and so exquisite that none of our conceptions can adequately describe it. It's overflowing life breaks through all intellectual barriers.

A simple childlike vision purified and purged of all prejudices, can get at it. When the soul is absorbed in God, it sees

Him. "The soul that knows Brahman becomes Brahman." Reasoning and argument are of no avail. Syllogism does not give us its spirit. It is deeper than demonstration. Intelligence cannot fathom the depths of that divine mystery. He is a God who hideth Himself. He can be "felt in the dark, but not seen in the day." He can only be known intuitively. Rabindranath says: "The vision of the Supreme One in our own soul is a direct and immediate intuition, not based on any ratiocination or demonstration at all."

To the eye of the finite intellect, it is darkness, impenetrable darkness. God is the King of the Dark Chamber. We are in a dark prison, surrounded by walls which our finiteness has raised, which separate us from others. Outside it there is light and no darkness. If suddenly the great vision appears to our untrained eyes, which can see objects only in the pleasure garden, if it reveals itself unexpectedly to our ordinary consciousness, sticking to the small strutting ego as if it were everything of consequence in the world, the vision will alarm the eyes and shake that consciousness to its foundations.

Even to the high-souled Arjuna, with his soul full of divine fire and heart full of devotion to God, the tremendous vision of the Universal Form of God was insupportable, too terrific and awful for him to look upon. By its exceeding brilliance it will dazzle the eyes of mortal man. God who shows himself in a moment of great suffering will look terrible. Black, black oh, thou art black like the everlasting night! I only looked on thee for one dreadful instant. The blaze of the fire fell on your features you looked like the awful night when a comet swings fearfully into our ken, and then I closed my eyes I could not look on you any more. Black as the threatening storm-cloud, black as the shoreless sea with the spectral red tint of twilight on its tumultuous waves!

For one awful moment the Princess saw into the heart of things with the eyes of eternity, and had visions of suns grown cold, universes frozen. We cannot see either in perfect darkness or in perfect light. Both are dark to us one with the excess of brightness, the other with the lack of it. We want a mixture of opposites everywhere, and that we have in our solid-seeming world.

The Princess in the drama of The King of the Dark Chamber, which describes the eternal quest of the soul for its kindred, wishes to see her husband and dear lord in the empirical world, where we have summer houses and motor cars, in the world of time, space, and causation. She wants to see him as an object among objects. She cannot reach him thus. The scientist says: You can sweep the wide heavens with the telescope but will not find God. Even so the Princess, when her vision is confined to the empirical world, may grow sceptic about the existence of God.

"It strikes me, Kaundilya that these people haven't got a King at all. They have somehow managed to keep the rumour afloat." The existence of God is put down for a fiction or a hypothesis, contrived by the cunning, perhaps to keep the wretch in good order. Life becomes a despairing question and God a problem. He is near to her if she looks from the proper angle of vision, but He is far off if she adopts the empirical standpoint. The Absolute is a phantom that eludes her grasp. So long as the Princess wants to find God, who is ever in love with her, where she sees trees and animals, birds and stones, she cannot find Him.

The reason is that the Supreme is not an object which we can see with our finite eyes. It is the very light by which we see all objects. How can we see it as an object when it is both the subject and the object, when it is the light by which we see and the light which we see? There is nothing else than light to see it by. If we turn ourselves rightly, we shall see it everywhere. We and the whole universe are eternal witnesses to its presence. It is the life of life, the self of self. It is in our very heart. We need not fathom the sea, or sweep the sky; we need not ascend into heaven or descend into the deep to reach it. A conversion of soul is what is needed. If we break through the ordinary gaze we shall find it. Our cherished illusions must go.

The vulgar wisdom of the masses should be recognised to be vulgar. An inversion of the secular into the religious consciousness is needed. If we get rid of the finiteness, and rise above the intellectual level and pierce behind the veil, we shall see it face to face. To see God we should transfer ourselves to another dimension of reality. We should break down the barrier of individuality and relax the despotism of the senses; our ignorance will then be removed. We escape from the light of separation and see God as the transcendent darkness in which the whole universe is bathed. Surangama says: "A day came when all the rebel in me knew itself beaten, and then my whole nature bowed down in humble resignation on the dust of the earth. And then I saw ... I saw that he was as matchless in beauty as in terror. Oh, I was saved, I was rescued."

We shall then see our ordinary consciousness to be the real darkness and the transcendent one to be the perfect radiance of Eternity. The Princess says: "Your sight repelled me because I had sought to find you in the pleasure garden, in my Queen's chambers: there even your meanest servant looks handsomer than you. That fever of longing has left my eyes for ever. You are not beautiful, my lord you stand beyond all comparisons! "While the supreme is bright and clear to the religious intuition, it is misty and dark to the cold intellect. It is "dark from its surpassing brightness ... as the shining of the sun on his course is as darkness to weak eyes." Vaughan in his "The Night" says:

There is in God, some say,
A deep but dazzling darkness, as men here
Say, it is late and dusky because they
See not all clear.
O for that night! where I in Him
Might live invisible and dim.

To the finite consciousness God is far away; to the religious soul He is quite near. God is present, yet absent. The *Bhagavad Gita* says: "Near and far away is That." The Isa Upanishad says: "He is far and also near." "When you think that He is not here, then you wander farther and farther away, and seek Him in vain with tears. Where He is far off, there He is unattainable: Where He is near, He is very bliss." "They have sung of Him as infinite and unattainable: but I in my meditations have seen Him without sight." Tukaram, the Indian saint, says: "O man, why do you travel from place to place to search God? As the deer does not know that it possesses an invaluable thing called kasthuri (musk), so you' do not know what is within you. Search God within you and you will find Him." Rabindranath says: "You were in the centre of my heart, therefore when my heart wandered she never found you."

The traveller has to knock at every alien door to come to his own, and one has to wander through all the outer worlds to reach the innermost shrine at the end. My eyes strayed far and wide before I shut them and said "Here art thou!" In thus transcending intellect by intuition we become childlike in our simplicity and innocence of the world's ways. Our knowledge is transformed into wisdom. "God waits for man to regain his childhood in wisdom."

The eyes of the body are closed as in sleep for the eyes of spirit to open as in dreams. "Yea, when it sleeps, the mind is bright with eyes." Thus Rabindrahath, in common with other mystics, discriminates between the path of intuition, which is the way of wisdom born of love, and the path of intellect, which is the way of knowledge born of observation. Intuition enables us to penetrate beneath outward appearances studied by science and see the life in things. It is a matter of experience or insight, which is coercive and certain. The design-argument, which makes God a matter of inference and not observation, is urged by Janardhan in *The King of the Dark Chamber*.

"But look at the nice order and regularity prevailing all over the place how do you explain it without a King?" This argument is put down for mere quibbling, as the question is to be decided by intuition. "Have you, or have you not, seen the King? Yes or no? "Kabir sings: "They are blind who hope to see it by the light of reason, that reason which is the cause of separation. The house of Reason is very far away." Reason, which can help us to weigh the dust or measure the air, cannot show us the face of God. The truly religious soul does not argue and infer, but meditates and waits for light. The poet, the artist, and the lover pursue this path of intuition; the mystic knows it, and lives in the full light of the vision.

In the characterisations of God in the Vedanta writings and Rabindranath's works we find an identity of thought. The popular idea that the Brahman of the Vedanta is an abstract beyond is incorrect. Rabindranath protests against such a misconception. He says: "The infinite in India was not a thin nonentity, void of all content. The Rishis of India asserted emphatically, ' To know Him in this life is to be true; not to know Him in this life is the desolation of death.' How to know Him then? 'By realising Him in each and all.' Not only in nature, but in the family, in society, and in the state, the more we realise the world -conscious in all, the better for us. Failing to realise it we turn our faces to destruction."

The Vedanta thinkers do not place God in the solitude of a world beyond. The hymn or mantra chanted every evening at the Bolpur school, " The God who is in fire, who is in water, who interpenetrates the whole world, who is in herbs, who is in trees, to that God I bow again and again," is from the Upanishads. The Vedantic Absolute as much as Rabindranath's God is a concrete spirit.

He is there where the tiller is tilling the hard ground and where the pathmaker is breaking stones. The mystics of all faiths and creeds, from the Rishis of Upanishads downwards, are at one in this belief in the immanence of God. St. Paul says: "He is above all, through all, and in all." So too we read: " Raise the stone, and there thou shalt find me; cleave the wood, and there am I." It is meaningless to argue that the Vedantic Absolute is a barren nothing and Rabindranath's God a concrete something, and therefore Rabindranath is no Vedantin. The logic is irresistible; only the premisses are false.

Critics may urge that the Vedanta philosophy is ambiguous about the nature of God. True it says, God is All, but it also says God is nothing. "It is not this, not this." This dilemma of mysticism which makes God sometimes the All, sometimes nothing, is not peculiar to the Vedanta writings, but runs through all mystic literature. Rabindranath's poems are full of it. In some pages the Absolute is an abstract, formless, featureless unity, not a God who deserves to be adored and worshipped. It is "the inscrutable without name and form."

But there, where spreads the infinite sky for the soul to take her flight in, reigns the stainless white radiance. There is no day nor night, nor form nor colour, and never, never a word. On the other hand, in the same poem Rabindranath makes the whole universe the manifestation of God:

Thou art the sky, and thou art the nest as well.

Much the same thing is true of Kabir's utterances.

He is neither manifest nor hidden; He is neither revealed nor unrevealed: There are no words to tell that which He is. He is without form, without quality, without decay. Only he knows it who has reached that region: it is other than all that is heard and said. No form, no body, no length, no breadth is seen there:

How can I tell you that which it is.

To represent the other current of his thought we may cite the following passage:

He Himself is the tree, the seed, and the germ.

He Himself is the flower, the fruit, and the shade.

He Himself is the sun, the light, and the lighted.

He Himself is Brahma, creature, and Maya.

He Himself is the manifold form, the infinite space;

He is the breath, the word, and the meaning.

He Himself is the limit and the limitless: and beyond both the limited and the limitless is He, the Pure Being. He is the Immanent Mind in Brahma and in the creature. The Upanishads are full of such apparently contradictory descriptions, for they are only the records of the spiritual experiences of the sages of India. "He is not this, He is not that." "It is neither coarse nor fine, neither sharp nor long, neither red like fire nor fluid like water; it is without shadow, without darkness, without air, without water, without attachment, without taste, without smell, without eyes, without ears, without speech, without mind, without light, without breath, without mouth, without measure, having no within and no without; it devours nothing and no one devours it."

To represent the other tendency we have the Chandogya, which says: "this entire universe has the Supreme deity for its life. That deity is truth. He is the Universal soul. Thou art He, Swethakethu." The Mundaka Upanishad says: " This immortal Brahma, to the right and the left, below and above, all pervading, Brahma is this All, this infinite world." The contradiction between the two accounts is only apparent and not real. If by means of our finite intellect we try to reach the Absolute we shall fail in our attempts. The Kena Upanishad says: "It is far from the known and above the unknown."

The Taittiriya says: "Words together with the mind return without comprehending it." The Absolute unity is opposed to the intellectual duality, and the intellectual account of the Absolute remains a negative one. But when we rise above the plane of intellect to religion, poetry, and philosophy we see it face to face. When we say that the Absolute is above the grasp of intellect, we do not mean that it is opposed to it. Only in the Absolute the intellectual is realised. "In love all the contradictions of existence merge themselves and are lost. Only in love are unity and duality not at variance."

At the intuitional level the Absolute is the all-comprehending love with whom we can commune, whom we can love, adore, and worship. The Absolute is the whole Universe. The creation is the dance, leela, or the play of the Absolute. "The Creator brought into being the game of joy. The Earth is his Joy. ... In play is the creation spread out. In play it is established."

Now the question arises, Is Rabindranath's God a person and not the impersonal Absolute of the Vedanta? Yes: *Gitanjali* makes of God a person. The Vedanta Philosophy in all its stages of development provides for such a conception. Art, philosophy, and religion are the specialised modes in which the Absolute presents itself to mankind. God is a trinity because man is. The human individual is a unity of intellect, emotion, and will, and the Supreme Ideal, to satisfy sentiment, will, and reason, appears as Supreme Beauty, Supreme Good, and Supreme Truth.

And as the human individual is a unity of the three, and as these elements cannot conflict with each other, and as no one of them can complete its idea except as it gathers into itself the two others, even so there is no discord between the different aspects of truth, beauty, and goodness in the Supreme Ideal. This ideal shows itself to man's capacity for joy as Supreme Beauty, to his capacity for knowledge as Supreme Truth, to his capacity to act, as Supreme Good. The contents of the three do not vary, though their form does. Art, philosophy, and religion are different forms and expressions of worship and different ways of approach to God.

The particular method depends upon the temperamental characteristics with which the Creator has enriched human nature. All souls, saints, sages, and seers seek union with God. Mystic souls of an emotional and imaginative cast of mind express their devotion by love, worship, and adoration. They make a person of the object of their love. In Rabindranath the art aspect predominates. His wealth of imagination, force of feeling, and intensity of passion turn his words into music and poetry. The poems of *Gitanjali* are the offerings of the finite to the infinite.

The relation between the two is conceived of as that between the lover and the beloved an analogy employed by the mystics the world over. Throughout oriental literature, this analogy is constantly used to express the true relationship between the human soul and God. Radha's passionate devotion to Krishna is the symbol of the soul's yearning for God. When Krishna, to draw all creation to him, sings the divine music of his flute, she listens to it and gives up her all for His sake. The analogy of human love holds, in that in perfect love we have two yet one, a single life led by a man and a woman. The surrender of the soul, the fulfilment of love, and the union with the other spirit, characteristic of human love, are present in the longing for the Absolute. But if we press this analogy too far we get all sorts of difficulties.

Ultimately there will be no divorce between head and heart, reason and faith. Rabindranath is intellectual enough to recognise that the Vedantic Absolute which he believes to be the ultimate philosophical unity does not lend itself to intellectual description. But being an artist, he translates his spiritual experience into material symbols. The language is metaphorical, and if literally interpreted would lead to absurdities and contradictions.

Miss Evelyn Underhill remarks in her admirable introduction to Kabirs Poems\ "It is a marked characteristic of mystical literature that the great contemplatives, in their effort to convey to us the nature of their communion with the supersensuous, are inevitably driven to employ some form of s ensuous imagery: coarse and inaccurate as they know such imagery to be, even at the best." If from the poems of *Gitanjali* we infer that God is a person over against man, we make a mistake.

To Rabindranath God is not a being seated high up in the heavens, but a spirit immanent in the whole Universe of persons and things. Rabindranath's love is a spiritual love above sex, unintelligible to the world at large, a love which loses itself in the sea of the Absolute to " melt and vanish away in the dark, or it may be in a smile of the white morning, in a coolness of purity transparent." The Absolute of philosophy becomes the God of religion, to all followers of the Bhakti school. Iswara, the highest manifestation of the Absolute, is the personal Lord of the Universe. The distinction of the lover and the loved is kept up till the last point, when in perfect love the two become one.

The personal God is then dissolved in the Absolute. If Rabindranath is viewed as a worshipper of a personal God, he may be looked upon as the living example of the long and noble succession of religious devotees of whom India is justly proud, including among others Manikkavasagar, Ramanuja, Maddhwa, Ramananda, Vedanta Desikar, Jnaneswar, Namdev, Vallabha Charya, Kabir, Chandidas, Chaithanya, Nanak, Dadu, Tulasidas, and Tukaram.

This Bhakti school has had a continuous history from the very beginnings of reflection in India. A Christian critic, Dr. Macnicol, says: "Theism is both ancient in the land and indigenous to the soil. . . . No one need suppose that the ideas that bhakti connotes are a foreign importation into India." The critics who make Rabindranath a borrower from Christianity betray an astonishing lack of "historic conscience" a charge generally urged against Indians. The Absolute of philosophy and the God of religion have both a place in the Vedanta system.

Those who draw a hard-and-fast line of distinction between the two will never be able to understand the Vedanta philosophy. What Richard Garbe says of the *Bhagavad Gita* is true of other Vedanta writings: "The doctrines which are here put into the mouth of Krishna present a remarkable combination of pantheistic and monotheistic ideas, of philosophical thoughts and of pure and deeply religious faith in God." The formless Absolute has to be conceived as a being of form by the finite individual. To put it the other way, we can say that the Absolute, which is above the pairs of opposites of beauty and ugliness, truth and error, good and evil, still appears for the sake of man as perfect Beauty, perfect Truth, and perfect Goodness. "The Perfect decks itself in beauty for the love of the Imperfect." The following words, quoted in Maharshi Devendranath Tagore's Autobiography, admirably depict the contrition of the devotee for the confusion of spirit due to his finiteness:

O spiritual guide of the Universe, Thou art without form:

Yet that I have conceived Thine image in the act of meditation;

That I have ignored Thine inexpressibility by words of praise;

That I have set at naught Thy omnipresence by making pilgrimages, and in other ways,

For these three transgressions committed through confusion of spirit, O Almighty God, I implore Thy forgiveness.

4

Rabindranath Tagore as Reformer

From this distance in time the eighty years of Rabindranath Tagore's life (1861-1941) are principally known for his work as a polymathic arts figure. He was not only a writer of novels, essays, and articles, a philosopher, a world-renowned poet and Nobel Prize winner. He also wrote songs and sang them; he wrote plays and acted in them; he wrote dance-dramas and danced in them. But, as they say, every schoolboy knows that. What Uma Das Gupta has done here is quite deliberately to by-pass most of this and to bring out some lesser known and unsung parts of Tagore's life and work, and to delineate the forces that shaped his thinking and his work.

The subjects examined here are his activities as an educator and rural reformer. His letters are evidence of how he longed only to be a poet, but they also reveal how he could not stay away from doing something practical and constructive for his country. Mr Gupta has chosen to write about these because; in his own words 'those aspects of his life are relatively unknown. We all know him as a poet but do not think of him as a man of action'. Mainly, the focus is on Tagore's practical actions in creating Visva-Bharati, an educational institution-even a university-in rural Bengal, and on his work to improve the economic, social, physical and cultural well-being of villagers in the countryside.

A secondary theme of the book is to identify and elaborate on the issues and beliefs that concerned Tagore all his life as a poet and a writer. This follows his privileged upbringing in British India and his travels all over the world to illustrate how his convictions were developed about Indian history, nationalism and internationalism, racial humiliation, self-esteem and humanism.

Rabindranath Tagore had sensible and clearly articulated views about nationalism in the light of cross-cultural knowledge, education for freedom of the mind, war and peace, the importance of reasonable criticism, the need for openness, and so on. His books show the influence of different parts of the Indian cultural background, as well as that of the rest of the world. People may be confused by Tagore's description of his Bengali family as the product of "a confluence of three cultures, Hindu, Mohammedan, and British," because the amalgamation of East and West may seem contradictory. Actually, Tagore did not support the idea of nationalism.

TAGORE'S CONCEPT OF NATIONALISM AND UNIVERSAL HUMANITY

Tagore's doctrine of universal humanity was to spread spiritual values among people and create a new world culture out of multi-culturism, diversity, and tolerance. When Gandhi took care of the political sector by essentially being and representing the everyman, Tagore served the spiritual and creative side of his countrymen, and possibly the whole world. Tagore's strongest expression comes not in nationalism but in creativity. The connotations of the term "nationalism" have changed a good deal since 1916.

Tagore has little to say about ethnic cultures, or about linguistic or religious communities or nationalist myths. His definition of a nation is the political and economic union of a people in that aspect that a whole population assumes when organised for a mechanical purpose. The emphasis falls upon organised and mechanical. The western nation is conterminous with the nation-state, the mechanical organisation of people in pursuit of material enhancement and hence aggressive and imperialist in character; in fact, for nationalism we might often read imperialism.

At other times, Tagore in his distrust of technology and impersonal bureaucracy, falls into a similar position to the western romantic critique of civilisation and modernisation as he said: "When this organisation of politics and commerce, whose other name is the nation becomes all-powerful, at the cost of the harmony of the higher social life, then it is an evil day for humanity ...This abstract being, the nation, is ruling India." This is very interesting that his thought continually moves between opposites-spiritual and materialist, East and West, nation and no-nation, masculine and feminine, abstract and personal and then seeks for ways to reconcile and harmonise the opposites.

According to him these don't need to compete but should eventually fall into equilibrium. In nationalism this is rarely more than wishful rhetoric. Moreover, Tagore stressed his international concerns, and shrewdly denounced the excesses of nationalism not only in India, but also in Japan, China, and the West. The following concepts and ideas of Tagore dominated his thoughts and principles far more than nationalism.

EDUCATION FOR FREEDOM OF MIND

Tagore published his first essay on Gandhi and Non-cooperation, "The Call of Truth," which argued that truth was of both the head and the heart; It was on education (and on the reflection, dialogue, and communication that are associated with it), rather than on, say, spinning "as a sacrifice" ("the charka does not require anyone to think"), that the future of India would depend. Tagore was concerned not only that there be wider opportunities for education across the country (especially in rural areas where schools were few), but also that the schools themselves be more lively and enjoyable.

He himself had dropped out of school early, largely out of boredom, and had never bothered to earn a diploma. He wrote extensively on how schools should be made more attractive to boys and girls and thus more productive. For Tagore it was of the highest importance that people be able to live, and reason, in freedom. His attitudes toward politics and culture, nationalism and internationalism, tradition and modernity, can all be seen in the light of this belief. Passion for freedom underlies his firm opposition to unreasoned traditionalism. His uncompromising belief was in the importance of "freedom of mind."

ANTI-WAR NOTION

Some argue that war is somewhat related to nationalism. But according to Tagore the word war is not a central theme of nationalism. It is, rather, ever present in the background, as proof of the self-destructive tendency of the organised modern nation. Throughout his adult political life, Rabindranath Tagore had been critical of using force, man against man, class against class, nation against nation. He had sharp words for the Japanese when he visited Japan at the time of the First World War and in the late 1930s; he was hostile towards their use of force in China.

CULTURAL CONVERGENCE

Tagore would oppose the cultural nationalism that has gained ground in India, along with an exaggerated fear of the influence of the West. He was uncompromising in his belief that human beings could absorb quite different cultures in constructive ways. He said: "Whatever we understand and enjoy in human products instantly becomes ours, wherever they might have their origin. I am proud of my humanity when I can acknowledge the poets and artists of other countries as my own.

Let me feel with unalloyed gladness that all the great glories of man are mine."

TAGORE AND PATRIOTISM

He had reservations about patriotism, which, he argued, can limit both the freedom to engage ideas from outside "narrow domestic walls" and the freedom also to support the causes of people in other countries. Tagore's criticism of patriotism is a persistent theme in his writings. His novel Ghare Baire (The Home and the World) has much to say about this theme. In the novel, Nikhil, who is keen on social reform, including women's liberation, was cool towards nationalism, and gradually loses the esteem of his spirited wife, Bimala, because of his failure to be enthusiastic about anti-British agitations, which she sees as a lack of patriotic commitment.

Bimala becomes fascinated with Nikhil's nationalist friend Sandip, who speaks brilliantly and acts with patriotic militancy, and she falls in love with him. Nikhil refuses to change his views: "I am willing to serve my country; but my worship I reserve for Right which is far greater than my country." As for the contrary evidence of Tagore's "patriotic" gesture, such as his renunciation of his knighthood, Tagore believes in protesting against injustice in the name of humanity, not in the hope of gaining concession. Tagore was the only one whose protests were motivated by a sense of moral duty. Rabindranath's qualified support for nationalist movements - and his opposition to the unfreedom of alien rule - came from the commitment that freedom is one of the most important priorities.

THOUGHT ON POLITICS AND CIVIL SOCIETY

While introducing a new edition of Tagore's Nationalism, E.P. Thompson wrote in 1991: "More than any other thinker of his time, Tagore had a clear conception of civil society, as something distinct from and of stronger and more personal texture than political or economic structure." He wanted his people of India to be left free by the British; he supported and praised Gandhi for his leadership. Tagore says E.P. Thompson "was a founder of anti-politics." This means that even during the phase of the most widespread political activities in India's struggle for independence, Tagore continued to maintain that village reconstruction in the dream to make a civil society was a more fruitful activity for the purpose of the real deliverance of the Indian people.

Tagore's commitment to anti-politics and his concern with civil society make him appear at times to be a markedly modern - or perhaps postmodern thinker. The assertive nationalisms and communalisms which mark our own time and which refuse any assent to universal value are not confined to the West. Tagore cannot resolve these problems but if we can share and apply his far-sighted intuitions he may help us do so.

SUPPORT FOR INTERNATIONAL COOPERATION

Tagore objected to the burning of foreign cloth because it was foreign. Gandhi stressed the need for Indian self-sufficiency in every sphere of life, while Tagore saw the need for international cooperation and sharing. In the modern age, the poet insisted, India must learn from abroad, for example, in science, as well as look inward. Tagore believed that India had a message for the world, but he thought India must also incorporate others' messages into her own cultural repertoire.

He warned his countrymen against accepting those evils, which the West has brought through the application of the great knowledge-the conquest of the vast spaces of the world and the upturning of man's moral balance, the liquidation of his human side under the shadow of the soulless organisation of the machine. Tagore exhorted: "You must apply your Eastern Mind, your spiritual strength, your love of simplicity, your recognition of social obligation in order to cut out a new path."

CRITICISM OF HIS BELIEFS AS ANTI-NATIONALIST

The contradiction between nationalism and no-nationhood did not admit of such a verbal reconciliation and this contradiction limited the success of Tagore's lectures on nationalism. It can be seen that he respects not only to the Japanese cultural inheritance but also the supposed presence of pan-Asian spiritual values which is contrasted against the aggressive materialism of the western nation. But later he observed the same features of material greed and imperialist aggression in the modernising Japan that he criticised. Japanese critics suggested that Tagore's praise for the lack of nationalism in India was the special pleading of a "defeated people."

Moreover, Tagore's diatribes against materialism, technology, mechanical organisation, and unbridled pursuit of wealth are criticised by many western people. Some people criticise him as saying Tagore had once been a nationalist but had withdrawn from this stance later. Tagore himself had passed through an ardent nationalistic phase in the first years of the century, the years of Swadeshi and of the agitation against the 1905 partition of Bengal, and then fell back into a more quietist stance in the next decade. His novel The Home and the World (1916 in Bengali) belongs to this latter phase, and it testifies to the ambivalence of Tagore's response to Indian Nationalism.

Nationalists accused him of apostasy, which seemed to be confirmed when he was awarded a knighthood in 1915; his renunciation of that honour in 1919, however, in protest at the massacre at Amtrisar and its aftermath, did something to repair his patriotic image. No matter what many critics state about him, it is well established that Rabindranath persisted on open debate on all subjects, and were wary of conclusions based on a mechanical formula, no matter how attractive it may seem separately. The question that repeatedly arises is whether we have sufficient reason to want what is proposed, taking everything into account. Important as history is, the reasoning must overshadow the past.

As Amartya Sen, Nobel laureate in economics (1998) well described him: "It is in the sovereignty of reasoning - fearless reasoning in freedom - that we can find Rabindranath Tagore's lasting voice." In my view, his valiant reasoning in self-determination prevails over extreme nationalism. The present world consists of the several aspects of globalisation that are being practiced through sharing knowledge and cross-cultural views by a globe-spanning network of communication, and it is me, a free mind, who is to decide what it is to acculturate.

PAN-ASIANISM

JAPANESE ASIANISM

Pre-World War II Japanese Pan-Asianism was, at its core, the idea that Asia should unite against European imperialism. Before and during World War II, this was a major element in Japanese propaganda to justify Japanese external invasions. The Greater East Asia Co-Prosperity Sphere was an example of this propaganda. Japanese Asianism developed in intertwining among debates on solidarity with Asian nations who were under pressure of the West and on aggressive expansion to the Asian continent.

The former debates originated from leftist liberalism. Their ideologues were Tokichi Tarui (1850-1922) who argued for equal Japan-Korea unionisation for cooperative defence against the Western powers, and Kentaro Oi (1843-1922) who attempted domestic constitutional government in Japan and reforms of Korea. Pan-Asian thought in Japan began to develop in the late nineteenth century and was spurred on particularly following the defeat of Russia in the Russo-Japanese War (1904 - 1905). This created interest from Rabindranath Tagore, Sun Wen and Sri Aurobindo.

However, Japanese society had been strongly inclined to ultranationalism from the Freedom and People's Rights Movement. The latter debates on aggressive expansionism to

Asia became clearly apparent. Their representatives were the Black Ocean Society and the Black Dragon Society. The Black Dragon Society (1933) argued for Japanese imperialism and expansionism, and they led to a debate on securing Asian continent under Japanese control. Exceptionally, Ryohei Uchida (1874-1937), who was a member of the Black Dragon Society, was a Japan-Korea unionist and activist of Philippine and Chinese revolutions.

Toten Miyazaki (1870-1922) consistently supported a Chinese revolution of Sun Wen with spiritual sacrifice and sympathy under imperial Japan. Tenshin Okakura (1862-1913) criticized Western imperialism as a destroyer of human beauty, and argued for romantic solidarity with diverse "Asia as one" against Western civilisation.

Asia is one. The Himalayas divide, only to accentuate, two mighty civilisations, the Chinese with its communism of Confucius, and the Indian with its individualism of the Vedas. But not even the snowy barriers can interrupt for one moment that broad expanse of love for the Ultimate and Universal, which is the common thought-inheritance of every Asiatic race, enabling them to produce all the great religions of the world, and distinguishing them from those maritime peoples of the Mediterranean and the Baltic, who love to dwell on the Particular, and to search out the means, not the end, of life.

In this Okakura was utilising the Japanese concept of *sangoku*, which existed in Japanese culture before the concept of Asia became popularised. *Sangoku* literally means the "three countries": *Honshû* (the largest island of Japan), *Kara* (China) and *Tenjiku* (India). However, most Asianists were nationalistic and imperialistic and were connected with rightist organisations. They discussed self-righteous solidarity which led to ideology such as a "new order" of East Asia and "Greater East Asia Co-prosperity Sphere" based on Japanese supremacy.

NEW GREATER ASIANISM FROM MODERN CHINA

In a Chinese perspective, Japanese Asianism was interpreted as a rationalized ideology for Japanese military aggression and political absorption (cf. Twenty-One Demands). In 1917, Li Dazhao (1889-1927) argued for liberation of Asian nations and equal greater Asian union. In 1924, Sun Yat-sen (1866-1925) stated that the West was hegemonic and the East was Confucian, and he argued for full independence by resisting colonialism with "Greater Asianism" which unionizes Asian nations.

THIRD WAY FROM THE POSTCOLONIAL WORLD

After the World War II, Jawaharlal Nehru (1889-1964) of India argued for neutral third way under the cold war. His assertion was: Asian nations should be fair to both American and Soviet sides, and the United Nations should be strong and independent who played a role to balance the world power politics. However, the North-South divide show that the postcolonial world has been confronted with economic independence and development. The growing official interest in broader Asian concerns was shown in the establishment of facilities for Indian Studies.

In 1899 Tokyo Imperial University set up a chair in Sanskrit and Pali, with a further chair in Comparative religion being set up in 1903. In this environment, a number of Indian students came to Japan in the early twentieth century, founding the Oriental Youngmen's Association in 1900. Their anti-British political activity caused consternation to the Indian Government, following a report in the London Spectator. Political leaders from Sun Yat-Sen in the 1910s and 20s to Lee Kuan Yew in the 1990s argue that the political models and ideologies of Europe lack values and concepts found in Asian societies and philosophies.

Some proponents argue that these values are better for all human societies. Some would argue that they are better or more suited for Asian societies. European values such as individual rights and freedoms would not be suited for Asian societies in this extreme formulation of Pan-Asianism. In the 1930s and 1940s this ideology was used by the Japanese government as part of a propaganda campaign against European (and U.S.) imperialism in support of its rival imperialist Greater East Asia Co-Prosperity Sphere.

During the Cold War Pan-Asianism took a back seat. Several countries like India, Cambodia and Indonesia advocated for greater ties with the rest of the developing world within and beyond Asia, while others were economically and politically more orientated towards either one of the superpowers. However ASEAN emerged in 1967, providing a framework for cooperation in South-East Asia. The idea of Asian values is somewhat of a resurgence of Pan-Asianism. One foremost enthusiast of the idea of Asian values is the former prime minister of Singapore, Lee Kuan Yew. In India, Rammanohar Lohia dreamt of a united socialist Asia.

5

The Distinctiveness of Rabindra Nath Tagore's view on Indian Renaissance

The work of Satyajit Ray presents a remarkably insightful understanding of the relations between cultures, and his ideas remain pertinent to the great cultural debates in the contemporary world, not least in India. I would like to pursue these ideas. In Ray's films and in his writings, we find explorations of at least three general themes on cultures and their interrelations: the importance of distinctions between different local cultures and their respective individualities; the necessity of understanding the heterogeneous character of each local culture (even the culture of a common, not to mention a region or a country); and the great need for intercultural communication, attended by a recognition of the barriers that make intercultural communication a hard task.

A deep respect for distinctiveness is combined, in Ray's vision, with recognition of internal diversity and an appreciation of the need for genuine communication. Impetuous cosmopolitans have something to learn from his focus on distinctiveness, but it is the growing army of communitarian and cultural "separatists"- increasingly more fashionable in India and elsewhere, that most needs to take note of the persistence of heterogeneity at the local level and the creative role of intercultural and intercommunal communication and learning. In emphasizing the need to honor the individuality of each culture, Ray saw no reason for closing the doors to the outside world. Indeed, opening doors was an important priority of Ray's work.

In this respect, Ray's attitude contrasts sharply with the increasing tendency to see Indian culture (or cultures) in highly conservative terms, to preserve it (or them) from the "pollution" of Western ideas and thought. He was always willing to enjoy and to learn from ideas, art forms, and styles of life from anywhere, in India or abroad. Ray appreciated the importance of heterogeneity within local communities. This perception contrasts sharply with the tendency of many communitarians, religious and secular, who are willing to break up the nation into communities and then stop dead there: "thus far and no further."

The great filmmaker's eagerness to seek the larger unit - to talk to the whole world - went well with his enthusiasm for understanding the smallest of the small - the individuality, ultimately, of each person. From such a vision, I believe, we have much to learn right now. There can be little doubt about the importance that Ray attached to the distinctiveness of cultures. He also discussed the problems that these divisions create in the possibility of communication across cultural boundaries. In *Our Films, Their Films*, he noted the important fact that films acquire "colour from all manner of indigenous factors such as habits of speech and behaviour, deep- seated social practices, past traditions, present influences and so on."

He went on to ask: "How much of this can a foreigner - with no more than a cursory knowledge of the factors involved - feel and respond to?" He observed also that "there are certain basic similarities in human behaviour all over the world" (such as "expressions of joy and sorrow, love and hate, anger, surprise and fear"), but "even they can exhibit minute local variations which can only puzzle and perturb - and consequently warp the judgment of - the uninitiated foreigner." The presence of such cultural differences raises many interesting problems.

The possibility of communication is only one of them. There is also the more basic issue of the individuality of each culture. How might this individuality be respected and valued, even as the world grows steadily smaller and more uniform? We live in a time in which many things are increasingly common, and the possibility that something important is being lost in this process of integration has aroused understandable concern. The individuality of cultures is a big subject now, and the tendency towards the homogenisation of cultures, particularly in some uniformly Western mode, or in the deceptive form of "modernity," has been sharply challenged.

Anxieties of this kind have been expressed in different forms in recent cultural studies, which flourish today in Western literary and intellectual circles. There is an irony, perhaps, in the fact that so much of the critique of "Western modernity" has come straight from the West to the Third World; but these questions are being plentifully asked in contemporary India as well.

En e separateness of "Asian values," and their distinction from Western norms, has often been asserted, particularly in East Asia, from Singapore and Malaysia to China and Japan. The invoking of Asian values has sometimes occurred in rather dubious political circumstances. It has been used to justify authoritarianism (and harsh penalties for alleged transgressions) in some East Asian countries.

In 1993, at the Vienna conference on human rights, the foreign minister of Singapore, along with the Chinese Foreign Minister, cited the differences between Asian and European traditions and argued that "universal recognition of the ideal of human rights can be harmful if universalism is used to deny or mask the reality of diversity." The championing of "Asian values" has typically come from governmental spokesmen and not from individuals opposed to the established regimes. Still, the general issue is important enough to deserve our attention; and so, in examining the implications of cultural diversity, I must also take up this question.

Even though he emphasized the difficulties of intercultural communication, Ray did not take cross-cultural comprehension to be impossible. He saw the difficulties as challenges to be surmounted rather than as strict boundaries that could not be breached. He did not propound a thesis of "incommunicability" across cultural boundaries; he argued instead that we need to recognize the difficulties that may arise. And on the larger subject of preserving traditions against foreign influence, Ray was not a cultural conservative. He did not give systematic priority to inherited practices. I find no evidence in Ray's films or in his writings that the fear of being too influenced by outsiders disturbed his equilibrium as an "Indian" artist.

He wanted to take full note of the importance of a particular cultural background without denying what there is to learn from elsewhere. There is much wisdom, I think, in this "critical openness," including the prizing of a dynamic, adaptable world over a world that is constantly "policing" external influences and fearing "invasion" of ideas from elsewhere. The difficulties of understanding each other across the boundaries of culture are undoubtedly great.

This applies to the cinema, but also to other art forms, especially literature. The inability of most foreigners, even of other Indians, to grasp the beauty of Rabindranath Tagore's poetry (a failure that we Bengalis find so exasperating) is a good illustration of this problem. Indeed, the thought that these non-appreciating others are being willfully contrary and obdurate (rather than being thwarted by the barriers of languages and translations) is a frequently aired suspicion.

The problem is perhaps less extreme in films, so far as film is less dependent on language. People can be informed by gestures and actions. Still, our day-to-day experiences generate certain patterns of reaction and non-reaction that can be mystifying for foreign viewers who have not had those experiences. The gestures - and the non-gestures - that are quite standard, and are "perfectly ordinary," in India may appear altogether remarkable when they are seen by others.

Also words have a function that goes well beyond the information that they directly convey. Much is communicated by the sound of the language, and a special choice of words conveys a particular meaning or creates a particular effect. As Ray observed, "in a sound film, words are expected to perform not only a narrative but a plastic function," and "much will be missed unless one knows the language, and knows it well." Even the narrative may be inescapably transformed by language barriers, owing to nuances that are missed in translations. I was reminded of Ray's remark the other day when I saw Tin Kanya again, in Cambridge, Massachusetts, at a recent festival of Ray's films (in their wonderful reissues by Merchant-Ivory).

When the obdurate Paglee at last decides to write a letter to her spurned husband, she conveys her new sense of intimacy by addressing him with the familiar form tumi rather than the formal apni. This could not be caught in the English subtitle. The translation had to show her sign the letter as "your wife," to convey this new sense of intimacy; but the Bengali original form in which she signs as "Paglee" but addresses him as tumi, is infinitely more subtle. Such difficulties cannot be altogether escaped. Ray did not design his movies for a foreign audience, and the Ray fans abroad who rush to see his films know that they are, in a sense, eavesdropping.

This relationship between the artist and the eavesdropper is by now very well established among the millions of Ray's admirers around the world. There is no expectation that his films are anything other than those of an Indian director - and a Bengali director - made for a local audience, and the attempt to see what is going on in these films is a decision to engage in a self-consciously "receptive" activity. In this sense, Ray has triumphed and on his own terms. This vindication of his belief that he will be understood, barriers notwithstanding, tells us about the possibility of understanding across cultural boundaries.

It may be hard, but it can be done; and the eagerness with which viewers with rich experience of Western cinema flock to see Ray's films (despite the occasional obscurities of a presentation tailored to an entirely different audience) indicates what may be accomplished when there is a willingness to go beyond the bounds of one's own culture. Satyajit Ray makes an important distinction between what is or is not sensible when one tries to speak across a cultural divide, especially across the divide between the West and India.

In 1958, two years after *Pather Panchali* won the Special Award in Cannes, and one year after he won the Grand Prix at Venice for Aparajito, Ray wrote the following, in an essay called *Problems of a Bengali Film Maker*: "There is no reason why we should not cash in on the foreigners' curiosity about the Orient. But this must not mean pandering to their love of the false-exotic. A great many notions about our country and our people have to be dispelled, even though it may be easier and - from a film point of view - more paying to sustain tile existing myths than to demolish them." Ray was not alone, of course, in pursuing such an approach.

There have been several other eminent directors from India who have essentially followed the same route as Ray. As an old resident of Calcutta, I am proud of the fact that some of the particularly distinguished ones have come - like Ray - from this very city. (I think of Mrinal Sen, Rhtwik Ghatak, Aparna Sen and others.) But what Ray calls pandering to the "love of the false-exotic" has clearly tempted many other directors. Many Indian films that can fairly be called "entertainment movies" have achieved great success abroad, including in the Middle

East and Africa, and Bombay has been a big influence on the cinematic world in many countries.

It is not obvious whether the imaginary scenes of archaic splendor shown in such "entertainment movies" should be seen as mis-descriptions of the India in which they are allegedly set or as an excellent portrayal of some non-existent "never-never land" that is not to be confused with any real country. As Ray notes in another context, quite a few of these traditional Indian films, which attract large audiences, "do away wholly with the bothersome aspect of social identification" and "present a synthetic, nonexistent society, and one can speak of credibility only within the norms of this make-believe world." Ray suggests that this feature "accounts for their countrywide acceptance."

This is true; but this quality of make-believe also contributes greatly to the appeal of these films to some foreign audiences, which are happy to see lavish entertainment in an imagined land. This is an easily understandable "success" story: acceptance abroad brings both reputation and revenue. In contemporary India, where "export promotion" is becoming a supreme value, who can deny such an achievement? In fact, the exploitation of the biases and the vulnerabilities of the foreign audience need not be concerned specifically with the "love of the false-exotic." Exploitation can take other forms - not necessarily false, nor especially exotic.

There is nothing false neither about Indian poverty nor about the fact- remarkable to others - that Indians have learned to live normal lives in the midst of this poverty, taking little notice of the surrounding misery. The graphic portrayal of extreme wretchedness, and of heartlessness towards the downtrodden, can itself be exploited, especially when supplemented by a goodly supply of vicious villains. At a sophisticated level, such exploitation can be seen even in *Salam Bombay!* the wonderfully successful film by Meera Nair.

Nair's film is powerfully constructed and deeply moving; and yet it mercilessly exploits not only the viewer's sympathy and sentimentality, but also her interest in identifying "the villain of the piece" who might be blamed for all this suffering. Since *Salam Bombay!* is full of villains, and of people totally lacking in sympathy and any sense of justice, the causes of the suffering portrayed in the film begin to look easily comprehensible even to distant foreigners. Given the lack of humanity around these Indian victims, what else can you expect? Nair's kind of exploitation draws simultaneously on the common knowledge that India has much suffering and on the common comfort - for which there is a demanding seeing the faces of the "baddies" who are causing all this trouble, as in, say, American gangster movies. (This easy reliance on villains is less present in Nair's subsequent film, *Mississippi Masala*, which raises some important and interesting issues of identity involving ex-Ugandans of Indian origin in the United States.)

At a more mundane level, *City of Joy* does the same with Calcutta, with clearly identified villains who have to be confronted. By contrast, even when Ray's films deal with problems that are just as intense (such as the coming of the Bengal famine in *Ashani Sanket*), the comfort of a ready explanation through the presence of villains is avoided. In Ray's films, villains are remarkably rare, almost absent. When terrible things happen, there may be nobody clearly responsible and even when someone is clearly responsible, as Dayamoyee's father-in-law most definitely is responsible for her predicament, and ultimately for her suicide, in *Devi*, he, too, is a victim, and by no means devoid of humane features.

If *Salam Bombay!* and *City of Joy* ultimately belong in the "cops and robbers" tradition (except that there are no "good cops" in *Salam Bombay!*), the Ray films which portray tragedies have neither cops nor robbers. Ray chooses to convey something of the complexity of social situations that makes such tragedies hard to avoid, rather than to supply easy explanations in the greed, the cupidity and the cruelty of "bad" people. While Satyajit Ray insists on retaining the real cultural features of the society that he portrays, his view of India - even his view of Bengal - recognizes a complex reality, with immense heterogeneity at every level. It is not the picture of a stylized East meeting a stereotypical West, which has been the stock-in-trade of so many recent writings critical of "Westernisation" and "modernity."

Ray emphasized that the people who "inhabit" his films are complicated and extremely diverse. Take a single province: Bengal. Or, better still, take the city of Calcutta where I live and work. Accents here vary between one neighbourhood and another. Every educated Bengali peppers his native speech with a sprinkling of English words and phrases. Dress is not standardized. Although women generally prefer the sari, men wear clothes, which reflect the style of the thirteenth century or conform to the directives of the latest Esquire. The contrast between the rich and the poor is proverbial. Teenagers do the twist and drink Coke, while the devout Brahmin takes a dip in the Ganges and chants his mantras to the rising sun.

It is important to note that the native culture which Ray stresses is not some pure vision of a tradition-bound society, but the heterogeneous lives and commitments of contemporary India. The Indian who does the twist is as much there as the one who chants his mantras by the Ganges. The recognition of this heterogeneity makes it immediately clear why Ray's focus on local culture cannot be readily seen as an "anti-modern" move. "Our culture" can draw on "their culture" and "their culture" can draw on our culture."

The emphasis on the culture of the people who inhabit Ray's films is in no way a denial of the legitimacy of the interest in things originating elsewhere. Indeed, Ray recollects with evident joy the time when Calcutta was full of Western (including American) troops, in the winter of 1942: Calcutta now being a base of operations of the war, Chowringhee was chock-a- block with GIs.

The pavement book stalls displayed wafer-thin editions of Life and Time, and the jam-packed cinema showed the very latest films from Hollywood. While I sat at my office desk ... my mind buzzed with the thoughts of the films I had been seeing. I never ceased to regret that while I had stood in the scorching summer sun in the wilds of Santiniketan sketching *simul* and *palash* in full bloom, *Citizen Kane* had come and gone, playing for just three days in the newest and biggest cinema in Calcutta. This interest in things from elsewhere had begun a lot earlier. Ray's engagement with Western classical music goes back to his youth, and his fascination with films preceded his involvement with music.

In his posthumously published book, *My Years with Apu: A Memoir* Ray recollects: "I became a film fan while still at school. I avidly read Picturegoer and Photoplay, neglected my studies and gorged myself on Hollywood gossip purveyed by Hedda Hopper and Louella Parsons. Deanna Derbin became a favourite not only because of her looks and her obvious gifts as an actress, but because of her lovely soprano voice. Also firm favourites were Fred Astaire and Ginger Rogers, all of whose films I saw several times just to learn the Irving Berlin and Jerome Kern tunes by heart."

Ray's willingness to enjoy and to learn from things happening elsewhere in India or abroad is plentifully clear in how he chose to live and what he chose to do. (In addition to Ray's own autobiographical accounts in *Our Films, Their Films* and *My Years with Apu: A Memoir* his involvements in ideas and arts from elsewhere are discussed in some detail in Andrew Robinson's *Satyajit Ray: The Inner Eye*, which appeared in 1989.) When Ray describes what he learned as a student at Santiniketan, where he studied fine arts at Tagore's distinguished center of education, the elements from home and abroad are well mixed together.

He learned a great deal about India's "artistic and musical heritage" (he got involved in Indian classical music, aside from being trained to paint in traditional Indian ways) and "far-eastern calligraphy" (particularly the use of "minimum brush strokes applied with maximum discipline"). When his teacher, Nandalal Bose, a great artist and the leading light of the Bengal school, taught Ray to draw a tree ("Not from the top downwards. A tree grows up, not down. The strokes must be from the base upwards..."), Bose was being critical of some Western conventions and introduced Ray to the styles and the traditions of China and Japan. (They got the tree right, Bose had decided.)

Ray does not hesitate to indicate how strongly *Pather Panchali* - the profound film that immediately made him a film maker of international distinction - was influenced by Vittorio De Sica's *The Bicycle Thief*. He saw *Bicycle Thief* within three days of arriving in London for a brief stay, and noted: "I knew immediately that if I ever made *Pather Panchali* - and the idea had been at the back of my mind for some time - I would make it in the same way, using natural locations and unknown actors." Despite this influence, *Pather Panchali*, of course, is a quintessentially Indian film, in subject matter and in style, and yet a major inspiration came from an Italian film.

The Italian influence did not make *Pather Panchali* anything other than an Indian film; it simply helped to make it a great Indian film. The growing tendency in contemporary India to champion the need for an indigenous culture that has "resisted" external influences and borrowings lacks credibility as well as cogency. It has become quite common to cite the foreign origin of an idea or a tradition as an argument against its use, and this has been linked to an antimodernist priority. Thus, even a social analyst as acute as Partha Chatterjee finds it impossible to dismiss Benedict Anderon's thesis linking nationalism and its "imagined communities" by referring to the Western origin of that "modular" form. I have a central objection to Anderson's argument.

If nationalisms in the rest of the world have to choose their imagined community from certain "modular" forms already made available to them by Europe and the Americas, what do they have left to imagine? Anderson's concept of "the nation as an imagined community" may or may not have much to commend it (I think that it does); but the fear that its Western origin would leave us without a model that is our "own" is a rather peculiar concern. Indian culture, as it has evolved, has always been prepared to absorb materials and ideas from elsewhere. Satyajit Ray's heterodoxy is not out of line with our tradition.

Even in matters of day-to-day living: the fact that the chili, a basic ingredient of traditional Indian cooking was brought to India by the Portuguese from the "New World" does not make Indian cooking any less Indian. Indeed, chili has now become an "Indian" spice. Of course, cultural influences are a two way process: India may have acquired the chili from abroad, but we have also given the world the benefits of our culinary traditions. While tandoori came from the Middle East to India, it is in its Indian form that tandoori has become a staple British diet. In London last summer I heard something described as being "as English as daffodils or chicken tikka masala."

The mixture of traditions that underlie the major intellectual developments in the world dictates strongly against taking a "national" (or "regional" or "local" or "community-based") view of these developments. The role of mixed heritage in a subject such as mathematics, for example, is well-known. The interlinkage between Indian, Arabic and European mathematics has been particularly significant in the development of what is now called Western mathematics. These connections are beautifully illustrated by the origin of the term "sine" in Western trigonometry.

That modern term came to India through the British, and yet in its genesis there is a remarkable Indian component. Aryabhata, an Indian mathematician and astronomer who lived in the fifth and early sixth centuries, discussed the concept of "sine," and called it Jyanardha, or "half-chord," in Sanskrit. From there the term migrated in an interesting way, as Howard Eves describes in *An Introduction to the History of Mathematics*: Aryabhata called it ardha-jya ("half-chord") and jya-ardha ("chord-half"), and then abbreviated the term by simply using jya ("chord").

From jya the Arabs phonetically derived jiba, which, following Arabic practice of omitting vowels was written as jb. Now jiba, aside from its technical significance, is a meaningless word in Arabic. Later writers who came across jb as an abbreviation for the meaningless word Jiba substituted Jaib instead, which contains the same letters, and is a good Arabic word meaning "cove" or "bay." Still later, Gherardo of Cremona (ca. 1150), when he made his translations from the Arabic, replaced the Arabian jaib by its Latin equivalent, sinus [meaning a cove or a bay], from whence came our present word sine. Given the and intellectual interconnections, the question of what is "Western" and what is "Eastern" (or Indian) is often hard to decide, and the issue can be discussed only in dialectical terms.

The characterisation of an idea as "purely Western" or "purely Indian" can be very illusory. The origin of ideas is not the kind of thing to which "purity" happens easily. This issue has some practical importance now, given the political developments of the last decade, including the increase in the strength of political parties focusing on the Indian - particularly the Hindu - heritage. There is an important aspect of anti-modernism, which tends to question, explicitly or implicitly, the emphasis to be placed on what is called "Western science." If the challenges from traditional conservatism grow, this can become quite a threat to scientific education in India, affecting what young Indians are encouraged to learn, and how much emphasis is put on science in the general curriculum.

The reasoning behind this "anti-foreign" attitude is flawed in several ways. First, so-called "Western science" is not the special possession of Europe and America. It is true that, since the Renaissance, the Industrial Revolution, and the Enlightenment, most scientific progress has occurred in the West; but these scientific developments drew substantially on earlier work in mathematics and science done by the Arabs, the Chinese, the Indians, and others. The term "Western science" is misleading in this respect, and misguided in its tendency to establish a distance between non-Western people and the pursuit of mathematics and science.

Second, irrespective of the location of the discoveries and the inventions, the methods of reasoning used in science and mathematics give them some independence of local geography and cultural history. To be sure, there are important issues of local knowledge, and of the varying perspectives regarding what is or is not important; but there is still much of substance that is shared in methods of argument, demonstration, and the scrutiny of evidence. The term "Western science" is misleading in this respect, too. Third, our decisions about the future need not be parasitic on the past we have experienced.

Even if there were no Asian or Indian component in the evolution of contemporary mathematics and science - this is not the case, but even if it were the case - their importance in the contemporary India need not be deeply undermined for that reason. Rabindranath Tagore nicely illustrated the tyranny of being bound to the past in his amusing but profoundly serious short story *Kartar Bhoot* ("The Ghost of the Leader"), in which the wishes of the respected but dead leader make the lives of others impossibly constrained. There is a similar issue, to which I referred earlier, about the role of "modernity" in contemporary India.

The recent attacks on modernity (especially on a "modernity" that is seen as coming to India from the West) draw greatly on the literature of "post-modernism" and on similar approaches that have been quite influential in Western literary and cultural circles, and in India, too. There is something interesting in this dual role of the West, the colonial metropolis supplying ideas to post-colonial intellectuals to attack the influence of the colonial metropolis; but there is no contradiction here. This dual role does suggest, however that the mere identification of the Western connections of an idea cannot be enough to damn it.

The critics of "modernism" often share with the advocates of "modernism" the belief that being "modern" is a well-defined concept - they are for "it" and we are against "it." But this type of identification is not at all easy, given the historical roots - the long and tangled roots - of recent intellectual developments, and given the mixture of origins in the genesis of the ideas and the methods that are typically taken to characterize modernism. The point is not that all modern things are good, or that there are reasons to doubt the wisdom of many developments that are justified in the name of modernity. Rather, the point is that there is no escape from the critical scrutiny of ideas, norms and proposals, no matter whether they are seen as pro-modern or anti-modern.

When we come to decide what policies to support in education, health care, or social security, the modernity or the non-modernity of a proposal is neither here nor there. The relevant question is how these policies would actually affect the lives of people. Similarly, when faced with communal tensions in contemporary India, there is much to be gained from reading the tolerant poems of Kabir, or studying the political priorities of Akbar, in contrast with, say, the intolerant approach of Aurangzeb. The discrimination among ideas must be made in terms of their worth, not on the basis of some claim that Kabir or Akbar was "more modern" or "less modern" than Aurangzeb. Modernity is not only a bewildering notion; it is also largely irrelevant as a measure of merit or demerit in assessing contemporary priorities.

What about the specialness of "Asian values," about which so much is now being said by the authorities in a number of East Asian countries? These arguments, used in Singapore and China, appeal to the differences between "Asian values" and "Western values" to dispute the importance of human rights and press freedoms in Asian countries. The resistance to Western hegemony - a perfectly respectable cause in itself - takes the form, under this interpretation, of justifying the suppression of journalistic freedoms and the violations of elementary political and civil rights on the grounds of the alleged unimportance of these freedoms in the hierarchy of what are claimed to be "Asian values."

There are two problems with this mode of reasoning. First, even if it were shown that freedoms of this kind have had less importance in Asian thought and tradition than in the West, this would still be an unconvincing way of justifying the violation of these freedoms in Asia. To see the conflict over human rights as a battle between Western liberalism and Asian authenticity is to cast the debate in a form that distracts attention from the central question: What is right, what makes sense, in contemporary Asia? The history of ideas, in Asia and the West, cannot decide this issue.

Second, it is by no means clear that historically there has been systematically greater importance attached to freedom and tolerance in the West than in Asia. Individual liberty, in its contemporary form, is a relatively new notion both in Asian and in the West; and while the West did get to these ideas earlier (through developments such as the Renaissance, the European Enlightenment the Industrial Revolution and so on), the divergence between the cultures is relatively recent. In answer to the question, "at what date, in what circumstances, the notion of individual liberty... first became explicit in the West," Isaiah Berlin has remarked that "I have found no convincing evidence of any clear formulation of it in the ancient world."

This view has been disputed by Orlando Patterson in *Freedom, Volume I: Freedom in the Making of Western Culture*. His historical arguments are interesting and forceful; but his thesis of a freedom-centered tradition in the West in contrast with what happened elsewhere seems to depend on attaching significance to particular elements of Western thought without looking adequately for comparable elements in non-Western intellectual traditions - for example, in the fairly extensive literatures on politics and governance in Sanskrit, Pali, Chinese, Arabic, and other languages. In the reading of Western tradition that sees it as the natural habitat of individual freedom and political democracy, there is a tendency to extrapolate backwards from the present.

Values that the European enlightenment and other relatively recent developments have made common and widespread can scarcely be seen as part of the long-run Western heritage, as if they were experienced in the West over millennia. In specific contexts in the Western classical tradition, of course, there have been championings of freedom and tolerance, but much the same can be said of many parts of the Asian tradition as well - not least in India, with Ashoka's inscriptions, Shudraka's drama, Akbar's pronouncements, or Kabir's poetry, to name a few examples. It is true that tolerance has not been advocated by all in the Asian traditions. Nor has that tolerance typically covered everyone (though some, such as Ashoka, in the third century BC, did insist on completely universal tolerance, without any exception).

But much the same can be said about the Western traditions as well. There is little evidence that Plato or Augustine were more tolerant or less authoritarian than Confucius. Aristotle certainly did write on the importance of freedom, but women and slaves were excluded from the domain of his concern. The allegedly sharp contrast between Western and Asian traditions on the subject of freedom and tolerance is based on the special nature of Asian values is particularly dubious. Further, even if it were the case that "Asian values" are more authoritarian, this would not have been grounds enough to reject tolerance and liberties in contemporary Asia.

The debate about "Asian values" draws attention to an important issue underlying attempts at generalisations about the East and West, about Europe and India, and so on. There are many sharp contrasts between Europe and India, but there are many sharp contrasts within India itself. And there are great differences between various parts of Indian intellectual and historical traditions. One of the things that go deeply wrong with grand contrasts between "our culture" and "their culture" is the neglect of the tremendous variety within each of these cultures. Joan Robinson, the Cambridge economist, used to say that whatever you can rightly say about India, the opposite is also true.

It is not that cultural differences are of no importance; but the contrasts do not come in the tailor-made form of some immense opposition between, say, the West and India, with relative homogeneity inside each. The problem is even greater, of course, when there are attempts at generalisations about "Asian values." Asia is where about 60 percent of the world's entire population lives. There are no quintessential values that apply to this immensely large and heterogeneous population, which separates them out as a group from the rest of the world. Those who have written on the importance of cultural divisions have been right to point to them, and yet the attempt to see these divisions in the over-aggregated form of a dichotomy between East and West conceals more than it reveals.

Indeed, even generalisations about a single religious community within India (the Hindus or the Muslims), or about a single language group (the Bengalis or the Punjabis or the Tamils), can be deeply misleading. Depending on the context, there may be more significant similarity between groups of people in different parts of the country who come from the same class, have the same political convictions, or pursue the same profession or work, and that similarity can hold across national boundaries as well. People can be classified in terms of many different criteria, and the recent tendency to emphasize some contrasts (religion or community,) while ignoring others has overlooked important differences even as it has capitalized on others.

The difficulties of communications across cultures are real, as are the normative issues raised by the importance of cultural differences; but these difficulties do not require us to accept the standard divisions between "our culture" and "their culture." Nor do they give us reason to overlook the demands of practical reason, and of political and social relevance, in favor of faithfulness to some alleged historical contrasts. Which brings us back to Satyajit Ray? His delicate portrayal of very different types that make us what we are cannot be matched.

Reflecting on what to include in his films, he posed the problem beautifully:

What should you put in your films? What can you leave out? Would you leave the city behind and go to the village where cows graze in the endless fields and the shepherd plays the flute? You can make a film here that would be pure and fresh and have the delicate rhythm of a boatman's song. Or would you rather go back in time - way back to the Epics, where the gods and demons took sides in the great battle where brother killed brother and Lord Krishna revivified a desolate prince with the words of the *Gita*? One could do exciting things here, using the great mimetic tradition of Kathakali, as the Japanese use their Noh and Kabuki.

Or would you rather stay where you are, right in the present, in the heart of this monstrous, teeming, bewildering city, and try to orchestrate its dizzying contrasts of sight and sound and milieu? The celebration of these differences - the "dizzying contrasts" - is far from what can be found in labored generalisations about the unique and fragile purity of "our culture," and in the vigorous pleas to keep "our culture", "our modernity", immune from "their culture", "their modernity." In our heterogeneity, and in our openness, lies our pride, not our disgrace. Satyajit Ray taught us this, and the lesson is profoundly important for India. And for Asia, and for the world.

BENGAL RENAISSANCE, INDIAN RENAISSANCE AND BRITISH INDIA

British India had brought together with their Occidental culture a new domain towards betterment in life, a breakaway from dark fashion. 'Renaissance' was that very domain that had infused India to its core, courtesy the reformist thinkers and intellectuals born prior to independence. And Bengal during those times was the pinnacle of culture and heritage, with the maximum of writers and fighters being bred from that part of eastern India. As such, Bengal was the foremost region which was inspired from their European counterpart in the renaissance and 'reawakening' regard.

Bengal Renaissance refers to a massive social reform movement during the nineteenth and early twentieth centuries in the region of Bengal in undivided India during the extensive period of British supremacy. In Bengal, the five fundamental influences led to the tremendous emergence of Bengal Renaissance, comprising; the boost of British-Bengali commerce, the introduction of English education, British Orientalism, Christianity and perhaps above all, how the Bengali intellectuals themselves responded to these influences.

The East India Company took control of Bengal, Bihar and parts of Orissa in 1765 from Shah Alam, the Mughal Emperor. As a result, Bengal and its environing lands became the first neighbourhoods in India to encounter the direct impact of British rule and the beginnings of modernisation. For the remaining eighteenth century and throughout the early decades of nineteenth century, the British laid solid foundations for civil administration.

They laid down communication and transportation systems, a modern bureaucracy, an army and a police.

They further established law courts and opened schools and colleges. The nineteenth century became the high point of British-Indian mutual reciprocation, especially within Bengal. Historians denote this era as the Bengal Renaissance, a period of passionate cultural and technological advancement, as well as a time of great social, cultural, and political metamorphosis. With the consolidation of British political power in India came the ascension of extensive trade and the establishment of large centres of administration and business. Calcutta in particular became the focus of British administration, trade and commerce. In the process a class of Bengali elite germinated that could mingle with the ruling British. This was the bhadraloka, a 'socially privileged and consciously superior group', economically dependent upon landed rents, professional and clerical employment.

During the second half of eighteenth century, this elite group started to reside in Calcutta as permanent residents. Some from this 'elite' bunch hurriedly acquired fortunes by working in partnership with the British. Bengal renaissance can be declared to have commenced precisely from this bunch, which including among other legends, started with Raja Ram Mohan Roy (1775-1833) and ended with Rabindranath Tagore (1861-1941). Nineteenth century Bengal was an unparalleled mish-mash of religious and social reformers, scholars, literary heavyweights, journalists, patriotic orators and scientists, all coalescing to form the image of a renaissance.

During the period designated as Bengal renaissance, Bengal witnessed an intellectual awakening that was in some way similar to the Renaissance in Europe during the 16th century. Indian renaissance severely questioned the existing orthodox customs, especially with respect to women (sati for instance), marriage, the dowry system, the caste system and religion. One of the earliest social movements that emerged during this time was the Young Bengal movement, that adopted rationalism and atheism as the common attributes of civil conduct among upper caste cultivated Hindus. The Brahmo Samaj, the parallel socio-religious movement had germinated during this time and banked upon many of the leaders of Bengal Renaissance amongst its followers.

Their version of Hinduism, or rather Universal Religion (likened to that of Ramakrishna), was entirely devoid of practices like sati and polygamy that had crept into the social aspects of Hindu life. Hinduism according to Brahmo Samaj was an unyielding impersonal monotheistic faith, which actually was quite dissimilar from the pluralistic and comprehensive nature of the way Hindu religion was practiced. Future leaders like Keshab Chandra Sen were as much devotees of Christ, as they were of Brahma, Krishna or Buddha.

The renaissance period after the Sepoy Mutiny of 1857, witnessed an outstanding overflow of Bengali literature. While Ram Mohan Roy and Ishwar Chandra Vidyasagar were the pioneers, others like Bankim Chandra Chatterjee broadened it and built upon it. The first significant nationalist detour to the Bengal Renaissance was given by the splendid writings of Bankim Chandra Chatterjee. Later writers of the British Indian period, who introduced panoptic discussions of social problems and more colloquial forms of Bengali into mainstream literature, included the great Sarat Chandra Chatterjee.

Later, Ramakrishna Paramahansa, the legendary saint from Bengal, is believed to have recognized the mystical truth of every religion and to have harmonised the conflicting Hindu sects ranging from Shakta tantra, Advaita Vedanta and Vaishnavism. In fact Ramakrishna made famous the Bengali saying: "Jato Mat, Tato Path" (All religions are different paths to the same God). The Vedanta movement flourished principally through his disciple and sage, Swami Vivekananda. He was one of the leading intellectuals who had carried the torch of Bengal

Renaissance towards the dazzling future of swaraj. On Vivekananda`s return from the highly acclaimed Parliament of the World`s Religions in Chicago in 1893 and subsequent lecture tour in America, he had become a revered national idol.

Ramakrishna Mission, the great organisation founded by Swami Vivekananda, was wholly non-political in nature. It must be stressed that the Ramakrishna Movement founded by Swami Vivekananda carried forward their Master's (Ramakrishna's) message of all religions being true. Next to this illustrious line of Bengalis, the Tagore family, including Rabindranath Tagore, were leaders of this period and shared a meticulous interest in educational reforms. Their contribution to Bengal Renaissance was multi-faceted and indeed priceless.

Tagore's 1901 Bengali novella, Nastanirh was penned as a critique of men who conceded to follow the ideals of Bengali Renaissance, but were unsuccessful to do so within their own families. Tagore's English translation of a set of poems titled the *Gitanjali* won him the Nobel Prize for Literature in 1913. He was the first Bengali, first Indian and first Asian to win the award. That was the only unparalleled example during that time, but the contribution of the Tagore family is mammoth. British Orientalism was another significant factor that worked to shape the Bengal Renaissance during the nineteenth century, particularly on religio-cultural matters.

As much as English language education brought the ideas of West to India, so did the era of Orientalism facilitate spread of innovative cultural attitudes to the bhadraloka? British Orientalism was an inimitable phenomenon in British Indian history that was inspired by the requirements of the East India Company to tutor a class of British administrators in the languages and customs of India. Intellectually, this was one of the most powerful ideas of nineteenth century India. In the political pre-independence scenario, a huge number of debating societies and newspapers appeared. Personalities like Kashi

Prasad Ghosh, Kristo Pal and Sisir Kumar Ghosh explicitly expressed their political opinions and would not hesitate to exercise their newspapers to achieve political ends, often in direct defiance to British rule. Ultimately the roots of Indian independence can be traced back to the Bengal Renaissance.

BENGAL RENAISSANCE

The Bengal Renaissance refers to a social reform movement during the nineteenth and early twentieth centuries in the region of Bengal during the period of British rule. The Bengal renaissance can be said to have started with Raja Ram Mohan Roy (1775-1833) and ended with Rabindranath Tagore (1861-1941), although there have been many stalwarts thereafter embodying particular aspects of the unique intellectual and creative output. Nineteenth century Bengal was a unique blend of religious and social reformers, scholars, literary giants, journalists, patriotic orators and scientists, all merging to form the image of a renaissance, and marked the transition from the 'medieval' to the 'modern'.

During this period, Bengal witnessed an intellectual awakening that is in some way similar to the Renaissance in Europe during the 16th century, although Europeans of that age were not confronted with the challenge and influence of alien colonialism. This movement questioned existing orthodoxies, particularly with respect to women, marriage, the dowry system, the caste system, and religion. One of the earliest social movements that emerged during this time was the Young Bengal movement, that espoused rationalism and atheism as the common denominators of civil conduct among upper caste educated Hindus.

The parallel socio-religious movement, the Brahmo Samaj, developed during this time period and counted many of the leaders of the Bengal Renaissance among its followers. In the earlier years the Brahmo Samaj, like the rest of society, could not however, conceptualize, in that feudal-colonial era, a free India as it was influenced by the European Enlightenment (and its bearers in India, the British Raj) although it traced its intellectual roots to the Upanishads. Their version of Hinduism, or rather Universal Religion (similar to that of Ramakrishna), although devoid of practices like sati and polygamy that had crept into the social aspects of Hindu life, was ultimately a rigid impersonal monotheistic faith, which actually was quite distinct from the pluralistic and multifaceted nature of the way the Hindu religion was practiced.

Future leaders like Keshub Chunder Sen were as much devotees of Christ, as they were of Brahma, Krishna or the Buddha. It has been argued by some scholars that the Brahmo Samaj movement never gained the support of the masses and remained restricted to the elite, although Hindu society has accepted most of the social reform programmes of the Brahmo Samaj. It must also be acknowledged that many of the later Brahmos were also leaders of the freedom movement. The renaissance period after the Indian Rebellion of 1857 saw a magnificent outburst of Bengali literature.

While Ram Mohan Roy and Iswar Chandra Vidyasagar were the pioneers, others like Bankim Chandra Chatterjee widened it and built upon it. The first significant nationalist detour to the Bengal Renaissance was given by the brilliant writings of Bankim Chandra Chatterjee. Later writers of the period who introduced broad discussion of social problems and more colloquial forms of Bengali into mainstream literature included the great Saratchandra Chatterjee. The Tagore family including Rabindranath Tagore were leaders of this period and had a particular interest in educational reform.

Their contribution to the Bengal Renaissance was multi-faceted. Indeed, Tagore's 1901 Bengali novella, Nastanirh was written as a critique of men who professed to follow the ideals of the Renaissance, but failed to do so within their own families.

In many ways Rabindranath Tagore's writings (especially poems and songs) can be seen as imbued with the spirit of the Upanishads. His works repeatedly allude to Upanishadic ideas regarding soul, liberation, transmigration and - perhaps most essentially - about a spirit that imbues all creation not unlike the Upanishadic Brahman. Tagore's English translation of a set of poems titled the Gitanjali won him the Nobel Prize for Literature in 1913. He was the first Asian to win this award. That was the only example at the time but the contribution of the Tagore family is enormous.

COMPARISON WITH EUROPEAN RENAISSANCE

The word "renaissance" in European history meant "rebirth" and was used in the context of the revival of the Graeco-Roman learning in the fifteenth and sixteenth centuries after the long winter of the dark medieval period. A serious comparison was started by the dramatis personae of the Bengal renaissance like Keshub Chunder Sen, Bipin Chandra Pal and M. N. Roy. For about a century, Bengal's conscious awareness and the changing modern world was more developed and ahead of the rest of India. The role played by Bengal in the modern awakening of India is thus comparable to the position occupied by Italy in the European renaissance.

Very much like the Italian Renaissance, it was not a mass movement; but instead restricted to the upper classes. Though the Bengal Renaissance was the "culmination of the process of emergence of the cultural characteristics of the Bengali people that had started in the age of Hussein Shah, it remained predominantly Hindu and only partially Muslim." There were, nevertheless, examples of Muslim intellectuals such as Saiyed Amir Ali, Mosharraf Hussain, Sake Dean Mahomed, Kazi Nazrul Islam, and Roquia Sakhawat Hussain. Some scholars in Bangladesh, now hold Bengal Renaissance in a different light.

As Professor Muin-ud-Din Ahmad Khan of the department of Islamic History and Culture of Chittagong University, observes:

"During nineteenth century A.D., Bengal produced a galaxy of reform movements among the Hindus as well Muslims... the Islamic reform movements such as Faraizi, Tariquah-i-Muhhamadiyah, and Taiyni and Ahl-i-Hadith, occupied a conspicuous position amongst them. These Islamic movements were revivalist in character... these Islamic movements were born of the circumstances, which had also given birth to the contemporary Hindu reform movements such as Brahmo Samaj and Arya Samaj, which thrived in Bengal side by side with them... Raja Ram Mohan Roy's movement is generally regarded as 'Renaissance movement'.

It is called by some as 'Hindu Renaissance' and by others as 'Bengali Renaissance' movement. It should nevertheless be observed that compared with the European 'Renaissance model', it was a Renaissance with a difference, especially, deeply inlaid by a revivalist make-up of pristine Hindu or Aryan religious spirit... Raja Ram Mohan Roy's Renaissance aimed at resuscitating the pristine Aryan spirit, 'Unitarianism of God', with the help of modern Western rationalist spirit."

SCIENCE

During the Bengal Renaissance science was also advanced by several Bengali scientists such as Satyendra Nath Bose and Jagadish Chandra Bose. Sir Jagadish Chandra Bose was a polymath: a physicist, biologist, botanist, archaeologist, and writer of science fiction. He pioneered the investigation of radio and microwave optics, made very significant contributions to plant science, and laid the foundations of experimental science in the Indian subcontinent. He is considered one of the fathers of radio science, and is also considered the father of Bengali science fiction. He was the first from the Indian subcontinent to get a US patent, in 1904.

Satyendra Nath Bose was a physicist, specializing in mathematical physics. He is best known for his work on quantum mechanics in the early 1920s, providing the foundation for Bose-Einstein statistics and the theory of the Bose-Einstein condensate. He is honoured as the namesake of the boson. Although more than one Nobel Prize was awarded for research related to the concepts of the boson, Bose-Einstein statistics and Bose-Einstein condensate-the latest being the 2001 Nobel Prize in Physics, which was given for advancing the theory of Bose-Einstein condensates-Bose himself was never awarded the Nobel Prize.

According to historian Romesh Chunder Dutt:

"The conquest of Bengal by the English was not only a political revolution, but ushered in a greater revolution in thoughts and ideas, in religion and society... From the stories of gods and goddesses, kings and queens, princes and princesses, we have learnt to descend to the humble walks of life, to sympathise with the common citizen or even common peasant ... Every revolution is attended with vigour, and the present one is no exception to the rule.

Nowhere in the annals of Bengali literature are so many and so bright names found crowded together in the limited space of one century as those of Ram Mohan Roy, Akshay Kumar Dutt, Isvar Chandra Vidyasagar, Michael Madhusudan Dutt, Hem Chandra Banerjee, Bankim Chandra Chatterjee and Dina Bandhu Mitra. Within the three quarters of the present century, prose, blank verse, historical fiction and drama have been introduced for the first time in the Bengali literature..."

SANTINIKETAN

Santiniketan is a small town near Bolpur in the Birbhum district of West Bengal, India, approximately 180 kilometres north of Kolkata (formerly Calcutta). It was made famous by Nobel Laureate Rabindranath Tagore, whose vision became what is now a university town (Visva-Bharati University) that attracts thousands of visitors each year. Santiniketan is also a tourist attraction because Rabindranath wrote many of his literary classics here, and his house is a place of historical importance.

Santiniketan was previously called Bhubandanga (named after Bhuban Dakat, a local dacoit), and owned by the Tagore family. Rabindranath's father, Maharshi Debendranath Tagore, found it very peaceful and renamed it Santiniketan, which means abode (niketan) of peace (shanti). It was here that Rabindranath Tagore started Patha Bhavana, the school of his ideals, whose central premise was that learning in a natural environment would be more enjoyable and fruitful. After he received the Nobel Prize (1913), the school was expanded into a university in 1921, but in 1951, it became one of the central universities of India. Many world famous teachers have become associated with it. Indira Gandhi, Satyajit Ray, Abdul Ghani Khan, Jahar Dasgupta and Nobel Laureate Amartya Sen are among its more illustrious students,

Kala Bhavana, the art college of Santiniketan, is still considered one of the best art colleges in the world. Other institutions here include Vidya Bhavana; the Institute of Humanities, Shiksha Bhavana; the Institute of Science, Sangit Bhavana; Institute of Dance, Drama and Music, Vinaya Bhavana; Institute of Education, Rabindra Bhavana, Institute of Tagore Studies and Research, Palli-Samgathana Vibhaga; Institute of Rural Reconstruction, and Palli Shiksha Bhavana; Institute of Agricultural Sciences.

There are also other centres, affiliated to major institutions such as Nippon Bhavana, the Indira Gandhi Centre for National Integration, Rural Extension Centre, Silpa Sadana; Centre for Rural Craft, Technology and Design, Palli-Charcha Kendra; Centre for Social Studies and Rural Development, Centre for Biotechnology, Centre for Mathematics Education, Centre for Environmental Studies, Computer Centre and Indira Gandhi Centre for National Integration. As well as Patha-Bhavana, there are two schools for kindergarten level education; Mrinalini

Ananda Pathsala, Santosh Pathsala; a school for primary and secondary education known as Shiksha Satra, and a school of higher secondary education known as Uttar-Shiksha Sadana. Santiniketan is also home to Amartya Sen, the 1998 Nobel Prize winner in Economics.

MAJOR EVENTS

Numerous social and cultural events taking place through out the year, have become part and parcel of Santiniketan.These include - Basanta Utsav, Barsha Mangal, Sharodutsav, Nandan Mela, Poush Mela, Magh Mela, Rabindra Jayanti to name a few. Of these, the Poush Mela deserves special mention, this being a major tourist attraction.

It is a 3-day fair (Bengali, mela means a fair),starting on the seventh day of the Bengali month Poush(usually, last week of December).It fetches not just tourists, but also artisans, folk singers, dancers, and the traditional Baul from the neighbourhood.

RECENT DEVELOPMENTS

Santiniketan has changed considerably since the days of Tagore. Although Visva-Bharati University still plays an active role, Santiniketan has become a haven for India's nouveau riche: large houses have been built on what used to be barren khoai (desert) and condominiums are becoming commonplace. But travel beyond the outskirts of the ever-expanding "small town" and one is soon back in village India.

The idyllic existence envisioned by Tagore in Santiniketan is rapidly disappearing, but it still maintains a "college town" feels, with many large shade-covered open spaces on campus where students can congregate. The student population remains international in origin, as does the faculty, and some of the best thinkers and intellectuals in India remember their college life in Santiniketan with fondness.

INDIA'S RENAISSANCE 1881-1905

By 1881 India had 253,890,000 people. Viceroy Ripon's finance minister, Major Evelyn Baring, lowered the duty on salt and removed all import duties except on alcohol, salt, opium, arms and ammunition, thus allowing free trade. Because very few Indians had been able to pass civil service exams in England by the age of 19, Ripon raised the age limit back to 21.

He added Oriental language as a subject, but the Secretary of State rejected these and other reforms. Ripon tried to ban employment of children under eight years, but Bengal's lieutenant governor Ashley Eden persuaded him to make it under seven; working hours were limited for children under twelve instead of fourteen.

In 1882 Prime Minister Gladstone told India to bear the £1.75 million cost of sending troops to Egypt, but Ripon got the Home Government to contribute £500,000. He appointed the Hunter Commission to look into educational reforms, but science was still preferred over literary and moral education. After consulting the provincial governments, in 1882 the Governor-General and his Council passed a resolution allowing much more self-government in local communities.

Within three years all the provinces were allowing local elections. In 1882 the Sirhind Canal was completed with a length of 3,700 miles. During Ripon's four years railways were extended by 2,000 miles to more than 11,500 miles in India. In 1883 Law Minister Courtenay Ilbert introduced a controversial bill that allowed Indian judges to hear cases of Europeans. Planters were so upset that Ripon was insulted in the streets of Calcutta. Finally they agreed to let Europeans request a jury of which half were to be Europeans. Ripon retired at the end of 1884 so that the liberal Gladstone could choose his successor, the Earl of Dufferin (Frederick Temple Blackwood), who had served in Egypt.

In 1876 the British Resident had refused to remove his shoes and kneel before King Mindon in Upper Burma, and his visits ceased. Thibaw became king of Burma in 1878, and British merchants and residents sent complaints to India. After Resident R. B. Shaw died in Upper Burma in June 1879, his successor Col. H. A. Browne and his staff left Mandalay. Two British steamers complained they were mistreated by Burmese officials. In 1881 the British set boundary pillars between Burma and Manipur, which the Burmese Government did not accept. King Thibaw tried to mollify the British by abolishing his monopolies in February 1882, but the next year he sent a trade mission to Paris.

France made a treaty with Burma in January 1885, and later the British learned of secret arms importing from Tonkin. Thibaw demanded a loan of £220,000 from the Bombay-Burma Trading Company for a royal concession in teakwood. When the Company refused, the Government of Burma fined the Trading Company ten lakhs of rupees (£230,000) in August for having bribed the governor of Ningyan to harvest the timber. Burma prepared to grant the concessions to France. In October the British sent Burma an ultimatum demanding a permanent Resident at Mandalay, control over Burma's foreign policy, arbitration of the timber case, and Burma's help trading with Yunnan.

King Thibaw rejected this on November 9, and General Prendergast with 10,000 men took over Mandalay on November 28. The Burmese army dispersed in the jungles and became robber bands. Thibaw had killed so many possible successors that on the first day of 1886 Viceroy Dufferin proclaimed the British annexation of Upper Burma into the Indian empire. As many as 30,000 troops and five years were needed to pacify the brigands. Six more years were spent trying to control the Shans and Chins on the borders.

The Russians occupied Merv in 1884, and General Komaroff drove the Afghans from Panjdeh with heavy losses in March 1885. The British mobilized for war, but Abdur Rahman was visiting Viceroy Dufferin and agreed to concede Panjdeh rather than precipitate an Anglo-Russian war in his country. Gladstone thus arranged to let the Russians keep Panjdeh in exchange for the Afghan Amir retaining the Zulfiqar Pass. In 1886 a commission agreed on an Afghan border running from the Oxus River to the Zulfiqar Pass. That year Dufferin replaced the license tax on trade with an income tax, and the age of admission to the Indian Civil Service was raised to 23.

Chandrakirtti ruled Manipur from 1850 until his death in 1886. He had ten sons by six queens. Sura-chandra became maharaja; Kula-chandra was named heir apparent; and after Jhala-kirtti died a few months later, Tikendrajit became Senapati (commander-in-chief). Tikendrajit was the only brother who knew Hindustani well and could converse with the British agent, F. S. C. Grimwood. At midnight on September 21, 1890 two other brothers, Angao Sena and Zilla Gumba, led several hundred men and took over the palace. The Maharaja gave no order for fighting, and the British political agent Grimwood had British sepoys disarm the Manipuri troops. The two brothers favored the popular Tikendrajit, but he waited for Kula-chandra to return and be crowned. Maharaja Sura-chandra went into exile but did not abdicate.

In February 1891 Viceroy Lansdowne and Chief Commissioner J. W. Quinton declared they would recognize Kula-chandra as maharaja of Manipur if he was advised by the British agent, deported Tikendrajit, and allowed 300 British soldiers in the Residency. Quinton went to Manipur with four hundred Gurkha soldiers under Col. Skene in March and planned to arrest Tikendrajit by inviting him to a durbar. Tikendrajit was kept waiting at the gate, learned of the extra soldiers, and returned home. A British attack on his house failed, but the British killed some people and burned down a dozen nearby houses. The Manipuris had four guns and began bombarding the Residency.

During a truce Tikendrajit and his brother Angao Mingto met with Quinton, Grimwood, Col. Skene, and two others; but as the five were leaving, they were attacked by a mob, which killed Grimwood. While Tikendrajit was sleeping, Tongol General had the four Englishmen and their bugler beheaded. When he awoke, Tikendrajit was angry at Tongol General and freed the other British soldiers and subjects. In a trial before a special court Tikendrajit was convicted of abetting Tongol General. The Governor-General commuted the death sentences of Kula-chandra and his brother Angao Sena to transportation for life and confiscation of property, but both Tongol General and Tikendrajit were hanged on August 13.

Accounts of Tikendrajit's trial indicate it was unfair, and his death had been called a judicial murder. The British recognized a five-year-old as maharaja and administered Manipur. After being governor-general of Canada for five years, the Marquess of Lansdowne became viceroy of India in December 1888. He extended British control into the Zhob Valley in northern Baluchistan in 1889 and into the Kurram Valley in 1892. Irrigation increased cultivated area, but the population of India was growing even faster, thirty million in a decade. The value of silver decreased almost in half as Germany demonetized silver, and Lansdowne closed down the free coinage of silver in Indian mints. Gold was made legal tender in India.

Lansdowne enacted a law to prevent cruelty to animals. He encouraged the election of local councils, and an act in 1892 allowed legislative councils to discuss the budget and public issues. However, by authorizing separate representation for Hindus and Muslims they practiced the imperial method of divide and rule. Communal conflicts between Hindus and Muslims increased between 1885 and 1893, breaking out in 1885 in Lahore and Karnal, in 1886 in Delhi, in 1889 in Hosiarpur, Ludhiana, Ambala, and Dera Ghazi Khan, and in 1891 in Madras.

During six days of riots in 1893 in Bombay 65 people were killed, and more than five hundred were injured. In the spring of 1893 riots erupted in Bihar over the killing of cattle. When the Chief Commissioners of Assam raised land assessments by more than seventy percent in 1893, people spontaneously revolted. They were suppressed by force, and leaders were arrested. On January 10, 1894 several thousand people gathered at Rangiya and refused to disperse until in the evening they were fired on by the military and police. A similar incident occurred in Darrang on January 28, but the police charged with fixed bayonets instead. The Deputy Commissioner was transferred, and the land revenue was reduced.

The Russians claimed the Pamirs in 1892, and the next year Mortimer Durand negotiated the Afghanistan boundary. Amir Abdur Rahman was allowed to import arms, and his annual subsidy was increased from 12 to 18 lakhs. The British tried to assert their authority over the Afridis, Mahsuds, Waziris, Swats, and the chiefs of Chitral and Gilgit. The tribal chiefs had not been consulted, and the boundary divided the Mohmand tribal area in two parts. Dr. Robertson was sent to help the new Mehtar of Chitral and decided to stay because of the hostility of Umra Khan of Jandol. In January 1895 the Mehtar was murdered, and Umra Khan proclaimed a jihad in Dir, Swat, and Bajaur.

The Chitralis and Pathans besieged Dr. Robertson at Fort Chitral in March. Col. Kelly marched 350 miles in 35 days from Gilgit in Kashmir, and Robert Low went by way of Malakand. Chitral was garrisoned, but Salisbury's government vetoed it in August. The boundary dispute was settled the next month. In June 1897 Dawaris in the Tochi Valley requested British aid, but the political officer's escort was attacked at Maizar. Sadullah Khan led an uprising in Swat and attacked Malakand and Chakdarra. Then the Mohmands led by Najm-ud-din revolted. The Orakzais and Afridis captured the Khyber forts, but a force of 35,000 men under Bruce Lockhart was used to subdue them. The British forward policy once again had provoked violence.

Victor Alexander Bruce (1894-99) was the ninth earl of Elgin and the son of a viceroy. He was inexperienced and depended on advice by telegraph from Whitehall. A five percent import duty was put on cotton in 1894, and the Lancashire interests quickly got a countervailing excise of five percent imposed on cotton manufactured in India. These were both reduced to 3.5 percent two years later. A drought began to spread in 1896, and sixty million people were affected in western and central India. By 1897 about 4,500,000 people had died.

A meteorologist called it the worst drought in two centuries. Bubonic plague spread from Bombay in August 1896 and took another 193,000 lives by 1898. This was followed by a second famine in 1899; despite extensive Government relief efforts spending more than £6,000,000, estimates of the number of people who died ranged from the Government's 1,250,000 to William Digby's 3,250,000. Shri Birsa revived the Munda faith in Chotanagpur and urged his followers to worship the one God he called Sing Bonga. They tried to purify their lives by being chaste and abstaining from intoxicants and animal food. Some of his followers were Christian converts, and they considered Birsa a prophet and an incarnation of God.

Thousands of Mundas made the pilgrimage to his village Chalkad. The British government believed their goal of self-government was dangerous, and they arrested Birsa and many followers at night on August 24, 1895. Birsa and fifteen followers were sentenced to a fine and two years imprisonment while others only had to pay a small fine. After Birsa was released in January 1898, he began training his followers to use swords and bows and arrows. They were urged to fight against their oppressors and planned an uprising for Christmas 1898. They attacked mission houses and fought police. On

January 7, 1899 about three hundred Mundas attacked the Khunti Police Station, killed a constable, and set houses on fire.

Troops were called in and killed about two hundred Mundas, including women and children. Complaints were later made that some wounded also had been buried in deep trenches. Birsa's general Gaya Munda was shot dead, but Birsa was not captured until February 2, 1900. He died of cholera in jail four months later. About 450 followers of Birsa were arrested, and 87 were tried; two received capital sentences and the rest were transported or imprisoned. From 1881 the number of students increased over the next twenty years by 49% in primary schools and 180% in secondary schools. By 1902 about four million students were being instructed in 105,000 schools, plus 600,000 pupils in 43,000 private schools.

The 145 arts colleges had 17,500 undergraduates. Yet with India's huge population this still meant that only one boy in six was in a primary school and only one out of forty girls. Twelve female colleges had only 177 students. Secondary schools had 9,800 girls, and primary schools had 380,000 girls. Dayananda Saraswati (1824-83) objected to idol worship at the age of fourteen. Five years later he ran away from home to avoid being married and became a sannyasi in the Saraswati Order. After fifteen years of ascetic wandering, he studied the ancient *Vedas* under a blind old teacher who beat them into him.

He learned that the *Vedas* did not sanction idol worship or child marriage or the subjection of women. He founded Arya Samaj in Bombay in 1875 to spread Hinduism in northern India, and he went to the Punjab in 1877. He took a more fundamentalist attitude toward the *Vedas* than the liberal Brahmo Samaj. His strict view of karma made forgiveness impossible. His Satyartha Prakash argued that Hinduism is better than other religions, and he founded the Cow Protection Association in 1882 to try to stop Muslims from slaughtering cattle.

Dayananda stated that the primary purpose of Arya Samaj is to improve the physical, spiritual, and social conditions of humanity by treating everyone with love, justice, and a due regard for their merits. He was attacked by the orthodox and was eventually poisoned by a woman after he had criticized the loose living of a prince. Mahadev Govind Ranade (1842-1901) enrolled in the first class at Bombay University in 1859. Two years later he was the English editor of the *Indu Prakash*, and he began teaching history at Elphinstone College in 1866. Ranade was a judge for thirty years and served on the High Court of Bombay. He urged Hindus to embrace all humanity, and he criticized asceticism and contempt for the world.

In his *Theist's Confession of Faith* he emphasized the unity of God, the reality of God's creation, and the spiritual nature of the human soul. Although he considered congregational worship and ceremonies helpful, he found asceticism, adoration of gurus, and belief in saviors and miracles unnecessary. Ranade led the Prarthana Samaj (Prayer Society), which began missionary work in 1882. He advised obeying conscience instead of expediency and urged social reforms because he believed that all humans are essentially equal. He justified reform as the work of liberation based on reason, and he emphasized the divine principle in everyone as more important than great and wise men.

Ranade founded the Indian National Social Conference in 1887. He advocated abolishing caste, recognizing inter-caste marriages, prohibiting child marriage, and legalizing widow's remarrying. He repudiated the seclusion of women, promoted female education, and opposed all irrational and cruel customs that degrade human beings. He argued that the law of karma could be controlled by making one's will serve the higher will and the law of duty (dharma).

Ranade urged Hindus and Muslims to work together as they did in Akbar's time; he warned against the mistakes of

Aurangzeb. In 1890 he inaugurated the Industrial Association of Western India. Two years later his essay on "Indian Political Economy" suggested that many economic functions such as education, postal service, telegraphs, railways, canals, and insurance could be discharged by the state. He noted that in India the state was the sole landlord and the largest capitalist in the country, being involved in iron and coal fields and experiments with cotton, tobacco, tea, coffee, and cinchona plantations. In 1900 his *Rise of the Maratha Power* was published.

CURZON'S VICEROYALTY 1899-1905

Viceroy George Nathaniel Curzon arrived at Calcutta on January 3, 1899, eight days before his 40th birthday. He was interested in every aspect of government and energetically worked for improvements. Sugar from imported European beets had increased tenfold in the previous decade, and so he imposed a duty on subsidized sugar-beet imports in order to protect Indian growers of sugar cane. The bill was passed in March, and Curzon, who believed in free trade, explained that the new duties made up for the sugar-beet bounties. He visited areas suffering from famine and pestilence. Three and a half million people were on Government relief, and he was severely criticized in the press for warning provincial governments against spending too much for famine relief. Curzon favored self-reliance and generally had a low opinion of Indians.

Yet he felt he was the only official willing to punish soldiers for killing Indians. He asserted his authority by punishing officers and the regiment that obstructed justice after a Burmese woman was raped by British soldiers in Rangoon. The Indian press praised this justice. However, he antagonized the Indian nationalists when he curtailed the elected officials in the 1899 Calcutta Municipal bill in order to make administration more efficient. Curzon traveled the country and encouraged the rajas to do their duty. The silver rupee had stabilized at 1s 4d, and with less military spending the economy prospered during his years.

Curzon opposed forward defenses on the borders and saved six lakhs of rupees on fortifications. He reduced the 10,200 troops in the northwest to 5,000 by 1904. He limited the importation of arms and encouraged the tribes to maintain peace and stop crime by granting them allowances. His policy was to let tribal forces defend their own country, and he concentrated British troops in the rear as a safeguard and support. During the previous five years military operations on the northwest frontier had cost £4,584,000, but in his nearly seven years they would spend only £248,000. He organized this region and five districts from the Punjab into the new North-West Frontier Province under a chief commissioner.

The old North-Western Provinces were renamed the United Provinces of Agra and Oudh. In 1900 India sent over 8,000 British troops for the Boer War in South Africa along with 3,000 Indians for non-combatant service. In 1901 Abdur Rahman died. His oldest son Habibulla insisted that his agreements with the British be continued, though he did not draw the subsidy for a few years. After the Boer War ended in 1902, Curzon refused to permit Indians to be recruited as indentured laborers for the Transv*a*l gold mines. He confirmed the principle that when India loaned troops for a colonial war, the imperial Government must pay the expenses.

Curzon sent Col. Francis Younghusband to Tibet in July 1903, and they killed at least 600 Tibetans who tried to stop them before they reached Gyantse in April 1904. While Curzon was in England, Younghusband pushed on to Lhasa. The Dalai Lama fled, but Younghusband got Tibetan officials to agree to a British official residing at Gyantse with the right to visit Lhasa, and he imposed an indemnity of three lakhs of rupees per year for the next 25 years. This violated his own instructions, and the British Government changed it to 25 lakhs of rupees to be paid in three years. Then the British troops would be withdrawn. The British Government reprimanded Curzon for his aggressive policy that turned a trade mission into an armed invasion.

The Punjab Land Alienation Act of 1900 limited the sale of land to agriculturalists so that moneylenders could not take over farms. In 1904 Curzon enacted Cooperative Credit Societies to address the problem of farmer's debts, and the next year he persuaded Henry Phipps to contribute £30,000 to establish the Agricultural Research Institute at Pusa in Bengal. In 1905 a report recommended that they spend £30,000,000 in the next twenty years to irrigate 6,500,000 acres. In the previous twelve years the area of food crops increased by only three percent while the area of non-food crops grew by 29 percent. As the population increased by fifteen million, the increased food was only half enough.

The Suspension and Remissions Resolution of 1905 allowed for flexibility in collecting land revenue in hard times, and Curzon established the principle that land taxes should not exceed ten percent of all revenues. In 1904 Viceroy Curzon appointed a commission that improved police training and increased their pay. The number of police expanded from 150,000 to 175,000. He also enacted a law to preserve and protect ancient monuments. However, his Universities Bill of 1904 aroused protests because they believed fixed fees would block new universities from starting. Curzon wanted to improve the teaching at institutions that had become primarily examining boards. In 1905 he created a Department of Commerce and Industry.

He encouraged mining by removing obstructive regulations. During his viceroyalty more than 6,000 miles of railway lines were added to the 27,000 miles already in India. Bengal contained 190,000 square miles, and the population had increased to 78 million. So in 1905 Curzon divided it into two parts, leaving Muslims the majority in the new province of Eastern Bengal and Assam. Hindu political leaders in Calcutta protested this because the Biharis and Oriyas now outnumbered those speaking Bengali in the province Western Bengal, Bihar and Orissa. They began boycotting British textiles and promoted the Swadeshi cloth made in India.

The partition took effect on October 16, 1905, and 50,000 people gathered at the Kali temple near Calcutta. They sang "Bande Mataram" and bathed in the Ganges. Sisters tied woolen threads around their brothers' wrists as they vowed to undo the partition of Bengal. This *rakhi-bandhan* ceremony became an annual ritual. Gurkha troops were stationed in East Bengal. Surendranath Banerji said that the agitation would not stop until the partition was cancelled. Two British titans clashed when H. H. Kitchener became commander-in-chief. He wanted to eliminate the military member on the Council who administered the military department and also offered the Viceroy a second opinion. Viceroy Curzon objected to the change because he thought the current system worked well by relieving the commander-in-chief of much administrative work.

When the British Government chose a compromise that favored Kitchener, Curzon resigned in August 1905, staying on for three more months. Ananda Mohan Bose had first suggested at the 1898 Indian National Congress that India should be represented in the British Parliament, and in 1905 the Congress passed a resolution that each province should have at least two members in the House of Commons. That year Gokhale founded the Servants of India Society to promote the national interests of the Indian people. He noted that the death rate in India had risen from 24 per thousand in 1883 to the current 34 per thousand. The 1905 partition of Bengal provoked Tilak into advocating a boycott of British goods that grew into a movement that swept the nation.

RAMAKRISHNA AND VIVEKANANDA

Gadadhar Chattopadhyaya (Chatterji) was born into a poor Brahmin family in a small village in western Bengal just before dawn on February 18, 1836. From the age of seven he had mystical experiences, often falling into trances. He attended school but preferred to spend his time with wandering *sadhus*.

He went to Calcutta when he was seventeen, and three years later he began assisting his older brother Ramkumar at a temple devoted to the goddess Kali at Dakshineswar. There he had more mystical experiences and eventually took the name Ramakrishna Paramahansa.

His life was devoted to God and searching continually for greater God realisation. He spent long hours in prayer and meditation or singing and wailing to Kali. Because he had so many peculiar trances and visions, he was relieved of the usual priestly duties. When Ramakrishna was 24, he was married to a girl who was only five years old. A Bhairavi yogi observed that Ramakrishna's odd behavior was similar to that of the famous Vaishnava Chaitanya, and she initiated him into Tantric *sadhana* (spiritual practice). He practiced this for two years, going through the stages.

Then in 1863 he became a Vaishnava and had a vision of Krishna. For a while he dressed and acted like a woman, longing for Krishna. The nondualist guru Tota-puri taught him how to practice Vedanta. Bhairavi warned him that if he became a nondualist, he would lose his devotion; but Ramakrishna went ahead. He could easily experience Kali, and by destroying her image in his consciousness he could empty his mind and attained *nirvikalpa samadhi* in one day.

Tota-puri was surprised because it took the guru forty years of ascetic practice. Ramakrishna believed that every religion is a path to God and proved it to himself by practicing the spiritual disciplines of various Hindu sects and other religions until he experienced God by their methods. When Ramakrishna was initiated as a Sufi, he ate and dressed like a Muslim and prayed to Allah. After three days he had a vision of God. Another three days of Christian practice resulted in his vision of Jesus Christ. When Ramakrishna's wife Sarada Devi came to Dakshineswar, he worshipped her as his mother.

They were celibate. She accepted this, served him, and asked him to teach her how to realize God. In 1867 Ramakrishna went on a pilgrimage for four months. He served as a sweeper and scavenger to clean up after outcastes and Muslims, and he became known as a saint. Keshab Chandra Sen, the influential leader of the Brahmo Samaj, visited him. In 1875 Ramakrishna went to see him and his disciples, speaking in parables. Keshab was won over and published an influential sketch of Ramakrishna's life and teachings. Keshab agreed that his daughter could marry the wealthy Maharaja of Cooch-Behar before she was fourteen years old. A split emerged in the Brahmo Samaj because Vijay Krishna Goswami and others accused Keshab of hypocrisy.

They adamantly opposed child marriage and formed General Samaj. Ramakrishna said he opposed hard and fast rules but remained friendly with both sides. Keshab liked Ramakrishna's universality and was impressed by his vision of Jesus. Keshab worked on integrating the teachings of Hinduism and Christianity as a way forward, and in 1879 he declared a "New Dispensation, the Religion of Harmony." He hoped that Europe would enter the heart of Asia, and Asia the mind of Europe in a universal synthesis. He suggested they include and absorb all humanity without hating or excluding anyone. He wanted to unite East and West in one undivided and universal church of God in order to reconcile faith and modern science, philosophy and inspiration, and asceticism and civilisation.

On October 27, 1883 Keshab invited Ramakrishna on a chartered steamer, and he brought Vijay with him. In this way the two leaders were reconciled, though, as Ramakrishna predicted, their followers still continued the feud. Many spiritual seekers came to see Ramakrishna, and he conversed with them. He accepted neither money nor expensive gifts. He could not even bear the touch of silver or gold coins. When he was asked how to eliminate passion, Ramakrishna asked why it should be eliminated. He recommended directing one's passion toward God.

He taught that God is both with form and formless. He warned against setting limits to God's nature, and he found by experience that various ways of worshipping God can be successful. He said that to gain a vision of God one must practice spiritual discipline because one "cannot see him just by wishing."

Kristodas Pal, editor of the *Hindu Patriot* newspaper, said that Ramakrishna's renunciation was an escape, and he believed in working to improve social conditions. Ramakrishna detected a note of egotism in "helping the world" and suggested that "serving the world" with less sense of self came from doing what the Divine Mother gave one to do. Ramakrishna practiced exceptional devotion; but he also emphasized that one must always speak the truth to find God because God is truth. He taught the golden rule of doing what you wish others to do to you. He warned that people are quick to blame or praise, and so you should not be concerned about what others say of you.

He noticed that people tend to develop the propensities of those around them, and they seek the company of those with similar propensities. Ramakrishna often taught in parables. He compared religion to the rain from heaven that becomes dirty depending on the medium through which it manifests. He said that as long as one lives, one may learn every day of the mysteries of love and devotion. He advised that the best course is to renounce desire and work unattached. Ramakrishna recognized Narendranath Datta as the one who would spread his teachings, but Ramakrishna himself never started a new religion or sect. He got cancer and finally departed from his body on August 16, 1886.

Narendranath Datta was born into a wealthy Kshatriya family in Calcutta on January 12, 1863. His family tried to get him to marry, but Narendra resolved to remain celibate and refused. He attended English schools and graduated from Calcutta University in 1883. He studied the writings of John Stuart Mill, David Hume, and Herbert Spencer. Narendranath liked Spencer's ideas on evolution, corresponded with him, and translated his book *Education* into Bengali. He attended the Brahmo Samaj and made contact with Keshab Chandra Sen.

When Narendranath first visited Ramakrishna in 1881, the saintly mystic told him that he was an incarnation of Narayana (Vishnu). Ramakrishna said that one can communicate with God. He asked Narendra to promise to come back soon. At the second visit Ramakrishna put his foot on him, and Narendra had an unusual experience. His consciousness changed so much that he thought he was dying and asked the master to stop it. Ramakrishna put his hand on Narendra's chest, and he returned to his normal awareness. On another occasion the master touched him, and Narendra realized that everything is part of God, that there is nothing in the universe but God.

He was impressed how Ramakrishna combined the devotion of *bhakti* with the knowledge of Vedanta. He once said that Ramakrishna was a *bhakt* outwardly and a *jnani* (knower) inwardly while he was a *jnani* outwardly and a *bhakt* inwardly. While Ramakrishna emphasized the devotion of *bhakti*, Narendra would practice the karma yoga of working. They both taught that human misery would continue until human character changed. Thus lasting social reform depends on spiritual and ethical culture. Narendra's father liked to spend money, and at his death in early 1884 he left behind more debts than assets.

Narendra had to give up his clerkship and was suddenly poor. He was studying law and asked Ramakrishna to pray so that he would get a job. Ramakrishna said he did not make such requests, but he urged the educated Hindu to pray to Kali. Despite his reluctance to worship an idol, Narendra did so and came to accept the Divine Mother. As he experienced her, he too only prayed for detachment, devotion, and knowledge. A few days before he died, Ramakrishna passed his energy to Narendra. Though other disciples went back to school or work, Narendra and a few others started a fraternity of monks in a dilapidated house in Baranagar near Kasipur. They barely survived on rice and salt, but eventually others joined.

In July 1890 Narendra began a pilgrimage and traveled around India for three years. The rajas of Ramnad and Khetri urged him to represent Hinduism at the Parliament of Religions meeting at the World Exposition at Chicago in 1893 in commemoration of Columbus, and they offered to pay his expenses. While meditating on the rock at Cape Comorin, the southern tip of India, Narendra realized that India needed food and the West needed spirituality. The Raja of Khetri suggested he call himself Swami Vivekananda, and he sailed from Bombay on May 31, 1893, stopping at Colombo, Hong Kong, and Japan before reaching Vancouver.

Vivekananda arrived at Chicago in mid-July but learned the Parliament was delayed until September. So he went to Boston, where he gave talks and became a local celebrity. The Swami spoke five times to the Chicago conference and was very well received. His comments before reading his paper on Hinduism were widely reported in the American press. He criticized the English Christians for putting their foot on the neck of 250 million Asians, and he reminded them of the Spanish conquest of America. He warned that the Muslim sword could destroy India, and he said, "Blood and sword are not for the Hindu, whose religion is based on the laws of love."

Swami Vivekananda suddenly became a world figure, and his intelligent interpretation of Hinduism lifted its philosophy to a new level of recognition in India and the world. A lecture tour was quickly organized for him, and in the next two years he spoke often in Chicago, Detroit, Boston, New York, and other cities. He preached self-reliance and individual effort. Scriptures can be a guide until one is strong enough to do without them. He believed that only the spiritually aware could be great teachers of humanity. In the summer and fall of 1895 he visited London and Paris, and he inspired Max Müller to publish

Ramakrishna - His Life and Teachings. He went back to New York and then returned to England in April 1896 on his way home. He had gained some western disciples who worked for Indian education and freedom in various ways.

Vivekananda believed that education is the key to the development of equality and democracy. When people develop their own inner powers, they will become free. Vivekananda observed that the western world especially had become very materialistic and so needed the spiritual understanding that India could offer. He combined the need for spiritual awakening with patriotic Indian nationalism. Yet he went beyond nationalism, which he considered an incomplete stage of development, to international solidarity with international laws as a more lasting solution to human conflicts. He believed that India is immortal because she persists in searching for God; but he warned that if they went in for politics and caused social conflicts, she would die.

Just as hatred cannot be conquered by hatred but by love, materialism cannot conquer materialism. When armies try to conquer others, armies multiply and make brutes of humanity. He suggested that spirituality will conquer the West. Western civilisation since the Greeks has sought happiness, but the Hindus seek spiritual liberation. Vivekananda observed how human societies had first been dominated by priests (Brahmins) and then by the nobility (Kshatriyas). In modern times the merchants (Vaishyas) had taken control. In 1896 he prophesied that the fourth epoch would bring domination by the workers (Sudras), and he predicted that the first proletarian state in the world would be Russia or China. He criticized the social Darwinism of competition, saying,

> The attempts to remove evil from the world
> by killing a thousand evil-doers,
> only adds to the evil in the world.

But if the people can be made to desist from evil-doing
by means of spiritual instruction,
there is no more evil in the world.

Now, see how horrible the Western struggle theory becomes!

In Vivekananda's idea of spiritual evolution the highest level is attained through sacrifice. He found that fighting put back human progress fifty years rather than moving it forward. He urged the other monks to become Christs themselves in order to aid in redeeming the world. They could deny themselves to realize God as Jesus had done.

Vivekananda landed on Ceylon in January 1897 and then returned to Calcutta. They had founded the Ramakrishna Order, and Brahmananda (Rakhal Chandra Ghosh) welcomed him home to the Alambazar monastery. Vivekananda handed him all the money he had raised and had to borrow pennies to take the ferry back across the Ganges. On May 1 Vivekananda spoke to the monks and announced his plans for the Ramakrishna Mission to teach the masses what they need for material and spiritual welfare. Their goals would be spiritual and humanitarian rather than political. The Ramakrishna Mission was instituted four days later, and monasteries were established throughout India.

They immediately began working on famine relief and plague relief, founding hospitals and schools. Vivekananda urged that the nation, like an individual, must learn to help itself. He said, "Modern India admits spiritual equality of all souls-but strictly keeps the social difference." He denounced untouchability and worked on raising the status of women and the masses. He recommended beginning slowly and working from the ground up. He believed that India needed to go beyond recalling her past by improving upon it. Vivekananda lectured tirelessly and published a book on Ramakrishna as well as *Jnanayoga*, *Rajayoga*, *Karmayoga*, and *Bhaktiyoga*.

He believed that removing poverty was more important than preaching. He found God in the poor, the miserable, and the weak. He suggested that everyone should be treated equally because God is in everyone. Every individual and nation must work out their own salvation. Having power in the world does not necessarily make one happy, but by conquering oneself one may find happiness. Vivekananda taught that God unifies the variety of the universe. In God all humans are one, though every person is different. In the summer of 1899 Vivekananda visited California.

There his health improved, and he began Vedanta centers in Los Angeles and San Francisco. After touring Europe he returned to India in December 1900. His health declined, but he taught a class and walked two miles on the day (July 4, 1902) he died with an expression of ecstasy on his face. Brahmananda had succeeded Vivekananda as president of the Mission in February 1901, and he continued to serve in that position for the next 21 years. He emphasized that more time should be spent on learning how to know God than on serving humanity.

THEOSOPHY AND BLAVATSKY 1875-88

Helena Petrovna von Hahn was born on August 12, 1831 in the Ukraine. Her mother was an excellent novelist, but she died at the age of 28. When her governess told Helena that because of her fiery temperament she could not even marry an old man she considered ugly, the 17-year-old got him to propose to her. Helena tried to get out of marrying the elderly Nikifor Blavatsky but could not and after two months of resisting his "conjugal rights" she escaped to her grandmother. Helena traveled to Turkey, Greece, Egypt, and France, and in London she met her Hindu master.

In 1852 Madam Blavatsky went to America and India but could not get into Tibet. She got the idea of combining science and religion and continued to travel around the world, sometimes dressing as a man. She participated in spiritualist experiments and astounded people by willing or evoking tapping sounds across a room that answered questions. In 1860 she began answering questions verbally or by writing. She volunteered to help Garibaldi, and at the battle of Mentana on November 3, 1867 she suffered five wounds.

Blavatsky claimed that she spent three years in Tibet studying with her masters, but this has been questioned. She lived in Cairo in 1871 and went to New York in 1873. On September 7, 1875 the Theosophical Society (TS) was founded in New York with Col. Henry Steel Olcott as chairman and William Quan Judge as secretary. At the first meeting the next day HPB (Blavatsky) agreed to be corresponding secretary. The main purposes are 1) to promote universal brotherhood without distinction of race, creed, sex, caste, or color; 2) to study ancient and modern religion, philosophy, and science; and 3) to investigate unexplained laws of nature and the divine powers latent in humanity. Blavatsky published *Isis Unveiled* in September 1877 in two long volumes entitled *Science* and *Theology*.

The first volume explores the occult sciences as an important part of psychology, and the second volume takes on traditional Christian theology as an obstacle to free thought in a society of "increasing materialism, worldliness and hypocrisy." In the last chapter HPB outlined the fundamental propositions of Oriental philosophy in ten points that are summarized as follows:

1. A "miracle" occurs because of eternal and immutable laws.
2. Nature has visible objectivity and an inner vital principle and above them eternal and indestructible spirit.
3. Humans have a physical body and an astral body but are sovereign and immortal spirits.

4.Magic is a science and an art for applying knowledge to control nature's forces.

5. Arcane knowledge may be misapplied as sorcery or be used beneficently as wisdom.
6. Mediums are passive, but adepts actively control inferior powers.
7. All things are recorded and can be known by an adept.
8. People differ in spiritual gifts.
9. Adepts can withdraw the inner person from the physical body consciously, but mediums do so unconsciously.
10. Magic is based on knowing how magnetism and electricity affect humans and animals.

Blavatsky concluded,

Magic is spiritual wisdom;

nature, the material ally, pupil and servant of the magician.

One common vital principle pervades all things,

and this is controllable by the perfected human will.

Madam Blavatsky became a citizen of the United States in July 1878. She and Olcott went to Bombay in January 1879 and announced that they were being guided spiritually by the mahatmas who live in the Himalayas. They recommended abstinence from alcohol and pure living in order to develop psychic and spiritual abilities. They taught occult science and considered clairvoyant intuition more important than rational analysis. The British secret service put HPB under surveillance because they thought she might be a Russian spy. She was the first editor of the monthly *Theosophist*, which began in October.

Alfred Percy Sinnett was the editor of *The Pioneer*, the most influential newspaper in India that was a mouthpiece for the Government. The Theosophists visited him and his wife Patience in Allahabad, and Allan Hume became interested in Theosophy. Blavatsky and Olcott first visited Ceylon in May 1880. The Sinnetts visited England and published *The Occult World* in June. Correspondence from Master KH helped Sinnett write *Esoteric Buddhism*. HPB said she met Master M in Lahore, and he told her to tour northern India. After that tour the Theosophists moved their headquarters from Bombay to Adyar in Madras in December 1882.

Theosophy has a special appeal in India because of its primary doctrines of karma and reincarnation that are universally accepted by Hindus, Buddhists, and Jains. Thousands of educated Indians joined the Theosophical Society. Olcott helped Ceylon increase the number of Buddhist schools there from two in 1880 to two hundred by 1900. He did so much to revive Buddhism in Burma that a national committee of Japanese priests sent a representative to escort him to Japan. HPB and Olcott traveled in Europe for seven months in 1884. Alexis Coulomb and his wife Emma had been expelled from the Theosophical Society in May for extortion, slander, and misuse of TS funds.

In October 1884 HPB replied to a scandalous article in the *London Times* based on their accusations of fraud saying that she never tried to gain money for herself or the Society by means of her psychic gifts. In December 1885 Richard Hodgson issued a report for the Society for Psychical Research (SPR) based on the Coulombs' charges and incriminating letters. This scandal was widely believed at the time. Olcott persuaded Blavatsky to accept the recommendation of the Theosophists committee not to sue her defamers because a trial might ridicule the sacred names of the Masters. Blavatsky nearly died from an illness, and in March 1885 she resigned as corresponding secretary of the TS.

Ironically this scandal gave Theosophy so much publicity that many more people joined. In 1884 the Theosophical Society had 104 chartered branches in the world, but by 1890 this had increased to two hundred. A century later handwriting expert Dr. Vernon Harrison made a thorough investigation for the SPR of the letters and concluded that the Coulombs had forged letters, that Hodgson was biased, and that the SPR had not checked his report critically. He also found that the letters attributed to the mahatmas were not written by HPB. From 1885 to 1888 Blavatsky worked on writing *The Secret Doctrine* while she was living in Germany and then in London. Letters were given to Dr. William Hübbe-Schleiden, president of the TS in Germany, from the masters M and KH saying that they wrote *The Secret Doctrine* with HPB.

The two long volumes on *Cosmogenesis* and *Anthropogenesis* contain many long quotations from other books that HPB copied and cited by psychic perception. Dr. Bertram Keightley had a typed copy of the manuscript made, looked them up in the British Museum, and found that most were accurate word for word. The first volume was published in October 1888, and the second volume came out three months later. HPB based her work on three premises: 1) that an "omnipresent, eternal, boundless, and immutable principle" is the basis "of all that was, is, or ever will be;" 2) that the eternal universe is a boundless plane in which the universal Spirit as souls (monads) experience a cycle of incarnations; and 3) that the souls are one with the universal over-soul.

The Secret Doctrine elucidates the mysteries and essential teachings of various religions in order to show their unity. Blavatsky also intended to reveal the occult side of Nature that modern science was not approaching. For HPB evolution is spiritual and mental as well as physical. She wrote of the one Universal Life, and she perceived that matter and force are two sides of the same substance. She explained karma as action and the universal law of cause and effect or ethical causation that governs the world of being. This law of retribution is unerring; but it does not predestine because humans plan and create the causes. Destiny is self-made.

The doctrine of karma explains the origin of evil, but all actions are resolved into universal harmony by the law of justice. Science by being too materialistic has left out the inner, spiritual, psychic, and moral aspects of human nature. The aggregate of individual karma becomes national karma, and the world is the total of national karma. Because of the principle of Harmony we reward and punish ourselves for our own actions. HPB wrote,

> With right knowledge,
>
> or at any rate with a confident conviction
>
> that our neighbors will no more work to hurt us
>
> than we would think of harming them,
>
> two-thirds of the World's evil would vanish into thin air.
>
> Were no man to hurt his brother,
>
> Karma-Nemesis would have neither cause to work for,
>
> nor weapons to act through.

When one breaks the laws of harmony and life, one falls into the chaos that is produced. Avenging angels only represent the reaction. The doctrines of karma and reincarnation explain the apparent injustices in life. When humans learn to act from their inner spiritual intuitions with real altruism instead of by the impulses of the selfish body, then brotherhood will become actual. Humans are their own destroyers but their own saviors as well. HPB warned that Europe was on the eve of a cataclysm because of its racial karma. In other writings she warned of future wars and an instantly devastating new weapon.

Mohandas Gandhi discovered Theosophy and met HPB in 1889 while he was studying law in London. He first read the *Bhagavad-Gita* in Edwin Arnold's English translation, and he joined the Blavatsky lodge in March 1891. In her last years HPB began a secret Esoteric Section for more than a thousand people. From *The Book of Golden Precepts* she wrote *The Voice of the Silence* and "The Seven Portals" with its seven keys of love (charity), harmony in word and action, patience, detachment, courage to find truth, meditation, and wisdom. She published *The Key to Theosophy* to answer basic questions. The motto of the

Theosophical Society is "There is no religion higher than truth." The Wisdom-Religion has been known since ancient times and is passed on by initiates, profound seekers of truth, in all cultures.

HPB divided human nature into seven levels: 1) physical body *(rupa)*, 2) vital principle *(prana)*, 3) astral body *(linga sharira)*, 4) animal desires *(kama rupa)*, 5) mind *(manas)*, 6) soul *(buddhi)*, and 7) Spirit *(atman)*. However, in Indian traditions *buddhi* usually means intuition; *atma* is soul, and *Brahman* is God or Spirit. Blavatsky rejected the dangerous doctrine of atonement that the sacrifice of Jesus can wipe out the enormous crimes against human and divine laws. Yet she described God's mercy as boundless. She opposed retaliating against evil and advised leaving people to their karma. Because others do evil is no reason for doing evil oneself. Blavatsky died on May 8, 1891, and her body was cremated. *The Theosophical Glossary* she wrote was published after her death.

BESANT AND THEOSOPHY 1889-1905

Annie Wood was born October 1, 1847 in London. She married the Anglican priest Frank Besant in 1867. They had two children, but he abused her. When he said that she must accept Church dogma to stay with him, she left him and Christianity in 1873. Annie Besant joined the National Secular Society the next year, wrote for the *National Reformer*, and worked for woman suffrage, penal reform, trade unions, birth control, and against vivisection. She lectured on the political status of women and called for "equality before the law for all in public and in private." She said,

> The man shall bring his greater strength
>
> and more sustained determination,
>
> the woman her quicker judgment and purer heart,
>
> till man shall grow tenderer, and woman stronger,
>
> man more pure, and woman more brave and free.

She was secretary of the Malthusian League and educated people about birth control. In 1877 she and her mentor Charles Bradlaugh were prosecuted for republishing *The Fruits of Philosophy* by Charles Knowlton, and their acquittal allowed information on contraception. Because of her work for birth control, she lost custody of her daughter. Besant wrote *The Law of Population: Its Consequences and Its Bearing upon Human Conduct and Morals*. She argued that celibacy is not natural to men or women, and bodily needs require legitimate satisfaction. She suggested that by limiting population they would deprive the capitalists of their crowded labor market.

Workers would have more opportunities with limited families. She was threatened with prosecution but not indicted, and the book eventually sold 175,000 copies. In February 1878 she helped organize the International Labor Union. Annie worked to stop the imminent war in Afghanistan by writing the pamphlets *Rushing into War* and *England, India, and Afghanistan.* During the elections of 1879 she published "The Story of Afghanistan: or, why the Tory Government Gags the Indian Press: A Plea for the Weak Against the Strong."

This excellent summary of British interventions in Afghanistan boldly criticized the crimes of the Tory Government that murdered men and froze women and children by burning villages. She accused Disraeli of bullying, boasting, and imperialism. She noted that Amir Sher Ali's delayed response in the summer of 1877 was because of the forty-day mourning period for his son Abdulla Jan. Public opinion in England was misled, and the Indian press was gagged. She concluded that the defeat of the Tory party would mean peace, liberty, and hope for South Africa, India, and Afghanistan.

Becoming a friend of George Bernard Shaw and Sidney and Beatrice Webb, Annie Besant joined the socialist Fabian Society in January 1885. She and Shaw were also on the executive committee of the Social Democratic Federation. She agreed with the Fabians' gradual approach to reform as evolution instead of revolution. Besant wrote pamphlets on why she was a socialist and on the socialist movement. During her atheistic phase she also wrote several pamphlets criticizing the Christian religion and in 1887 *Why I Do Not Believe in God*. She formed the short-lived Law and Liberty League in November 1887 with Jacob Bright and William Morris.

She was one of the leaders of the Social Democratic Federation that organized a march in Trafalgar Square with 10,000 people on November 13. Two thousand police and four hundred troops beat people, and one was killed on this "Bloody Sunday." Two leaders and hundreds of others were arrested, but police refused to detain Besant. In 1888 Besant and Willam T. Stead began editing *The Link* for humanitarian purposes. The Government issued an order against collecting money at public meetings; but Besant defied it in June 1888, and the rule was rescinded.

She was in love with the socialist Herbert Burrows, and they helped organize a strike by women who worked at the Bryant and May match factory in East London and suffered terribly from starvation wages and phosphorus fumes that caused cancer. Shaw explained why Annie was different than himself and the Fabians when he wrote, "Injustice, waste, and the defeat of noble aspirations did not revolt her by way of irony and paradox; they stirred her to direct and powerful indignation and to active resistance." In 1889 Besant was elected to the London School Board, and her reforms included free meals and medical examinations for children in the elementary schools.

Annie Besant discovered Theosophy in 1889 when William Stead asked her to write a review of *The Secret Doctrine*. Like Shaw, she became a vegetarian. He asked her if she knew that Madam Blavatsky had been exposed by the Society for Psychical Research, and Blavatsky herself asked her to read the SPR report. Annie found that the allegations were not credible, and even if true they did not affect the teachings of

Theosophy. She studied *The Secret Doctrine* and wrote a favorable review. In May 1889 she became a Fellow of the Theosophical Society and was blessed by Blavatsky and her master KH (Kuthumi). Besant became his disciple and soon was co-editing the magazine *Lucifer* (Light-bringer).

She spoke on "Why I Became a Theosophist" and published it as a pamphlet, explaining that materialism had failed and that she was trying to follow the truth. In 1890 she published "The Trades Union Movement" pamphlet in which she wrote,

> Now Trades Unionism is spreading among women,
> and large and powerful unions
> are springing up among unskilled workers;
> so that there is hope that at last
> all workers will be enrolled in disciplined hosts,
> and there will be no stragglers from the army of labor.
> When each Trade Union comprises
> the majority of the workers in its Trade,
> and when these unions are united
> in a National Trade Federation,
> then will come the time for the International Federation,
> which will mean the triumph of labor
> and the freedom of the workers everywhere.

Besant gave her farewell speech to the secularists on August 30, 1891. She defended Blavatsky and said she had letters from the mahatmas in the same handwriting after her death. Besant, G. R. S. Mead, and Herbert Burrows emphasized that the principles of Theosophy were more important than occultism, but people still wanted to hear more about the mahatmas than brotherhood. Besant succeeded Blavatsky as head of the Esoteric Society in Europe, and she went on a speaking tour in the United States in 1892. She and her guru Gyanendra N. Chakravarti spoke at the Parliament of Religions in Chicago the next year.

After spending a week in Ceylon and visiting a Theosophical college there, Besant arrived with Olcott in India on November 16, 1893. Many Indians joined the Theosophical Society because they did not have to give up their religion. Some Hindu women came out of purdah to attend a convention, but Muslim women were more reluctant. Besant spoke to three thousand people in Madras on "India and Its Mission." Olcott gave her the Hindu name Annabai, and she followed most Hindu customs. Olcott had been reviving Buddhism and Zoroastrianism, and she hoped to do the same for Hinduism. She gave several lectures in Calcutta and stayed with Dr. Bhagavan Das.

The *London Times* quoted her as telling Bengalis, "If the youths of India would act up to the traditions of their past, instead of fawning on a foreign power, they would not long remain under a foreign yoke." However, she explained in a letter that she came to India as a spiritual and educational worker rather than for political work. In four months she gave 121 lectures to audiences ranging from 600 to 6,000. Besant would spend the rest of her life as a resident of India, but she would travel to England annually for conferences and occasionally to America.

Besant learned from her own master that the mahatma letters she had found had been written by W. Q. Judge, who engaged in a struggle for power in the TS with Olcott and her. Judge was suspended and then reinstated as the head of the American TS. Besant widened her base of support by traveling to Australia and New Zealand in 1894. On October 29 the *Westminster Gazette* began a series of articles on "Isis Very Much Unveiled: The Truth about the Great Mahatma Hoax." The Theosophical Society in America declared itself the original and genuine TS. President Olcott in India expelled Judge and cancelled the American charters.

Many branches in America formed independent associations. Besant learned Sanskrit and translated the *Bhagavad-Gita* in 1895. In *The Ancient Wisdom* she explained that on the higher planes whether a motive is good or bad can be even more important than whether the action is beneficial or not because one can learn from the results. She worked with the clairvoyant Charles W. Leadbeater and published books on thought forms and other spiritual studies. Judge died on March 21, 1896, and the spiritualist Katherine A. Tingley became Besant's rival by traveling to Europe and India. Leadbeater got into trouble by advising boys to use sexual self-gratification and for having close relations with them. Besant repudiated these, and they continued to work together.

In 1898 Besant founded the Central Hindu College, which became Benares Hindu University. She believed that the spiritual wisdom in India's philosophies could help the entire world. Theosophists started 250 schools that included women and the poor. They opposed caste restrictions and child marriage while helping outcasts and widows. To discourage child marriage she refused to admit married boys to the elementary departments and doubled the fees for boys who married in college. In 1903 Besant said that India must be governed by Indians and Indian ideas.

However, in 1905 she refused to allow students to attend the college without shoes as part of the Swadeshi protest. In her book *A Study in Consciousness*, which was first published in 1904, Besant observed that our knowledge of right and wrong comes from many experiences; but it can be guided by ideals. She suggested that studying divine teachers such as Krishna, Buddha, and Christ could be helpful.

Evil desires will fall away if good desires are fostered. One way to avoid bad desires is to imagine the likely consequences that bring misery. The emotion of love directed to a living being is virtue, and vices springing from hate can be eradicated. What is right is in harmony with the great law and brings bliss, but what is wrong brings unhappiness. Love draws people together, whether it be a family, tribe, or nation. Right reason works actions of love into permanent obligations or duties. The will expressing as desire is not free but bound by those impulses. When the will is directed as love, the self-determined person is free. She served as the president of the Theosophical Society from 1907 until her death in 1933.

BESANT, KRISHNAMURTI, AND BHAGAVAN DAS

Surendranath Banerjea (1848-1926) was one of only a handful of Indians who qualified for the Indian Civil Service, but he was dismissed for failing to correct the false report of a subordinate. He went to London to appeal and was not even allowed to take the bar examinations. He decided to dedicate his life to redressing wrongs and protecting rights, both personal and collective. When he was arrested for criticizing a judge, he began the Indian tradition of welcoming imprisonment in order to expose the injustice of the Government's policies. In 1876 he founded the Indian Association of Calcutta to work for a united India.

The next year he launched a national campaign against the reduction of the age limit for the Civil Service Examination, holding large meetings in Calcutta, Agra, Lahore, Amritsar, Mirat, Allahabad, Delhi, Kanpur, Lakhnau, Aligarh, and Benares. They petitioned for a higher age and exams in India as well as England, and they sent the Bengali barrister Lalmohan Ghosh to England as their representative. In 1878 Banerjea urged college graduates to dedicate their lives to helping their country. He argued that violence was not necessary to redress grievances. He believed that under the British they could secure their rights by constitutional agitation.

He noted that Nanak, who founded the Sikh empire, did much to unite Hindus and Muslims, and he preached good will between all religions. By living worthy, honorable, and patriotic lives they could live and die happily while making India great. Their next protest was against the oppressive Vernacular Press Act. During the debate over the controversial Ilbert Bill in 1883 they formed an All-India National Fund and the Indian National Conference. Allan Octavian Hume had been secretary to the Government of India, but in 1879 Viceroy Lytton removed him for asserting his independent views. After he retired from the Indian Civil Service in 1882, Hume worked on forming a political organisation that would unite the efforts of Indians.

His idea was to have leading Indian politicians meet annually to discuss issues and plan strategies. He founded the Indian National Union in March 1885, and they planned a conference for the last week of December. Because of a cholera epidemic in Poona, the conference was moved to Bombay, and 72 volunteer delegates to the first Indian National Congress met on December 28. Bengali barrister W. C. Bonnerjea presided, and they passed nine resolutions that called for a royal commission to investigate the Indian administration, abolishing the Secretary of State's Indian Council, creating more legislative councils and allowing more elected members and discussion of budgets, reducing military spending, and simultaneous public service examinations in England and India with older candidates.

They also protested the annexation of Upper Burma as part of India and sent the resolutions to political associations. Coincidentally in 1885 the second session of the Indian National Conference was meeting in Calcutta. This group merged with the Indian National Congress, which met annually the last week in December in various cities, followed by second and third sessions in Calcutta and Madras. Hume served as general secretary of the Congress for 21 years, and he often went to England to promote their causes. The second annual Congress at Calcutta was attended by 434 delegates, 230 of them from Bengal. Dadabhai Naoroji presided and called for unity on the political program even though communities have social differences.

They wanted India to have the same representative institutions as the British colonies of Canada and Australia. Madan Mohan Malaviya made his first speech and said there should be "no taxation without representation." Viceroy Dufferin invited members of Congress to a garden party as did the Governor of Madras the next year. In 1886 Dufferin appointed six Indians among the fifteen members of the Public Service Commission. The Civil Service was reorganized, and more Indians were recruited into the provincial and subordinate services.

However, before leaving office in December 1888, Viceroy Dufferin objected to the methods of the Indian Congress and called them a "microscopic minority" of educated Indians. In 1888 the Congress demanded that the minimum taxable income be raised to 1,000 rupees. The fifth annual Congress in 1889 was attended by 1,502 delegates, including 254 Muslims. Congress used constitutional agitation, and they published the journal *India*. Its editor William Digby established the Congress Agency in London, and William Wedderburn was elected chairman of the British Committee of the Indian National Congress and served in that position until his death in 1918.

In 1890 Charles Bradlaugh introduced a bill in the House of Commons to expand the legislative councils. When an eleven-year-old bride died after intercourse in Calcutta, agitation increased to raise the age of marriage for girls from ten to twelve or fourteen. Behramji Merwanji Malabari was a Parsi and had published *Notes on Infant Marriage and Enforced Widowhood* in 1884. This reform campaign led in 1891 to the Age of Consent Act that prohibited marriage before the age of twelve. In 1892 Naoroji was elected as a Liberal to the British House of Commons, and he argued that Europeans were not natural leaders of India because they did not belong to the people.

Malaviya noted at the eighth Congress that it was unjust to compel Indians to travel 10,000 miles to take an examination for service in their own country. In 1893 the House of Commons favored simultaneous exams in India and England for the Civil Service, but all the governments of India except Mysore opposed this, believing it would exclude Muslims and Sikhs. In the Congress that year Malaviya spoke about the miserable poverty of fifty million Indians because of British exploitation. In 1894 a delegate from Natal persuaded the Congress to pass a resolution asking the British Government to veto a law disenfranchising the Indians in South Africa.

In 1895 "Surrender-not" Banerjea suggested that they could transplant the spirit of free institutions that made England a great nation. Never before had an ancient civilisation been so influenced by modern ideas. Civilisation had moved, like the sun, from east to west, and the west owes a great debt to the east. He hoped that the debt would be repaid by the enfranchisement of their people. In 1896 the Congress sponsored an Industrial Exhibition and a Social Conference. Although they encouraged Muslims to attend and chose Badruddin Tyabji as president for their third annual meeting, only a few Muslims joined the Congress.

Tyabji urged all educated and public-spirited citizens to work together for reforms to benefit all. He tried to persuade Muslims that Congress would not interfere with their religion. Sayyid (Syed) Ahmad Khan emphasized education and had founded the Muhammadan Anglo-Oriental College at Aligarh in 1877. He advocated working with Hindus to support each other; but he generally opposed the Indian National Congress because he believed the Hindus and Muslims had conflicting interests. He trusted the British more than the Hindus. He formed the Annual Muslim Educational Congress in 1886, and they held their sessions at the same time of year as the Indian Congress.

Theodore Beck was the first principal of the Aligarh College, and he devoted his career to serving the Muslims in India. He was instrumental in forming the United Indian Patriotic Association in 1888 and the Muhammadan Anglo-

Oriental Defence Association of Upper India in 1893. These organisations were parallel to the Indian National Congress and were intended to protect the political rights of Muslims by strengthening British rule in India. Sayyid Ahmad was concerned that Muslims as only one-fourth of the population of India would be outvoted by Hindus in a democratic government. His writings in Urdu in a clear style were influential. Beck died in 1899, and Theodore Morison was the principal of Aligarh College until 1905.

He continued the hostility toward the Indian Congress, emphasizing educational and economical development rather than political agitation. Sayyid Ahmad died in 1898, and his policies were also followed by his successor, Nawab Mohsin-ul-Mulk. Gopal Krishna Gokhale (1866-1915) was strongly influenced by his teacher Ranade and carried on his work. When he graduated from Elphinstone College in 1885 he joined the Deccan Education Society in Poona, taking a vow of poverty for twenty years and dedicating his life to public service. That year Fergusson College was founded, and he began teaching English and mathematics.

Gokhale first spoke at the Indian National Congress in 1889 and his annual speeches at Calcutta on the budget began in 1902. They called for self-government in the central and provincial governments, abolishing the India Council, spreading education, reducing military expenditures and military training for Indians, separating the judicial and executive functions in criminal justice, employing more Indians in higher public offices, reducing taxes, and using surpluses to promote medical relief, scientific agriculture, and industrial education. He argued that the large annual surpluses of the Government did not indicate success but that taxes on the people were much too high.

In 1903 Gokhale spoke about how they must improve the conditions of the low-caste Hindus by helping them get education and employment to improve their social standing and self-respect. He said it was monstrous that a class of people should be condemned to utter wretchedness, servitude, and degradation by permanent barriers that were impossible for an individual to overcome. He recalled how Gandhi had reported on the discrimination Indians were suffering in South Africa and how Ranade became an advisor to Gandhi. Ranade pointed out that Indians should correct the disgraceful oppression and injustice in their own country.

Modern civilisation is making greater equality a priority over the privilege and exclusiveness of the old world. Gokhale asked how they could realize their national aspirations if so many of their countrymen remained in ignorance and degradation. He served on the Bombay Legislative Council from 1902 until his death, and Gandhi considered him his political guru. Gokhale declined a position on the Secretary of State's Council and a knighthood. He urged the Parliament to pass mandatory education for boys and educational provisions for girls.

In 1905 Gokhale founded the Servants of India Society for those willing to take vows of poverty to serve the poor and help India to achieve self-government. Their five goals were to create love of the motherland, organize political education and agitation, promote goodwill and cooperation among different communities, assist in educating women and the poor, and lift up the depressed classes. Each member joining the Society took a vow to think of one's country first, serve it without seeking personal advantage, regard all Indians as brothers, be content with provisions provided by the Society, lead a pure life, quarrel with no one, and always work for the aims of the Society.

Bal Gangadhar Tilak was born on July 23, 1856 as a Maratha Brahmin. He earned a university degree and taught mathematics in Poona. He founded the Deccan Education Society and Fergusson College in 1884; but he resigned in 1890 after his associates gave up the ideal of selfless service by keeping their outside earnings. Tilak advocated action for political reforms and published two weekly newspapers - *Kesari* (which means "The Lion") in Marathi and *The Mahratta* in English. He argued that no alien government has the right to interfere in social customs no matter how worthy the cause. As a Hindu nationalist he opposed all British laws that restricted their religion, including banning the marriage of young girls.

Yet he led by example and did not allow his own daughters to marry until they were at least sixteen. Tilak suggested self-help and national revival. He considered untouchability a cancer in the body of Hindu society and said it must be eradicated at all costs. He was so opposed to the Indian National Congress letting the Indian National Social Conference use their tent that he threatened to burn it down. Tilak began organizing Ganapati festivals in 1893 to worship the popular Hindu god Ganesha. Tilak admired the Maratha warrior Shivaji and began the annual Shivaji festival in 1895. Rabindranath Tagore wrote a famous poem about the 17th-century hero of Maharashtra.

Tilak urged civil disobedience for political change years before Gandhi began his experiments in South Africa; but he was a freedom fighter and considered nonviolence only a strategy, not a moral principle. Gandhi would later call Tilak the "maker of modern India." Tilak favored revolutionary action in politics but moderate evolution in social reforms. When the famine occurred in 1896, he demanded that victims receive the benefits mandated by the Famine Relief Code. In May 1897 Tilak wrote in *Kesari* that Shivaji was justified in murdering the Mughal general Afzal Khan and he suggested that it was not wrong to kill "for the good of others." He objected to the destruction of Hindu property as a means to prevent the bubonic plague from spreading.

The Plague Commissioner W. C. Rand ordered stringent inspections and measures in Poona, and the next week on June 22 he and his assistant were shot after celebrating Queen Victoria's diamond jubilee. Both died, and two Natu brothers were detained. Tilak was tried in September, and six Europeans on the jury found him guilty of sedition while the three Indian jurors voted not guilty; the judge sentenced him to eighteen months. The Indian newspapers censured the Government and praised Tilak.

Eventually Balkrishna Chapekar and his brother Damodar Chapekar confessed and were hanged. Because of public pressure, Tilak was released early on September 6, 1898. The two Dravid brothers who informed on the Chapekar brothers were murdered on February 8, 1899 by a third brother, Vasudev Chapekar, and his friend, and they were also hanged. Going to prison made Tilak a hero, and he was given the name Lokamanya, which means "leader of the people." He demanded self-government *(swaraj)* and coined the slogan, "*Swaraj* is my birthright, and I will have it."

Using Government records, William Digby calculated that the capital drained out of India in the 19th century was £6,080,172,021. This figure represents how much the Europeans were exploiting the natural and human resources of India. India's public debt increased from 94 crores of rupees in 1860 to 312 crores by 1901. Arabinda Ghose (later called Sri Aurobindo) was born on August 15, 1872 in Calcutta. His father was a barrister, and in 1879 he sent him to Manchester, where he was taught English, Latin, and French by Mr. and Mrs. Drewett. In 1884 Aurobindo went to St. Paul's in London and then to King's College at Cambridge in 1890 on a classics scholarship.

He learned more languages and liked writing poetry. He passed his examination in only two years but did not apply for the degree he had earned. Not wanting to be in the Indian Civil Service nor disobey his father, he failed the examination by not showing up for the horse-back riding test. Aurobindo returned to India at the beginning of 1893. When his father heard that the ship his son was sailing on had sunk, he died of heart failure; but Aurobindo had taken another ship. He taught college in Baroda and was described as speaking little, being desireless, self-controlled, and always given to study. In his series of articles "New Lamps for Old" in Induprakash he ridiculed those who talked about "the blessings of British rule."

He criticized the Congress for being too middle-class and selfish without being a popular organisation. Ranade warned the editor that he might be prosecuted for sedition, and young Aurobindo had to tone down his rhetoric. He and others began to form secret societies dedicated to Indian freedom such as the Lotus and Dagger Society. His poetry was published as *Songs to Myrtilla* in 1895. No press would publish his pamphlet "No Compromise" in 1903, but the Maratha revolutionary Kulkarni printed a few thousand copies at night and freely distributed them.

Aurobindo became vice principal of the college in 1904 and began yoga. By practicing breath control *(pranayama)* five hours a day he found his mind worked much better, enabling him to write two hundred lines of poetry in a half hour. Aurobindo tried to remain hidden behind the scenes. During the time of the Bengal partition, he wrote the revolutionary booklet *Bhawani Mandir* arguing that India needed to be reborn by developing the Shakti power of the Divine Mother. He wrote that we are all gods and creators with the energy of God within us. He noted that Ramakrishna came, and Vivekananda preached. Now it was up to them to work for progress. Influenced by Bankim Chandra's novel *Anandamath* and the "Bande Mataram" anthem, he devised rules for a new Order of Sannyasis that would practice strict discipline and work to instruct and help the poor, educate the middle class, and persuade the rich to benefit the public for the general welfare of the country.

6

Indian Literature through the Ages

Indian literature includes everything which is included in the word 'literature' in its broadest, sense: religious and mundane, epic and lyric, dramatic and didactic poetry, narrative and scientific prose, as well as oral poetry and song. In the Vedas (3000 BC-1000 BC), when one finds such expressions, "I am standing in water but I am very thirsty", one marvels at the continuity of a rich heritage which is both modern and traditional. It is, therefore, not very correct to say that ancient Indian literature includes only the religious classics of Hinduism, Buddhism and Jainism. Jain narrative literature in the Prakrit language is full of erotic stories and realism. It is not true to say that the Vedas are a series of sacred texts used in religious rituals and sacrifices.

The Vedas are essentially archetypal poetry of high literary value. They are mythical in nature and their language is symbolic. Being mythical, they have multiple meanings, and, therefore, the theologian moulds his rites, the preacher seeks his belief, the philosopher finds the clues for his intellectual speculation and the law-makers work out the social and political life-style in accordance with the archetypal truths of the Vedas.

Vedic poets are called the rishis, the seers who visualized the archetypal truths of cosmic functioning at all levels of existence. Devatas of the Vedic poetry symbolise the manifestations of the divine force of the One Supreme. Vedas give importance to yajna (sacrifice). Purusa sukta of the Rigveda (10.90) describes the whole creation as a yajna extended by the divine forces of nature. Etymologically yajna means the worship of the divine, coordination and giving (sacrifice). These three elements together, vision, coordination and giving provide a basic paradigm for any creative act. The Yajur Veda is related to yajna, which is not just sacrifice, but also means creative reality.

The mantras (verse with archetypal meanings) of the Rig Veda are adapted to certain melodies and this collection is named Sama Veda, and the Atharva Veda deals with the peace and prosperity of human society and is concerned with the daily life of man. Vedic ritual is preserved in literary texts called the Brahmanas. The main division of the contexts of these extensive texts is twofold – the ritualistic injuction and discussions on the meaning of Vedic ritual and all that is related to it. The Aranyakas or the treatises of the forest present secret explanations of the ritual, have their origin in the philosophical discussions of the Brahmanas, find their culmination in the Upanishads and represent the transitional phase between the ritualistic symbolism of the Brahmanas and the philosophical doctrines of the Upanishads.

The Upanishads, written both in prose and poetry, are expressions of philosophical concepts. In the literal term, it means that knowledge which is imparted to the student who is sitting very near to the teacher and the knowledge by which all ignorance is destroyed. The knowledge of the identity of the self (Atman) with the eternal (Brahman). The Upanishads are the end of the Vedas. This is the literature in which ancient sages realised that in the final analysis, man has to know himself. The great epics (Mahakavya), the *Ramayana* (1500 BC) and the *Mahabharata* (1000 BC) are the, repositories of the ethnic memory of the Indian people. Valmiki, the poet of the *Ramayana*, is known as Adikavi (first among the poets), and the story of Rama is occasionally referred to in the *Mahabharata*.

But both these epics were composed over a long passage of time, not by one poet, but by many poets, for the purpose of oral transmission by singers and story tellers. Both are epics of the people, and as such, reflect the ethos and the psyche of a group of people, not only in a given temporal frame, but have a universal human context. The *Ramayana* tells us about how a man can achieve divineness, as Rama achieves divinity through righteous action. It also tells us about how to achieve the fourfold objectives (Purushartha) of human life, Dharma (righteousness, or loosely, religion), Artha (worldly achievement, mainly wealth and prosperity), Kama (fulfilment of all desires), and Moksha (liberation).

Inwardly it is a quest to know oneself. The *Ramayana* consists of 24,000 verses and is divided into seven books, called Kandas, and known as Kavya (poetry), which means that it instructs while it entertains. The *Mahabharata* consists of a 1,00,000 verses divided into 10 books, parvas, with many interpolations, known an Itihasa Purana (mythical history). Both are long, continuous narratives and deal with war. The king Rama fights a battle with the demon king Ravana, who steals his wife, Sita, and holds her captive in his palace at Lanka (now Sri Lanka). Rama, with the help of the monkey army and Hanuman, rescues Sita. His triumph over Ravana symbolises the victory of virtue over evil. This pattern, at the individual level, is a fight going on within the self between vice and virtue.

With the change in the social structure at the time of the *Mahabharata*, the fight now takes place between the human beings between Pandavas and the Kauravas, family members of the same royal clan, over succession to the throne. Written by Vyasa (Vyasa means a collector), the *Mahabharata* is mythical history, because history here does not denote merely an event that took place, but events that will always happen and repeat itself.

The Pandavas are assisted by Lord Krishna, who is metamorphosed into Godhead, and is shown as descending into the cycles of cosmic history to assist man in his struggle against the forces of evil. He recites the Bhagavad *Gita* (the song of the lord) just before the war to the Pandava Prince Arjuna, who is unwilling to fight because he feels that victory in the battle is not desirable. Thus begins the debate on an epic scale regarding the problems of action versus non-action, of violence versus non-violence, and ultimately about Dharma.

The *Gita* is incorporated in the *Mahabharata* primarily to give an integrated view of Dharma. Dharma means to perform righteously one's duty in a selfless way (Nishkama Karma) with complete dedication to the will of God. The survivors of the epic war discover that public esteem and power are no more than hollow victories in an illusory struggle. It is not bravery but knowledge which is the key to the mystery of life. These two epics of ancient India are practically transcreated in almost in all Indian languages, and have also crossed the borders of this sub-continent and became popular in foreign lands, where they eventually get more or less adopted and adapted and recreated. This became possible because both these epics are rich in motifs which have universal appeal.

THE PURANA

The word Purana means 'that which renews the old' and is almost always mentioned alongwith Itihasa. The Puranas were written to illustrate and expound the truth of the Vedas. The fundamental abstruse philosophical and religious truths are expounded through popular legends or mythological stories. Nothing can exert grater credence on the human mind than when it is described as having happened. Thus, Itihasa combined with narration makes a story seem credible. Together with the two epics, the *Ramayana* and the *Mahabharata*, they are the origins of many of the stories and anecdotes of the social, religious and cultural history of India. The main Puranas are 18 encyclopaedic collections of legend and myth.

Though the archaic form of the genre might have existed as early as the fourth or the fifty century B.C., the famous names of the 18 Mahapuranas were not discovered earlier than the third century A.D. The phenomenal popularity of these Mahapuranas gave rise to yet another sub-genre known as the Upapuranas or minor Puranas. They are also 19 in number. The Mahapuranas have five subjects. These are : (1) Sarga, the original creation of the universe, (2) Pratisarga, the periodical process of destruction and re-creation, (3) Manvantara, the different eras or cosmic cycles, (4) Surya Vamsha and Chandra Vamsa, the histories of the solar and lunar dynasties of Gods and sages, (5) Vamshanucharita, the genealogies of kings.

Around this core skeleton of the five subjects any Purana adds other diverse materials like matters of religious concern, customs, ceremonies, sacrifices, festivals, the duties of various castes, different types of donations, details of the construction of temples and images, and descriptions of places of pilgrimage. The Puranas are the meeting point of diverse religious and social beliefs, are linked with the vital spiritual and social needs and urges of the people, and are a unique outcome of the ever-continuing synthesis based on an understanding between various groups of Vedic Aryans and non-Aryans.

CLASSICAL SANSKRIT LITERATURE

The Sanskrit language is divided into the Vedic and the classical. The great epics, the *Ramayana* and the *Mahabharata* and the Puranas are part of the classical period, but are discussed separately because of their enormity and importance, and are undoubtedly the precursors of Sanskrit Kavya (epic poetry), nataka (drama) and other literature. Classical Sanskrit literature includes the Kavyas (epic poetry), the Nataka (drama), lyric poetry, romance, popular tales, didactic fables, gnomic poetry, scientific literature on grammar, medicine, law, astronomy, mathematics, etc. Classical Sanskrit literature is on the whole secular in character. During the classical period, language was regulated by the rigid rules of Panini, one of the greatest Sanskrit grammarians.

The tallest figure in the sphere of epic poetry is Kalidasa (between A.D. 380-A.D. 415). He wrote two great epics, *Kumarasambhava* (the birth of Kumar), and Raghuvamsa (the dynasty of the Raghus). In the Kavya tradition, more care is bestowed on the form, such as the style, figure of speech, conceits, descriptions, etc., and the story-theme is pushed to the background. The overall purpose of such a poem is to bring out the efficacy of a religious and cultured way of life, without flouting any ethical norms. Other distinguished poets, like Bharavi (550 A.D.), wrote *Kiratarjuniyam* (Kirat and Arjun) and Magha (65-700 A.D.) wrote *Sishupalavadha* (the killing of Shishupal).

There are several other poets like Sriharsha and Bhatti who are of great merit. The main purpose of Kavya or even Nataka (drama) is to offer the reader or spectator diversion or entertainment, (Lokaranjana), and also stimulate his feelings, and ultimately give him a perspective to illuminate his vision of life. The drama is, therefore, stylized and is packed with poetry and descriptive prose. It moves on a level of worldliness as well as on another level of other-worldiness. Therefore, the symbolism of Sanskrit drama reveals that man's journey is complete when he moves from attachment to non-attachment, from temporality to eternity, or from flux to timelessness.

It is achieved in Sanskrit drama by arousing Rasa (theatrical experience or aesthetic sentiment) in the minds of the spectators. The rules and prescriptions regarding performance, the theatre hall, acting, gestures, Rasa, stage direction, are all given in the first book of dramaturgy, *Natyashastra*, by Bharata (1st century B.C.-1st century A.D.). Kalidasa is the most distinguished dramatist and his treatment of the rasa of love in all its possible manifestations in the three plays *Malavikagnimitra* (Malavika and Agnimitra), *Vikramorvasiya* (Vikram and Urvasi) and *Abhigyana Shakuntala* (the recognition of Shakuntala) is unparalleled. He is the poet of love and beauty, and believes in the affirmation of life, the joy of which lies in pure, sacred and ever-widening love. The *Mricchakatika* (the clay-cart) by Sudraka (248 A.D.) presents a remarkable social drama with touches of grim reality.

The characters are drawn from all stratas of society, which include thieves and gamblers, rogues and idlers, courtesans and their associates, police constables, mendicants and politicians. In Act III an interesting account of a burglary is given in which stealing is treated as a regular art. The interlinking of a political revolution with the private affairs of the two lovers adds new charm to the play. The 13 plays of Bhasa (4th century B.C.-2nd century A.D.), which were discovered at the beginning of the 20th century, are accepted as the most stagable plays of Sanskrit theatre.

The most popular is *Swapnavasavadatta* (Vasavadatta in dream) where the playwright has displayed his skill of characterisation and a fine manipulation of the plot. Bhavabhuti (700 A.D.), another great dramatist, is well known for his play *Uttara-Ramacharitam* (the later life of Rama), which contains a play within it in the last act of a love of exquisite tenderness. He is also well known for directly rebuking his critics by saying that his work was not intended for them, and that some kindred soul would surely be born; time is endless and the earth broad. These are some of the best dramas out of more than six hundred written during that period.

Sanskrit literature is replete with lyrical poetry of great merit. This poetry constitutes a fusion of erotic and religious sentiments. In fact, division between art and religion in Indian culture seems to be less sharp than in Europe and China. In Kalidasa's narrative lyric poem, *Meghaduta* (the cloud messenger), the poet makes a cloud a messenger to tell the story of two lovers who are separated. This is also quite in keeping with the sublime conception of love, which looks dark in separation, like a black cloud with a silver lining. Jayadeva (12 century A.D.) is the last great name in Sanskrit poetry, who wrote the lyric poetry *Gitagovinda* (the song of Govinda) to describe every phase of love beween Krishna and Radha – longing, jealousy, hope, disappointment, anger, reconciliation and fruition – in picturesque lyrical language.

The songs describe the beauty of nature, which plays a prominent part in the description of human love. The didactic fable Panchatantra (five chapters), dealing with politics and practical wisdom, which was written by Vishnu Sharma, and the Hitopadesha, the bird, animal-human and non-human stories of advice for the benefit of the listeners, which was written by Narayan Pandit, are literary masterpieces which cross the borders of the sub-continent and became popular in foreign lands. These books of fables also indicate that the whole of Sanskrit literature was just not religious or elitist. These popular fables are obviously a retelling of folklore.

LITERATURE IN PALI AND PRAKRIT

Pali and Prakrit were the spoken languages of Indians after the Vedic period. Prakrit in the widest sense of the term was indicative of any language that in any manner deviated from the standard one, i.e. Sanskrit. Pali is archaic Prakrit. In fact, Pali is a combination of various dialects. These were adopted by Buddhist and Jain sects in ancient India as their sacred languages. Lord Buddha (500 B.C.) used Pali to give his sermons. All the Buddhist canonical literature is in Pali which includes Tipitaka (threefold basket). The first basket, Vinaya Pitaka, contains the monastic rules of the Order of Buddhist monks. The second basket, Sutta Pitaka, is the collection of the speeches and dialogues of the Buddha.

The third basket, the Abhidhamma Pitaka, elucidates the various topics dealing with ethics, psychology or theory of knowledge. The jataka Kathas are non-canonical Buddhist literature in which stories relating to the former births of the Buddha (Bodhi-sattva or the would-be Buddha) are narrated. These stories propagate Buddhist religious doctrines and are available in both Sanskrit and Pali. As the jataka tales grew in bulk, they assimilated popular tales, ancient mythology, stories from older religious traditions, etc. Jatakas are, in fact, based on the common heritage of the Indian masses. Buddhist literature is also abundantly available in Sanskrit, which includes the great epic *Buddhacharita* by Aswaghosha (78 A.D.).

Like the Buddhist stories, the Jain tales in general are didactic in character. They are written in some forms of Prakrit. The word Jain is derived from the root ji (to conquer) and signifies the religion of those who have conquered the lust for life. Jain canonical literature by Jain saints, as well as a large number of works on lexicography and grammar by Hemachandra (1088 A.D.-?), is well known. Much also in the way of moral tale and poetry are to be found. However, Prakrit is well known for Gathasaptashati (700 verses) by Hala (300 A.D.), the best example of erotic literature.

It is a compilation of 700 verses along with his own contribution of 44 poems. It is interesting to note that quite a few poetesses like Pahai, Mahavi, Reva, Roha and Sasippaha are included in the anthology. The vast Katha (story) literature of Prakrit, written with a conspicuous religious overtone, even by Jain saints, is full of erotic elements. The author of the Vasudevahindi ascribes this changed approach of the Jain authors to the fact that it is easy to teach religion cloaked by erotic episodes, like sugar-coated medicine. The characteristic of Prakrit poetry is its subtlety; the inner meaning (Hiy*a*li) is its soul. Jain literature is available in Sanskrit too, like the *Upamitibhava Prapancha Katha* of Siddharasi (906 A.D.).

EARLY DRAVIDIAN LITERATURE

The Indian people speak languages belonging to major four distinct speech families: the Austric, Dravidian, Sino-Tibetan and Indo-European. In spite of these four different language groups, there is an Indian characteristic running through these language groups, which forms one of the bases of that certain underlying uniformity of life described by Pandit Jawaharlal Nehru as unity in the midst of diversity. Dravidian literature mainly consists of the four languages, Tamil, Telugu, Kannada and Malayalam. Out of these, Tamil is the oldest language which preserved its Dravidian character the most. Kannada, as a cultured language, is almost as old as Tamil.

All these languages have borrowed many words from Sanskrit and *vice versa*. Tamil is the only modern Indian language which is recognizably continuous with a classical past. Early classical Tamil literature is known as Sangam literature meaning 'fraternity', indicating mainly two schools of poets, aham (subjective love poems), and puram (objective, public poetry and heroic). Aham deals purely with the subjective emotions of the lover, and puram with all kinds of emotions, mainly the valour and glory of kings, and about good and evil. The Sangam classics, consisting of 18 works (eight anthologies of lyrics and ten long poems), are well known for their directness of expression.

These were written by 473 poets, among whom 30 were women, the famous poetess Avvaiyar being one of them. In the case of 102 poems, the authors are unknown. Most of these anthologies are of the 3rd century B.C. During this time, a Tamil grammar *Tolkappiyam* was written, to understand early Tamil poetry. *Tolkappiyam* indicates five landscapes or types of love, and outlines their symbolic conventions. Critics say that Sangam literature is not just the earliest evidence of the Tamil genius. The Tamils, in all their 2000 years of literary effort, wrote nothing better. The famous *Thirukkural* by Thiruvalluvar, in the 6th century A.D., serves as a manual of precepts to guide one to noble living.

It expounds a secular, moral and practical attitude towards life. The twin epics, *Silappadhikaram* (the story of the anklet), written by Ilango-Adigal, and *Manimekalai* (the story of *Manimekalai*) by Chattanar, were written sometimes in A.D. 200-300 and give vivid accounts of Tamil society during that period. These are valuable storehouses and epics of dignity and sublimity, laying stress on the cardinal virtues of life. In *Manimekalai* there is an elaborate exposition of the doctrines of Buddhism. If Tamil reveals a triumph of Brahmanic and Buddhist knowledge, Kannada shows Jain ascendency in its ancient phase. Malayalam absorbed a rich treasure contained in the Sanskrit language. Nannaya (A.D.1100) was the first Telugu poet. In ancient times, Tamil and Telugu spread to distant places.

If one were to identify another striking feature of ancient Tamil literature, the obvious choice would be Vaishnava (pertaining to Vishnu) bhakti (devotional) literature. In Indian literature the effort has been to find out how a man can achieve divinity. The secret behind a tendency for hero worship is love and regard for humanity. In Vaishnava bhakti poetry, God descends on this earth as a human being, to share with us our suffereing and turmoil, our happiness and prosperity. Vaishanava bhakti literature was an all-India phenomenon, which started in the 6th-7th century A.D. in the Tamil-speaking region of South India, with twelve Alvar (one immersed in God) saint-poets, who wrote devotional songs.

They revitalized Hinduism and checked the spread of Buddhism and Jainism, while absorbing some of their features. The religion of Alvar poets, which included a woman peot, Andal, was devotion to God through love (bhakti), and in the ecstasy of such devotions they sang hundreds of songs which embodied both depth of feeling and felicity of expressions.

Devotional songs in praise of the Hindu god Shiva (the worship of Shiva and Vishnu forms the basis of the broad division of Hindus into Shaiva and Vaishnava sects) were also written by Tamil saint poet Nayanar (leader, master) in the 6th-8th Century A.D. Besides its importance as poetry of emotional bhakti, it guides us into the world of classical Tamil civilisation and explains to us the ethnic-national consciousness of the Tamils as a whole. The flowering of bhakti literature as a pan-Indian consciousness took place in almost all the Indian languages during medieval times.

MEDIEVAL LITERATURE

Around 1000 A.D. local differences in Prakrit grew more and more pronounced which later came to be known as Apabhramsa, and this led to the modern Indian languages taking shape and being born.

These languages, conditioned by the regional, linguistic and ethnic environment, assumed different linguistic characteristics. Constitutionally recognised modern Indian languages and Konkani, Marathi, Sindhi, Gujarati (Western); Manipuri, Bengali, Oriya and Assamese (Eastern); Tamil, Telugu, Malayalam and Kannada (Southern) and Hindi, Urdu, Kashmiri, Dogri, Punjabi, Maithali, Nepali and Sanskrit (Northern). Two tribal languages, Bodo and Santhali are also recognised by the Constitution.

Out of these 22 languages, Tamil is the oldest modern Indian language maintaining its linguistic character with little change for about 2000 years. Urdu is the youngest of the modern Indian languages, taking its shape in the 14th century A.D., deriving its script from an Arabic-Persian origin, but vocabulary from Indo-Aryan sources, i.e. Persian and Hindi. Sanskrit, though the oldest classical language, is still very much in use, and hence is included in the list of modern Indian languages by the Constitution of India.

The most powerful trend of medieval Indian literature between 1000 and 1800 A.D. is devotional (bhakti) poetry which dominates almost all the major languages of the country. Unlike the dark middle ages of Europe, India's middle ages brought about a very rich tradition of devotional literature of remarkable merit which dispels the superstitious assumption of a dark period of India's history. Bhakti literature is the most important development of the medieval period. It is love poetry. Love for one's Lord, Krishna or Rama, the two main incarnations of the great God Vishnu.

This love is depicted as love between husband and wife, or between lovers, or between servant and master, or between parents and child. This is personalisation of the godhood, which means a truthful perception of God residing in you, and also harmony in life which only love can bring. Worldly love is Kama (Eros) and divine love is Prema (mystic Eros). The dominating note in bhakti is ecstasy and total identity with God. It is a poetic approach to religion and an ascetic approach to poetry. It is poetry of connections – connecting the worldly with the divine, and as a result, the old form of secular love poetry began to have a new meaning in all languages.

The rise of bhakti poetry gave rise to regional languages (Bhasa). The conception of bhakti did away with the elite tradition of Sanskrit and accepted the more acceptable language of the common man. Kabir (Hindi) says that Sanskrit is like water of a well stagnant, Bhasa like flowing water. A seventh century Shaiva Tamil writer Manikkarvachakar has something similar to say about in his book of poetry Thiruvachakam. Bhakti also attacked the age-old caste system and devoted itself to the worship of humanity, because the catch-word of bhakti is that God is there in every human being. The movement was in essence subaltern, as most of its poets belonged to the so-called 'lower' castes. Bhakti is antitheology and against any kind of conceptual erudition.

The power of ancient bhakti poetry in Tamil set in motion what might well be considered a pan-Indian efflorescence? After Tamil, Pampa's great court epics were composed in Kannada in the 10th century. Devotional literature in Kannada, the Vachanas (sayings) of the various saints of the Krishna, Rama and Shiva cults, is well known. Basavanna was a famous Kannada poet, a Shiva devotee and a great social reformer. Allama Prabhu (Kannada) wrote great poetry under the garb of religion. Chronologically, Marathi, the close successor of Kannada, became the next venue for bhakti. Gyaneswar (1275 A.D.) is the first and foremost bhakti poet in Marathi. In his teens (he died at the age of 21) he became famous for his poetic contribution to bhakti for Vithal (Vishnu).

Eknath wrote his short poetic narratives and devotional abhangas (a literary form), and after him it was Tukarram (1608-1649 A.D.) whose songs cast a spell all over Maharasthra. And then it is Gujarati in the 12th century. Gujarati poets like Narsi Mehta and Premananda occupy a prominent place in the galaxy of the Vaishnava poets. Afterwards, the sequential order is as follows: Kashmiri, Bengali, Assamese, Manipuri, Oriya, Maithili, Braj, Avadhi (the last three languages come under the umbrella language, Hindi) and other languages of India. Chandidas, a Bengali poet, is acclaimed as a great genius for the lucidity and sweetness of his poems.

Similarly, Vidyapati in Maithili created a new poetic language. Lal Ded, a Kashmiri Muslim poetess, gave a new dimension to mystical bhakti. Jayadeva, a Sanskrit lyric poet of the 12th century, influenced a large number of devotional Bengali poets like Govinda Das (16th century), Balaram Das and others. Sri Chaitanya (1486-1533), a great Bengali saint, helped Vaishnavism to turn into a religious and literary movement, made it a living faith and became a source of never-ending inspiration to a host of Bengali poets, including Jiva Goswami. Sankardev (1449-1568), an Assamese devotional poet, used plays (Ankiya-Nat) and Kirtan (devotional songs) to propagate Vaishnavism and became a legend.

Similarly, Jagannath Das is a legendary devotional poet in Oriya who wrote *Bhagavat* (the story of Krishna), which has spiritually united all the people of Orissa and created a living consciousness. Muslim and Hindu saint-poets of rural Bengal known as Bauls (mad lovers) created oral poetry of divine intoxication under the influence of both Vaishnava and Sufi (Islamic mysticism which enunciates the doctrine of divine love) philosophy. Medieval Muslim Bengali poets like Daulat Kazi and Saiyad Alaoal (17th Century A.D.) wrote narrative poems based on Sufistic philosophy, betraying a happy cultural and religious synthesis of Islam and Hinduism.

In fact, bhakti became a great platform for Hindu-Muslim unity. Kabir (Hindi) is the foremost among the poets of the sant tradition (faith in one omnipresent god and not in many gods like Rama and Krishna). Kabir's poetry touches upon the various aspects of devotion, mysticism and social reforms. Hindi literature, with its supra-regional character, attracted Namdev (Marathi) and Guru Nanak (Punjabi) and others to write in Hindi, which by then had developed into a conglomeration of many languages and dialects, and came to be known as an umbrella language.

The centrality of Hindi and its vast geographical area was the reason for it. Surdas, Tulsidas and Meera Bai (15th to 16th Century A.D.) point to the great heights of Vaishnavite lyricism achieved by Hindi. Tulsidas (1532 A.D.) was the greatest of the Rama-bhakti poets who wrote his famous epic, the Ramacharit Manas (the lake of the deeds of Rama). In fact, epics like the *Ramayana* and the *Mahabharata* received a rebirth in the new languages. These languages gave a fresh life, a renewed relevance, and a meaningful reincarnation to the great Sanskrit epics, and these epics in their turn provided substance and style to the new languages too.

Kamban in Tamil, Krittibasa Ojha in Bengali, sarala Das in Oriya, Ezhuttacchan in Malayalam, Tulsidas in Hindi and Nannaya in Telugu are well knoown and legion. Muslim poets like Malik Muhammad Jayasi, Raskhan, Rahim and other wrote Sufi and Vaishnava poetry. The religious and cultural synthesis that was a special feature of medieval India finds abundant expression in its literature. The Islamic element is all-pervasive, next only to the Upanishadic Hindu element. Nanak, the first Sikh Guru, wrote in many languages, but mostly in Punjabi, and was a great poet of inter-religious communication.

Nanak says truth is supreme, but above truth is truthful living. Guru Nanak and other Sikh Gurus belong to the sant tradition, which believes in one omnipresent God, and not in many gods like Rama and Krishna. The poetry of the Sikh Gurus is collected in the *Guru Granth Sahib* (the Revered Book), a multilingual text which talks about the unchanging one reality (Sat) the cosmic law (Hukum), meditation (Satnam), compassion and harmony (Daya and Santosh). Bulleh Shah, the most famous Muslim Punjabi poet, popularised Sufism through Punjabi Kafi (verse-form). Kafi is a small poem in stanzas followed by refrain and is sung in a dramatic way. Shah Latif, the famous Sindhi Muslim poet (1689 A.D.) in his sacred work Risalo explained Sufi mystic love as the divine truth.

WOMEN POETS OF BHAKTI

The contribution of women writers in different languages during that period deserves special attention. Women writers like Ghosha, Lopamudra, Gargi, Maitreyi, Apala, Romasha Brahmavadini, etc., right from the days of the Vedas (6000 B.C. – 4000 B.C.), focused on the image of women in mainstream Sanskrit literature. The songs of Buddhist nuns (6th century B.C.) like Mutta and Ubbiri and Mettika in Pali express the torment of feelings for the life left behind. The Alwar women poets (6th century A.D.), like Andal and others, gave expression to their love for the divine.

Lal Ded (1320-1384), the Muslim poetess from Kashmir Lalded & Habba Khatun, represented the sant tradition of bhakti and wrote Vakhs (maxims), which are peerless gems of spiritual experience. Meera Bai, in Gujarati, Rajasthani and Hindi (she wrote in three languages), Avvayyar, in Tamil, and Akkamahadevi in Kannada, are well known for their sheer lyrical intensity and concentrated emotional appeal. Their writings speak to us about the social conditions prevailing at that time, and the position of woman at home and in society. They all wrote small lyrics or poems of devotional fervour, metaphysical depth, and with a spirit of dedication and utmost sincerity. Behind their mysticism and metaphysics is a divine sadness. They turned every wound inflicted by life into a poem.

OTHER TRENDS IN MEDIEVAL LITERATURE

Bhakti was not the only aspect of medieval literature. Love ballads and heroic poetry in Punjabi, known as Kissa and Var, were popular Punjabi medieval forms. The most famous Punjabi love ballad is Hir Ranjha, an immortal book by a Muslim poet called Warris Shah. A popular Punjabi heroic ballad, sung by village bards orally, is Najabat's Var of Nadir Shah. Var is the most popular form of Punjabi poetry, music and drama, all rolled into one, and has been in vogue since the earliest times. In Hindi, between 1700 and 1800 A.D., many poets like Bihari Lal and Keshav Das created secular poetry of Sringara (erotic sentiment), and a large number of other poets, wrote academic accounts of the entire range of poetry, in verse form.

During the medieval period, Urdu, as a language, came into being. It was Amir Khusro (1253 A.D.), an early architect of India's composite culture, and a great Sufi poet, who first experimented with Persian and Hindi (then known as Hindavi) mixed poetry, which was the genesis of a new language, subsequently recognised as Urdu. Urdu has largely followed Persian forms and metres in poetry, but it has adopted some of the purely Indian forms also. Ghazals (lyrical couplets), marsia (elegy) and qasidah (ode of praise) are of Iranian origin. Sauda (1706-1781) was the first among the late medieval poets who gave vigour and versatility to Urdu poetry, which his predecessors had been struggling to accomplish. Then, it was Dard (1720-1785) and Mir Taqi Mir (1722-1810) who gave Urdu maturity and class, and ushered it into the modern period.

MODERN INDIAN LITERATURE

THE 19TH CENTURY INDIAN RENAISSANCE

In almost all the Indian languages, the modern age begins with the first struggle for India's freedom in 1857, or near that time. The impact of western civilisation, the rise of political consciousness, and the change in society could be seen in what was written during that time. Contact with the western world resulted in India's acceptance of western thought on the one hand, and rejection of it on the other, and resulted in an effort made to revive her ancient glory and Indian consciousness. A large number of writers opted for a synthesis between Indianisation and westernisation, in their search for a natinal ideology.

All these attitudes were combined to bring about the renaissance in 19th century India. But it was a renaissance in a country which was under foreign domination. So it was not that kind of renaissance which had spread in 14th-15th century Europe, where scientific reasoning, individual freedom and humanism were the dominant characteristics.

The Indian renaissance took a different shape, in the context of the Indian race, moment and milieu, and as a result, nationalistic, reformistic and revivalistic thinking found its way into literature, which slowly turned itself into a pan-Indian movement, spearheaded in different parts of the country by renaissance leaders like Raja Rammohun Roy (1772-1833), Bankim Chandra Chatterjee, Vivekananda, Madhav Govind Ranade, U.V. Swaminatha Aiyer, Gopal Krishna Gokhale, K.V.

Pantulu, Narmada Shankar Lalshankar Dave and othrs. The leaders of the renaissance, in fact, succeeded in instilling nationalistic fervour in the people, and induced in them a desire for social reform and a sentimental yearning for their past glory.

The most important literary event that revolutionalised literature was the emergence of literary prose in all the modern Indian languages, and the advent of the printing press, under the patronage of an Englishman, William Carey (1761-1834), at Serampore, Bengal. It is true that Sanskrit and Persian had a vast body of prose, but the necessity for prose in modern Indian languages, for use in administration and higher education, led to the emergence of prose in different languages at the beginning of the modern period.

The birth of newspapers and periodicals in Indian languages between 1800 and 1850 was extremely important for the development of prose and the missionaries of Serampore started off Bengali Journalism on its career. The emergence of prose as a powerful medium brought a kind of change that coincided with the process of modernisation.

THE EMERGENCE OF NATIONALISM

It is true that the idea of a modern state took root in Indian society because of India's contact with western ideas, but very soon, Indian writers like Bankim Chandra Chatterjee (Bengali, 1838-1894) and others made use of this newly acquired concept of nationalism to attack colonial rule, and in the process created their own brand of nationalism, rooted in the soil. Bankim Chandra wrote many historical novels like *Durgesh Nandini* (1965), and *Anand Math* (1882), acquired a pan-Indian popularity and made nationalism and patriotism a part of dharma. This alternative was a distinctive civilisational concept of universalism that was accepted by many as a reply to western colonialism.

Revivalism and reformism were natural corollaries of the newly emerging idea of nationalism. Rabindra Nath Tagore (Bengali, 1861-1942), the greatest name in modern Indian literature, made federalism an important part of his concept of national ideology. He said that the unity of India has been and shall always be a unity in diversity. The foundation for this tradition had been laid in India at the social level, not the political, by saints like Nanak, Kabir, Chaitanya and others.

It is this solution-unity through acknowledgement of differences- that India has to offer to the world. As a result, India's nationalism is mingled with its spiritual tradition, with truth and tolerance preached by Mahatma Gandhi, and non-alignment advocated by Pandit Jawaharlal Nehru, showing India's concern for its pluralism. Modern Indian pluralism is multi-lingual, multi-cultural, secular, national-state concept.

THE LITERATURE OF NATIONALISM, REFORMISM AND REVIVALISM

Patriotic writings proliferated almost spontaneously in different languages, as the resistance of a community against foreign rule. Rangalal in Bengali, Mirza Ghalib in Urdu and Bharatendu Harishchandra in Hindi expressed themselves as the patriotic voice of that era. This voice was, on the one hand, against colonial rule, and on the other, for the glorification of India. Besides, Mirza Ghalib (1797-1869) wrote ghazals in Urdu, about love, with unusual imagery and metaphors. He accepted life both as a joyous existence and as a dark and painful experience.

Michael Madhusudan Dutt (1824-73) wrote the first modern epic in an Indian language, and naturalised blank verse in Bengali. Subramania Bharati (1882-1921) was the great Tamil patriot-poet, who revolutionized the poetic tradition in Tamil. Themes from mythology or history were taken to write epics, by Maithili Saran Gupta (Hindi, 1886-1964), Bhai Vir Singh (Punjabi, 1872-1957), and others, with the express purpose of fulfilling the needs of the patriotic reader.

The birth of the novel is associated with the social reform-oriented movement of the 19th century. This new genre, borrowed from the West, is characterized by a spirit of revolt, right from its adoption into the Indian system. The first Tamil novel, *Pratap Mudaliyar Charitram* (1879) by Samuel V. Pillai, the first Telugu novel, *Sri Ranga Raja Charitra* (1872) by Krishnamma Chetty, and the first Malayalam novel, *Indu Lekha* (1889) by Chandu Menon were written with didactic intentions and to re-examine evil social customs and practices like untouchability, caste distinctions, denial of remarriage of widows, etc.

In other first novels, like the Bengali novel, *Phulmani O Karunar Bibaran* (1852), by an Englishwoman, H. Catherine Mullens, or the Hindi novel, Pariksha Guru (1882) by Lala Sriniwas Das, one can discover shared patterns of response and articulation towards social problems. Historical novels were written by Bankim Chandra Chatterjee (Bengali), Hari Narayan Apte (Marathi), and others, to describe the glorious past of India, and to instill nationalist fervour in her people.

Novels were found to be the most appropriate medium to eulogize the intellectual and physical richness of the past, and reminded Indians about their obligations and rights. In fact, in the 19th century, the idea of national identity emerged from literature, and most Indian writings turned into the voice of enlightment. This paved the way for India to understand the real, factual position by the time it reached the threshold of the 20th century. It was during this time that Tagore started writing the novel *Gora* (1910), to challenge colonial rule, colonial criteria and colonial authority, and to give new meaning to Indian nationalism.

INDIAN ROMANTICISM

The trend of Indian romanticism ushered in by three great forces influenced the destiny of modern Indian literature. These forces were Sri Aurobindo's (1872-1950) search for the divine in man, Tagore's quest for the beautiful in nature and man, and Mahatma Gandhi's experiments with truth and non-violence. Sri Aurobindo, through his poetry and philosophical treatise, 'The Life Divine', presents the prospect of the ultimate revelation of divinity in everything. He wrote mostly in English.

Tagore's quest for beauty was a spiritual quest, which attained fruition in the final realisation that service to humanity was the best form of contact with God. Tagore was aware of a supreme principle pervading nature and the entire universe. This supreme principle, or the unknown mystique, is beautiful, because it shines through the known; and it is only in the unknown that we have perpetual freedom.

Tagore, a many-splendoured genius, wrote novels, short stories, essays and dramas, and never ceased to try out new experiments. His collection of poetry in Bengali, *Gitanjali* (song offerings), received the Novel Prize in 1913. Tagores' poetry, after the award, inspired writers of different Indian languages to popularize the age of romantic poetry. The age of romantic poetry in Hindi is known as Chhayavad, the age of romantic mystery, in Kannada, is Navodaya, the rising sun, and in Oriya, it is known as Sabuj, the age of green.

Jaishankar Prasad, Nirala, Sumitra Nandan Pant and Mahadevi (Hindi); Vallathol, Kumaran Asan (Malayalam); Kalindi Charan Panigrahi (Oriya); B.M. Srikantayya, Puttappa, Bendre (Kannada); Viswanath Satyanarayana (Telugu); Uma Shankar Joshi (Gujarati), and poets of other languages highlighted mysticism and romantic subjectivity in their poetry. The poets of Ravikiran Mandal (a group of six poets of Marathi) searched for the hidden reality in nature. Indian romanticism is fraught with mysticism – not like English romanticism, which wants to break puritanic shackles, seeking joy in Hellenism.

In fact, the romantic trend of the modern times follows the tradition of Indian poetry, where romanticism indicates the

Vedantic (the philosophy of one Reality) oneness between Nature and man, more along the lines of Vedic symbolism and not Paganism. Muhammad Iqbal (1877-198), the greatest poet that Urdu had produced, second only to Ghalib, went through initially a romantic-cum-nationalistic phase in his poetry. His best collection of Urdu poems is *Bang-i-Dara* (1924). His quest for Pan-Islamism did not deter him in his concern for humanity at large.

THE ADVENT OF MAHATMA GANDHI

The emergence of Mohandas Karamchand Gandhi (Gujarati, English, and Hindi, 1869-1948) and Tagore, influencing Indian life and literature, were quite often complementary to one another. Gandhi spoke the language of the common man, and was for the outcasts. His weapon was the weapon of truth and non-violence. He was for traditional values and against industrialisations. He very soon turned himself into a medieval saint and a social reformer. Tagore called him Mahatma (saint). Gandhi became the theme of both poetry and fiction of cultural nationalism. He became an apostle of peace and idealism.

Poets like Vallathol (Malayalam), Satyendranath Datta (Bengali), Kazi Nazrul Islam (Bengali) and Akbar Allahabadi (Urdu) accepted Gandhi as a challenge to western civilisation, and as an assertion of the dignity of Asian values. Gandhian heroes swamped the fictional world of that time. Raja Rao (English), Tara Shankar Bandyopadhyay (Bengali), Premchand (Hindi), V.S. Khandekar (Marathi), Sarat Chandra Chatterjee (Bengali), Lakshmi Narayan (Telugu) all created Gandhian protagonists as rural reformers or social workers with moral and religious commitments. It was not the writers, but the people, who created the Gandhi myth, and the writers, in their turn, used it effectively to mark a period of great awakening.

Sarat Chandra Chatterjee (1876-1938) was one of the most popular Bengali novelists, whose popularity continues unabated even today, not only among Bengali readers, but also among people in other parts of India, by means of the numerous translations of his books, which are available in various Indian languages. His pet theme was the man-woman relationship, and he was well known for his portrayal of women, their sufferings and their often unspoken love. He was both a Gandhian and a socialist.

Premchand (1880-1936) wrote novels in Hindi. He was a true son of the soil, deeply attached to the Indian earth. He was the finest literary exponent of the Indian peasantry in Indian literature. As a true Gandhian, he believed in the idealistic theory of 'a change of heart' in the exploiters. But, in his magnum opus, Godan (1936), he becomes a realist and records the suffering and struggle of the Indian rural poor.

PROGRESSIVE LITERATURE

The advent of Marxism on the Indian literary scene in the thirties is a phenomenon which India shared with many other countries. Both Gandhi and Marx were driven by opposition to imperialism and concern for the dispossessed sections of society. The Progressive Writers Association was originally established in 1936 by some expatriate writers in London, like Mulk Raj Anand (English). However, soon it became a great pan-Indian movement that brought together Gandhian and Marxist insights into society.

The movement was especially conspicuous in Urdu, Punjabi, Bengali, Telugu and Malayalam, but its impact was felt all over India. It compelled every writer to reexamine his/her relationship with social reality. In Hindi, Chhayavad was challenged by a progressive school that came to be known as Pragativad (progressivism). Nagarjun was undisputedly the most powerful and noted Hindi poet of the progressive group. The Bengali poets, Samar Sen and Subhas Mukhopadhyay, added a new socio-political outlook to their poetry. Fakir Mohan Senapati (Oriya, 1893-1918) was the first Indian novelist of social realism. Rootedness to the soil, compassion for the wretched, and sincerity of expression are the qualities of the novels of Senapati.

Manik Bandyopadhyay was the most well-known Marxist Bengali novelist. Malayalam fiction writers like Vaikkom Muhammed Basheer, S.K. Pottekkat and Thakazhi Sivasankara Pillai, made history by writing progressive fiction of high literary value. They covered fresh ground exploring the life of ordinary men and the human relations that economic and social inequalities fostered. Shivaram Karanath, the most versatile fiction writer in Kannada, never forgot his early Gandhian lessons.

Sri Sri (Telugu) was a Marxist, but showed interest in modernism at a later stage in his life. Abdul Malik, in Assamese, writes with an ideological bias. The critical norms of progressive literature were established by the pioneer of this phase in Punjabi by Sant Singh Sekhon. The progressive writers' movement attracted the attention of eminent poets of Urdu, like Josh Malihabadi and Faiz Ahmad Faiz. Both imbued with the Marxist spirit, infused in the age-old love symbolism a political meaning.

MAKING OF MODERN THEATRE

Sanskrit drama after the 10th century lost its tenor. It strove no more through symbol and gesture to realize the truth behind human experience. Medieval Indian literature was glorious, but it was an era of devotional poetry, which was a little indifferent to secular representation of life on stage. The Islamic taboo against such forms of entertainment was also responsible for the decline of Indian theatre, and, therefore, drama remained in a state of oblivion. However, folk plays continued to entertain the audience.

With the advent of the modern period and the impact of western literature, drama took a new turn and developed as a form of literature. The Parsi theatre, around 1850, started staging plays based on Indian mythology, history and legends. With its moving troupes, they travelled to different parts of the country and made a tremendous impact on their audience. Agha Hashr (1880-1931) was an imporant playwright of the Parsi theatre. But Parsi plays were mostly commercial and cheap In fact, modern Indian theatre grew mainly as a reaction against its initial crudity and superficiality.

Baratendu Harishchandra (Hindi), Girish Chandra Ghosh (Bengali), Dwijendra Lal Roy (Bengali), Dinabandhu Mitra (Bengali, 1829-74), Ranchodbhai Udayram (Gujarati, 1837-1923), M.M. Pillai (Tamil), Balvant Padurang Kirloskar (Marathi, 1843-1885) and Rabindra Nath Tagore delved into our folk tradition to create plays to protest against colonialism, social injustice and westernisation. Jaishankar Prasad (Hindi) and Adya Rangacharya (Kannada) wrote historical and social plays to highlight the clash between idealism and the harsh realities by which they were surrounded. P.S. Mudaliyar gave Tamil stage respectability and new direction. But in all, Indian literature before Independence is generally poor in drama. The making of modern theatre became complete only after India achieved independence in 1947.

SEARCH FOR MODERNITY

A great work of art, in the Indian context, is the expression of both the traditional and the actual. As a result, the concept of modernism grew in the Indian context along different lines. The urge was to create something new. Even the imitations of western modernist came as a challenge to understand their own realities. Writers during this time presented their manifestos, explaining their ideas of modernity. A new language was found to articulate their own historical position. Jibanananda Das (1899-1954) was the most important Bengali poet after Tagore who had a total sense of poetry. He was an imagist and used language not just to communicate, but to grasp reality.

Bibhuti Bhushan Bandyopadhyay (1899-1950) the Bengali fiction writer, whose novel *Pather Panchali* (The Saga of the Road) was filmed by Satyajit Ray, and which received international acclaim, presents the unsophisticated and warmhearted village life that is passing away. In his quest for identification with man's everyday relation with nature, he proved himself to be no less modern. Tara Shankar Bandyopadhyay (Bengali 1898-1971) depicts in his novels the pulsating life of a whole generation staying in a village or a city, where society itself becomes the hero. In depicting regional life, the social change and human behaviour, he achieves utmost success. Uma Shankar Joshi (Gujarati) initiated new experimental poetry and spoke of the shattered self in the modern day world.

Amrita Pritam (Punjabi) creates an intensely personal poetry of an unearthly glory, without losing contact with the earth. B.S. Mardhekar (Marathi, 1909-1956) reflects in his poetry contemporary reality with the help of images, indicating the limitations of man and the inevitable despair arising from them. Gopal Krishna Adiga (1918-92), the famous modern Kannada poet, developed his own personal idiom, and became mystical. He also displays the agony of his time. Practically all the writers reflect the despair of man, arising out of his sense of helplessness in society and in the larger sphere of history.

The limitation of the West, the degeneration of canons and the disillusionment of the middle-class psyche, are some of the characteristics of Indian modernity. However, the tradition of humanism is also very much alive and hopes for a better future is not discarded. In western terminology, modernism is a breaking away from established rules, traditions and conventions, but in India, it is a search for alternatives to existing literary models. But one cannot identify one single reference point of modernity and, therefore, one may conclude that Indian modernity is like a mosaic.

THE INDIAN LITERARY SCENE AFTER INDEPENDENCE

After independence, in the fifties, the disillusionment became more vivid because of the pressure of the disintegration of society and a broken relationship with India's past heritage. In 1946, India witnessed the worst bloodbath in the memory of the sub-continent, just before it became Independent, after the partition of the country. India's nationalism at that juncture was a nationalism of mourning. At that time, a majority of new writers portrayed a dreadful artificial world, based on the formulas of western modernism. There were experimentalists who showed concern for the inner reality – intellectualism entered the realm of modernity.

In a culture like India's, the past does not pass off. It keeps on providing paradigms for the present, but the rhythm broke down because of modernistic experimentations. Most Indian poets looked outside, and accepted T.S. Eliot, Malarme, yeats or Baudelaire as their masters, and in the process, rejected Tagore, Bharati, Kumaran Asan, Sri Aurobindo and Gandhi. But then, these poets of the fifties, and even the sixties of 'dark modernism', developed an identity crisis. This specific identity crisis, the conflict between traditional Indianness and western modernity, is discernable in the writings of the major language areas in India during those days.

Those who adhered to western modernity separated themselves from the common masses and their reality. But the concept of experimentation (Prayog) sometimes developed independent of western influence, as a quest for new values and a searching examination of the basic sanctions or sources of value. S.H. Vatsyayan Ajneya (Hindi), Navakanta Barua (Assamese), B.S. Mardhekar (Marathi), Harbhajan Singh (Punjabi), Sharatchandra Muktibodh (Marathi) and V.K. Gokak (Kannada) emerged with a distinct voice and vision, enriching the new movement.

Besides, the literature of social realism, having its roots in the soil, became a dominant trend in contemporary literature. It was a continuation of the progressive literature of the thirties and forties, but definitely more militant in its approach. G.M.

Muktibodh (Hindi), Bishnu Dey (Bengali) or the Telugu naked (Digambar) poets revealed the poet's solitary struggle in opposition to the mounting crisis of uprooted identity. They wrote political poetry on the theme of agony and struggle. It was poetry of commitment. Literature now moved to the downtrodden and the exploited.

The Kannada Bandaya (the rebels) were concerned with forms of violence in a class society. People like Dhumil (Hindi) showed a great range of social realism. O.N.V. Kurup (Malayalam) added to his lyricism the sharpness of anger towards social injustice. Then came the Naxalite movement of the seventies, and with it post-modernism entered the Indian literary scene. In the Indian context, post-modernism arrived as a reaction to media-operated and market-guided reality – a reaction to the modernism of the sixties of the existential anguish, of the crisis of identity, and of the frustration of the idealist, but it carried with it the trend of progressive literature of protest and struggle.

DALIT LITERATURE

One of the most significant features of the post-modernist era was the emergence of writings of the outcasts, as a major literary force. The word Dalit means the downtrodden. The literature which is concerned with the socially underprivileged, and which asserts the socio-political stature of the underdogs, is known by this name. The Dalit movement was started in literature by Marathi, Gujarati and Kannada writes under the leadership of Dr. B.R. Ambedkar. It came into the limelight because of progressive literature moving nearer to the downtrodden. It is a literature of militant protest against upper caste literature upholding Brahmanical values.

Marathi poets, Namdev Dhasal or Narayan Surve, or novelists like Daya Pawar, or Laxman Gaikwad, reflect in their writings the anguish of a community, and demand the shaping of a just and realistic future for the underprivileged and the outcast in society. Mahadev Devanur (Kannada) and Joseph Macwan (Gujarati), in their novels, deal with the experience of violence, protest and exploitation. It challenges the tone and context of existing literary canons and decentralises the whole process of a literary movement. It creates an alternative aesthetics and extends the linguistic and generic possibilities of literature. Dalit literature introduces a new world of experience in literature, widens the range of expression, and exploits the potentiality of the language of the outcasts and underprivileged Dalits.

In order to bridge the gap between urban and rural consciousness, between the past and the present, another trend which is very much visible in the post-modernist poetry scene is the use of mythology to present the modern predicament. Mythic thoughts, in fact, are attempts to mediate the gaps between continuity and change, thereby authenticating the idea of 'total poetry'. By using similar mythological situations, a broader dimension is given to the present-day chaotic condition in which humanity is living today. The mythical past affirms man's relationship to the transcendent. It has a value-structure. It is a rediscovery of the past for the present, and an adaptation for the future.

In Ajneya's (Hindi) poetry, one finds a shift towards the realisation that the individual's entity is just a humble part of a larger reality. Ramakanta Rath (Oriya) and Sitakant Mahapatra (Oriya) use mythology or folk legends to contemplate on man's alienation from a life of nourishment and grace. One comes across many instances of writers trying to explore their roots, find their moorings, and probe whole areas of experience, blurred during a period of extreme modernism during the last several decades. In contemporary Indian poetry, along with a sense of urbanity, an attitude of irony, frequent use of mythological sequences as structural images, and a continuous involvement with the problems of expediency and eternity, are very visible.

Playwrights like Girish Karnad, Kambar (Kannada), Mohan Rakesh, Mani Madhukar (Hindi), G.P. Satish Alekar (Marathi), Manoj Mitra and Badal Sircar (Bengali) are using myths, folk legends and religio-centric tradition to understand India's present-day existence. The departure from Euro-centric modernism has created a new socio-cultural mythical code, which is used in the poetry of Kunwar Narayan (Hindi), Dilip Chitre (Marathi) and Sankho Ghosh (Bengali), and in novels by Bhyrappa (Kannada), Prapancham (Tamil) and others.

Myth is now accepted as a meaningful sub-text of the literary text. U.R. Anantha Murthy (Kannada), in his stories, explores the relevance of some traditional values in today's changed context. His novel, *Samskara*, is a world classic, which portrays the spiritual struggle of man in terms of the urgency of life's demands. These writers have made an effort to retrieve, rediscover, and redefine elements of culture in a creative way, by a return to pride in one's roots, while looking ahead.

CONTEMPORARY LITERATURE

In the uttara Adhunika (post-modern) era the effort is to be natural, to be Indian, to be near to the common man, to be socially conscious. The third generation of Malayalam writers like N. Prabhakaran, and P. Surendran prefer the term anti-modernism to post-modernism and are content simply to narrate human tales without any explicit social message or philosophical pretensions. Vijayadan Detha (Rajasthani, under the umbrella language Hindi) and Surendra Prakash (Urdu) are now writing stories without any ideological prejudices.

The modernist idea that anything simple should not be accepted is now questioned. It is established now that simple texts may present complex extra-textual structures. Even cultural references simply stated in poetry can have different semantic values. In the contemporary Indian novels by Jayamohan (Tamil), Debes Ray (Bengali) and Shivprasad Singh (Hindi), dealing with various neglected regions, and the spoken dialect of that area, a composite picture of a total India, pulsating with new experience and struggling to hold on to the old values, and in the process sometimes discarding them, is also easily discernible.

In this period of Uttara Adhunikta (post-modernism), these novels dramatise the shift of the dominant from problems of knowing to problems of modes of being. It gives a glimpse of the actual India of the villages, and also makes it amply clear that this country belongs to the Hindus, Muslims, Sikhs and Christians. Its culture is a composite culture. These regional novelists have forcefully demolished the myths created by the western Indologists that Indianness is just fatalism, or that Indianness is to be identified with harmony and order, and Indian vision cannot perceive its own reality.

The central tension experienced by the vast majority of contemporary Indian novelists is that of transition from the rural and traditional to an urban and post-modern situation, expressed either through a romantic nostalgia for the village left behind, or through fear and hatred of the cruel impersonal city, with all its sex, horror, murder and cruelty. Birendra Kumar Bhattacharya (Assamese), Sunil Gangopadhyay (Bengali), Pannalal patel (Gujarati), Mannu Bhandari (Hindi), Nayantara Sahgal (English), V. Bedekar (Marathi), Samaresh Basu (Bengali) and others, with their rural-urban sensitivity, have portrayed the Indian experience in its totality.

Some fiction writers, with the help of symbols, images and other poetic means, magnify a particular moment in life. Nirmal Verma (Hindi), Moni Manikyam (Telugu) and many others have made their presence felt in this area. Emancipatory women's writing has emerged strongly in all Indian languages, seeking to subvert the man-dominated social order, forging revisionary myths and counter-metaphors by women writers like Kamala Das (Malayalam, English), Krishna Sobti (Hindi), Ashapurna Devi (Bengali), Rajam Krishnan (Tamil) and others.

The present-day crisis in India is the conflict between expediency and universality, and as a result, a large number of writers are in the process of identifying a pattern of problem-solving within the traditional system, vigorous enough to generate and sustain an indigenous process of modernisation, which does not need readymade external solutions, and is in accord with indigenous needs and attitudes. The new crops of writers are concerned with truth as they see it in life around them.

Even for the Indian English writers, English is no more a colonial language. Amitabh Ghosh, Shashi Tharur, Vikram Seth, Upamanyu Chatterjee, Arundhati Roy and others are using it without showing a lack of commitment to Indianness. Those writers who are aware of their inheritance, complexity and uniqueness, express in their work without any conscious effort both tradition and the actual. One may conclude that no single Indian literature is complete in itself, and hence no study of it, within a single language context, can do justice to it, or even to its writers, who grow in a common cultural ambience. What is noteworthy is that Indian literature is written in many languages, but there is a vital, living relationship among them, because of polyglot fluidity, inter-language translations, shared themes, forms, concerns, direction and movements. All these keep the ideals of Indian literature dynamically alive even today.

7

The Western Imperialistic Challenge: Rabindra Nath Tagore, Aurobindo, Tilak and Gokhale

Lokmanya Bal Gangadhar Tilak (1856-1920) is modern India's first National Leader and Father of the Indian Revolution. He has also been described as Architect of Indian Nationalism, Maker of Modern India and Patron and Prince of revolutionaries. "The conditions of things in India being given, this man had to come and, once in the field, had to come to the front. He could not but stand in the end where he stands today, as one of the two or three leaders of the Indian people who are in their eyes, the incarnation of the national endeavour and the God-given captains of the national aspiration .... He had that closeness of spirit to the mass of men, that unpretentious openness with them, that faculty of plain and direct speech which interprets their feelings and shows them how to think out what they feel .... For this reason he had always been able to unite all classes of men behind him, to be the leader not only of the educated, but of the people, the merchant, the trader, the villager, the peasant." – Sri Aurobindo.

"For us, he will go down to the generations yet unborn as maker of Modern India. They will revere his memory as of a man who lived for them and died for them .... Let us erect for the only Lokmanya of India an imperishable monument by weaving into our own lives, his bravery, his simplicity, his wonderful industry and his love for his country." – Mahatma Gandhi.

"We have here, in Lokamanya, a symbol of India's struggle for freedom, and a man who was not only a brave soldier but a great captain, not a captain of an organised Government, but a captain of the unorganised masses of India, a captain who had to deal with India as it was in his day .... the first great mass leader of this new stage of our revolutionary movement was Lokmanya Tilak .... Lokmanya blazed the trail in so many directions in this country, laid the foundations of our struggle and brought about, I repeat, for the first time this mass consciousness, political consciousness, this dynamic energy, because he was a tremendously dynamic person. So, there can be no fitter person whose picture should adorn this hall, which represents the achievement of that freedom and independence .... Therefore, we meet here not only to unveil the picture of this great man and Father of India's Revolution, but to remember him and to be inspired by him."– Jawaharlal Nehru.

"Such was the secret hand of that great patron and prince of revolutionaries working behind all the various activities on different fronts, in the fight for freedom against the British Empire" – Balshastri Hardas.

A true revolutionary and freedom fighter, Lokmanya Tilak was born on the eve of the 1857 Revolutionary War of Independence against British imperialist occupation. His extraordinary life began in the village of Chikalgaon in Ratnagiri district, Maharashtra, as the son of Gangadharpant Ramachandra Tilak, a Brahmin schoolteacher and Sanskrit scholar (and later, Assistant Deputy Educational Inspector for the districts of Pune and Thane) and his wife, Parvati Bai Gangadhar.

From an early age, Lokmanya Tilak had absorbed the spirit of anti-British resistance, not least from his grandfather, Ramachandra Pant, who inspired him with stories about the heroic deeds of leading revolutionary figures (Ramachandra Pant had taken the vows of *Sannyas* and lived at Kashi during the 1857 Revolution). Not surprisingly, Lokmanya soon clashed with his English headmaster, a Mr Jacob, as a result of which he was forced to leave high school for a year.

Following traditional custom, Lokmanya married his bride, Tapibai, at the age of fifteen, returning to his native village for the ceremony. He then continued his studies, graduating from high school in 1872 and enrolling at Deccan College, Pune, in 1873. In 1876 he completed his BA at Elphinstone College, Mumbai, with first-class honours. Already in his student years he displayed a sharp intellect, good memory and keen interest in various traditional subjects such as mathematics, astronomy, astrology, Sanskrit and law. He took his LL B degree in law in 1879.

Tilak was also a born fighter and took martial arts lessons from the famous revolutionary and hero Vasudeo Balwant Phadke (1845-1883). His fighting spirit, together with his keen sense of justice (indicated by his interest in law, in particular, traditional Hindu law), made him well qualified to be a leader of men. In addition, he was soon presented with the opportunity to demonstrate his aptitude as a schoolteacher – which he did exceptionally well.

In 1880, together with Mahadev Ballal Namjoshi, Lokmanya responded to the call of Vishnu Krishna Chiplunkar, the Hindu nationalist and educator, and volunteered to participate in the founding of the private New English School, Pune, working without remuneration for the first year. In 1881, Lokmanya founded the publishing house Kitabkhana and was joined by Gopal Ganesh Agarkar in the publication of two newspapers, the *Marathi Kesari* and the English-language *Mahratta*. Thus, Lokmanya began his life as educator, journalist and revolutionary leader, for which he had been destined in those trying years of national struggle.

From the very beginning, Lokmanya Tilak had been aware of the corrupting and stultifying effect British-inspired education exerted on the Indian people, which was based on the racist assumption of Western cultural superiority over Eastern races. Education, therefore, had always been at the heart of his strategy for national awakening and liberation. Tilak and Agarkar's popularity as teachers increased greatly not least due to their journalistic publications in which they fearlessly attacked the British imperialist order and its Indian collaborators.

Their school had become so successful that in 1884, they were able to establish the Deccan Education Society (DES) and in 1885 they founded the Ferguson College which was to become one of India's foremost institutions of higher learning. The Ferguson College was dedicated to providing Western and, above all, Sanskrit learning, the lack of which had been correctly identified by Tilak as one of the causes of India's downfall: "That which gives us a knowledge of the experience of our ancestors is called education .... How can a person be proud of his religion if he is ignorant of it?

The want of religious education is one of the causes that brought the missionary influence all over our country." ("National Education", speech delivered at Barsi, February 27, 1908, *Bal Gangadhar Tilak: His Writings and Speeches*, pp. 81). In short, the national education promoted by Tilak was Hindu Nationalist, thus initiating a revolutionary trend in education, away from the British-founded, Western-only Government schools. Unfortunately, the cynical intrigues of "Moderate" DES-members like Gopal Krishna Gokhale forced Tilak to resign from the Society in 1890 and he dedicated himself to journalism and politics, activities he used with great skill and success to further the revolutionary cause.

As a counter-measure to the rise of Hindu Nationalism, in 1885, the Indian National Congress was founded by Alan O. Hume, William Wedderburn and others for the express purpose of controlling India's awakening political consciousness and directing it along lines that were convenient to British interests. The British imperialist authorities knew full well that they could not keep India in a position of domination for much longer. They were fully aware that they represented an unwanted foreign body, standing on the brink of a volcano ready to erupt and blow them to pieces. Thus, all the British could do was to take off some of the anti-Colonialist, revolutionary pressure which was building up in Indian society, by channeling it in a less dangerous direction.

Having failed in their strategy of outright repression, the British were now resorting to controlled reform as a substitute for revolution. On their part, Hindu revolutionaries were aware of the British imperialist game and played along with the intention of subverting the British plan and eventually beating the British at their own game.

As Lokmanya Tilak warned his compatriots in his paper, "Old people always used to advise us never to get enamoured of the sentences full of good words used cheaply and the glamour of the English. Though the exterior may look beautiful, Ram only knows what is going on inside .... We must behave towards these people with cunning and shrewdness". In consequence, in addition to his work as teacher and journalist, Lokmanya began his political career by joining the Congress – he attended the annual session for the first time in 1889 – where he soon became leader of the extremist wing of the organisation, agitating against the moderate elements in the Congress, many of whom were outright collaborators and agents of British interests.

THE REBIRTH OF POLITICAL HINDUISM

One of the most important contributions Lokmanya Tilak made to the Hindu revolutionary movement was to assist in the reawakening of the political consciousness of the Hindus. Under Muslim Imperialism, Hindus had often been forced into a defensive position from which they had begun to extricate themselves under the leadership of the Maratha King Chhatrapati Shivaji Maharaj (1630-1680). However, British occupation forced them into a defensive position again and many adopted a reactionary attitude of resignation and collaboration. Lokmanya was one of the key figures who were instrumental in turning the situation around.

Traditional Hindu statecraft recognises three logical states in the dynamic situation between two opposing parties: (1) a state of decline arising when one's opponent occupies a position of relative progress; (2) a state of stagnation, equilibrium or "no-change" arising from an absence of either progress or decline; and (3) a state of progress arising when the opponent occupies a position of relative decline. As the *Arthashastra* of Kautilya explains, "From decline a position of no change should be reached and from that a state of progress".

In other words, it is a ruler's duty to ensure that the nation advances from a state of decline to one of equilibrium and from a state of equilibrium to one of progress. This applies to both internal (national) and external (international) situations. In keeping with this fundamental principle, Hindu revolutionary leaders sought to lift the nation out of a position of decline to one of progress, in particular, *vis-à-vis* the British occupation forces. On account of his traditional Hindu education, which made him aware of India's past greatness, Lokmanya was in a particularly favourable position to rationally analyse the historical situation of the Hindus and diagnose a state of decline in the nation's condition.

His vast knowledge of Indian history and culture also enabled him to identify the causes of India's decline as well as reflect upon a strategy whereby the nation could extricate itself from the situation into which it had fallen. Finally, he was in a position to proceed with the practical planning and implementation of his strategy. It is a common misconception among those who look upon religion as mere belief in the supernatural, that religion is incapable of resolving any problems in practical life. It was Lokmanya's special merit to demonstrate that religion did have a practical value, in particular, in resolving India's problems caused by foreign domination and exploitation.

Therefore, the key to the correct understanding of Lokmanya's revolutionary work as well as his importance in Indian and even world history is the fact that he regarded the revival of Hindu religion as the answer to India's problems. While other revolutionary movements such as Marxism and Social Democracy were based exclusively on economic and other materialist considerations, Lokmanya rightly insisted on the primacy of religion as the foundation of India's Revolution. Lokmanya was not only a schoolteacher, journalist, politician, freedom fighter and revolutionary but also, and above all, a Hindu scholar.

His interest in Hindu religion did not stem from mere pride in his Hindu heritage but from a profound scholarly knowledge and understanding of India's timeless spiritual tradition. Therefore, while it had become fashionable among the degenerate sections of Western-educated Indian society to regard religion as "ignorance" and "superstition", Lokmanya recognised true religion as that which gave meaning and direction to human life. Hindu religion was especially relevant to India's situation of domination, dependence, oppression and exploitation at the hands of predatory and imperialistic foreign powers.

In the first place, for Lokmanya Tilak, Hindu religion represented an inalienable part of the Indian nation which provided all Indians with a link to God, that is, a higher truth, as well as with a link to their fellow-citizens: "Religion is an element in nationality. The word *Dharma* [Religion] means a tie and comes from the root *dhri* to bear or hold. What is there to hold together? To connect the soul with God and man with man".

Indeed, the word *Dharma* means that which upholds and supports everything that exists. *Dharma* is the Eternal Law of the Universe, the Universal Order (*Rta*) which supports and holds everything together and enables all things, from the universe itself to human society, to function in an ordered, harmonious and efficient way in accordance with the Will of the Creator (*Ishwara*). In the Hindu tradition, therefore, Religion or Dharma stands for everything that is right, including Righteousness (Truth, Order and Justice) itself. Being a Law, Dharma also implies a Duty to obey and carry it out incumbent upon all living beings:

"Dharma means our duties towards God and duty towards man. Hindu religion as such provides for a moral as well as social tie. This being our definition we must go back to the past and see how it was worked out. During Vedic times India was a self-contained country. It was united as a great nation. That unity has disappeared, bringing on us great degradation and it becomes the duty of the leaders to revive that union" ("The Bharata Dharma Mahamandala"). The above definition of religion makes it clear why there was no distinction between religion and ethics for the Hindu revolutionary movement in general and for the Lokmanya, in particular: ethical values such as right, freedom, law, order and justice, were the values of Hindu religion.

They were the expressions of the Supreme Eternal Law of the Universe (*Sanatana Dharma*) which was the very essence of Hindu religion. The corrupt and degenerate segments of Indian society, represented by the Moderate faction in the Congress, were insisting upon the introduction of Western values only because their European education had rendered them ignorant of the values of authentic Hindu tradition. By contrast, Hindu-educated leaders like Tilak clearly understood that there was absolutely no need for imported Western values and even less for Western laws, since everything that was necessary for the building of a harmonious, just, civilised and prosperous society was already present in the Hindu tradition which in the past had made India a leading nation in the world.

Lokmanya Tilak correctly regarded Hindu civilisation as a solid and well-built house (or temple) that was in need of some external repair but was otherwise structurally sound. On the occasion of the celebration of the Ganapati festival, he remarked: "Though the heads of some have been agitated by the unhampered ravings of the missionaries and the atheistic reformers, and though our heart may be shocked in seeing a crack or a crevice in the wall of our house, it again becomes calm on seeing that the stones of the foundation and the pillars of the hall are in good condition".

Tampering with this sound structure was unwarranted and could only result in a weakening of the original building and, ultimately, its collapse. Indeed, Tilak's stance proved to be not only prudent and wise but also prophetic: the Great Depression of the 1930s, the two World Wars, the collapse of India's economy under the Socialist Indira Gandhi regime, the destruction of the New York World Trade Centre on September 11, 2001 and the US-engineered global banking crisis of 2008 have demonstrated that Western civilisation is not something Hindus ought to emulate.

Furthermore, just as there could be no separation of religion and ethics, there could be no separation of religion and politics. God and His Eternal Principle of Dharma (Righteousness) stood at the very centre of Hindu culture and civilisation. From that spiritual centre proceeded the values which formed the ethical and moral foundation of Hindu society and from that ethical and moral foundation proceeded all the duties, rights and actions in the civic sphere on which public life was based. Indeed, Hindu religion was a practical system which inspired and directed all spheres of human knowledge and activity. Politics, therefore, was clearly inseparable from Hindu religion. It must be noted that Mahatmạ Gandhi, too, had come to the realisation that "those who say that religion has nothing to do with politics do not know what religion means".

ACTIVISM VS. QUIETISM

In the past, anti-imperialist Hindu movements initiated by Shivaji Maharaj, the Sannyasi leadership of Bengal and others had shown that Hinduism was not separated from political and military activities. Unfortunately, by the 19th century, due to Islamic, British and Indian quietist (anti-activist) influence, Hindu religion had come to be looked upon as apolitical. Naturally, this was acknowledged by Hindu revolutionary leaders as a highly dangerous and undesirable trend that had to be stopped by all means. Lokmanya, in particular, took it upon himself to demonstrate that authentic Hindu tradition was neither quietist nor apolitical but activist and political.

His vast knowledge of Hinduism enabled him first of all to show that Hindu religion was an activist religion and not a religion of *sannyasis* or renunciants. Indeed, even *sannyasis* were not inactive – as demonstrated by the anti-British Sannyasi Uprising of Bengal. In his scholarly commentary on the *Gita* (*Gita Rahasya*) which he composed in 1910-11, he shows in a lucid and systematic manner that the path to Liberation or God-realisation (*Mukti*) was a path of action. At that time, the debate revolved around the teachings of Shri Adi Shankara which were given a quietist interpretation by certain Hindu philosophical schools.

However, it should be noted that Shri Adi Shankara, the main exponent of the renunciant (*sannyas*) interpretation of Hindu Scriptures such as the Upanishads, the Vedantasutra (Brahmasutra) and the *Gita*, was not a practitioner of quietism or inaction. On the contrary, as observed by the Lokmanya himself, "After 600 years of chaos rose one great leader, Shankaracharya and he brought together all the common philosophical elements of our religion and proved and preached them in such a way that Buddhism [which was believed to promote quietism] was swept away from the land".

Indeed, in his own commentary on the *Gita* (*Bhagavad Gita Bhashyam*) Shri Adi Shankara clearly states: "By doing works for the sake of God (Ishvarartham), man attains Supreme Liberation or God-realisation (Param Moksham)". True renunciation, therefore, is not inaction but selfless action in service of God. Tilak himself said in a speech on February 1908: "Religion and practical life are not different. To take to *sannyasa* (renunciation) is not to abandon life. The real spirit is to make the country your family instead of working only for your own. The step beyond it is to serve humanity and the next step is to serve God".

Another important point that should be noted is that nowhere did Shri Adi Shankara claim that the Path of Renunciation should or could be followed indiscriminately by all and sundry. Only those who had purified their mind through constant selfless action in the service of God and society in this and previous lifetimes and had attained the required degree of spiritual maturity, were fit for the Path of Knowledge and Renunciation and not others: "Among men, one in many thousands strives to win perfection. And even among those who know and strive ... only one rare soul indeed comes to know Me [God] in truth". "At the end of many births, devoted to self-purification resulting in greater knowledge, the man of knowledge gains full illumination and directly reaches Me [God] .... There is none like him or excelling him. Hence he is *extremely rare*", etc.

It is very true that the Upanishads gave priority to spiritual knowledge and that many Upanishadic texts advocated or appeared to advocate renunciation of the world. But not all Upanishads advocated renunciation. Those that did so were the textbooks of renunciant schools – which are why they are known as Samnyasa Upanishads. Moreover, these were secret teachings to be imparted by a Guru exclusively to a small group of disciples. At no time were they meant for the whole Hindu community. Indeed, preaching world-rejection and inaction to the wide world would be unreasonable and suicidal. Ordinary Hindus have always understood this fact full well and the topic was never a subject of debate among the masses who led a normal life and remained in touch with reality and common sense.

It was only the degenerate and misguided elements among the idle and unproductive intellectual elites who manufactured this unwarranted and harmful controversy which should never have arisen in the first place. The fact is that *Shruti* (the highest Scriptural authority, such as the Rg Veda) does not advocate renunciation, its main concern being worship of God (or Gods). Furthermore, the Rg Veda mentions *Dharma* in the sense of "religious rite" and "established principle or rule of conduct". It is, therefore, undeniably an Activist Scripture.

Even the spiritual centres (maths) established by Shri Adi Shankara, although based on *sannyasi* membership, were not meant for the promotion of renunciation. Their true function was to preserve and consolidate Hindu religion. It is clear from this that the Path of Knowledge and Renunciation was never intended for the majority of the population (not even among the Buddhists) and that those who wished to turn India into a nation of world-renouncers were acting contrary to both the teachings of Scripture and the teachings of Shri Adi Shankara himself.

Finally, it must be remembered that according to Shri Adi Shankara God is the supreme spiritual and ethical authority who decides the fate of all creatures: "Samsara and Moksha come from the Supreme Lord, because Scripture teaches that", etc. The results of man's efforts, physical, mental and spiritual, depend on God and on Him alone. On his part, man can only do his duty to God and society according to scriptural injunction or divine command: "If killed, you will attain Heaven; if victorious, you will enjoy this world. Therefore, stand up, determined to fight" (*Bhagavad Gita* 2. 37). As Shri Adi Shankara observes, "In either case, you stand only to gain – this is the Lord's idea".

What is certain is that for doing his duty to God and society, man will be rewarded with either: (a) earthly enjoyments, (b) Heaven, or (c) God-realisation or Liberation. On the other hand, for neglecting his duty, man will be punished either in this world or the next and, possibly, in both: "The renunciation of duties that ought to be performed is not proper. Such renunciation is due to delusion and is well known to be *tamasic* (of inferior mental quality)" (*Bhagavad Gita* 18. 7 and *Shankara Bhashyam*); "... if you refuse to fight this righteous war, then casting away your own duty (svadharma) and your reputation, you will incur sin" (*Bhagavad Gita* 2.33 and *Shankara Bhashyam*), etc.

It follows that in practice there is no escape from one's duty to God and society: "One cannot escape Action ... the Blessed Lord, Who is the most supreme Jnanin (Knower), continues to perform Action". Quoting the *Gita* 3.5, Lokmanya writes: "in this world, no one can for a single moment remain without performing Action". Therefore, even the God-realised man continues to be bound by this duty: "It has been stated in the Yoga-Vasistha that even a Jnanin, who is a 'jivan-mukta' (Released in this life) must perform action".

This is in complete agreement with Shri Adi Shankara: "The man of wisdom should not bewilder the mind of the [spiritually] ignorant attached to works [with talk of renunciation]. Himself steadily performing all actions, let him [by his own example] cause them to do likewise" (*Bhagavad Gita* 3.26 and *Shankara Bhashyam*). Also, "if you think you have reached life's goal of being a knower of self in your own right, you may have no duty to perform; *still you should work to promote others' well-being*".

Lokmanya with irrefutable logic asks, "If a Jnanin [Knower] becomes uniform with the Parameshvara [Supreme Lord] as a result of Jnana [Spiritual Knowledge], how will he escape the necessity of performing that Action which is performed by the Parameshvara?" Evidently, he cannot escape it. Thus, it must be admitted that Lokmanya Tilak and Shri Adi Shankara both agree that even the God-realised man continues to act for the following reasons:

- For the welfare of the world.
- To set an example to the unawakened.
- Because God Himself acts for the above reasons and one who has attained Unity with God necessarily acts in complete unity and harmony with Him, in the same way as a drop of water which has merged with the ocean stands still and moves with the ocean at all times.

True, Lokmanya emphasised action (karma) whereas Shri Adi Shankara had highlighted the importance of knowledge (jnana) in respect of attaining God-realisation. Yet in practical life, no proper action is possible without knowledge just as knowledge is worthless if not put into practice. Therefore, it is clear that, in essence, Lokmanya was confirming what Shri Adi Shankara had taught centuries earlier, with special emphasis on the necessity of action in accordance with the needs of the time. For, it should be remembered that India's situation under British imperialist occupation was vastly different from that of Shankara's time.

Having exposed the fallacy of the quietist or anti-activist position, Lokmanya next demonstrated, again on the basis of Hindu Scripture, that Hindu religion is not only activist but also political. For example, in his speech, "Tenets of the New Party" he observes that "A story in the *Mahabharata* tells that Sri Krishna was sent to effect a compromise, but the Pandavas and Kauravas were both organizing their forces to meet the contingency of failure of the compromise. This is politics". In other words, Hindu Scripture itself teaches politics and even God engages in political acts.

In the *Gita*, God declares: "There is no action in the three worlds that I need to do … nevertheless, I engage in action …. If I do not work, the worlds will perish". Moreover, in the *Gita* (as in the *Ramayana*, Puranas, etc.) God takes the side of the righteous, which is a political act. He praises King Janaka for his (political) actions. It follows that Hindu religion is inseparable from politics and those who insist on separating the two are doing a great disservice to the Hindu cause.

The Lokmanya clearly understood that, without politics, there is no political power and without political power the Hindu community is bound to become dominated by the surrogate power-holders (the predatory foreign imperialists and other subversive and anti-Hindu elements). Thus the reawakening of the political consciousness of the Hindus was itself a revolutionary project which, however, did not aim to invent something new, but to restore the Hindu nation to its original state which was a state of independence, self-determination and progress as defined by traditional Hindu statecraft.

REVOLUTIONARY HINDUISM

Inattentive students of Indian history sometimes doubt the fact that Tilak wanted a revolution. However, such unwarranted doubts are dispelled by Tilak's own writings and speeches from which it is absolutely clear that he wanted the Indian people to take power into their own hands. Thus in "The Political Situation" he stated: "Do not expect much from a change of Government. Three P's – pray, please and protest – will not do unless backed by solid force. Look to the examples of Ireland, Japan and Russia and follow their methods [of armed struggle]".

In 1908 he declared in very clear terms that "An opposition has arisen between the national character of India and the institutions of [British] Government, and the time is approaching for action being taken to bring about its harmony – an action of revolution". Furthermore, he repeatedly gave as example the revolutions of other nations, such as the 1642 English Revolution, and stressed the right of the people to oppose and, when necessary, remove an unjust ruler or government. Another important point which is conveniently overlooked by left-wing historians who believe that revolution can only come from atheist Marxism is that, having shown that Hindu religion was activist and political; Lokmanya Tilak also demonstrated in very clear terms that Hindu religion was revolutionary.

On the revolutionary implications of Hindu teachings, he observed: "When a Raja held as a God, starts behaving unjustly, another *Raja* emerges and replaces the former, by engaging him in a sustained struggle. Both Lord Parashurama and Lord Rama were incarnations of Lord Vishnu. Parashurama, however, had to surrender to Rama.

At that moment, it is said, a luminous flame, symbolic of Divinity, left Parashurama's and entered the mouth of Rama". Furthermore, in the *Bhagavad Gita*, God Himself declares: "Whenever there is a decline in Righteousness and a rise in Unrighteousness .... I take birth (or manifest Myself) for the protection of the righteous, for the destruction of the unrighteous and for the establishment of Righteousness" (*Bhagavad Gita* 4.7-8 and *Shankara Bhashyam*).

Lokmanya Tilak in his 1906 speech, *The Bharata Dharma Mahamandala*, refers to precisely this promise which God has given to the Hindus: "We have the grand and eternal promise Shri Krishna has given in the *Gita* that whenever there is a decay of Dharma, He comes down to restore it. When there is decay owing to disunion, when good men are persecuted, then Shri Krishna comes down to save us. It is because of this that the Hindu religion is not dead. We are never without hope. Let the heretics say what they may. A time will come when our religious thoughts and our rights will be vindicated".

It must be noted that the revolutionary concept of God as Destroyer of Evil and Restorer of Righteousness goes back to the Rg Veda itself where God (Indra) is eulogised as *Vrtrhan* (Slayer of the Demon *Vrtra*). The theme of God as Saviour of the oppressed and Supreme Champion of Righteousness is repeated in different forms in all major Hindu Scriptures (the *Mahabharata*, *Ramayana*, Puranas) and is the central theme, implied or express, of the Ganapati and Shivaji festivals initiated by Lokmanya Tilak. Although Scripture does not specify the time when God will come to re-establish Righteousness on Earth, the current state of the world logically leads us to infer that this will be soon.

Lokmanya himself gave King Shivaji as a historical example of divine intervention in the cause of Righteousness. However, it was self-evident that Righteousness could not be restored without the active participation and co-operation of human society. Hindus could not sit idly by and wait for God to restore Righteousness on their behalf. Such an attitude would have been a blatant contradiction of the doctrine of activism (*Karma-Yoga*) as expounded by God in the *Gita* and in Lokmanya's own *Gita Rahasya*. Accordingly, the Ganapati and Shivaji festivals served a very clear political and revolutionary as well as cultural and psychological purpose, being meant to revive Hindu culture, give emotional encouragement and inspiration and, above all, provide a model of action to the Hindu masses.

Apart from the fact that other religions were "partial truth while our Hindu religion is based on the whole, the Sanatan [Eternal] truth, and therefore, it is bound to triumph in the end", what was needed was for Hindus to unite, organise themselves and channel their efforts in a direction that would turn their situation around from a state of domination and exploitation to one of freedom and independence: "All that is required for our glorious triumph and success is that we should unite all the different sects on a common platform and let the stream of Hindu religion flow through one channel with mighty consolidated and concentrated force.

This is the work that the Bharata Dharma Mandala has to do and accomplish. Let us be all united." And, "God does not become incarnate for nothing. God does not become incarnate for idle people. He becomes incarnate for industrious people. Therefore begin work". It is also imperative to take note of the fact that the Hindu Revolution as understood by Lokmanya Tilak differed from those of the West (such as Marxist revolution) in that it did not aim to bring about a new political system, but to restore India's original form of government that would operate in accordance with Hindu laws and customs based on the universal principle of Dharma or Righteousness (Truth, Order and Justice).

We may observe in this context that in his 1848 *Manifesto of the Communist Party*, Karl Marx laments the fact that the dispossessed workers of Capitalism "seek to restore by force the vanished status of the workman of the middle Ages". This was an admission to the fact that Europe's dispossessed masses did not want a new, invented system (like Marxism), but a restoration of pre-Capitalist conditions in which the peasantry owned its own land and its own means of production (agricultural implements, etc.). In blatant disregard of the will of the people, Marx opposed a return to pre-Capitalist conditions and sought to abolish all private property and even trade in order to promote his own fraudulent and criminal agenda.

By contrast, the Hindu Revolution as understood by Lokmanya and by the Indian masses themselves stood in opposition to Marxist theories and in agreement with the aspirations of the European peasantry and, we may add, with the aspirations of the peasantry everywhere. In short, the Hindu Revolution had much more in common with China's nationalist Boxer Revolution of 1900 than with any Marxist-inspired counterfeit "revolutions". We have seen that, as observed by Lokmanya Tilak, Hindu Scripture promises that Righteousness (Dharma) will be restored after having reached a state of decline.

The Scripture-based definition of the Hindu Revolution, therefore, is the reversal or restoration of conditions as they obtained prior to the present state of decline caused by foreign rule. This definition must be accepted not only "because Scripture says so", but because it follows a very clear and irrefutable logic. Hindu religion, culture and civilisation are based on Truth which manifests itself as Righteousness (Law, Order and Justice). When this Truth, or Righteousness (Dharma), becomes distorted, corrupted or suppressed, the obvious remedy is its restoration to the original state. The Hindu Revolution being a True Revolution, Truth or Righteousness (Dharma) is its point of departure and Truth or Righteousness (Dharma) is its point of arrival.

This is why the Hindu Revolution is the only true one and others, in particular those of the Marxist variety, are false. It should be noted that Shri Adi Shankara himself was a Hindu revolutionary as defined above in as far as, as acknowledged by the Lokmanya; he tirelessly worked for the restoration of Hindu religion and the refutation of heretical views which had become prevalent in the country and were in the process of eroding and corrupting India's authentic religious tradition. In this respect, Lokmanya had much in common with Shri Adi Shankara, as becomes evident from his *Gita Rahasya.*

Indeed, the very fact that Lokmanya was a follower of Advaita Vedanta necessarily implies fundamental agreement with Shri Adi Shankara (the exception, as indicated earlier, being that the one emphasised action while the other emphasised knowledge, as a means of God-realisation). In addition, although he has been compared with Shivaji and he himself often gave the latter as a historical example of revolutionary leadership, the fact is that Lokmanya was not a military leader – although he did advocate the militarisation of the Hindus and would have liked to see an armed insurgency against the repressive British regime if all other means failed.

Finally, Lokmanya regarded National Independence (*Swaraj*) as a manifestation of the Vedantic ideal of inner self-realisation: "The two ideals [of Vedanta and Nationalism] are mutually consistent and both of them demand a kind of self-sacrifice and self-control .... The feeling is one of love for humanity, for the equality of man before God, and it is the spirit of that feeling that governs the two ideals, Vedantic and National". Self-realisation, that is, awareness of one's true identity and of one's situation was the first step towards Liberation on the personal, national and world levels.

Indeed, Lokmanya did not believe in the political liberation of India only, but in the political and spiritual liberation of the entire human race. Thus, he observed that once India had gained her own independence, "we Indians would like to help other nations which have lost their freedom". In consequence, personal liberation was the first step towards national liberation and national liberation was a preliminary step towards the liberation of mankind and the establishment of an Universal Brotherhood of Man (Vishwa-Bandhutva) according to the Hindu concept of the world as one family (Vasudha eva Kutumbakam). Thus the three steps for the realisation of universal welfare and happiness were:

- Personal liberation.
- National liberation.
- World liberation.

In conclusion, the Rule of Righteousness promised by God in the *Gita* had to be extended to the whole world. As Lokmanya observed, a time will come "when instead of Christians preaching Christianity here we shall see our preachers preaching Sanatan Dharma all over the world. It must be added that this is entirely consistent with the teachings of other followers of the "School of Renunciation", such as Swami Vivekananda who in similar terms called upon Hindus to "conquer the world with their spirituality". Significantly, Swami Vivekananda's Irish disciple, Sister Nivedita was a co-founder of the revolutionary organisation Anushilan Samiti.

Indeed, if the world was a family and the Hindu Community as a member of this family was in possession of the whole Truth in the form of Sanatana Dharma or the Supreme Eternal Law of the Universe, while the others were in possession of the partial Truth only, then the Law of Karma-Yoga which demanded that Hindus strive for the material and spiritual welfare of the world (lokasamgraha) logically obliged them to spread knowledge of the Truth to all corners of the world.

This was the only way of bringing about the spiritual liberation of mankind and establishing the Rule of Righteousness on Earth as commanded by God. Furthermore, this was a legitimate and necessary defensive measure. For, so long as the other nations remained ignorant of the Truth of Sanatana Dharma, they would be inclined to follow evil ways, such as Imperialism, and attack the Hindu Community which was the Community of the Righteous, as the unrighteous nations, the Muslim Arabs, the Mongols and the Christian Europeans had already done for centuries. Therefore, the restoration of Hindu Dharma at home and the spread of Hindu Dharma abroad was the inescapable revolutionary implication of Hindu teachings.

SWARAJ AND TRISUTRI

It is generally acknowledged by both Indian and Western historians that India's economy suffered a dramatic setback under foreign occupation. For example, the *Dufferin Report* published in 1888 by Lord Dufferin, the Viceroy of India, describes in very clear terms the appalling poverty suffered by the Indian masses under British occupation. The British historian of empire, Professor Niall Ferguson, in his book *Empire* (2003) writes that British Colonialism "reduced India and China from being quite possibly the world's most advanced economies in the sixteenth century to relative poverty by the early twentieth".

Indeed, under British imperialist rule India had become one of the poorest nations in the world. Thus, India had lost not only her political independence, but had become reduced to economic dependence and exploitation by predatory and parasitical Western powers. Already under Muslim (Mughal) occupation the people of India – the majority of which were peasants – had been reduced to growing poverty by the revenue-appropriating classes, the *jagirdars* and the *zamindars* of the Mughal system. With the assumption of *Diwani* by the British East India Company in Bengal, Bihar and Orissa in 1765 and, even more so, after the British made India their colony in 1858, oppression and exploitation on the Subcontinent reached intolerable levels.

The British oppressors and their native collaborators had completely monopolised the national economy which allowed them to exact extortionate taxes, control the production and marketing of commodities, engage in predatory moneylending activities, expropriate those who were unable to pay taxes or debts, etc. Famine and accompanying outbreaks of plague were frequent and widespread. In Bengal alone, in 1769-1770 a third of the population (some ten millions) perished of starvation and malnutrition. Apart from the humiliating experience of being enslaved by European barbarians, it was a matter of cultural, intellectual and physical survival of the Indian nation.

Indeed, it was evident that co-existence with the British imperialists was not possible under any circumstances and that the only remedy was independence from foreign rule. As observed by Tilak, British Imperialism was an evil conspiracy of the military and merchant classes of European society (British

Colonialism being financed by British and other European banks). Superior military technology such as cannon, monopoly of international markets and bribing of the upper classes of colonised nations enabled them to dominate much of the world by military and economic means.

The British education system was another instrument of domination by which the British constructed for themselves a bureaucracy from pro-British elements of the local population. The British military, economy and education system, therefore, were identified as the foundation of the British Empire and these were the areas where the Empire had to be hurt. Military efforts such as the 1761-1800 Sannyasi Revolution of Bengal and the 1857 War of Independence were unable to throw off the heavy yoke of British Imperialism.

In consequence, without ruling out the military option, Hindu revolutionary leaders, Lokmanya Tilak in particular, resolved to concentrate on achieving their objective of Self-rule (*Swaraj*) through the immediate strategy of attacking British economic interests on the Subcontinent. This was to be implemented with the weapons of *bahishkar* and *swadeshi*. As a long-term strategy, the British education system was to be attacked with the weapon of national education. Thus, *bahishkar*, *swadeshi* and national education became the *Trisutri* (three-point) programme of India's revolutionary effort against British Imperialism.

- Bahishkar: the boycott of British goods, in particular, textiles.
- Swadeshi: promotion of Indian goods, industries and commerce.
- National education: This entailed the founding of national schools throughout the country including in villages, which would be independent of the British Government and use their own textbooks.

The main points outlined by Tilak were: (1) religious education which was necessary to give young Indians knowledge of their spiritual heritage and build up their character; (2) education in vernacular languages instead of English (as Tilak observed, "Under the Mohammedan rule we were required to learn Persian but we were not compelled to study it"); (3) industrial education which would help India become independent from foreign-controlled industries; (4) political education that would raise the nation's consciousness of its situation. For example, pupils should be taught that "Every year some thirty or forty crores of rupees are drained out of India without any return".

In short, the purpose of national education was to inspire patriotic sentiments among the people which would eventually lead them to challenge the legitimacy of British rule and shake off the chains of foreign subjugation and exploitation. It must be added that Tilak also campaigned for the militarisation of the Indian people, demanding the establishment of military colleges and a militia force. The above were not only measures for bringing down the British regime but also the pillars of the future independent Hindu State (*Hindu Rajya*).

THE ENEMY WITHIN

Although the Congress styled itself "Indian" and "National", the fact is that it was anything but that. Not only were many of its leading members British or pro-British, but it represented a cacophony of alien political views ranging from Christian Evangelism to Islamism, Capitalism, Imperialism, Liberalism, Fabian Socialism, Social Democracy and Free Masonry which were united by the singular fact that they were all fundamentally un-Indian and, above all, anti-Hindu. The Hindu masses, who were the true Indian people, were completely excluded from this strange English-style gentleman's club and no Indian could ever dream of attending a Congress session unless he dressed like an Englishman and spoke fluent English.

For a correct understanding of Indian history, in general, and of the Hindu Revolution, in particular, it is imperative to bear in mind that the Indian National Congress (INC) was founded by the British in 1885 as a counter-revolutionary measure designed to subvert and undermine the emerging Hindu Nationalist movement. Together with the English education system introduced by the British imperialist order in the first half of the 19th century, the Indian National Congress gave birth to a political and bureaucratic elite of degenerate elements which was the instrument by which the imperialist order was able to ruthlessly subjugate, oppress and exploit the people of India.

In his *Autobiography*, the Martyr of the Hindu Revolution, Damodar Hari Chapekar, exposed the fraudulence of the Congress in very clear terms, correctly identifying its objective as being "to deceive the Hindu*s* and give a harmless turn to their activities" (the use of the word "Hindus" in this context demonstrates the anti-Hindu agenda harboured by the Congress from its very inception). On his part, Hindu revolutionary leader Lokmanya Tilak reminded the people time and again that the British did not rule alone but with the help of the parasitical elite (represented by the Congress Moderates) which in turn could only operate with the consent and co-operation of the people themselves – hence it was for the people to challenge and resist the system.

It must be noted that this British-created political and bureaucratic instrument of oppression never left India even after the British did. It was simply taken over by the Congress Party and used in the same way as the British had done to keep the people down, in particular, the Hindu majority which continues to be oppressed and exploited as before. As a result, Western culture in India is spreading everywhere, Christianity, Islam, Capitalism and Communism are on the rise and Hindu Dharma is on the decline. This makes it clear why the Hindu Revolution is an ongoing process and why committed and patriotic Hindus must double their efforts in the cause of the national struggle of liberation from foreign domination.

Indeed, it was evident that it was the intention of the leading Congress clique to make India and her people as European and, by implication, as acceptable to the British imperialist order as possible. In these circumstances, it is easy to understand why the Hindu masses – represented by Lokmanya Tilak and other Hindu revolutionary leaders – felt alienated and marginalised. While earlier they had only one master, the English authorities, now they had a second one, the dominant Congress clique, who aimed to emulate the former in all respects and as faithfully as possible. Tilak clearly understood that the total exclusion of the masses from the political process resulted in apathy among them, which in turn resulted in a dangerous weakening of the national strength as well as loss of revolutionary potential and initiative.

With the exception of sporadic outbursts of anger and violence against the imperialist system, the masses seeing that they had been let down even by the "Indian" Congress leadership, naturally suffered from a lack of confidence, depression and apathy – quite apart from unbearable poverty and starvation. Unlike the parasitical majority in the Congress who treated the Hindu masses like an alien and inferior race, Tilak understood that the involvement of the masses in the political system was the only cure for the disease that had befallen the nation and the only means of uplifting it from a state of decline to one of progress in its struggle against the British oppression.

As a true man of the people, Tilak understood that the Hindu masses were the true Indian nation and that there could be no national movement of resistance to foreign occupation without the masses. As a true national leader, Tilak took it upon himself to cure the degenerate Moderates of the malady of anti-people elitism and sectarianism by inculcating in them an awareness of the need to co-operate democratically with the masses. He therefore reminded the Congress that "The illiterate are our brethren.

They have the same rights and are activated by the same aspirations. It is therefore our bounden duty to awaken the masses". He pointed out the inherently schizophrenic position of the Congress in its exclusive reliance for support on the English-educated classes (who were by definition pro-British) and exclusion of the Hindu masses (who were the true Indian people whom the Congress was supposed to represent before the British). He demanded that "the Ryot – the common toiling people – [be allowed to] come forward to give vent to their grievances in the conferences, openly" and that "these people – on whose behalf the educated are voicing the grievances – should at least be present at these conferences".

Tilak clearly did not believe in the moral legitimacy, let alone the competence, of the British Government. He believed in a system of mutual and reciprocal obligations and duties based on close co-operation between the Raja (Government) and Praja (the governed) as had obtained during the golden age of Hindu Rule and as prescribed in the Shastras (Scriptures). Under Islamic and British rule, such a system was completely absent. For Tilak, the imperialist order ruling India was a criminal regime guilty of the capital crime of Praja-droha (treason to the people).

Therefore, his entire life was dedicated to involving the common people in the political process. He was painfully aware of the fact that the degenerate and parasitical English-educated political elites of the time, which were on the payroll of the imperialist regime, were not the right material for carrying on the national struggle of liberation. The involvement of the masses in the national struggle was paramount if the struggle was at all to succeed. The national schools founded by

Lokmanya Tilak were not for the elites but for the people. So were his newspapers, the *Kesari* and the *Mahratta*, the annual Ganapati and Shivaji festivals, and a wide range of other initiatives he introduced for the sake of awakening and empowering the people.

During the famine of 1896-97 Lokmanya demonstrated his deep concern for the welfare of the suffering masses and his great skills in educating, organising and mobilising them. Under his instruction, the workers of the socio-political organisation Sarvajanik Sabha would go from village to village, explaining to the helpless peasants the causes of their situation, the Government's duties and obligations in respect of relief measures and advised them not to pay the land revenue to the authorities. In other words, Lokmanya tried his utmost to awaken the masses to the fact that they could expect no improvement in their situation unless and until they actively participated in the political process and, through political action, forced the arrogant and cruel Government to mend its ways. As immediate relief measures, Lokmanya started Fair Price grain shops and founded people's co-operatives.

In short, he organised the peasants' movement in Maharashtra. On its part, the imperialist regime understood the challenge to its tyrannical rule posed by Lokmanya's revolutionary agitation among the masses. Therefore, in 1897, the regime arrested him and sentenced him to eighteen months rigorous imprisonment. Lokmanya had already served a four-month sentence in 1882 for his "defamatory articles" in support of the Maharaja Shivaji Rao of Kolhapur. He thus showed that he was prepared to sacrifice his own health, well-being and even life for the sake of the people. It is no surprise, therefore, that he came to be known as "the Lokmanya" ("Revered by the People").

As pointed out by the historian R. C. Majumdar in his *History of the Indian Freedom Movement*, Lokmanya's trial and conviction in 1897 "may be regarded as a landmark in the history of Indian nationalism" for, from that moment on, "it was not eloquence and debating skills, but sacrifice and sufferings in the cause of the country that came to be regarded as the badge of honour and distinction". However, what was badge of honour and distinction for Lokmanya Tilak must be regarded as badge of dishonour and shame for the Congress majority who opposed him and branded him an "extremist".

Indeed, Tilak's popularity as a revolutionary leader exposed the complete failure of the Congress Party to do anything for the masses. The Moderate majority in the Congress was happy to lead a parasitical life of leisure as "British citizens" and meeting once a year to pass resolutions, which the Government ignored and no one bothered to implement. Tilak strongly criticised this irresponsible inactivity of the Congress, remarking that it was not enough to croak once a year like a frog and that "By now (1896) a large number of organised groups, associations and institutions, ready to undertake public cause, should have emerged .... It is not late, even now, to make a beginning in this direction".

Instead of pointless conferences and resolutions, Tilak logically wanted an organisation that would engage in direct action and work for the national cause on a day-to-day basis. In particular, he was looking for young men prepared to work as Hindu missionaries or "*Ramdasis*" (disciples of Shri Samartha Ramdas) "who, like the zealous Christian missionaries, working day in and day out, would be ready to go to the villages and work for the upliftment of their compatriots". What becomes apparent is that the contrast between the approach of the Congress Moderates and that of Tilak's Extremists could hardly have been greater.

Whether from ill will, naivety or sheer stupidity, the fact is that the Congress majority was dragging its feet on all issues that were of importance to the suffering people and to the national struggle of liberation. In effect, the "National Indian

Congress" was systematically acting as a brake on India's national movement, pushing it in a counter-revolutionary, reactionary direction that went against the interests of the people. Exasperated by this impossible situation, Tilak exclaimed that the movement had become like a yoke of oxen, one of which was straining to move ahead while the other (the Congress Moderates) remained stuck in the mud.

Indeed, there can be little doubt that in any other political set-up Tilak would have long formed an independent party of his own and would have become unchallenged leader of the nation. Unfortunately, under the repressive regime of imperialist Britain, he was forced to operate in tandem with the Congress which had been set up by the British for the purpose of obstructing the national movement led by Hindu revolutionary leaders like Tilak. In a letter of March 5, 1891, to Lord Lansdowne, A. O. Hume wrote: "Every adherent of the Congress, however noisy in declamations, however bitter in speech, is safe from burning bungalows and murdering Europeans, and the like. His hopes are based upon the British nation, and he will do nothing to invalidate these hopes and anger that nation".

Evidently, as founder of the Congress, Hume was in a position to know that he could rely on the pro-British credentials of Congress leaders. This once again confirms the view of Hindu revolutionaries such as Hutatma Damodar Hari Chapekar, that the Congress was founded for the purpose of watering down the national struggle of liberation and pushing it in a direction that was harmless to the British regime. Indeed, apart from Hume's admissions and Hindu revolutionaries' own observations, the counter-revolutionary intentions of the Congress founders become apparent if we consider that: (a) the Congress was established after Hindu Nationalism began to organise itself; and (b) the Congress was established in opposition to Hindu Nationalism which was the primary moving force behind the national struggle. Therefore, regardless of its official declarations, as an organisation that opposed Hindu Nationalism, the Congress was an organisation opposed to the national independence movement.

It becomes clear from the above why leading Congress Moderates like Gopal Krishna Gokhale (Tilak's adversary) claimed that the ruthless and systematic economic exploitation of India by the British was a "genuine mistake". Incredible though this may sound, even after the 1905 partition of Bengal, when the evil intentions of the British imperialist order had become obvious to all, the Congress Moderates objected that "the word 'Boycott' implies a vindictive desire to injure another". Thus for the Congress Moderates, the concern not to appear to "desire to injure" the barbaric alien regime had more weight than the suffering of the people it was supposed to represent.

Fortunately, the Lokmanya was not a man to rely on irresponsible elements like the Congress Moderates (although he needed them for political purposes) and valiantly carried on his revolutionary work without them. In addition to the official Three-point (*Trisutri*) Programme of Boycott, *Swadeshi* and National Education described above, Lokmanya devised the following revolutionary programme which he implemented with the assistance of other Nationalist leaders:

- Religious-political education and awakening of the masses. This entailed inculcation of the concept of economic, political and, when necessary, military struggle against oppression as a religious duty.
- Organisation. Forming self-help groups, organising mass agitations and protest movements.
- Unification. Religious, cultural and economic initiatives that brought people together, such as the Bharata Dharma Mahamandala, the Ganapati and Shivaji festivals and social-work projects for combating famine and plague. The Ganapati and Shivaji festivals were especially important

in uniting the Hindu masses around the concept of righteous struggle against evil, as illustrated by Lord Ganapati's slaying of the demon Gajasura and King Shivaji's slaying of the Muslim General Afzal Khan.

·Mobilisation. Carrying out of boycott, strikes and other economic and political actions of resistance and protest against the repressive imperialist regime.

THE STRUGGLE OF 1905-1908

The revolutionary policies conceived by Lokmanya Tilak began to find large-scale practical application in 1905, during the national unrest provoked by the partition of Bengal. The partition came into effect on October 16, 1905, which coincided with the appointment of Lord Curzon's friend, Joseph Bampfylde Fuller, as Lieutenant-Governor of the new province of East Bengal and Assam.

Although ostensibly introduced for reasons of "administrative efficiency", that is, to facilitate imperialist control and exploitation of the Subcontinent, as far as Hindus were concerned (who were the original and legitimate inhabitants of the country), the effect of the partition was to divide their ancestral homeland and to make Hindus a minority in Muslim-majority areas. To add insult to injury, pro-Muslim Fuller roused the Muslim mobs in support of the partition in order to stifle Hindu protests and launched an administrative terror campaign against Hindus. Muslim opposition to national independence was used against Hindu revolutionaries, many of whom were attacked by gangs belonging to the Muslim League (founded in 1906 with British support) protected by the police.

Naturally, this led to widespread unrest throughout the country and to a sharp rise in Hindu militancy which in turn was met with severe repression by the criminal imperialist order. Anti-partition meetings and protests were brutally broken up by the police, there were regular *lathi* (bamboo-stick) charges on peaceful demonstrators, beatings, flogging and torture, as well as arrest and harassment of leaders. While the partition of Bengal was being brutally enforced, moderate leader Gopal Krishna Gokhale was in England as official representative of the Congress, trying to plead with the English for self-government for India.

In contrast, as a true leader Tilak was fully aware of the fact that "eloquence" and "begging" would not lead anywhere and that the partition was bound to result in violence. In keeping with the strategic policies conceived by Tilak, the most basic form of action was propaganda and agitation (the reading aloud of revolutionary papers like the *Kesari* and the *Jugantar* in public places; political meetings, demonstrations and protest marches; Hindu revolutionary songs were sung at festivals like that of Shivaji; and, notably, foreign cloth was collected by Vinayak Damodar (Veer) Savarkar with his fellow-students of Fergusson College and burned in public ceremonies).

The next step was direct action in the form of boycott (picketing of shops and stores selling British goods, especially textiles; refusal by merchants to sell food to the British; refusal by servants to serve British masters) and strike (by shopkeepers, factory, mill and railway workers, etc.). Apart from the preparatory aspect (propaganda, agitation, organisation), a notable factor in the movement that is immediately apparent was the participation of the masses – peasants, workers, merchants, politicians, intellectuals and students of all castes and occupations, all took active part.

Nor did the movement stop at this. Punitive action was taken against traitors, collaborators and spies; Englishmen were pelted with mud and stones and forced to sing Hindu revolutionary songs; there were attacks on British offices, businesses and missionary houses; town halls, court-houses and police stations were attacked and burned down; and there were bloody battles with the police and armed forces in which Hindu revolutionaries responded to imperialist bullets with stones and sticks. Thus the next logical level was that of armed struggle and the evidence shows that despite the situational limitations imposed upon the revolutionaries, this was not entirely left out.

For example, bomb-making technology was acquired in London and Paris by Savarkar (whom Tilak had sent to London on the Shivaji Scholarship of Shyamaji Krishna Varma), Hemchandra Das (Kanungo) of Bengal and P. M. Bapat of Maharashtra. Copies of bomb-making manuals were sent for the use of revolutionary organisations like Abhinava Bharat Samaj back in India and bomb factories were soon established in Nashik, Kothure Pen and Vasai.

As part of his anti-partition campaign, Tilak visited Bengal in 1906 and 1907 and distributed pamphlets on the history of the Irish revolutionary movement Sein Fein and delivered fiery speeches against the imperialist regime. In Kolkata, Ullaskar Dutt had been experimenting with explosives since 1906 and on 30 April 1908 revolutionaries from the Jugantar group hurled a bomb at a carriage mistakenly believed to belong to the Chief Presidency Magistrate Kingsford. An attempt was also made on the life of the hated Lieutenant-Governor Fuller. Upon his return from Paris in December 1908, Hemchandra Das produced his own bombs.

The degenerate Congress Moderates of course opposed all forms of action that would upset their English masters. However, the Hindu majority was beginning to understand that force was the only language the tyrannical and illegal regime was prepared to understand. Tilak himself had long argued that in the same way as French revolutionaries had resorted to violence against oppression, Indians too, were now entitled to do the same. Indeed, it must be noted that Europeans themselves were routinely using violence to further their own imperialist interests.

Therefore, it was unreasonable to deny Indians the right to take up arms in self defence. On this point, Rabindranath

Tagore, who was far from being an extremist, said: "May I ask, who is the original and most stubborn extremist? …. Is it not the sign of an extremist administration to allow the distress of the people to reach an extreme height and to remain althrough indifferent to it? …. We, of course, know how to react when we are struck" The fact is that Lokmanya Tilak and other Hindu revolutionaries could only be regarded as "extremist" in the corrupt and twisted world of Abrahamic Imperialism in which Western (Christian and Islamic) aggressors could do as they pleased whereas non-Abrahamic Eastern nations had no right to exist and were expected to be grateful for being invaded, occupied and "civilised" by their oppressors and exploiters.

In reality, Lokmanya always favoured non-violent over violent means. Times and again he would tell his followers: "Every patriotic Indian should resort to Boycott. There is no need of violence either; we have a stronger weapon, a political weapon in Boycott". However, as the imperialist regime refused to give in to the demands of the people, it was becoming more and more clear with each passing day that a revolution was inevitable: "The time of revolution has not yet begun in India, but it is to begin hereafter".

It is evident; therefore, that Lokmanya approved of violence only as a last resort and his words or actions in the direction of armed struggle must be understood on this background. The view that armed insurrection was inevitable was shared by many others. For example, an article in the *Marathi Vihari* stated: "But there is no doubt that eventually the sword itself has to be unsheathed". At the same time, Lokmanya was aware of the fact that the nation had not been sufficiently prepared and equipped for an all-out armed struggle against British Imperialism.

A time of preparation was necessary. Among other methods, this preparation was carried out through publications in India and abroad. In his newspaper *Kesari*, Lokmanya published a series of nine editorials entitled *Guerrila Warfare* between June and August 1902, in which he compared the guerrilla tactics employed by the Boers of South Africa against the British with similar tactics used in the past by Maratha forces against the Muslims. Outside India, publications like the *Indian Sociologist*, *Gaelic American* and *Justice* similarly propagated a doctrine of armed struggle for the liberation of India from foreign occupation.

In addition, attempts were made in 1902 to build an arms factory in Nepal with the co-operation of the German company Krupps and to send some Nepalese revolutionaries for military training to Japan. In 1905 he established contact with the Russian consulate in Mumbai with a view to arrangements for military training for Hindu revolutionary forces. Similar contacts were made with the US and Swiss representatives. Lokmanya's solidarity with other Eastern nations is of particular interest.

Already on April 28, 1903 the *Kesari* had carried an article stressing the need for the co-operation of India with other Eastern nations like China and Japan against the common British enemy. In 1904 Lokmanya collected money for Japan's Relief Fund Committee and sent it to the Japanese consul in Mumbai as a neighbourly gesture from his party. Following Japan's brilliant victory over Russia in 1905, the *Kesari* published a series of articles congratulating the Japanese for exposing the lie of Western invincibility. Thus Lokmanya's revolutionary programme evidently was extensive and systematic, not leaving out even international relations.

The general revolutionary strategy being formulated, the 1905 partition of Bengal was an opportunity to rouse the people to action. However, although Tilak enjoyed the support of the masses, the Congress Moderates demonstrated their anti-national intentions by stubbornly holding on to their refusal to co-operate. To make matters worse, the British regime deployed its tried divide-and-rule tactics to weaken the national-liberation struggle by bribing the upper sections of Indian society (the princes, the zamindars and the English-educated intelligentsia) with concessions or promises of concessions.

In particular, the Congress Moderates who represented these degenerate sections, decided in India's hour of need to go back on their promise made at the 1906 Kolkata Congress to support the Extremist policies of Boycott and Swaraj which had been adopted in the presidential address (written by Congress president Dadabhai Naoroji and, due to the latter's ill health, delivered by Gokhale himself).

As the Moderates held the majority in the Congress, the Extremists were in the minority despite the fact that they enjoyed the support of the nation's majority. As a result, at the Surat Conference of December 27, 1907, it became evident that the Congress majority was not representing the interests of the Indian people, but those of the degenerate and corrupt pro-British classes. This exposed the Congress as an anti-national and, in particular, anti-Hindu scam, making a mockery of the demands of the suffering Indian people for an urgent solution to the rising imperialist oppression.

In consequence, it was decided to split away from the Moderates and form a separate Nationalist Party led by Lokmanya Tilak. Earlier that year, in his famous speech, "Tenets of the New Party", the Lokmanya had reviewed the disastrous situation of the country under British occupation and criticised the irresponsible policy of Moderate leaders like Gokhale who irrationally clung to petitioning (or "begging") the British Government with no apparent results. "The remedy", Lokmanya reiterated, "is not petitioning but boycott ... What the New Party wants you to do is to realise the fact that your future rests entirely in your own hands. If you mean to be free, you can be free; if you do not mean to be free, you will fall and be forever fallen .... We shall not give them [the British regime] assistance to collect revenue and keep peace.

We shall not assist them in fighting beyond the frontiers or outside India with Indian blood and money. We shall not assist them in carrying on the administration of justice. We shall have our own courts, and when time comes we shall not pay taxes. Can you do that by your united efforts? If you can, you are free from tomorrow". In May 1908, Lokmanya reminded the nation that its aspirations could not be realised "unless a spoke is put somewhere into the wheel of the car of the administration". Thus, it becomes once again evident that although he was prepared to consider advocating violent means when all other methods had failed, Lokmanya (rightly) stood by his view that Liberation could be achieved as soon as the people stopped co-operating with the illegitimate imperialist regime.

A nationwide general strike would have been sufficient to bring the criminal administration down and achieve freedom from foreign occupation, domination and exploitation once and for all. At the same time, in reference to the actions of the more impatient among the revolutionaries (such as the 30 April assassination attempt on Kingsford) he was warning the imperialist Government that it would not be possible to indefinitely "stop or do away with the bomb by means of laws or the supervision of officials or the busy swarming of the detective police", for "The bomb has more of the form of knowledge than a bullet, it is "magic", it is a mantra, an amulet". However, true to its evil character, the imperialist order refused to fulfil the legitimate demands of the people and instead resorted to its usual repressive and inhuman measures against the people and their leaders.

On June 24 1908, Lokmanya Tilak was arrested, brought before the Bombay High Court on July 13, and after a six-day show trial, sentenced to six years of transportation to Mandalay jail in Burma. To ensure the desired verdict, the court had appointed a jury consisting exclusively of Europeans and Parsis. While the two Parsis insisted on acquittal, the Europeans decided on a guilty verdict as expected. It was, therefore, a classic show trial and a travesty of justice in every respect. It was an insult not only to the Indian nation which stood firmly behind its leader, but also to the very "democratic" principles upon which the British Empire was ostensibly built. The Russian Communist leader, Lenin, aptly described the trial as "a reprisal against a democrat by the lackeys of the money-bags [the Capitalist oppressors and exploiters of the Indian people]".

It should be noted that even Lenin regarded the Leader of the Hindu Revolution as a democrat, whereas the degenerate Congress leadership liked to attack him for being an "extremist". As for the evil British regime which the Congress Moderates and Loyalists believed to be a "gift from God" it demonstrated its cowardice and its hatred of the Indian people by turning the whole of Mumbai into a heavily armed military camp and stealthily taking the Lokmanya by special train to Sabarmati Central Jail (Gujarat) from where he was later taken to Rangoon and Mandalay.

Outraged by this heinous crime, between 23 and 28 July the people of Mumbai, Pune, Chennai (Madras) and other cities rose up in protest, staging general strikes, mass demonstrations and battles with the police and the armed forces which the cowardly regime called in to suppress the people's righteous anger. It is right; indeed, necessary to ask at this point, where were India's traditional leaders, the Hindu rajas and maharajas? As the great Hindu nationalist poet and educator Vishnu Krishna Chiplunkar had said in 1881 in his Marathi magazine *Nibandhamala*, "In the last century, terms like Hindu people's rule, Hindu people's wealth, Hindu people's learning, etc., had some meaning. Have they any meaning today?

At present our grand and minor kings are almost like pawns in a game of chess – they cannot move, cannot talk, and are always under the control of the big Sahibs with troops at their side! And now for some time even this has become an eyesore to Government!". Indeed, under British imperialist occupation,

Hindu rulers had been reduced to a mere shadow of their former glory. The Maharaja of Kolhapur, a royal house tracing its origin to Shivaji Maharaj had even been put under medical arrest by the British resident (the British Government's local political agent) on the ground that "medical opinion amounts to his being occasionally insane". Thus, the Hindu kings who were India's legitimate rulers had been deliberately reduced to a condition of almost complete domination and dependence by the British imperialist machinery.

There were of course other able and charismatic Hindu revolutionary leaders like Aurobindo Ghose, Bipin Chandra Pal and Lala Lajpat Rai. Yet Lokmanya Tilak, the "Beloved of the People" and "Lion of Maharashtra" was the undisputed Leader not only of the Hindu revolutionary movement but of the entire nation. Mahatma Gandhi himself, who often referred to the Lokmanya as "Maharaj" conceded that "There is only one person in India over whom millions are crazy, for whom millions of countrymen would lay down their lives. That person is Tilak Maharaj".

1914 – 1920

Despite the hardships and deprivation of Mandalay jail which the cowardly and cruel British had imposed on him, Lokmanya Tilak was able to write his great scholarly commentary on the *Bhagavad Gita*, the *Gita Rahasya* (published in 1915) in which he expounded the philosophy of Karma-Yoga or the Doctrine of Selfless Action which is the path to God-realisation and Liberation. This great treatise has provided spiritual guidance to millions of Hindus ever since, enabling them to return to the pure roots of Hindu religion as a means of regaining their true cultural and spiritual identity and gaining authentic knowledge of how to build a righteous and truly Hindu society that will one day be an example to the world.

Upon his return from Mandalay in June 1914, Lokmanya was met with a hero's reception by thousands of followers who came to see him at his home in Pune and he announced his determination to resume political life immediately. Anti-revolutionary propagandists and second-rate "historians" have maliciously circulated the rumour that the six years of imprisonment had somehow "weakened" Lokmanya's resolve to continue his heroic struggle against foreign occupation. There are two important points that must be considered in answer to this.

Firstly, Lokmanya had more than once proved his readiness to sacrifice his own health and liberty for the sake of the national struggle. Another show trial and spell of incarceration would have done little to advance the revolutionary cause. He had been officially declared "an enemy of the British Government" and put under the strictest surveillance by the cowardly and criminal regime which took the trouble to build one police station on either side of his house and surrounded him with hundreds of informers and spies. In these circumstances, he naturally thought it prudent to use careful language in all his public communications. However, his speeches are incontrovertible proof that his central message remained as revolutionary and incisive as ever till the very end.

Secondly, regarding his co-operation with the Congress, it must be recalled that the Congress was India's officially approved framework for political work. Lokmanya's logical strategy, therefore, was to rebuild his Nationalist Party with the help of Congress and ultimately take control of the latter from within. The problems associated with this strategy are obvious. However, it was the only option available in the political situation of the time. To accuse Lokmanya of unwarranted collaboration with the Congress is as absurd as accusing him of collaboration with the prison in which he had been locked up by his British enemies. In summation, Lokmanya's activities in the last phase of his political life can only be correctly understood on the background of these facts.

Unfortunately, during Lokmanya's six years of absence, the political situation in India had changed for the worse. The absence of its leader and Government repression and harassment had left the Nationalist Party weakened and this in turn had had an adverse effect on the national freedom movement, including the Congress. In addition, there were growing tensions between different religious denominations (notably, between Hindus and Muslims) as well as between different provinces, different castes and different social classes, which the imperialist rulers were using to their own advantage while stepping up repression and exploitation at the same time.

In other words, there was a growing fragmentation and Balkanisation of Indian politics which represented a serious impediment to the national struggle of liberation. Lokmanya's return to political life proved providential. His sharp analytical mind enabled him to identify the new dangers and bring the revolutionary process back on course by stressing the need for (1) resistance to foreign rule, (2) national unity and (3) the creation of a righteous society free from discrimination, oppression and injustice.

At Lokmanya's request, the Congress Party at the 1915 Mumbai Session amended its constitution to allow the election of delegates to the Congress from any public body irrespective of whether it was registered or not. In the following year Lokmanya persuaded his Nationalist Party colleagues to join the Congress. He also established the Indian Home Rule League and joined forces with Annie Besant's All-India League. This lead to the adoption of the goal of Home Rule for India by the Congress. In his characteristic manner, Lokmanya ridiculed the Government's claim that Indians needed to be taught how to rule themselves: "How long will you teach us? We ask. For one generation, two generations, or three generations! Is there any end to this? Set some limit".

Furthermore, he pointed out that "We in India are not children to be promoted from standard to standard until we pass our graduation either in Arts or in Law. We are full-grown people.

We have had experience of governing Empires and Kingdoms in the past .... Add to it that we have received Western education which lays down certain principles of Government. We have learned those principles and how to use those principles, having watched them so far in civilised countries. Are we not capable of carrying on the Government of India from tomorrow if the Government is given into our hands?"

The death of Lokmanya's adversary and Congress leader Gokhale in 1915; his legal victory over the imperialist regime (which in 1916 had dragged him before the courts on sedition charges for the third time); and his election as President of the Delhi Congress in 1918, enhanced his authority and prestige among the people and demonstrated his growing political power. There could be no doubt that under Lokmanya's able leadership, the National Movement was back on course again. However, serious difficulties still remained. In his 1906 speech at the Varanasi Bharata Dharma Mahamandala, Lokmanya had identified Christianity and Science as the main forces threatening Hindu culture and civilisation.

Christianity aimed to convert India to an alien and fraudulent cult, while Science destroyed traditional ways of life and promoted materialism and unbelief. At the same time, Western science refuted key Christian teachings, while confirming Hindu doctrines such as Karma and the all-pervasiveness of Consciousness (Chaitanya). Indeed, since then, Western scientific research (notably the work of Professor Ian Stevenson) has also confirmed the Hindu doctrine of Reincarnation. Lokmanya pointed out the fact that Science forced Westerners to accept the teachings of Vedanta and Yoga.

Science, therefore, was a two-edged sword that Hindus had to learn how to wield correctly to defeat the enemy and further their own cause. In economic terms, Lokmanya identified Western Imperialism as a conspiracy to take over India's traditional occupations of the military and merchant classes

(*Kshatriyas* and *Vaishyas*) in order to dominate and exploit the Indian people. For, while the Four Castes (*Varnas*) of traditional Hindu society worked together for the harmonious and efficient functioning of society for the benefit of all, in Western society each class, in particular, the ruling classes, were out to further their own interests at the expense of the others.

It must be noted that the social reformer Bhimrao Ramji (Babasaheb) Ambedkar (1891-1956) himself admitted that the "prevalence of abject poverty should be a sufficient convincing reason for you to opt for Swaraj. It is a deliberate policy with the British Government to secure benefits for themselves at the cost of the Indian .... The Britishers have stakes in keeping India under-developed and, thus, securing a ready market". Indeed, the East India Company which controlled much of India's economy until 1858 was a commercial organisation (founded in 1600 by influential London merchants, including Mayor Stephen Soame).

As its power and influence grew, the Company established for itself a standing army for which it paid enormous sums to maintain. Thus the architect of India's (and Asia's) enslavement by the West was Britain's predatory merchant class (consisting mainly of Englishmen) which had become the dominant element in British society and used the military (of which it was the employer) to enslave and exploit the other classes, in particular, the peasantry and industrial workers. Just as this dominant merchant class had enslaved the Scottish, Irish and Welsh nationalities in Britain, it was now enslaving the Indians, the Chinese and other Eastern nations.

Even after the dissolution of the Company and take-over by the Crown, India continued to be ruled by the same merchant class – the capitalist "money-bags" behind the repressive bureaucracy which, as remarked by Lenin, had sent Lokmanya to jail in 1908. The same European merchant class was behind the London-based League of Nations (precursor of the United

Nations), established in January 1920, of which Lokmanya observed that it was a "political institution started by the powerful countries to enable themselves to keep under their rule the countries which they (already) hold". Thus, although the League ostensibly intended to "guarantee political independence and territorial integrity to great and small States alike", Lokmanya identified it as a "club of dacoits" and "White man's club".

He also correctly diagnosed Western expansionism as a threat to the whole of Asia: "The Asian people are threatened by one common danger. The political activities, as are taking shape in this Eastern sphere, indicate the possibility of their being totally conquered on the lines of America and Africa, by the European-Christian nations". Indeed, other Eastern nations such as China, in particular, were similarly suffering under Western imperialist domination and exploitation and there was growing resentment of European-Christian rule as demonstrated by China's Boxer Revolution of 1900.

Nor was the danger emanating from the West exclusively Christian. According to Jewish sources, "Jews played a prominent part wherever the European East India Companies established factories and trading posts ... many became extremely wealthy .... British Jews rose to high rank and distinction in the civil administration of India, especially Sir Robert Nathan ... [and] ... Rufus Daniel Is*a*cs, Marquis of Reading, viceroy and governor-general of India from 1921 to 1926". It is well known that Nathan, who was appointed Private Secretary to Lord Curzon in 1905 and Police Commissioner of Dhaka in 1908, was responsible for the suppression of Indian revolutionary groups, while Viceroy Is*a*cs ordered the imprisonment of Mahatma Gandhi in 1922.

In addition to Jewish-Christian Capitalism, another Western danger was Marxism which, according to its London-based inventor Karl Marx, aimed to start Communist revolutions in

India and China and establish a worldwide "dictatorship of the proletariat" (following the Russian Communist Revolution of 1917, Communist parties were formed simultaneously in India and China in 1920-1921 for this purpose). However, even more dangerous than Capitalism and Marxism was Fabianism. Like Capitalism and Marxism, Fabianism aimed to establish cultural, economic and political supremacy of the West over the rest of the world.

What was different about the Fabian approach was its doctrine of Socialist Gradualism, a particularly obnoxious and subversive form of Western Imperialism which under the banner of "social and economic progress" aimed to destroy non-Western culture and civilisation so gradually that the changes would either go unnoticed or appear as desirable "progressive" developments. The London-based Fabian Society was founded in 1884 as an offshoot of utopian philosopher Thomas Davidson's Fellowship of the New Life. Through its London School of Economics (founded in 1895) and other institutions, the Fabian Society was able to infiltrate government agencies, political parties and educational institutions in India and elsewhere.

Among its more prominent members were Annie Besant, Motilal and Jawaharlal Nehru and Mohammad Ali Jinnah. Jinnah's notorious partition of India and creation of Islamic Pakistan and the Socialist dictatorship established in India by the Nehru-Gandhi clan provide a sample of the unsavoury characters spawned by the neo-Imperialism of the Fabian Society. It must be recalled that not long ago even Colonialism and Imperialism were openly constructed as "progressive" and necessary to civilise the "uncivilised" and "backward" Hindoos, Negroes and Redskins. In the light of these facts it becomes apparent that all so-called "progressive" trends emanating from the West were in reality nothing but different forms of Western Imperialism and Racism under different guises.

The precedent for these trends had of course been set by Islam as evidenced by Mahmud of Ghazni's declaration that "since India's inhabitants were "unbelievers" and "idolaters" it was right by the command of God and of the Prophet to conquer them" and, before that, by Christianity and Judaism. In the final analysis, therefore, we are dealing with the same pathological drive for world domination that has emanated from the Western (Abrahamic) world for over two millennia.

The difficulty was that in his quest for national unity as a means of driving out the British imperialists, Lokmanya could ill afford to antagonise the Muslim minority (who could have sided with the British against the Hindus). Thus, for the sake of creating a united national front against the imperialist regime, Lokmanya even went so far as to agree to the 1916 Lucknow Pact between the Congress and the Muslim League granting the Muslims' demand for separate electorates in the elections to the Central and Provincial legislatures.

Although the wisdom of separate electorates has been much debated, the concept was based on the expectation that Muslims would join the Hindus in the national struggle of liberation and that the British would grant "responsible government" to the Indians after the First World War. As neither expectation was fulfilled, support for separate electorates could have been withdrawn. Even on the assumption that Lokmanya's co-operation with the Muslim League had somehow weakened the Hindu position vis-à-vis the Muslims, it must be understood that this would only have been a passing phase which was in agreement not only with logic but also with traditional Hindu strategic theory according to which a state of temporary parity and even decline in relation to the adversary is acceptable or desirable if it serves the long-term purpose of achieving progress.

At any rate, Lokmanya's position at the time was absolutely clear from an article in the *Kesari* he wrote after the Pact: "The Hindus and the Muslims have forgotten their differences. We have no hesitation in issuing a warning to the bureaucracy that its days are numbered now that the united voice of India has given it the final notice to quit".

As to the British role in this matter, it has been claimed that the British did not originally intend to divide Indians along Muslim-Hindu lines. However, the fact is that the British imperialists were mostly Christians and it had been Christian imperialist policy from the very inception of Colonialism to convert India's Hindu majority to Christianity. Hindu temples (but not mosques) were singled out for desecration and conversion into churches by Portuguese and French colonialists. It is on record that Lord Olivier, Secretary of State for India 1924, openly admitted in a letter to the London *Times* that: "No one with a close acquaintance with Indian affairs will be prepared to deny that on the whole there is a predominant bias in British officialism in favour of the Moslem community, partly on the ground of closer sympathy but more largely as a make-weight against Hindu nationalism". Thus there was an undeniable degree of Abrahamic solidarity between Christian European colonialists and Indian Muslims on religious grounds.

In addition, collaboration with the Muslims was a vital strategic policy in Britain's "Great Game", the British-Russian race for supremacy in the region. That some of India's Muslim radicals did not wish to be part of an independent Hindu India and opposed the national freedom struggle was a separate issue which – although the British were quick to exploit – was subordinate to the British Empire's regional and global strategic policy of collaboration with Muslim populations against third parties. Middle Eastern Oil interests, for example, caused the British to initially oppose Jewish settlements in Palestine prior to the 1917 Balfour Declaration so as not to antagonise the Muslim Arabs. What becomes indisputable is that British-Muslim collaboration was motivated by three important factors:

- Religious solidarity (or "sympathy") between fellow-Abrahamic traditions.
- Defence of strategic geo-political interests.
- The need of a political ally against India's Hindu majority.

Christian-Capitalist collaboration with Islamic regimes like Pakistan continued without interruption even after Independence and remains a key factor in British and American global strategy to the present day. In any case, Muslim-Hindu division formed an integral part of the British agenda by 1905 and needed no encouragement from Lokmanya Tilak. Nor could he do anything about the fact that Muslims after 1930 (when Muslim League president Mohammad Iqbal proposed a Muslim India) began to agitate for a separate Islamic state. This was an expression of the fact that Indian Muslims had never given up their imperialist ambitions or their dreams of restoring Muslim supremacy on the Subcontinent. Their own fantasies of past Islamic glory had rendered them psychologically incapable of accepting Hindu political primacy in India and acknowledging their true status as an alien minority.

Another source of division that was a serious impediment to the Hindu revolutionary cause was differences related to Caste issues. It is essential to understand that Lokmanya firmly believed in a just society based on the Hindu principle of Righteousness or Dharma. He strongly condemned all forms of oppression and injustice and opposed caste-restriction, caste-discrimination and untouchability. With regard to Caste-restriction he observed that "It would be advisable to allow such persons as would wish to change their hereditary occupations, to do so" (*Samagra Tilak*, Vol. p. 117, in *Lokmanya Tilak*, p. 178) and "It is here that Caste starts getting determined not by birth but by merit and deed (*guna-karma*). And, it should really get determined like that".

His position on Caste-discrimination was equally unequivocal: "Every sensible person will have to accept that caste-discrimination in the past and, especially more so in the present, has led to a feeling of hatred among the different castes, ultimately affecting adversely, the sense of unity among the people". Needless to say, Lokmanya was even more strongly opposed to Untouchability: "The Dharma Shastras of the Hindus do not support the notion of treating any class of human beings as untouchables .... Whatever may be the genesis of Untouchability, the sinful nature of the notion is beyond dispute. Untouchability must go".

At the same time, however, Lokmanya acknowledged the indisputable fact that the Caste System (*Varna Dharma*) had essential positive elements and could play a useful role in society once the negative aspects that had come to be associated with it under foreign rule were removed. Indeed, if we consider the matter carefully, it will become clear that the existence of and harmonious interaction between occupational classes like priests, armed forces, merchants, farmers and labourers constitute essential elements in the structure of a stable and sound society. By contrast, Western societies where there was a dictatorship of the merchant class over other classes were structurally unstable and plagued by repressive regimes.

Even such societies where "Democracy" had been established at home, could only survive by imposing domination, oppression and exploitation on other nations abroad – as demonstrated by the British Empire itself. Those who advocated the import of Western systems into India failed to take note of the fact that the life of luxury led by the unproductive sections of Western societies was based entirely on the suffering of other classes and other nations. Even today, when the more obvious and politically incorrect (or inconvenient) forms of Colonialism and Imperialism have been abolished, the "developed" societies of England, Russia and USA, which anti-casteists wish to imitate and reproduce in India, are far from being harmonious and egalitarian.

Not all members of these societies lead an easy life as left-wing journalists or politicians. Construction work, harvesting of crops, sweeping the streets, waste collection and hundreds of similar forms of "menial" labour are still carried out as always, only not by the native population, but by foreign migrants who are often treated in a similar way as India's own depressed classes. This clearly indicates a widespread underlying psychological bias against a certain type of work and those associated with it. If we now take into consideration that even in Islamic societies, which under European and American influence have embraced Capitalism (such as Saudi Arabia, etc.), foreign migrants are often treated similarly, it becomes evident that oppression and exploitation of, and discrimination against, low-paid workers by higher-earning ones, is nearly universal and has nothing to do with caste.

Furthermore, the import of cheap labour upon which these "developed" societies depend for the maintenance of their standard of living is perpetuated by keeping other nations sufficiently poor for their citizens to feel moved to emigrate and provide cheap labour to the "developed" societies. In India, even the limited reproduction of Western systems such as Capitalism introduced late in the 20th century has created a higher standard of living for certain sections of society only through the (largely illegal) import of cheap labour from poorer nations like Pakistan, Bangladesh and Nepal. As the import of cheap labour into India is mainly from neighbouring Islamic states, it becomes obvious that in India's case the imitation of Western practices is counter-productive and self-destructive, indeed, suicidal.

Two facts become apparent from the above: (1) Western systems are unstable constructs based on exploitation of other nations and (2) social discrimination is not a product of the Caste System but of degenerate and corrupt human nature. In consequence, discrimination cannot be removed by abolishing castes but through social and moral education. As Lokmanya put it in his address to the 1918 All-India Depressed Classes Conference in Mumbai, "Untouchability is a matter of social usage and the social usage should change". Even then there is no guarantee that discrimination will be removed completely.

In the final analysis, therefore, a social system like that of Ancient India is the most likely to produce a harmonious, stable and just society if correctly implemented.

Furthermore, it is essential to understand that what differentiated leading Eastern nations (India, China, Japan) from those of the West (Portugal, Spain, The Netherlands, France and Britain) was the historical absence in the former of Capitalism and its external manifestations, Colonialism and Imperialism. This was due to the fact that in the East, the merchant class had retained a subordinate position vis-à-vis the traditional ruling classes, the military and the priesthood.

This prevented the merchant classes of the East from following in the footsteps of their European counterpart which had practically monopolised political power and established a dictatorship over all other classes. There is no doubt that at least in India, the Hindu Caste System or, more correctly, Caste Duty (Varna Dharma) has played an important role in the prevention of Capitalism. In rejecting the traditional Indian caste-based structure, the anti-Brahmin Movement limited itself to two alternative options: (1) Capitalism or the dictatorship of the merchant class and (2) Socialism or the dictatorship of the administrative bureaucracy.

In either case, the "rule of the people" was condemned to remain an utopian fantasy from the outset. In particular, if it is considered that Capitalist America and Britain had fast-disappearing farming communities while Socialist Russia (and later, China) had poor and starving farming communities (Stalin's agrarian policies claimed 25-50 million lives and Mao Zedong's 60-80 million), the inescapable conclusion is that an improved Caste System (with all inequality and discrimination removed) would have benefited India's rural masses far more than any other alternative. In Lokmanya's living years, Socialism or Marxism had never been practically applied anywhere. Russia's Communist Revolution had only taken place in 1917.

After the Revolution, Russia's land reforms and other Socialist innovations pushed the economy to the verge of collapse, industrial and agricultural production fell to an unprecedented low and the leaders were squabbling over what to do. A panic-stricken Lenin was forced to reintroduce private agriculture and other Capitalist measures to keep the economy going until Stalin put an end to it in 1929 and introduced mass murder as a method of governance.

Those who suffered most were the farmers. It is important to understand in this context that under Russian Stalinist (and, subsequently, Chinese Maoist) rule, farmers were not sacrificed to the demon of Socialism by accident, but knowingly and deliberately. As the ruling Socialist clique wanted to keep up with the dominant Capitalist powers, it embarked on a gigantic industrialisation programme. The question was who was to pay for it? The Socialist State had no money; the bourgeoisie or capitalist merchant class had been liquidated; the industrial workers could not be expected to bear the burden as they were the class which Socialism had promised to raise to the status of ruling class; hence it was consciously decided by leading Socialist "economists" that the farmers (the majority of the population) were to bear the brunt of Socialist "modernisation".

With the coming to power of Stalin in 1929, this criminal anti-farmer decision was ruthlessly implemented. Millions of Russia's big and middle farmers were executed, imprisoned or exiled and their property was confiscated by the State. The remaining small farmers, the peasants and rural labourers, were forced to work not only on their own small plots of land to sustain them, but also on unprofitable State-owned co-operatives. In addition, they were so heavily taxed that they were left with nothing to eat. This of course was in keeping with Karl Marx's ideas for, as he wrote in his *Manifesto of the Communist Party*, "... the following will be pretty generally applicable: 1. Abolition of property in land and application of all rents of land to public purposes. 2. A heavy progressive or graduated income tax ..." etc.

Russia's poor peasants and labourers, some of whom had supported the Revolution, could not have known what Socialism meant in practice (no one knew, as Socialism had never before been applied anywhere in the world). India's own peasants and depressed classes knew even less than the Russians what Western-style innovations would mean in practice. But their leaders should have known better as they were educated men. On the whole, it must be admitted that they behaved in an irresponsible and anti-national way by advocating the introduction of reforms the practical application and results of which they were ignorant of.

At any rate, it is evident that Socialism was a particularly risky enterprise which would have been worse even than British Imperialism. It was only through Hindu opposition that India's Socialist dictatorship introduced by the Nehru-Gandhi clique was eventually swept away. In the light of these facts, the special merit of Lokmanya Tilak was to reject Western innovations and recognise that traditional Hindu society was based on the concept of *Dharma* or Duty according to which the individual had a duty towards society and society had a duty towards the individual.

Thus Duty or Obligation was the binding force that held society together: "Therefore, when this Dharma ceases to be observed, the binding ropes of society may be said to have become loose, and when these binding ropes are loosened, society will be in the same position as the planetary system consisting of the Sun and the planets would be in the sky without the binding force of gravitation or as a ship would be on the ocean without a rudder". Indeed, without a sense of Social Obligation and Social Morality, society would disintegrate. Therefore, unlike Western Liberal society which gives priority to "rights", Hindu society emphasises duties or obligations the universal discharge of which automatically ensures that all citizens' rights are respected and enforced for the benefit of all.

Lokmanya also understood that Western concepts such as "social reform", "progress", "class consciousness" and "class struggle" were used for subversive purposes by anti-national interests aiming to divide and rule India as before. As he pointed out, "It was because of the dissentions among the different Castes that the British entrenched themselves here, and if these were to continue, we would remain equally backward even under *Swaraj*". The implication was that it was not Caste which was the problem but caste-related tensions, which the anti-casteists (the Christian Capitalists, the Fabian Socialists and the Marxists) sought to exploit for their own agenda.

Indeed, "class consciousness" and "class struggle" were the terms in which Socialism sought to interpret (or distort) history for its own agenda: "The history of all hitherto existing society is the history of class struggles" claimed Marx in his *Manifesto*. But if class antagonism was the problem, why make it worse by encouraging "class consciousness" and "class struggle"? Why not encourage class unity, class harmony and class co-operation? Evidently, the motive was to divide and rule society. The true intention of Socialist fraudsters, indeed criminals, like Marx was to deepen the social divisions that had developed under Capitalism in order to play off one class against another and seize political power.

For, a dictatorship of the proletariat over other classes meant, above all, the dictatorship of the criminal clique which had appointed itself leader of the proletariat. Thus, from a Hindu revolutionary perspective, replacing discrimination against untouchables with discrimination against priests and military persons, for example, was both irrational and counter-productive. It could only lead to the disintegration of Indian society and its enslavement by anti-Indian powers. The creation of separate electorates and separate political identities for different social classes would likewise have the same disastrous result.

Finally, in Hindu revolutionary terms, the important thing was to create an anti-imperialist outlook in the masses in order to speed up the process of national unification and liberation. National unity was paramount in achieving political independence. Once this was achieved, all social and economic issues would be resolved in accordance with the Hindu principle of Righteousness or Dharma. Anti-Brahmin agitation was not only unjustified, but it was positively counter-productive in that (1) it took the pressure off the foreign imperialists who were the real enemies, (2) it created national division and (3) it slowed down the process of national liberation.

As conceded by leaders of the non-Brahmin Movement like Keshavrao Jedhe, their main concern was to obtain concessions from the imperialist order: "The non-Brahmin Movement totally neglected the issue of generating the spirit of nationalism. It worked only for acquiring favour of the (foreign) government ...: The attitude of the leaders of the movement was not national". The critical analysis of the various currents in India's political process demonstrates that Lokmanya's anti-imperialist strategy put the interests of the nation first. It therefore provided a logical basis for national unity.

In contrast, the reformists inspired by Western ideologies like Christian Capitalism, Marxism and Fabianism sought to change the character and direction of the national movement from anti-imperialist to anti-Brahmin and anti-Hindu. Such misguided elements were in effect making peace with Western Imperialism while attacking their own compatriots and undermining the national cause. Equally significant is that many advocates of Socialistic innovations (like Nehru) were connected with the British Fabian Socialists. This suggests that there was a wider Western-inspired conspiracy at work.

Being aware of the divisive and anti-national character of Western-inspired reformist trends, Lokmanya demonstrated his unique leadership qualities by urging all Indians to put their differences aside and join forces in the common cause of national liberation. The First World War (1914-1918), in particular, was identified by Lokmanya as a unique opportunity for India to force the imperialist order to grant her the Independence or Self-rule (Swaraj) her people were fighting for.

Indeed, Lokmanya saw the War as an opportunity for all subjugated nations of Asia to rise against their Western oppressors. Time and again, Lokmanya reminded the nation of the need to avoid behaving "like a frog in a well", that is in a selfish and sectarianist way and strive to acquire a wider and more comprehensive perspective of the situation. Only such a perspective, which rose above narrow individual or class considerations, would enable the nation to march united towards a common goal which was the defeat of the imperialist enemy and the building of a free and just society for all. That Lokmanya's ultimate goal was such a society is evident not only from his speeches and writings, in particular the *Gita Rahasya*, but also from the *Manifesto of the Congress Democratic Party* which he published on April 18, 1920.

LOKMANYA VS. GANDHI

The main political opponent of the Hindu revolutionary movement, in general, and of Lokmanya Tilak, in particular, had been the Moderate leader of the Congress, Gopal Krishna Gokhale. Following the latter's death in 1915, Lokmanya naturally assumed his rightful role of national leader. However, another source of opposition was soon to arise in the person of Mahatma Gandhi (1869-1948), who was Gokhale's disciple and political reincarnation. Some of Gandhi's main merits were: (1) his emphasis on the importance of Hindu religion in politics, (2) his insistence on boycott of foreign goods, including foreign dress (he even inspired Nehru to take to wearing traditional Indian dress) and (3) the mobilisation of the rural masses which had been started by Lokmanya. All these were positive initiatives.

Unfortunately, Gandhi failed to grasp the need of subordinating personal and sectarian interests to the common cause of the national movement. He failed to understand that although Gokhale was his political guru, Lokmanya was the National Leader and that, therefore, his allegiance to Gokhale had to be subordinated to his allegiance to Lokmanya. Following in the footsteps of Gokhale, Gandhi committed many errors resulting in serious consequences for the national cause. His main error was to oppose Lokmanya's revolutionary views which he openly criticised. He also sought to establish his own political base and disrupted the unity of the national movement of liberation.

As a result, the movement became embroiled in factional struggles which prevented Lokmanya from concentrating all his energy on his revolutionary work in the last years of his life, and set the trend for the development of divisive and counter-revolutionary trends that were to dangerously weaken the Hindu cause long after Independence had been won. Mohandas Karamchand Gandhi was a newcomer to Indian politics, having spent a period of time in South Africa until 1914, and distinguished himself by developing a novel approach to the freedom struggle.

His notorious insistence on a policy of "truth and non-violence" as a means of furthering the national cause set him on a course which conflicted with that of Lokmanya in many important respects. This was particularly deplorable as Lokmanya and his Extremist wing were the vanguard not only of the Hindu revolutionary movement but also of the national freedom struggle. Whatever else may be said of Gandhi, the fact is that his opposition to Lokmanya had the unfortunate effect of derailing the clear trajectory which the movement's vanguard had taken and of giving birth to a trend in Indian politics that has not always worked to India's advantage.

Lokmanya was a pragmatic revolutionary leader. In the same way as he accepted the ancient Vedic precept that there was "one truth but the wise called it by many names" (Ekam Sat, Viprah Bahudha Vadanti), he believed in unity of purpose but plurality of means (sadhananam anekata). On his part, while acknowledging Lokmanya's superior scholarly knowledge as well as political experience and authority, Gandhi attacked his revolutionary views. Already in 1908, Gandhi declared: "What we need to consider is whether Indians should accept the views of Mr Tilak and his party. We submit, after great deliberation, that Mr Tilak's views should be rejected".

To understand the motives behind Gandhi's ideological opposition to Lokmanya, it is necessary to understand his psychology. We have seen that Lokmanya had enjoyed a solid traditional Hindu education which provided him with unshakable faith in Hindu religion, philosophy and way of life. The truths taught by Lokmanya were the truths of Hindu Scripture as understood and accepted by most Hindus. In contrast, Gandhi confessed that "With much striving I have formulated some principles for my life and put them into practice. The happiness I have found that way, I think, I have not seen in others".

The implications arising from this are (1) that these principles were Gandhi's own creation or "formulation" and (2) that the practical value of these principles was judged by their ability to give peace of mind or "happiness" to their creator. It was apparently irrelevant whether or not such principles were accepted by, and brought happiness to, the people. By contrast, Lokmanya saw no need of formulating any new principles. On the contrary, his method was to go back to the truth already laid down in Hindu Scripture and his position was that any new ideas had to be integrated with established tradition. Nor did he judge the value of his actions by the happiness they brought to himself. His sole aim was the happiness of the nation. And this could only be achieved by adherence to the eternal truths of Hindu Dharma.

One of the more exotic theories developed by Gandhi was that "Freedom gained through violence would not endure …. As for the masses, they would merely pass from one form of slavery to another". It must be noted that this was Gandhi's personal opinion which had no basis in historical fact and, moreover, was contradicted by Gandhi's own actions: Shivaji's war of liberation from Islamic Imperialism had not resulted in a "new form of slavery" and Gandhi himself had advocated the use of violence by the British against the South African Boers. In addition, after Independence, India was enslaved not by Lokmanya's Hindu Extremists but by the pacifist Congress Moderates who embraced the Fabian Socialist dictatorship of Nehru and Indira Gandhi.

Gandhi further claimed that "My purpose in life is to demonstrate that the strongest physical force bends before moral force when it is used in defence of truth" (*Young India*, Aug 9, 1919). If this was the purpose of Gandhi's life, then once again, he was proved wrong. For, the bullets that took his life in January 1948 were one physical force which did not bend before Gandhi's moral force. And, if Gandhi's moral force could not protect his own life, it is difficult to see how the moral force of the less spiritually-accomplished masses could have protected theirs. The logical and revolutionary implication was that, in the real world, the barrel of the gun still possessed a power that not even the Mahatma could afford to ignore.

It must be noted that, in principle, Lokmanya, too, believed in non-violence. He also accepted that Adherence to Truth (Satyagraha) was the remedy for all ills India was suffering from (as stated by Gandhi). However, he also recognised that, in certain circumstances, strict adherence to non-violence was counter-productive and that in such cases violence was not only acceptable, but a moral and religious duty as laid down in Hindu Scripture. To deny this fact was to raise one's personal opinion above Scripture and above God – which was unacceptable.

It is indisputable that Lokmanya was firmly established in the authentic Hindu tradition which he had absorbed as a child from his learned father and grandfather and studied as an adult. He exhibited an authenticity of beliefs that only traditional upbringing can provide. By contrast, despite his ascetic appearance and ostensible adherence to "Truth", Gandhi was less in touch with authentic Hindu tradition. He was less logical than Lokmanya and was full of contradictions. He was an English-educated man who only later in life re-discovered Hinduism which he sought to reconstruct according to his own psychological needs with the help of Buddhism, Christianity, Tolstoyism and other innovative trends. Thus his philosophy was artificial and eclectic.

As he himself conceded, Gandhi could not compete with Lokmanya in matters of religion and philosophy. As becomes apparent, he could not compete with the latter in matters of logic, either. Although he insisted on interpreting *Satyagraha* (Adherence to Truth) as "Truth and non-Violence", there was no logical correlation between the two: non-Violence does not logically follow from Truth, nor is Truth necessarily to be found in non-Violence. A pacifist person is not always motivated by Truth. He may be motivated by fear, selfishness, self-interest, self-conceit and many other ignoble sentiments. He may even be motivated by a false feeling of superiority and self-satisfaction derived from his adherence to pacifism. All of which has nothing to do with Truth.

Gandhi also erroneously believed that for Lokmanya, "everything is fair in politics". This charge was not only unfair, but was based on a fundamental misunderstanding of Lokmanya's political philosophy which can only be correctly understood on the background of established Hindu tradition, in particular, the tradition of Advaita Vedanta of which Lokmanya was a faithful follower. As explained by Shri Adi Shankara, Advaita Vedanta draws a clear distinction between

Absolute Truth (Paramartha-Satya) and Conventional Truth (Vyavahara-Satya), Conventional Truth being relative and therefore subordinate to Absolute Truth. For Lokmanya, Adherence to Truth (Satyagraha) meant specifically Adherence to Absolute Truth.

Like all things in the sphere of Maya, Conventional Truth could be manipulated in the higher cause of Absolute Truth. In political terms, the Highest Truth was that Independence was India's divine birthright and that the goal was to attain Liberation from foreign rule. To attain this Higher Truth it was legitimate to manipulate Conventional Truth if and as necessary, according to circumstances. Quoting the *Mahabharata*, Lokmanya wrote: "Religion and Morality consist in behaving towards others in the same way as they behave towards us; one must behave deceitfully towards deceitful persons and in a saintly way towards saintly persons".

Thus, in a Hindu revolutionary context, the use of deception to overcome a political adversary was not a violation of Absolute Truth but a violation of the Untruth represented by the enemy of the people, that is, the British imperialist order who as per Gandhi's own admission, was "satanic". Nor was Lokmanya telling any untruth in his dealings with his political opponents. He had always stated very clearly that his ultimate goal was Independence and that every compromise was only temporary and tactical according to his well-known motto, "Accept what you get, but exert yourselves to get more". Even on the assumption that Lokmanya had ever consciously spoken an untruth, it is indisputable that an untruth spoken in the cause of Truth is a truth.

While Gandhi unreasonably believed that "non-Violence was the highest religion" ("ahimsa paramo dharma"), Lokmanya understood that the highest religion was absolute adherence to Duty which man was obliged to carry out according to the example given by God Himself in Scripture. The proper performance of one's duty was the high road to Spiritual Salvation and Political Liberation (Mukti). This involved fighting for the defence of oneself and one's country as taught in the *Gita* and other Shastras: "Parameshvara [the Supreme Lord], than Whom nobody's Reason can be more equable, Himself takes incarnations from time to time for protecting saints and destroying evil-doers, and thereby brings about universal welfare (lokasamgraha); then how can the case of ordinary persons be different?"

For Lokmanya, adherence to Scriptural Teaching was true Adherence to Truth. Adherence to Truth (Satyagraha) could only be of value if the Truth was correctly assessed and verified against the teachings of Scripture and practical experience. Otherwise, Adherence to Truth could easily become Adherence to Untruth (Asatyagraha). It should be noted in this connection that Gandhi's views on non-Violence (Ahimsa) had been inspired by the teachings of Count Tolstoy and Jainism, rather than mainstream Hinduism. It is significant that at the 1893 Parliament of Religions in Chicago, Gandhi chose to represent Jainism.

At any rate, his views on this subject were clearly not shared by the broad masses and found many opponents even among the Moderate Congress leadership. In particular, his neurotic fixation with his own interpretation of truth caused him to behave more and more like an obstinate child. In 1940, exasperated by Gandhi's behaviour, the Muslim President of the Congress, Maulana Abul Kalam Azad, reminded him in very clear terms that the purpose of the Congress was not to promote pacifism but to achieve India's Independence.

Regarding the question of whether Gandhi can be regarded as a "Saviour of the Nation" in any concrete sense, the critical analysis of the facts indicates that, as Lokmanya had often pointed out, imperialist powers like Britain never granted concessions to subject-nations of their own free will, but only when forced to do so. From America to Ireland and Palestine, the British did not quit their colonial possessions except for fear of violence. In consequence, there is no reason to believe that India was any different. Indeed, had Gandhi's Adherence to Truth, Pacifism and "Fasting to the Death" been the only anti-imperialist trend on the Subcontinent, one might be justified in believing that this was the cause for Britain's withdrawal.

However, in view of the well-known activities of less-pacifistic movements, it becomes clear that it was these and not Gandhi's pacifism that forced the British to quit. Thus, in the final analysis, it was Lokmanya's strategy which proved correct and not Gandhi's. It is difficult to gauge the exact type of government Gandhi had envisaged for India, although his insistence on decentralising political power and according more independence to villages has been interpreted as indicative of a form of "Philosophical Anarchism" that left little room for a strong State. By contrast, Lokmanya's model of government was characteristically pragmatic, coherent and clear.

It is evident from his speeches and writings, in particular, from his 1920 *Manifesto of the Congress Democratic Party*, that he opposed Gandhi's Russian-inspired utopian-anarchistic tendencies. Like Gandhi, Lokmanya also favoured a high degree of independence for villages which were to be governed by strong *panchayats* (councils) with judicial powers. This was only natural, as this had been established practice in Hindu India since ancient times. However, in Lokmanya's scheme the State had an important role to play, in particular, in matters of maintenance of law and order, economic development, tariff protection, taxation, investment, education, social welfare and medical care.

This, too, was in keeping with traditional Hindu political practice where the duty, indeed the very *raison d'etre* or purpose, of the State was to ensure the protection and welfare of the people: "God created the King [or institution of Kingship] for the protection of the whole world" (*Manu Smrti* 7.3). Indeed, the state under the traditional Hindu Monarchy system ensured that law, order and justice prevailed in society for the benefit of all and in accordance with the universal principle of Dharma (Righteousness) and its correlative Lokasamgraha (Universal Welfare) as enshrined in Scripture.

Thus, Lokmanya's revolutionary ideal was a balanced and harmonious collaboration of State (Raja) and People (Praja) in the Hindu tradition: (1) Governance had to be conducted according to the wishes of the people; (2) the wishes of the people had to be harmonious with the principle of Righteousness (Dharma) as enshrined in Hindu Scripture; (3) Government was necessary to enforce points (1) and (2). No doubt, Lokmanya was referring to Russian-inspired anarchistic and nihilistic trends in vogue at the time, when he observed that "The case of anarchical nations is different. These nations can never rise .... There must be a king, there must be state administration. Both these propositions are true from a historical point of view. Of a country where there is no order, where there is no king, that is where there is no supervising body, the *Mahabharata* says: A wise man should not live even for a moment at that place .... There must be a government .... There must be some control or other. Control cannot be exercised always by all people assembling together at one place. Hence, sovereign authority is always divided into two parts: one the Advisory body and, the other, Executive body" (Swarajya, speech delivered at Belgaum, May 1, 1916). It follows that in Lokmanya's political philosophy there was absolutely no question of abolishing the State.

So, what kind of State did he have in mind? It is true that officially Lokmanya advocated a constitutional, parliamentary democracy with a federal structure of the type of that of Britain, Canada and Australia, and that this may appear to be inconsistent with the old system of Hindu tradition. However, the British system was a Monarchy just like the traditional Hindu one. In addition, Ancient Hindu Monarchy was constitutional to the extent that it operated according to established laws. Nor can we lose sight of the fact that in 1920 the situational constraints under which Lokmanya was forced to operate, left him with hardly any other option.

The Congress Democratic Party had been formed for the purpose of contesting the elections to the legislatures under the reformed Act. Apart from that, its goal was to acquire political power. Campaigning for a Western-style parliamentary democracy would have ensured the support of the majority of Indians, including the English-educated Congress Moderates. Above all, it would have ensured the approval of the British regime itself which in the long run could hardly have objected to Indians being ruled according to British-style, parliamentary democracy. At the same time, quoting Herbert Spencer, Lokmanya condemned Britain's Parliament as a "Commissariat sanctioning the financial demands of the Imperialist Army". Indeed, it must be recalled that the British Parliament (originally the King's Council) was an institution created by the capitalist merchant class as an instrument for the domination of other classes.

It was the British Parliament that had approved Britain's imperialist policies which reduced India to a condition of domination, dependence and abject poverty. Thus, advocating parliamentary democracy as a political goal was a means of obtaining liberation from British rule. It did not necessarily mean that Western-style parliamentary democracy had to be the model for Indian governments after Independence. After all, the Muslims had campaigned for Western-style democracy only to demand an Islamic State at the first opportunity. There was no reason why Hindus should not have equally demanded a Hindu State. Indeed, considering where parliamentary democracy has brought India today, it is to be doubted that this was what Lokmanya had intended.

According to Lokmanya, "A very simple definition of Home Rule which any of you including a peasant can understand is that I should be in my own country what an Englishman feels to be in England and in the Colonies. The simplest definition is that, and that is the whole of it .... I want to be in my country not as outlander but as master in the same sense that an Englishman is his own master in his own country and in the Colonies. That is Complete Home Rule". On this definition, it is clear that Complete Home Rule, Self-Government or Swaraj for Hindus has not been achieved. For, a Hindu is not his own master, nor does he feel like an Englishman in early 20th century England, in Pakistan, Bangladesh, Kashmir and many other places that were once Hindu but are now dominated by Christianity, Islam, Capitalism or Maoism.

Furthermore, India's Independence in 1947 really meant no more than legal independence from Britain. In view of the fact that the current political system is a carbon copy of Britain's, we cannot claim that India is politically independent. Full Independence (Purna Swaraj) means not only legal but also political, economic, cultural, religious and psychological Independence. This can only be achieved when Indians stop aping the West and learn to stand on their own feet. India can only become Independent in the true sense of the word when Indians start resisting Western imitation and return to the time-honoured values of Hindu Dharma. It is on this basis alone that a righteous and truly Indian society can be established. This was the original goal of the Hindu Revolution.

Lokmanya Tilak's departure from this world in August 1920 was a heavy blow to the nation which was left in a state of shock and grief. As bereaved people often do, many Indians transferred their reverence for Lokmanya on to Gandhi. Thus, the mantle of national leadership was uncritically conferred upon Gandhi in spite of obvious differences in personality and political approach. Although he must have been aware of this fact, Gandhi does not appear to have raised any objections. On the contrary, he used Lokmanya's political heritage to launch a Tilak Swaraj Fund through the Congress. On its part, the Congress was not slow in taking advantage of the new situation.

In 1922, Motilal Nehru, father of Jawaharlal and, like the latter, an unreformed agent of British Fabian Socialism, founded the "Swaraj Party" in an obvious attempt to gain political capital from Lokmanya's enduring popularity (the party, however, failed to achieve its proposed object). What becomes evident is that the Socialist Congress leadership under the Nehru clique fraudulently sought to lay a moral claim to Lokmanya's political legacy in order to monopolise power and divert the national movement in a counter-revolutionary Socialist direction. As for Gandhi, he was cleverly cast in the role of a saintly Saviour of the Nation, similar to the Moses of the Bible, in spite of the fact that the drawbacks of his obsessive pacifism had soon become clear to all.

Without Lokmanya's leadership, it was left for others, like Vinayak Damodar (Veer) Savarkar and Madhav Sadashiv (Guru) Golwalkar to carry on the struggle in the Hindu cause. Yet no other leader could match Lokmanya. Left without its beloved Leader, the nation slid from the pure and authentic revolutionary Hinduism of Lokmanya Tilak to the artificial, eclectic and self-serving spirituality of Gandhi and from that, to the atheistic Fabian Socialism of Nehru. As observed by Golwalkar in his *Bunch of Thoughts* (1966), "Our [Congress] leaders say that they will achieve Socialism by the ballot-box, and not by the bullet as was done in Russia and China .... With such docile people, why is the bullet required? A ballot-box is sufficient.

If the leader says, 'Vote for Socialism', the people will vote for it. If tomorrow they find that having voted for Socialism their independence is gone, and as individuals they have become only dead parts of a machine, they will take it as an ordinance of fate and submit to it". Indeed, while the politics of Lokmanya had been a politics inspired by Hindu religion, the politics of Nehru was devoid of spiritual meaning. The imposition of Socialism led to the spiritual degeneration and political fragmentation of the Indian nation and the loss of its cultural identity and independence.

It is ironic that even while he was converting the country to Socialism, the surrogate leader Jawaharlal Nehru was eventually obliged by public opinion (and, perhaps, conscience) to acknowledge the Lokmanya as the Father of India's Revolution, calling upon those present (on the occasion of the unveiling of an oil-portrait of Lokmanya Tilak in the Centrai Hall of Parliament on 28th July 1956) to remember and be inspired by him. On his part, Bengal's own great Nationalist leader, Aurobindo Ghose, aptly described the Lokmanya as one of India's "incarnations of the national endeavour and God-given captains of the national aspiration".

Lokmanya's powerful and stirring slogans such as, "Swaraj is India's Birthright", "Educate, Agitate, Organise" and "Militancy – not Mendicancy" electrified and awakened India. They remain as potent and valid today as they were when first announced. By his life, his character, his work and his teachings, Lokmanya Tilak has shown that the true purpose of Divine Avatars and other pure and great souls is to provide pure and authentic revolutionary leadership in the building of a Divine Society (or Kingdom of God) on earth according to the divine eternal principle of Righteousness or Dharma which is Truth, Order and Justice. This leadership is spiritual, political, social or military according to the needs of the time.

Shri Adi Shankara's leadership was spiritual, Shivaji's leadership was military and Lokmanya's leadership was political. However, even divine leadership cannot lead anywhere without the effective commitment and full co-operation of human society. In Lokmanya's words, "It is for man to work and for Providence to bless his work with success"; "God helps those who help themselves"; and "God does not help the indolent". While God always fulfils His promise of providing leadership to man, man does not always fulfil his duty of following that divine leadership.

Although pure and clear leadership was provided by revolutionary leader Lokmanya Tilak, the Hindu Community did not respond unanimously and unequivocally to his leadership. Some chose to follow the leadership of false leaders and this created division and strife in Hindu society which was exploited by counter-revolutionary elements to their advantage. As a result, the long-suffering Hindu People found itself under a new dictatorship, the dictatorship of Nehruvian Socialism and its associate, Fundamentalist Islam, which was imposed by the anti-Hindu agents of Western Imperialism on the Hindus to prevent them from achieving their aim of building a Divine Society on earth.

The critical analysis of the fateful historical events of the 20th century shows that Hindus were deprived of the Hindu State they had aspired for. Today, while the international community has come to accept the existence of a growing number of Islamic states (Saudi Arabia, Pakistan, Iran), a Hindu State remains unacceptable to a world dominated by Western (Abrahamic) ideologies. As long as this anti-Hindu discrimination persists, the struggle of the Hindu Community for religious equality and for a State of its own must go on. It is not too late even now, to go back to the authentic roots of the Hindu Revolution, understand its pure and true character as the expression of the Supreme Eternal Law of Dharma and put it into practice according to the teachings of Scripture and the guidance of the Hindu revolutionary leadership.

Bibliography

Binodini: a Novel translated by Krishna Kripalani. New Delhi: Sahitya Akademi, 1959.

Crisis in Civilization: A Message on Completing His Eighty Years translated by Kshitis Roy and Krishna R. Kripalani. – Santiniketan: Santiniketan Press, 1941.

Essays on Rabindranath Tagore: In Honour of D.M. Gupta edited by T.R. Sharma. Ghaziabad: Vimal Prakashan, 1987.

Four Chapters translated from the Bengali Novel Char Adhyaya (1934) by Surendranath Tagore. Calcutta: Visva-Bharati, 1950.

Gitanjali (Song Offerings) with an Introduction by W. B. Yeats. London, 1913.

Glimpses of Bengal Life: Being Short Stories from the Bengali of Rabindranath Tagore translated by Rajani Ranjan Sen. Madras; Chittagong, 1913.

In Your Blossoming Flower-Garden: Rabindranath Tagore and Victoria Ocampo. Dyson, Ketaki Kushari. New Delhi: Sahitya Akademi, 1988.

Letters from Russia edited by Sasadhar Sinha. Calcutta: Visua-Bharati, 1960.

Mashi and Other Stories translated from the original Bengali by various writers. London: Macmillan. 1918.

My Reminiscences translated by Surendranath Tagore. New York: Macmillan, 1917.

Rabindranath Tagore: Prophet Against Totalitarianism. Rajendra Verma. London, 1964.

Rabindranath Tagore: The Myriad-Minded Man. Krishna, Dutta. London: Bloomsbury, 1995.

Rabindranath Tagore: Poet and Dramatist. Thompson, Edward John. London: Oxford University Press, 1948

Rabindranath Tagore: The Man and His Poetry. Roy, Basanta Koomar. New York, 1915.

Selected Letters of Rabindranath Tagore edited by Krishna Dutta and Andrew Robinson, with a foreword by Amartya Sen. Cambridge University Press, 1997.

Six Portraits of Rabindranath Tagore. Rothenstein, William. London, 1915.

Social Thinking of Rabindranath Tagore. Sasadhar, Sinha London, 1962.

Song Offerings (Gitanjali) translated and Introduced by Joe Winter. London: Anvil, 2000.

Talks in China: Lectures Delivered in April and May, 1924. Calcutta: Visva-Bharati Book-Shop, 1925.

The Curse at Farewell translated by Edward Thompson. London: Harrap, 1924.

The Cycle of Spring translated by Andrews and Nishikanta Sen. London: Macmillan, 1917.

The Golden Boat translated by Bhabani Bhattacharya. London: Allen & Unwin, 1932.

The Golden Book of Tagore: Homage to Rabindranath Tagore, From India and the World, in Celebration of His Seventieth Birthday edited by Ramananda Chatterjee. Calcutta: The Golden Book Committee, 1931

The Home and the World translated by Surendranath Tagore, translation revised by Rabindranath Tagore. London: Macmillan, 1919.

The Hungry Stones and Other Stories translated from the original Bengali by various writers. London: Macmillan, 1916.

The Later Poems of Tagore. Ghose, Sisirkumar. London, 1961.

The Parrot's Training translated by Debjani Chatterjee. London: Tagore Centre U.K.. 1993.

The Philosophy of Rabindranath Tagore. Radhakrishnan, Sarvapalli. London: Macmillan, 1918.

The Post Office: A Play translated by Devabrata Mukerjea. London: Macmillan, 1914.

The Religion of Man: Being the Hibbert Lectures for 1930. London: Allen & Unwin, 1931.

Wings of Death: The Last Poems of Rabindranath Tagore translated by Aurobindo Bose. London: Murray, 1960.

INDEX

Encyclopaedia on Tagore and Contemporary Thinkers

Encyclopaedia on Tagore and Contemporary Thinkers

(Vol. 2)

Avinash Kumar Jha

KUNAL BOOKS

New Delhi-110002 , India

KUNAL BOOKS
4596/1A, First Floor,
11, Daryaganj, New Delhi-110002
Phones: 011-30125412, 9811043697
E-mail: *Kunalbooks@gmail.com*

Encyclopaedia on Tagore and Contemporary Thinkers

First Published 2011

ISBN - 978-93-80752-13-6

Published in India by Prem Singh Bisht for Kunal Books, and printed at **Asian Offset Press**, Delhi.

PREFACE

Rabindranath Tagore also known as Gurudev, was a Bengali poet, philosopher, religious thinker and intellectual leader, artist, playwright, composer, educationalist and novelist whose works reshaped Bengali literature and music in the late nineteenth and early twentieth centuries. A celebrated cultural icon in India, he became Asia's first Nobel laureate when he won the 1913 Nobel Prize in Literature. He is regarded as a towering cultural figure in all Bengali-speaking regions.

Tagore was not only a creative genius; he was a great man and friend to many. For instance, he was also a good friend from childhood to the great Indian Physicist, Bose. He was educated and quite knowledgeable of Western culture, especially Western poetry and Science. This made him a remarkable person, one of the first of our planet to combine East and West, and ancient and modern knowledge. Tagore had a good grasp of modern - post-Newtonian - physics, and was well able to hold his own in a debate with Einstein in 1930 on the newly emerging principles of quantum mechanics and chaos. His meetings and tape recorded conversations with his contemporaries such Albert Einstein and H.G. Wells, stand as cultural landmarks, and show the brilliance of this great man. Although Tagore is a superb representative of his country - India - the man who wrote its national anthem - his life and works go far beyond his country. He is truly a man of the whole Earth, a product of the best of both traditional Indian, and modern Western cultures. The School of Wisdom is proud to have him as part of its heritage.

In India, Rabindranath Tagore has transcended, as often happens in the Indian paradigm, the simple position of a writer-philosopher. Especially among bodies, he is revered as a Guru. Since great thinkers, who are often religious in their purview, are seen as gurus and close to Bhagavan (God) by Hindus, Rabindranath Tagore is especially revered. Hindus believe that by listening to the words of such wise and enlightened men, people are brought closer to Bhagavan. For this reason, he is affectionately known as Gurudeb (or Gurudev in Hindi), which means, literally, Teacher-God.

During his lifetime, Rabindranath Tagore was a towering and epochal figure of legendary proportions not only within the bounds of his native Bengal, or his beloved India, but to a considerable extent, throughout the world. As a multifaceted genius and renaissance man par excellence, he not only carried the literature and arts of Bengal, virtually single-handedly, to dizzying heights of creativity, but, by his inspiring words, his lyrically unequalled songs, his unstinting support for the cause of India's freedom during a long and turbulent phase of her history, he lifted Indian culture and the Indian psyche to an unprecedented level of revitalization.

CONTENTS

1

Tagore and Nationalism

Rabindranath Tagore, who died in 1941 at the age of eighty, is a towering figure in the millennium-old literature of Bengal. Anyone who becomes familiar with this large and flourishing tradition will be impressed by the power of Tagore's presence in Bangladesh and in India. His poetry as well as his novels, short stories, and essays are very widely read, and the songs he composed reverberate around the eastern part of India and throughout Bangladesh. In contrast, in the rest of the world, especially in Europe and America, the excitement that Tagore's writings created in the early years of the twentieth century has largely vanished.

The enthusiasm with which his work was once greeted was quite remarkable. *Gitanjali,* a selection of his poetry for which he was awarded the Nobel Prize in Literature in 1913, was published in English translation in London in March of that year, and had been reprinted ten times by November, when the award was announced. But he is not much read now in the West, and already by 1937, Graham Greene was able to say: "As for Rabindranath Tagore, I cannot believe that anyone but Mr. Yeats can still take his poems very seriously."

THE MYSTIC

The contrast between Tagore's commanding presence in Bengali literature and culture, and his near-total eclipse in the rest of the world, is perhaps less interesting than the distinction between the view of Tagore as a deeply relevant and many-sided contemporary thinker in Bangladesh and India, and his image in the West as a repetitive and remote spiritualist. Graham Greene had, in fact, gone on to explain that he associated Tagore "with what Chesterton calls 'the bright pebbly eyes' of the Theosophists."

Certainly, an air of mysticism played some part in the "selling" of Rabindranath Tagore to the West by Yeats, Ezra Pound, and his other early champions. Even Anna Akhmatova, one of Tagore's few later admirers (who translated his poems into Russian in the mid-1960s) talks of "that mighty flow of poetry which takes its strength from Hinduism as from the Ganges, and is called Rabindranath Tagore."

CONFLUENCE OF CULTURES

Rabindranath did come from a Hindu family- one of the landed gentry who owned estates mostly in what is now Bangladesh. But whatever wisdom there might be in Akhmatova's invoking of Hinduism and the Ganges, it did not prevent the largely Muslim citizens of Bangladesh from having a deep sense of identity with Tagore and his ideas. Nor did it stop the newly independent Bangladesh from choosing one of Tagore's songs-the "Amar Sonar Bangla" which means "my golden Bengal"-as its national anthem.

This must be very confusing to those who see the contemporary world as a "clash of civilisations"-with "the Muslim civilisation," "the Hindu civilisation," and "the Western civilisation," each forcefully confronting the others. They would also be confused by Rabindranath Tagore's own description of his Bengali family as the product of "a confluence of three cultures: Hindu, Mohammedan, and British".

Rabindranath's grandfather, Dwarkanath, was well known for his command of Arabic and Persian, and Rabindranath grew up in a family atmosphere in which a deep knowledge of Sanskrit and ancient Hindu texts was combined with an understanding of Islamic traditions as well as Persian literature.

It is not so much that Rabindranath tried to produce-or had an interest in producing-a "synthesis" of the different religions (as the great Moghul emperor Akbar tried hard to achieve) as that his outlook was persistently non-sectarian, and his writings-some two hundred books-show the influence of different parts of the Indian cultural background as well as of the rest of the world.

ABODE OF PEACE

Most of his work was written at Santiniketan (Abode of Peace), the small town that grew around the school he founded in Bengal in 1901, and he not only conceived there an imaginative and innovative system of education, but through his writings and his influence on students and teachers, he was able to use the school as a base from which he could take a major part in India's social, political, and cultural movements.

The profoundly original writer, whose elegant prose and magical poetry Bengali readers know well, is not the sermonizing spiritual guru admired-and then rejected-in London. Tagore was not only an immensely versatile poet; he was also a great short story writer, novelist, playwright, essayist, and composer of songs, as well as a talented painter whose pictures, with their mixture of representation and abstraction, are only now beginning to receive the acclaim that they have long deserved

His essays, moreover, ranged over literature, politics, culture, social change, religious beliefs, philosophical analysis, international relations, and much else. The coincidence of the fiftieth anniversary of Indian independence with the publication of a selection of Tagore's letters by Cambridge University Press brought Tagore's ideas and reflections to the fore, which makes it important to examine what kind of leadership in thought and understanding he provided in the Indian subcontinent in the first half of this century.

GANDHI AND TAGORE

Since Rabindranath Tagore and Mohandas Gandhi were two leading Indian thinkers in the twentieth century, many commentators have tried to compare their ideas. On learning of Rabindranath's death, Jawaharlal Nehru, then incarcerated in a British jail in India, wrote in his prison diary for August 7, 1941: "Gandhi and Tagore.

Two types entirely different from each other, and yet both of them typical of India, both in the long line of India's great men... It is not so much because of any single virtue but because of the *tout ensemble,* that I felt that among the world's great men today Gandhi and Tagore were supreme as human beings. What good fortune for me to have come into close contact with them."

Romain Rolland was fascinated by the contrast between them, and when he completed his book on Gandhi, he wrote to an Indian academic, in March 1923: "I have finished my *Gandhi,* in which I pay tribute to your two great river-like souls, overflowing with divine spirit, Tagore and Gandhi."

The following month, he recorded in his diary an account of some of the differences between Gandhi and Tagore written by Reverend C.F. Andrews, the English clergyman and public activist who was a close friend of both men (and whose important role in Gandhi's life in South Africa as well as India is well portrayed in Richard Attenborough's film Gandhi [1982]). Andrews described to Rolland a discussion between Tagore and Gandhi, at which he was present, on subjects that divided them:

"The first subject of discussion was idols; Gandhi defended them, believing the masses incapable of raising themselves immediately to abstract ideas. Tagore cannot bear to see the people eternally treated as a child. Gandhi quoted the great things achieved in Europe by the flag as an idol; Tagore found it easy to object, but Gandhi held his ground, contrasting European flags bearing eagles, etc., with his own, on which he has put a spinning wheel. The second point of discussion was nationalism, which Gandhi defended. He said that one must go through nationalism to reach internationalism, in the same way that one must go through war to reach peace."

Tagore greatly admired Gandhi but he had many disagreements with him on a variety of subjects, including nationalism, patriotism, the importance of cultural exchange, the role of rationality and of science, and the nature of economic and social development. These differences, I shall argue, have a clear and consistent pattern, with Tagore pressing for more room for reasoning, and for a less traditionalist view, a greater interest in the rest of the world, and more respect for science and for objectivity generally.

Rabindranath knew that he could not have given India the political leadership that Gandhi provided, and he was never stingy in his praise for what Gandhi did for the nation (it was, in fact, Tagore who popularized the term "Mahatma"-great soul-as a description of Gandhi). And yet each remained deeply critical of many things that the other stood for. That Mahatma Gandhi has received incomparably more attention outside India and also within much of India itself makes it important to understand "Tagore's side" of the Gandhi-Tagore debates.

In his prison diary, Nehru wrote: "Perhaps it is as well that [Tagore] died now and did not see the many horrors that are likely to descend in increasing measure on the world and on India. He had seen enough and he was infinitely sad and unhappy." Toward the end of his life, Tagore was indeed becoming discouraged about the state of India, especially as its normal burden of problems, such as hunger and poverty, was being supplemented by politically organized incitement to "communal" violence between Hindus and Muslims.

This conflict would lead in 1947, six years after Tagore's death, to the widespread killing that took place during partition; but there was much gore already during his declining days. In December 1939, he wrote to his friend Leonard Elmhirst, the

English philanthropist and social reformer who had worked closely with him on rural reconstruction in India (and who had gone on to found the Dartington Hall Trust in England and a progressive school at Dartington that explicitly invoked Rabindranath's educational ideals):

"It does not need a defeatist to feel deeply anxious about the future of millions who, with all their innate culture and their peaceful traditions are being simultaneously subjected to hunger, disease, exploitations foreign and indigenous, and the seething discontents of communalism."

How would Tagore have viewed the India of today? Would he see progress there, or wasted opportunity, perhaps even a betrayal of its promise and conviction? And, on a wider subject, how would he react to the spread of cultural separatism in the contemporary world?

2

East and West: W B Yeats and Rabindranath Tagore

Given the vast range of his creative achievements, perhaps the most astonishing aspect of the image of Tagore in the West is its narrowness; he is recurrently viewed as "the great mystic from the East," an image with a putative message for the West, which some would welcome, others dislike, and still others find deeply boring.

To a great extent this Tagore was the West's own creation, part of its tradition of message-seeking from the East, particularly from India, which- as Hegel put it-had "existed for millennia in the imagination of the Europeans." Friedrich Schlegel, Schelling, Herder, and Schopenhauer were only a few of the thinkers who followed the same pattern. They theorized, at first, that India was the source of superior wisdom. Schopenhauer at one stage even argued that the New Testament "must somehow be of Indian origin: this is attested by its completely Indian ethics, which transforms morals into asceticism, its pessimism, and its avatar," in "the person of Christ."

But then they rejected their own theories with great vehemence, sometimes blaming India for not living up to their unfounded expectations. We can imagine that Rabindranath's physical appearance-handsome, bearded, and dressed in non-Western clothes-may, to some extent, have encouraged his being seen as a carrier of exotic wisdom. Yasunari Kawabata, the first Japanese Nobel Laureate in Literature, treasured memories from his middle-school days of "this sage-like poet":

> His white hair flowed softly down both sides of his forehead; the tufts of hair under the temples also were long like two beards, and linking up with the hair on his cheeks, continued into his beard, so that he gave an impression, to the boy I was then, of some ancient Oriental wizard. That appearance would have been well-suited to the selling of Tagore in the West as a quintessentially mystical poet, and it could have made it somewhat easier to pigeonhole him.

Commenting on Rabindranath's appearance, Frances Cornford told William Rothenstein, "I can now imagine a powerful and gentle Christ, which I never could before." Beatrice Webb, who did not like Tagore and resented what she took to be his "quite obvious dislike of all that the Webbs stand for" (there is, in fact, little evidence that Tagore had given much thought to this subject), said that he was "beautiful to look at" and that "his speech has the perfect intonation and slow chant-like moderation of the dramatic saint."

Ezra Pound and W. B. Yeats, among others, first led the chorus of adoration in the Western appreciation of Tagore, and then soon moved to neglect and even shrill criticism. The contrast between Yeats's praise of his work in 1912 ("These lyrics...display in their thought a world I have dreamed of all my life long," "the work of a supreme culture") and his denunciation in 1935 ("Damn Tagore") arose partly from the inability of Tagore's many-sided writings to fit into the narrow box in which Yeats wanted to place-and keep-him.

Certainly, Tagore did write a huge amount, and published ceaselessly, even in English (sometimes in indifferent English translation), but Yeats was also bothered, it is clear, by the difficulty of fitting Tagore's later writings into the image Yeats had presented to the West. Tagore, he had said, was the product of "a whole people, a whole civilisation, immeasurably strange to us," and yet "we have met our own image,...or heard, perhaps for the first time in literature, our voice as in a dream."

Yeats did not totally reject his early admiration (as Ezra Pound and several others did), and he included some of Tagore's early poems in *The Oxford Book of Modern Verse,* which he edited in 1936. Yeats also had some favorable things to say about Tagore's prose writings. His censure of Tagore's later poems was reinforced by his dislike of Tagore's own English translations of his work ("Tagore does not know English, no Indian knows English," Yeats explained), unlike the English version of *Gitanjali* which Yeats had himself helped to prepare.

Poetry is, of course, notoriously difficult to translate, and anyone who knows Tagore's poems in their original Bengali cannot feel satisfied with any of the translations (made with or without Yeats's help). Even the translations of his prose works suffer, to some extent, from distortion. E.M. Forster noted, in a review of a translation of one of Tagore's great Bengali novels, *The Home and the World,* in 1919: "The theme is so beautiful," but the charms have "vanished in translation," or perhaps "in an experiment that has not quite come off."

Tagore himself played a somewhat bemused part in the boom and bust of his English reputation. He accepted the extravagant praise with much surprise as well as pleasure, and then received denunciations with even greater surprise, and barely concealed pain. Tagore was sensitive to criticism, and was hurt by even the most far-fetched accusations, such as the charge that he was getting credit for the work of Yeats, who had "rewritten" Gitanjali. (This charge was made by a correspondent for The Times, Sir Valentine Chirol, whom E.M. Forster once described as "an old Anglo-Indian reactionary hack.") From time to time Tagore also protested the crudity of some of his overexcited advocates. He wrote to C.F. Andrews in 1920: "These people...are like drunkards who are afraid of their lucid intervals."

GOD AND OTHERS

Yeats was not wrong to see a large religious element in Tagore's writings. He certainly had interesting and arresting things to say about life and death. Susan Owen, the mother of Wilfred Owen, wrote to Rabindranath in 1920, describing her last conversations with her son before he left for the war which would take his life. Wilfred said goodbye with "those wonderful words of yours-beginning at 'When I go from hence, let this be my parting word.'"

When Wilfred's pocket notebook was returned to his mother, she found "these words written in his dear writing-with your name beneath." The idea of a direct, joyful, and totally fearless relationship with God can be found in many of Tagore's religious writings, including the poems of *Gitanjali.* From India's diverse religious traditions he drew many ideas, both from ancient texts and from popular poetry. But "the bright pebbly eyes of the Theosophists" do not stare out of his verses.

Despite the archaic language of the original translation of *Gitanjali,* which did not, I believe, help to preserve the simplicity of the original, its elementary humanity comes through more clearly than any complex and intense spirituality:

Leave this chanting and singing and telling of beads! Whom dost thou worship in this lonely dark corner of a temple with doors all shut?

Open thine eyes and see thy God is not before thee!

He is there where the tiller is tilling the hard ground and where the pathmaker is breaking stones.

He is with them in sun and in shower, and his garment is covered with dust.

An ambiguity about religious experience is central to many of Tagore's devotional poems, and makes them appeal to readers irrespective of their beliefs; but excessively detailed interpretation can ruinously strip away that ambiguity. This applies particularly to his many poems which combine images of human love and those of pious devotion. Tagore writes:

I have no sleep to-night. Ever and again I open my door and look out on the darkness, my friend!

I can see nothing before me. I wonder where lies thy path!

By what dim shore of the ink-black river, by what far edge of the frowning forest, through what mazy depth of gloom, art thou threading thy course to come to see me, my friend?

I suppose it could be helpful to be told, as Yeats hastens to explain, that "the servant or the bride awaiting the master's home-coming in the empty house" is "among the images of the heart turning to God." But in Yeats's considerate attempt to make sure that the reader does not miss the "main point," something of the enigmatic beauty of the Bengali poem is lost - even what had survived the antiquated language of the English translation. Tagore certainly had strongly held religious beliefs (of an unusually nondenominational kind), but he was interested in a great many other things as well and had many different things to say about them.

Some of the ideas he tried to present were directly political, and they figure rather prominently in his letters and lectures. He had practical, plainly expressed views about nationalism, war and peace, cross-cultural education, freedom of the mind, the importance of rational criticism, the need for openness, and so on. His admirers in the West, however, were tuned to the more otherworldly themes which had been emphasized by his first Western patrons.

People came to his public lectures in Europe and America, expecting ruminations on grand, transcendental themes; when they heard instead his views on the way public leaders should behave, there was some resentment, particularly when he delivered political criticism "at $700 a scold."

REASONING IN FREEDOM

For Tagore it was of the highest importance that people be able to live, and reason, in freedom. His attitudes toward politics and culture, nationalism and internationalism, tradition and modernity, can all be seen in the light of this belief. Nothing, perhaps, expresses his values as clearly as a poem in *Gitanjali:*

> Where the mind is without fear
> and the head is held high;
> Where knowledge is free;
> Where the world has not been
> broken up into fragments
> by narrow domestic walls;...
> Where the clear stream of reason
> has not lost its way into the
> dreary desert sand of dead habit;...
> Into that heaven of freedom,
> my Father, let my country awake.

Rabindranath's qualified support for nationalist movements-and his opposition to the unfreedom of alien rule-came from this commitment. So did his reservations about patriotism, which, he argued, can limit both the freedom to engage ideas from outside "narrow domestic walls" and the freedom also to support the causes of people in other countries. Rabindranath's passion for freedom underlies his firm opposition to unreasoned traditionalism, which makes one a prisoner of the past (lost, as he put it, in "the dreary desert sand of dead habit").

Tagore illustrates the tyranny of the past in his amusing yet deeply serious parable "Kartar Bhoot" ("The Ghost of the Leader"). As the respected leader of an imaginary land is about to die, his panic-stricken followers request him to stay on after his death to instruct them on what to do. He consents. But his followers find their lives are full of rituals and constraints on everyday behavior and are not responsive to the world around them.

Ultimately, they request the ghost of the leader to relieve them of his domination, when he informs them that he exists only in their minds. Tagore's deep aversion to any commitment to the past that could not be modified by contemporary reason extended even to the alleged virtue of invariably keeping past promises. On one occasion when Mahatma Gandhi visited Tagore's school at Santiniketan, a young woman got him to sign her autograph book.

Gandhi wrote: "Never make a promise in haste. Having once made it fulfill it at the cost of your life." When he saw this entry, Tagore became agitated. He wrote in the same book a short poem in Bengali to the effect that no one can be made "a prisoner forever with a chain of clay." He went on to conclude in English, possibly so that Gandhi could read it too, "Fling away your promise if it is found to be wrong."

Tagore had the greatest admiration for Mahatma Gandhi as a person and as a political leader, but he was also highly skeptical of Gandhi's form of nationalism and his conservative instincts regarding the country's past traditions. He never criticized Gandhi personally. In the 1938 essay, "Gandhi the Man," he wrote:

Great as he is as a politician, as an organizer, as a leader of men, as a moral reformer, he is greater than all these as a man, because none of these aspects and activities limits his humanity. They are rather inspired and sustained by it.

And yet there is a deep division between the two men. Tagore was explicit about his disagreement:

We who often glorify our tendency to ignore reason, installing in its place blind faith, valuing it as spiritual, are ever paying for its cost with the obscuration of our mind and destiny. I blamed Mahatmaji for exploiting this irrational force of credulity in our people, which might have had a quick result [in creating] a superstructure, while sapping the foundation. Thus began my estimate of Mahatmaji, as the guide of our nation and it is fortunate for me that it did not end there.

But while it "did not end there," that difference of vision was a powerful divider. Tagore, for example, remained unconvinced of the merit of Gandhi's forceful advocacy that everyone should spin at home with the "charka," the primitive spinning wheel. For Gandhi this practice was an important part of India's self-realisation. "The spinning-wheel gradually became," as his biographer B.R. Nanda writes, "the center of rural uplift in the Gandhian scheme of Indian economics."

Tagore found the alleged economic rationale for this scheme quite unrealistic. As Romain Rolland noted, Rabindranath "never tires of criticizing the charka." In this economic judgment, Tagore was probably right. Except for the rather small specialized market for high-quality spun cloth, it is hard to make economic sense of hand-spinning, even with wheels less primitive than Gandhi's charka. Hand-spinning as a widespread activity can survive only with the help of heavy government subsidies.

However, Gandhi's advocacy of the charka was not based only on economics. He wanted everyone to spin for "thirty minutes every day as a sacrifice," seeing this as a way for people who are better off to identify themselves with the less fortunate. He was impatient with Tagore's refusal to grasp this point:

The poet lives for the morrow, and would have us do likewise.... "Why should I, who have no need to work for food, spin?" may be the question asked. Because I am eating what does not belong to me. I am living on the spoliation of my countrymen. Trace the source of every coin that finds its way into your pocket, and you will realise the truth of what I write. Every one must spin. Let Tagore spin like the others. Let him burn his foreign clothes; that is the duty today. God will take care of the morrow.

If Tagore had missed something in Gandhi's argument, so did Gandhi miss the point of Tagore's main criticism? It was not only that the charka made little economic sense, but also, Tagore thought, that it was not the way to make people reflect on anything:

"The charka does not require anyone to think; one simply turns the wheel of the antiquated invention endlessly, using the minimum of judgment and stamina."

CELIBACY AND PERSONAL LIFE

Tagore and Gandhi's attitudes toward personal life were also quite different. Gandhi was keen on the virtues of celibacy, theorized about it, and, after some years of conjugal life, made a private commitment-publicly announced-to refrain from sleeping with his wife. Rabindranath's own attitude on this subject was very different, but he was gentle about their disagreements:

[Gandhiji] condemns sexual life as inconsistent with the moral progress of man, and has a horror of sex as great as that of the author of *The Kreutzer Sonata,* but, unlike Tolstoy, he betrays no abhorrence of the sex that tempts his kind. In fact, his tenderness for women is one of the noblest and most consistent traits of his character, and he counts among the women of his country some of his best and truest comrades in the great movement he is leading.

Tagore's personal life was, in many ways, an unhappy one. He married in 1883, lost his wife in 1902, and never remarried. He sought close companionship, which he did not always get (perhaps even during his married life-he wrote to his wife, Mrinalini: "If you and I could be comrades in all our work and in all our thoughts it would be splendid, but we cannot attain all that we desire").

He maintained a warm friendship with, and a strong Platonic attachment to, the literature-loving wife, Kadambari, of his elder brother, Jyotirindranath. He dedicated some poems to her before his marriage, and several books afterward, some after her death (she committed suicide, for reasons that are not fully understood, at the age of twenty-five, four months after Rabindranath's wedding).

Much later in life, during his tour of Argentina in 1924-1925, Rabindranath came to know the talented and beautiful Victoria Ocampo, who later became the publisher of the literary magazine

Sur. They became close friends, but it appears that Rabindranath deflected the possibility of a passionate relationship into a confined intellectual one. His friend Leonard Elmhirst, who accompanied Rabindranath on his Argentine tour, wrote:

> Besides having a keen intellectual understanding of his books, she was in love with him-but instead of being content to build a friendship on the basis of intellect, she was in a hurry to establish that kind of proprietary right over him which he absolutely would not brook.

Ocampo and Elmhirst, while remaining friendly, were both quite rude in what they wrote about each other. Ocampo's book on Tagore (of which a Bengali translation was made from the Spanish by the distinguished poet and critic Shankha Ghosh) is primarily concerned with Tagore's writings but also discusses the pleasures and difficulties of their relationship, giving quite a different account from Elmhirst's, and never suggesting any sort of proprietary intentions.

Victoria Ocampo, however, makes it clear that she very much wanted to get physically closer to Rabindranath: "Little by little he [Tagore] partially tamed the young animal, by turns wild and docile, who did not sleep, dog-like, on the floor outside his door, simply because it was not done." Rabindranath, too, was clearly very much attracted to her. He called her "Vijaya" (the Sanskrit equivalent of Victoria), dedicated a book of poems to her, Purabi-an "evening melody," and expressed great admiration for her mind ("like a star that was distant"). In a letter to her he wrote, as if to explain his own reticence:

> When we were together, we mostly played with words and tried to laugh away our best opportunities to see each other clearly... Whenever there is the least sign of the nest becoming a jealous rival of the sky[,] my mind, like a migrant bird, tries to take... flight to a distant shore.

Five years later, during Tagore's European tour in 1930, he sent her a cable: "Will you not come and see me." She did. But their relationship did not seem to go much beyond conversation, and their somewhat ambiguous correspondence continued over the years.

Written in 1940, a year before his death at eighty, one of the poems in Sesh Lekha ("Last Writings"), seems to be about her: "How I wish I could once again find my way to that foreign land where waits for me the message of love!/... Her language I knew not, but what her eyes said will forever remain eloquent in its anguish." However indecisive, or confused, or awkward Rabindranath may have been, he certainly did not share Mahatma Gandhi's censorious views of sex. In fact, when it came to social policy, he advocated contraception and family planning while Gandhi preferred abstinence.

SCIENCE AND THE PEOPLE

Gandhi and Tagore severely clashed over their totally different attitudes toward science. In January 1934, Bihar was struck by a devastating earthquake, which killed thousands of people. Gandhi, who was then deeply involved in the fight against untouchability (the barbaric system inherited from India's divisive past, in which "lowly people" were kept at a physical distance), extracted a positive lesson from the tragic event.

"A man like me," Gandhi argued, "cannot but believe this earthquake is a divine chastisement sent by God for our sins" - in particular the sins of untouchability. "For me there is a vital connection between the Bihar calamity and the untouchability campaign." Tagore, who equally abhorred untouchability and had joined Gandhi in the movements against it, protested against this interpretation of an event that had caused suffering and death to so many innocent people, including children and babies. He also hated the epistemology implicit in seeing an earthquake as caused by ethical failure. "It is," he wrote, "all the more unfortunate because this kind of unscientific view of [natural] phenomena is too readily accepted by a large section of our countrymen."

The two remained deeply divided over their attitudes toward science. However, while Tagore believed that modern science was essential to the understanding of physical phenomena, his views on epistemology were interestingly heterodox.

He did not take the simple "realist" position often associated with modern science. The report of his conversation with Einstein published in The New York Times in 1930, shows how insistent Tagore was on interpreting truth through observation and reflective concepts.

To assert that something is true or untrue in the absence of anyone to observe or perceive its truth, or to form a conception of what it is, appeared to Tagore to be deeply questionable. When Einstein remarked, "If there were no human beings any more, the Apollo Belvedere no longer would be beautiful?" Tagore simply replied, "No." Going further-and into much more interesting territory-Einstein said, "I agree with regard to this conception of beauty, but not with regard to truth." Tagore's response was: "Why not? Truth is realized through men."

Tagore's epistemology, which he never pursued systematically, would seem to be searching for a line of reasoning that would later be elegantly developed by Hilary Putnam, who has argued: "Truth depends on conceptual schemes and it is nonetheless 'real truth.'" Tagore himself said little to explain his convictions, but it is important to take account of his heterodoxy, not only because his speculations were invariably interesting, but also because they illustrate how his support for any position, including his strong interest in science, was accompanied by critical scrutiny.

NATIONALISM AND COLONIALISM

Tagore was predictably hostile to communal sectarianism (such as a Hindu orthodoxy that was antagonistic to Islamic, Christian, or Sikh perspectives). But even nationalism seemed to him to be suspect. Isaiah Berlin summarizes well Tagore's complex position on Indian nationalism:

Tagore stood fast on the narrow causeway, and did not betray his vision of the difficult truth. He condemned romantic overattachment to the past, what he called the tying of India to the past "like a sacrificial goat tethered to a post," and he accused men who displayed it - they seemed to him reactionary - of not knowing what true political freedom was, pointing out that it is from English thinkers and English books that the very notion of political liberty was derived. But against cosmopolitanism he maintained that the English stood on their own feet, and so must Indians. In 1917 he once more denounced the danger of 'leaving everything to the unalterable will of the Master,' be he brahmin or Englishman.

The duality Berlin points to is well reflected also in Tagore's attitude toward cultural diversity. He wanted Indians to learn what is going on elsewhere, how others lived, what they valued, and so on, while remaining interested and involved in their own culture and heritage. Indeed, in his educational writings the need for synthesis is strongly stressed.

It can also be found in his advice to Indian students abroad. In 1907 he wrote to his son-in-law Nagendranath Gangulee, who had gone to America to study agriculture:

> To get on familiar terms with the local people is a part of your education. To know only agriculture is not enough; you must know America too. Of course if, in the process of knowing America, one begins to lose one's identity and falls into the trap of becoming an Americanised person contemptuous of everything Indian, it is preferable to stay in a locked room.

Tagore was strongly involved in protest against the Raj on a number of occasions, most notably in the movement to resist the 1905 British proposal to split in two the province of Bengal, a plan that was eventually withdrawn following popular resistance. He was forthright in denouncing the brutality of British rule in India, never more so than after the Amritsar massacre of April 13, 1919, when 379 unarmed people at a peaceful meeting were gunned down by the army, and two thousand more were wounded.

Between April 23 and 26, Rabindranath wrote five agitated letters to C.F. Andrews, who himself was extremely disturbed, especially after he was told by a British civil servant in India that thanks to this show of strength, the "moral prestige" of the Raj had "never been higher."

A month after the massacre, Tagore wrote to the Viceroy of India, asking to be relieved of the knighthood he had accepted four years earlier:

> The disproportionate severity of the punishments inflicted upon the unfortunate people and the methods of carrying them out, we are convinced, are without parallel in the history of civilized governments, barring some conspicuous exceptions, recent and remote. Considering that such treatment has been meted out to a population, disarmed and resourceless, by a power which has the most terribly efficient organisation for destruction of human lives, we must strongly assert that it can claim no political expediency, far less moral justification.... The universal agony of indignation roused in the hearts of our people has been ignored by our rulers - possibly congratulating themselves for imparting what they imagine as salutary lessons.... I for my part want to stand, shorn of all special distinctions, by the side of those of my countrymen who for their so-called insignificance are liable to suffer a degradation not fit for human beings.

Both Gandhi and Nehru expressed their appreciation of the important part Tagore took in the national struggle. It is fitting that after independence, India chose a song of Tagore ("Jana Gana Mana Adhinayaka," which can be roughly translated as "the leader of people's minds") as its national anthem. Since Bangladesh would later choose another song of Tagore ("Amar Sonar Bangla") as its national anthem, he may be the only one ever to have authored the national anthems of two different countries.

Tagore's criticism of the British administration of India was consistently strong and grew more intense over the years. This point is often missed, since he made a special effort to dissociate his criticism of the Raj from any denigration of British-or Western-people and culture. Mahatma Gandhi's well-known quip in reply to a question, asked in England, on what he thought of Western civilisation ("It would be a good idea") could not have come from Tagore's lips. He would understand the provocations to which Gandhi was responding - involving cultural conceit as well as imperial tyranny. D.H. Lawrence supplied a fine example of the former: "I become more and more surprised to see how far higher, in reality, our European civilisation stands than the East, Indian and Persian, ever dreamed of.... This fraud of looking up to them-this wretched worship-of-Tagore attitude is disgusting." But, unlike Gandhi, Tagore could not, even in jest, be dismissive of Western civilisation.

Even in his powerful indictment of British rule in India in 1941, in a lecture which he gave on his last birthday, and which was later published as a pamphlet under the title *Crisis in Civilisation,* he strains hard to maintain the distinction between opposing Western imperialism and rejecting Western civilisation. While he saw India as having been "smothered under the dead weight of British administration" (adding "another great and ancient civilisation for whose recent tragic history the British cannot disclaim responsibility is China"), Tagore recalls what India has gained from "discussions centred upon Shakespeare's drama and Byron's poetry and above all...the large-hearted liberalism of nineteenth-century English politics."

The tragedy, as Tagore saw it, came from the fact that what "was truly best in their own civilisation, the upholding of dignity of human relationships, has no place in the British administration of this country." "If in its place they have established, baton in hand, a reign of 'law and order,' or in other words a policeman's rule, such a mockery of civilisation can claim no respect from us."

CRITIQUE OF PATRIOTISM

Rabindranath rebelled against the strongly nationalist form that the independence movement often took, and this made him refrain from taking a particularly active part in contemporary politics. He wanted to assert India's right to be independent without denying the importance of what India could learn-freely and profitably-from abroad.

He was afraid that a rejection of the West in favor of an indigenous Indian tradition was not only limiting in itself; it could easily turn into hostility to other influences from abroad, including Christianity, which came to parts of India by the fourth century; Judaism, which came through Jewish immigration shortly after the fall of Jerusalem, as did Zoroastrianism through Parsi immigration later on (mainly in the eighth century), and, of course-and most importantly-Islam, which has had a very strong presence in India since the tenth century.

Tagore's criticism of patriotism is a persistent theme in his writings. As early as 1908, he put his position succinctly in a letter replying to the criticism of Abala Bose, the wife of a great Indian scientist, Jagadish Chandra Bose: "Patriotism cannot be our final spiritual shelter; my refuge is humanity. I will not buy glass for the price of diamonds, and I will never allow patriotism to triumph over humanity as long as I live." His novel *Ghare Baire* (The Home and the World) has much to say about this theme.

In the novel, Nikhil, who is keen on social reform, including women's liberation, but cool toward nationalism, gradually loses the esteem of his spirited wife, Bimala, because of his failure to be enthusiastic about anti-British agitations, which she sees as a lack of patriotic commitment. Bimala becomes fascinated with Nikhil's nationalist friend Sandip, who speaks brilliantly and acts with patriotic militancy, and she falls in love with him. Nikhil refuses to change his views: "I am willing to serve my country; but my worship I reserve for Right which is far greater than my country. To worship my country as a god is to bring a curse upon it."

As the story unfolds, Sandip becomes angry with some of his countrymen for their failure to join the struggle as readily as he thinks they should ("Some Mohamedan traders are still obdurate").

He arranges to deal with the recalcitrants by burning their meager trading stocks and physically attacking them. Bimala has to acknowledge the connection between Sandip's rousing nationalistic sentiments and his sectarian - and ultimately violent-actions. The dramatic events that follow (Nikhil attempts to help the victims, risking his life) include the end of Bimala's political romance.

This is a difficult subject, and Satyajit Ray's beautiful film of *The Home and the World* brilliantly brings out the novel's tensions, along with the human affections and disaffections of the story. Not surprisingly, the story has had many detractors, not just among dedicated nationalists in India. Georg Lukács found Tagore's novel to be "a petit bourgeois yarn of the shoddiest kind," "at the intellectual service of the British police," and "a contemptible caricature of Gandhi."

It would, of course, be absurd to think of Sandip as Gandhi, but the novel gives a "strong and gentle" warning, as Bertolt Brecht noted in his diary, of the corruptibility of nationalism, since it is not even-handed. Hatred of one group can lead to hatred of others, no matter how far such feeling may be from the minds of large-hearted nationalist leaders like Mahatma Gandhi.

ADMIRATION AND CRITICISM OF JAPAN

Tagore's reaction to nationalism in Japan is particularly telling. As in the case of India, he saw the need to build the self-confidence of a defeated and humiliated people, of people left behind by developments elsewhere as was the case in Japan before its emergence during the nineteenth century. At the beginning of one of his lectures in Japan in 1916 ("Nationalism in Japan"), he observed that "the worst form of bondage is the bondage of dejection, which keeps men hopelessly chained in loss of faith in themselves."

Tagore shared the admiration for Japan widespread in Asia for demonstrating the ability of an Asian nation to rival the West in industrial development and economic progress. He noted with great satisfaction that Japan had "in giant strides left centuries of inaction behind, overtaking the present time in its foremost achievement." For other nations outside the West, he said, Japan "has broken the spell under which we lay in torpor for ages, taking it to be the normal condition of certain races living in certain geographical limits."

But then Tagore went on to criticize the rise of a strong nationalism in Japan, and its emergence as an imperialist nation. Tagore's outspoken criticisms did not please Japanese audiences and, as E.P. Thompson wrote, "the welcome given to him on his first arrival soon cooled." Twenty-two years later, in 1937, during the Japanese war on China, Tagore received a letter from Rash Behari Bose, an anti-British Indian revolutionary then living in Japan, who sought Tagore's approval for his efforts there on behalf of Indian independence, in which he had the support of the Japanese government. Tagore replied:

Your cable has caused me many restless hours, for it hurts me very much to have to ignore your appeal. I wish you had asked for my cooperation in a cause against which my spirit did not protest. I know, in making this appeal, you counted on my great regard for the Japanese for I, along with the rest of Asia, did once admire and look up to Japan and did once fondly hope that in Japan Asia had at last discovered its challenge to the West, that Japan's new strength would be consecrated in safeguarding the culture of the East against alien interests. But Japan has not taken long to betray that rising hope and repudiate all that seemed significant in her wonderful, and, to us symbolic, awakening, and has now become itself a worse menace to the defenceless peoples of the East.

How to view Japan's position in the Second World War was a divisive issue in India. After the war, when Japanese political leaders were tried for war crimes, the sole dissenting voice among the judges came from the Indian judge, Radhabinod Pal, a distinguished jurist. Pal dissented on various grounds, among them that no fair trial was possible in view of the asymmetry of power between the victor and the defeated.

Ambivalent feelings in India toward the Japanese military aggression, given the unacceptable nature of British imperialism, possibly had a part in predisposing Pal to consider a perspective different from that of the other judges.

More tellingly, Subhas Chandra Bose (no relation of Rash Behari Bose), a leading nationalist, made his way to Japan during the war via Italy and Germany after escaping from a British prison; he helped the Japanese to form units of Indian soldiers, who had earlier surrendered to the advancing Japanese army, to fight on the Japanese side as the "Indian National Army."

Rabindranath had formerly entertained great admiration for Subhas Bose as a dedicated nonsectarian fighter for Indian independence. But their ways would have parted when Bose's political activities took this turn, although Tagore was dead by the time Bose reached Japan. Tagore saw Japanese militarism as illustrating the way nationalism can mislead even a nation of great achievement and promise.

In 1938 Yone Noguchi, the distinguished poet and friend of Tagore (as well as of Yeats and Pound), wrote to Tagore, pleading with him to change his mind about Japan. Rabindranath's reply, written on September 12, 1938, was altogether uncompromising:

It seems to me that it is futile for either of us to try to convince the other, since your faith in the infallible right of Japan to bully other Asiatic nations into line with your Government's policy is not shared by me.... Believe me, it is sorrow and shame, not anger, that prompt me to write to you. I suffer intensely not only because the reports of Chinese suffering batter against my heart, but because I can no longer point out with pride the example of a great Japan.

He would have been much happier with the postwar emergence of Japan as a peaceful power. Then, too, since he was not free of egotism, he would also have been pleased by the attention paid to his ideas by the novelist Yasunari Kawabata and others.

INTERNATIONAL CONCERNS

Tagore was not invariably well-informed about international politics. He allowed himself to be entertained by Mussolini in a short visit to Italy in May-June 1926, a visit arranged by Carlo Formichi, professor of Sanskrit at the University of Rome. When he asked to meet Benedetto Croce, Formichi said, "Impossible! Impossible!" Mussolini told him that Croce was "not in Rome." When Tagore said he would go "wherever he is," Mussolini assured him that Croce's whereabouts were unknown.

Such incidents, as well as warnings from Romain Rolland and other friends, should have ended Tagore's flirtation with Mussolini more quickly than it did. But only after he received graphic accounts of the brutality of Italian fascism from two exiles, Gaetano Salvemini and Gaetano Salvadori, and learned more of what was happening in Italy, did he publicly denounce the regime, publishing a letter to the *Manchester Guardian* in August.

The next month, Popolo d'Italia, the magazine edited by Benito Mussolini's brother, replied: "Who cares? Italy laughs at Tagore and those who brought this unctuous and insupportable fellow in our midst."

With his high expectations of Britain, Tagore continued to be surprised by what he took to be a lack of official sympathy for international victims of aggression. He returned to this theme in the lecture he gave on his last birthday, in 1941:

While Japan was quietly devouring North China, her act of wanton aggression was ignored as a minor incident by the veterans of British diplomacy. We have also witnessed from this distance how actively the British statesmen acquiesced in the destruction of the Spanish Republic.

But distinguishing between the British government and the British people, Rabindranath went on to note "with admiration how a band of valiant Englishmen laid down their lives for Spain." Tagore's view of the Soviet Union has been a subject of much discussion. He was widely read in Russia. In 1917 several Russian translations of *Gitanjali* were available, and by the late 1920s many of the English versions of his work had been rendered into Russian by several distinguished translators. Russian versions of his work continued to appear: Boris Pasternak translated him in the 1950s and 1960s.

When Tagore visited Russia in 1930, he was much impressed by its development efforts and by what he saw as a real commitment to eliminate poverty and economic inequality. But what impressed him most was the expansion of basic education across the Old Russian Empire. In Letters from Russia, written in Bengali and published in 1931, he unfavorably compares the acceptance of widespread illiteracy in India by the British administration with Russian efforts to expand education:

In stepping on the soil of Russia, the first thing that caught my eye was that in education, at any rate, the peasant and the working classes have made such enormous progress in these few years that nothing comparable has happened even to our highest classes in the course of the last hundred and fifty years....

The people here are not at all afraid of giving complete education even to Turcomans of distant Asia; on the contrary, they are utterly in earnest about it.

When parts of the book were translated into English in 1934, the under-secretary for India stated in Parliament that it was "calculated by distortion of the facts to bring the British Administration in India into contempt and disrepute," and the book was then promptly banned. The English version would not be published until after independence.

EDUCATION AND FREEDOM

The British Indian administrators were not, however, alone in trying to suppress Tagore's reflections on Russia. They were joined by Soviet officials. In an interview with *Izvestia* in 1930, Tagore sharply criticized the lack of freedom that he observed in Russia:

I must ask you: Are you doing your ideal a service by arousing in the minds of those under your training anger, class-hatred, and revengefulness against those whom you consider to be your enemies?... Freedom of mind is needed for the reception of truth; terror hopelessly kills it.... For the sake of humanity I hope you may never create a vicious force of violence, which will go on weaving an interminable chain of violence and cruelty.... You have tried to destroy many of the other evils of [the czarist] period. Why not try to destroy this one also?

The interview was not published in *Izvestia* until 1988-nearly sixty years later. Tagore's reaction to the Russia of 1930 arose from two of his strongest commitments: his uncompromising belief in the importance of "freedom of mind" (the source of his criticism of the Soviet Union), and his conviction that the expansion of basic education is central to social progress (the source of his praise, particularly in contrast to British-run India). He identified the lack of basic education as the fundamental cause of many of India's social and economic afflictions:

In my view the imposing tower of misery which today rests on the heart of India has its sole foundation in the absence of education. Caste divisions, religious conflicts, aversion to work, precarious economic conditions - all centre on this single factor.

It was on education (and on the reflection, dialogue, and communication that are associated with it), rather than on, say, spinning "as a sacrifice" ("the charka does not require anyone to think"), that the future of India would depend. Tagore was concerned not only that there be wider opportunities for education across the country (especially in rural areas where schools were few), but also that the schools themselves be more lively and enjoyable.

He himself had dropped out of school early, largely out of boredom, and had never bothered to earn a diploma. He wrote extensively on how schools should be made more attractive to boys and girls and thus more productive. His own co-educational school at Santiniketan had many progressive features. The emphasis here was on self-motivation rather than on discipline, and on fostering intellectual curiosity rather than competitive excellence.

Much of Rabindranath's life was spent in developing the school at Santiniketan. The school never had much money, since the fees were very low. His lecture honoraria, "$700 a scold," went to support it, as well as most of his Nobel Prize money. The school received no support from the government, but did get help from private citizens-even Mahatma Gandhi raised money for it.

The dispute with Mahatma Gandhi on the Bihar earthquake touched on a subject that was very important to Tagore: the need for education in science as well as in literature and the humanities. At Santiniketan, there were strong "local" elements in its emphasis on Indian traditions, including the classics, and in the use of Bengali rather than English as the language of instruction.

At the same time there were courses on a great variety of cultures, and study programs devoted to China, Japan, and the Middle East. Many foreigners came to Santiniketan to study or teach, and the fusion of studies seemed to work. I am partial to seeing Tagore as an educator, having myself been educated at Santiniketan. The school was unusual in many different ways, such as the oddity that classes, excepting those requiring a laboratory, were held outdoors (whenever the weather permitted).

No matter what we thought of Rabindranath's belief that one gains from being in a natural setting while learning (some of us argued about this theory), we typically found the experience of outdoor schooling extremely attractive and pleasant. Academically, our school was not particularly exacting (often we did not have any examinations at all), and it could not, by the usual academic standards, compete with some of the better schools in Calcutta. But there was something remarkable about the ease with which class discussions could move from Indian traditional literature to contemporary as well as classical Western thought, and then to the culture of China or Japan or elsewhere.

The school's celebration of variety was also in sharp contrast with the cultural conservatism and separatism that has tended to grip India from time to time. The cultural give and take of Tagore's vision of the contemporary world has close parallels with the vision of Satyajit Ray, also an alumnus of Santiniketan who made several films based on Tagore's stories. Ray's words about Santiniketan in 1991 would have greatly pleased Rabindranath:

> I consider the three years I spent in Santiniketan as the most fruitful of my life.... Santiniketan opened my eyes for the first time to the splendours of Indian and Far Eastern art. Until then I was completely under the sway of Western art, music and literature. Santiniketan made me the combined product of East and West that I am.

INDIA TODAY

At the fiftieth anniversary of Indian independence, the reckoning of what India had or had not achieved in this half century was a subject of considerable interest: "What has been the story of those first fifty years?" (as Shashi Tharoor asked in his balanced, informative, and highly readable account of *India: From Midnight to the Millennium*). If Tagore were to see the India of today, more than half a century after independence, nothing perhaps would shock him so much as the continued illiteracy of the masses. He would see this as a total betrayal of what the nationalist leaders had promised during the struggle for independence-a promise that had figured even in Nehru's rousing speech on the eve of independence in August 1947 (on India's "tryst with destiny").

In view of his interest in childhood education, Tagore would not be consoled by the extraordinary expansion of university education, in which India sends to its universities six times as many people per unit of population as does China. Rather, he would be stunned that, in contrast to East and Southeast Asia, including China, half the adult population and two thirds of Indian women remain unable to read or write. Statistically reliable surveys indicate that even in the late 1980s, nearly half of the rural girls between the ages of twelve and fourteen did not attend any school for a single day of their lives.

This state of affairs is the result of the continuation of British imperial neglect of mass education, which has been reinforced by India's traditional elitism, as well as upper-class-dominated contemporary politics (except in parts of India such as Kerala, where anti-upper-caste movements have tended to concentrate on education as a great leveller).

Tagore would see illiteracy and the neglect of education not only as the main source of India's continued social backwardness, but also as a great constraint that restricts the possibility and reach of economic development in India (as his writings on rural development forcefully make clear). Tagore would also have strongly felt the need for a greater commitment-and a greater sense of urgency-in removing endemic poverty. At the same time, Tagore would undoubtedly find some satisfaction in the survival of democracy in India, in its relatively free press, and in general from the "freedom of mind" that post-independence Indian politics has, on the whole, managed to maintain.

He would also be pleased by the fact noted by the historian E.P. Thompson (whose father Edward Thompson had written one of the first major biographies of Tagore:

> All the convergent influences of the world run through this society: Hindu, Moslem, Christian, secular; Stalinist, liberal, Maoist, democratic socialist, Gandhian. There is not a thought that is being thought in the West or East that is not active in some Indian mind.

Tagore would have been happy also to see that the one governmental attempt to dispense generally with basic liberties and political and civil rights in India, in the 1970s, when Prime Minister Indira Gandhi (ironically, herself a former student at Santiniketan) declared an "emergency," was overwhelmingly rejected by the Indian voters, leading to the precipitate fall of her government.

Rabindranath would also see that the changes in policy that have eliminated famine since independence had much to do with the freedom to be heard in a democratic India. In Tagore's play *Raja O Rani* ("The King and the Queen"), the sympathetic Queen eventually rebels against the callousness of state policy toward the hungry. She begins by inquiring about the ugly sounds outside the palace, only to be told that the noise is coming from "the coarse, clamorous crowd who howl unashamedly for food and disturb the sweet peace of the palace."

The Viceregal office in India could have taken a similarly callous view of Indian famines, right up to the easily preventable Bengal famine of 1943, just before independence, which killed between two and three million people. But a government in a multi-party democracy, with elections and free newspapers, cannot any longer dismiss the noise from "the coarse, clamorous crowd."

Unlike Gandhi, Rabindranath would not resent the development of modern industries in India, or the acceleration of technical progress, since he did not want India to be shackled to the turning of "the wheel of an antiquated invention." Tagore was concerned that people not be dominated by machines, but he was not opposed to making good use of modern technology.

"The mastery over the machine," he wrote in *Crisis in Civilisation,* "by which the British have consolidated their sovereignty over their vast empire, has been kept a sealed book, to which due access has been denied to this helpless country." Rabindranath had a deep interest in the environment - he was particularly concerned about deforestation and initiated a "festival of tree-planting" (vriksha-ropana) as early as 1928. He would want increased private and government commitments to environmentalism; but he would not derive from this position a general case against modern industry and technology.

ON CULTURAL SEPARATION

Rabindranath would be shocked by the growth of cultural separatism in India, as elsewhere. The "openness" that he valued so much is certainly under great strain right now - in many countries. Religious fundamentalism still has a relatively small following in India; but various factions seem to be doing their best to increase their numbers. Certainly religious sectarianism has had much success in some parts of India (particularly in the west and the north). Tagore would see the expansion of religious sectarianism as being closely associated with an artificially separatist view of culture.

He would have strongly resisted defining India in specifically Hindu terms, rather than as a "confluence" of many cultures. Even after the partition of 1947, India is still the third- largest Muslim country in the world, with more Muslims than in Bangladesh, and nearly as many as in Pakistan. Only Indonesia has substantially more followers of Islam. Indeed, by pointing to the immense heterogeneousness of India's cultural background and its richly diverse history, Tagore had argued that the "idea of India" itself militated against a culturally separatist view-"against the intense consciousness of the separateness of one's own people from others."

Tagore would also oppose the cultural nationalism that has recently been gaining some ground in India, along with an exaggerated fear of the influence of the West. He was uncompromising in his belief that human beings could absorb quite different cultures in constructive ways:

Whatever we understand and enjoy in human products instantly becomes ours, wherever they might have their origin. I am proud of my humanity when I can acknowledge the poets and artists of other countries as my own. Let me feel with unalloyed gladness that all the great glories of man are mine. Therefore it hurts me deeply when the cry of rejection rings loud against the West in my country with the clamour that Western education can only injure us.

In this context, it is important to emphasize that Rabindranath was not short of pride in India's own heritage, and often spoke about it. He lectured at Oxford, with evident satisfaction, on the importance of India's religious ideas-quoting both from ancient texts and from popular poetry (such as the verses of the sixteenth-century Muslim poet Kabir).

In 1940, when he was given an honorary doctorate by Oxford University, in a ceremony arranged at his own educational establishment in Santiniketan ("In Gangem Defluit Isis," Oxford helpfully explained), to the predictable "volley of Latin" Tagore responded "by a volley of Sanskrit," as Marjorie Sykes, a Quaker friend of Rabindranath, reports. Her cheerful summary of the match, "India held its own," was not out of line with Tagore's pride in Indian culture.

His welcoming attitude to Western civilisation was reinforced by this confidence: he did not see India's culture as fragile and in need of "protection" from Western influence. In India, he wrote, "circumstances almost compel us to learn English, and this lucky accident has given us the opportunity of access into the richest of all poetical literatures of the world."

There seems to me much force in Rabindranath's argument for clearly distinguishing between the injustice of a serious asymmetry of power (colonialism being a prime example of this) and the importance nevertheless of appraising Western culture in an open-minded way, in colonial and postcolonial territories, in order to see what uses could be made of it.

Rabindranath insisted on open debate on every issue, and distrusted conclusions based on a mechanical formula, no matter how attractive that formula might seem in isolation (such as "This was forced on us by our colonial masters - we must reject it," "This is our tradition-we must follow it," "We have promised to do this-we must fulfill that promise," and so on).

The question he persistently asks is whether we have reason enough to want what is being proposed, taking everything into account. Important as history is, reasoning has to go beyond the past. It is in the sovereignty of reasoning-fearless reasoning in freedom-that we can find Rabindranath Tagore's lasting voice.

RABINDRANATH TAGORE'S POLITICAL VIEWS

Tagore's politics exhibited a marked ambivalence - on the one hand, he denounced European imperialism, occasionally voicing full support for Indian nationalists; on the other hand, he also shunned the Swadeshi movement, denouncing it in his acrid September 1925 essay "The Cult of the Charka" (an allusion to elements of Gandhism and the Non-Cooperation Movement).

For example, in reaction to a July 22, 1904 suggestion by the British that Bengal should be partitioned, an upset Tagore took to delivering a lecture - entitled "Swadeshi Samaj" ("The Union of Our Homeland") - that instead proposed an alternative solution: a self-help based comprehensive reorganisation of rural Bengal. In addition, he viewed British control of India as a "political symptom of our social disease", urging Indians to accept that "there can be no question of blind revolution, but of steady and purposeful education".

In line with this, Tagore denounced nationalism, deeming it among humanity's greatest problems. "A nation," he wrote, "... is that aspect which a whole population assumes when organized for a mechanical purpose", a purpose often associated with a "selfishness" that "can be a grandly magnified form" of personal selfishness. During his extensive travels, he formed a vision of East-West unity.

Subsequently, he was shocked by the rising nationalism found in Germany and other nations prior to the World War II. Tagore thus delivered a series of lectures on nationalism; although well-received throughout much of Europe, they were mostly ignored or criticized in Japan and the United States. Yet Tagore wrote songs lionizing the Indian independence movement. On 30 May 1919, he renounced the knighthood that had been conferred upon him by

Lord Hardinge in 1915 in protest against the Amritsar massacre (Jallianwallah Bagh), when British soldiers killed at least 1526 unarmed civilians.

He was also instrumental in resolving a dispute between Gandhi and Bhimrao Ramji Ambedkar; it involved Ambedkar's insistence on separate electorates for untouchables and Gandhi's announcement - in protest against the concession - of a fast "unto death" beginning on 20 September 1932. Tagore also lashed out against the orthodox rote-oriented educational system introduced in India under the Raj.

He lampooned it in his short story "The Parrot's Training", where a bird - which ultimately dies - is caged by tutors and force-fed pages torn from books. These views crystallised in his experimental school at Santiniketan, ("Abode of Peace"), founded in 1901 on the site of a West Bengal estate inherited from his father.

Established in the traditional *brahmacharya* structure - whereby students live under a *guru* in a self-sustaining community - became a magnet for talented scholars, artists, linguists, and musicians from diverse backgrounds. Tagore spent prodigious amounts of energy fundraising for Santiniketan, even contributing all his Nobel Prize monies. Today, Tagore's school is a Central University under the Government of India.

TAGORE, HISTORY AND CULTURAL STUDIES

There was a time when in Europe, shattered by the torment of the First World War, the name Rabindranath Tagore (1861-1941) could evoke an enthusiasm bordering on idolatry. This is no longer the case. Today many people have perhaps heard the name but few will associate it with a famous Bengali poet on whom the Nobel Prize for literature was conferred in 1913. The basis for foreign recognition has been fragile as the non-Bengali-reading public only knew Tagore's work either from the few clipped paraphrases in English made by him, or from some later, fairly weak, translations done by others in the forties and the fifties.

It seems that until recently the personality cult of Tagore prevented a more sober and critical assessment of his Bengali works, while the available English texts do not do him full justice. After all, the original Bengali works run into thousands of pages and cover almost every literary genre. However, to date they are known only to the Bengali-reading public both in India and Bangladesh. A new impulse to produce better translations of and to encourage a less mawkish involvement with Tagore arose in the mid-eighties.

The first fruits of this new preoccupation can be seen in the recent works published by such people as William Radice, Martin Kämpchen, and Ketaki Kushari Dyson. As Tagore was and still is known mainly as a poet, these translations are for the most part (on the whole rather well executed) renderings of poetry. But Tagore wrote more than poems and songs, more than short stories, novels, travelogues, plays and letters.

As a perceptive intellectual of his times he also commented on politics, social questions and religious and cultural matters in numerous essays and lectures. This body of religious, cultural and political writings has been little studied so far, in spite of the fact that it made an important contribution to the canon of Bengali nationalist literature of the late nineteenth and the early twentieth century, a truth to which Tapan Raychaudhuri in his book *Europe Reconsidered, Perceptions of the West in Nineteenth Century Bengal*, frankly testifies.

SUBALTERN STUDIES

Also in the two recent books by Partha Chatterjee on Bengali and Indian nationalism in the colonial nineteenth century we find only scant reference to Tagore. Chatterjee, belonging to the prestigious historiographical school of the *Subaltern Studies* and now one of the editors of the volumes bearing the same name, prefers to analyse the conceptualisations of Indian nationalism by the earlier great Bengali writer Bankimchandra. In this Chatterjee follows the current postmodern, text-based trend of writing cultural history within the Subaltern Studies.

The latter's founder, Ranajit Guha, frequently refers to Bankimchandra, while Sudipta Kaviraj, also belonging to the Subaltern Studies group, has devoted a fresh study to this writer. The above-mentioned niche of Subaltern Studies seems to be meandering along slowly to join the field of Cultural Studies proper. The latter is a multidisciplinary attempt at writing and interpreting human culture.

After it sprang up formally in Birmingham at the Centre for Contemporary Cultural Studies and gained importance in the seventies, it is now rising to prominence in the North American, and Australian human sciences. Largely an outcome of the postmodern experience, it seems to hold out credible but heavily contested promises to build novel and creative passages towards a more refined, if fragmented, understanding of how cultural production comes about and what forces make it 'work' in human societies.

Its early theoretical 'canon' of Cultural Studies embraces among other schools Marxism, the Frankfurter Schule, English literary theory and a bit of classical Anarchist thought, as well as authors like Clifford Geertz, Bourdieu, and Stuart Hall. This canon is now expanding in various directions and incorporates many new fields of sociological and historical study such as women's and minority studies.

The most recent unfolding of Cultural Studies can be grasped from a number of anthologies, among which the ones edited by Lawrence Grossberg, Cary Nelson, Paula Treichler (1992); Simon During (1993); and Valda Blundell, John Shepherd, Ian Taylor (1993), are the more prominent.

The monographs by Norman K. Denzin (1992) and Fred Inglis (1993) offer vigorously critical and historical surveys of the entire field.

THE LEIDEN TAGORE PROJECTS

The Leiden projects on Tagore, which are conducted draw critically upon the theoretical frameworks and possibilities offered by both the Subaltern Studies and Cultural Studies. Thus the present Tagore projects will be drawn into the orbits of these fields. This will widen the horizons of the study of Bengali culture as well as those of Cultural Studies as a whole. Fragments of Tagore's poetry, nationalist and religious thought will be presented in this light as instances of Bengali cultural studies.

The first result, to appear in the course of 1995, is a translation from Bengali into Dutch of the *Gitali* (1914), a volume of Tagore's poetry which has hitherto been translated into English only once and that somewhat poorly. The Gitali is the last of three consecutive volumes of which the first, *Gitanjali* (1910), partly paraphrased into English by Tagore himself in 1912, brought his fame to the attention of the Western world. My translation of the Gitali will appear in the series 'Kern Institute Miscellenea'.

This literary presentation will soon be followed by two studies in English. The first one (with translations from various Bengali sources) will deal with the constructions of nineteenth century Indian nationalism, understood by its protagonists as being of a predominantly Hindu-cultural character, and its diverse ideological and political perspectives within the context of the British Raj. This volume will bring to light certain aspects of the (cultural) nationalism of this period, which neither Tapan Raychaudhuri, Partha Chatterjee, nor Sudipta Kaviraj have treated in detail in their respective explorations.

Around the turn of the century Tagore wrote with penetrating insight about European nationalism and its relevance to the Indian reality. Tagore wrote in a period in which what Benedict Anderson 1993) calls 'print capitalism' was already well established in India. The printed word had become a major vehicle for spreading ideology among the educated middle class, using not only English, but also the vernaculars. By means of the printed word Tagore tried to disseminate a distinctive brand of nationalism in which cultural theories, (mainly liberal Hindu) religious inspiration, historical imagination as well as invention and humanist ethos blended almost inseparably. This blend with its shifting accents forms the subject of the second publication. It will contain a full English translation from Bengali with annotations of *Dharma*, a volume of Tagore's early religious essays, published in book form in 1908.

In these essays Tagore construes a national religious ideology with different strands, ranging from utterly individualistic religious experience to broad concepts of a unitary Indian nation whose predominant flavour is humanist religious and spiritual. The exercise of translation and annotation (a rather traditional performance) is refined by commentatorial readings of the texts themselves. These readings will highlight some disturbing problems of the original texts and pose some disagreeable questions about the texts.

It will be underscored that these problems and questions have not lost much of their historical and social pertinence. Among the more agonizing problems is the present rise of religious political discourse, commonly labelled fundamentalism and communalism. But also nationalism with its seeming pretensions to secular religiosity shakes the (post)modern worldview down to its very roots.

Within the context of modern Indian political and cultural history, I will extract the genealogy of these phenomena right back to the period in which Tagore was active. This will to some extent enable us to gain a better understanding of the way in which Indian cultural productions exerted their influence in colonial society and in whose interest, and how various politically motivated readings of the same cultural product evokes different responses and different re-readings.

3

The Letters between Tagore and Noguchi

RABINDRANATH TAGORE AND JAPAN

Coincidentally, a quiet announcement in a distant country served to put the familiar debate over Japanese military affairs and ambitions in a longer perspective - and to remind Japan of the usefulness of seeing itself through others' eyes. According to a report from the Press Trust of India, a new museum commemorating the connection between Japan and India's Nobel Prize-winning poet and philosopher, Rabindranath Tagore (1861-1941), is due to open in November at Rabindra Bharati University in Calcutta, West Bengal, Tagore's birthplace.

Established with a grant from Mitsubishi Corp. India, the museum will house "rare memorabilia that chronicle [the poet's] many visits to Japan and its deep influence" on him. That influence was mostly literary and spiritual, reflecting Tagore's personal bent, yet any chronicle of his relationship with Japan will surely also have to mention his discreetly expressed dismay at what he saw as signs of militant nationalism, especially during his visit of 1916.

It reminded him of the unthinking, belligerent chauvinism that he, and others, felt had led to the outbreak of war in Europe two years earlier and did not, he believed, represent the best of Japan. While the nation's present political situation is light years removed from that of the Taisho Era, it could be said that the renunciation of militarism, as enshrined in the postwar Constitution, still represents the best of Japan - the things that the distinguished Indian visitor celebrated so long ago.

There are arguments to be made for recognizing the nation's Self-Defense Forces as a full-fledged conventional military, of course - the main one being that they are already a full-fledged conventional military in all but name, as the prime minister has pointed out. But the new reminder of Tagore's sojourns here suggests that, before such a step is taken, lawmakers should also remember that it is important how other countries see Japan, and what it is they think this country stands for.

Tagore was an interesting and thoughtful man. Born into a wealthy Hindu family,.he grew up as part of privileged, highly educated elite and drew on that background to become a virtual citizen of the world. From the school he founded at Santiniketan, in West Bengal, in 1901, he traveled much and wrote more, becoming a passionate - and passionately nonsectarian - champion of better understanding between East and West. When he finally came to Japan in 1916, at the urging of a Japanese friend, he found much to admire: the country's economic, industrial and scientific advances, for one thing, but also its cultural and literary traditions and the values he felt those traditions represented.

The verse form of haiku, for instance, he appreciated for its emotional restraint, Japan's "great Art" for its emphasis on simplicity and harmony. The seeds of divergence that he sensed between those values and the strident patriotism of the new Japan made him uneasy. Twenty-two years later, he saw the fruit of those seeds in Japan's military adventures in China.

In a remarkable correspondence in 1938 with the poet Yone Noguchi, who had become an apologist for Japan's expansionist aims in Asia, Tagore expressed his "utter sorrow" at these developments and also made a prediction. "I know that one day the disillusionment of your people will be complete," he wrote, "and through laborious centuries they will have to clear the debris of their civilisation wrought to ruin by their own warlords run amok.

They will realize that the aggressive war on China is insignificant as compared to the destruction of the inner spirit of chivalry of Japan, which is proceeding with a ferocious severity." Although he did not live to see it, Japan's postwar Constitution would surely have struck him as an attempt to restore and express that spirit. But he also understood that it would take time - not the centuries he foresaw, perhaps, but much more than the six or so decades that have passed - for the country to undo the damage it had done in Asia, including the damage to its own image.

The truth is that Japan's skeptical Asian neighbors still see the nation that grew from the seeds Tagore observed here in 1916 - nationalistic, scheming, aggressive - and not the nation whose culture he praised as the embodiment of totally opposite qualities: harmony, forbearance and benevolence.

Such perceptions are important, arguably more important than any of the pragmatic arguments for restoring the military's conventional status. The pacifist Constitution was a brave, although sometimes misunderstood, step toward changing those perceptions, permanently. As the new museum opens in Calcutta, it's hard to imagine Tagore, who loved Japan so well, thinking there would ever be a time to let it go.

TAGORE-NOGUCHI CORRESPONDENCE ON JAPANESE AGGRESSION, 1938

Dear Rabindranath,

When I visited you at Shantiniketan a few years ago, you were troubled with the Ethiopian question, and vehemently condemned Italy. Retiring into your guest chamber that night, I wondered whether you would say the same thing on Japan, if she were equally situated like Italy. I perfectly agreed with your opinion and admired your courage of speaking, when in Tokyo, 1916, you censured the westernisation of Japan from a public platform. Not answering back to your words, the intellectual people of my country were conscious of its possible consequence, for, not only staying as an unpleasant spectacle; the westernisation had every chance for becoming anything awful.

But if you take the present war in China for the criminal outcome of Japan's surrender to the West, you are wrong, because, not being a slaughtering madness, it is, I believe, the inevitable means, terrible it is though, for establishing a new great world in the Asiatic continent, where the "principle of live-and-let-live" has to be realized. Believe me, it is the war of "Asia for Asia." With a crusader's determination and with a sense of sacrifice that belongs to a martyr, our young soldiers go to be front. Their minds are light and happy, the war is not for conquest, but the correction of mistaken idea of China, I mean Kuomingtung government, and for uplifting her simple and ignorant masses to better life and wisdom. Borrowing from other countries neither money nor blood, Japan is undertaking this tremendous work single-handed and alone. I do not know why we cannot be praised by your countrymen. But we are terribly blamed by them, as it seems, for our heroism and aim.

Sometime ago the Chinese army, defeated in Huntung province by Hwangho River, had cut from desperate madness several places of the river bank; not keeping in check the advancing Japanese army, it only made thirty hundred thousand people drown in the flood and one hundred thousand village houses destroyed. Defending the welfare of its own kinsmen or killing them, - which is the object of the Chinese army, I wonder? It is strange that such an atrocious inhuman conduct ever known in the world history did not become in the west a target of condemnation. Oh where are your humanitarians who profess to be a guardian of humanity? Are they deaf and blind? Besides the Chinese soldiers, miserably paid and poorly clothed, are a habitual criminal of robbery, and then an everlasting menace to the honest hard-working people who cling to the ground. Therefore the Japanese soldiers are followed by them with the paper flags of the Rising Sun in their hands; to a soldierly work we have to add one more endeavour in the relief work of them. You can imagine how expensive this war for Japan is. Putting expenditure out of the question, we are determined to use up our last cent for the final victory that would ensure in the future a great peace of many hundred years.

I received the other day a letter from my western friend, denouncing the world that went to Hell. I replied him, saying: "Oh my friend, you should cover your ears, when a war bugle rings too wild. Shut your eyes against a picture of your martial cousins becoming a fish salad! Be patient, my friend, for a war is only spasmodic matter that cannot last long, but will adjust one's condition better in the end. You are a coward if you are afraid of it. Nothing worthy will be done unless you pass through a severe trial. And the peace that follows after a war is most important." For this peace we Japanese are ready to exhaust our resources of money and blood.

Today we are called under the flag of "Service-making," each person of the country doing his own bit for the realisation of idealism. There was no time as today in the whole historyM of Japan, when all the people, from the Emperor to a rag-picker in the street, consolidated together with one mind. And there is no more foolish supposition as that our financial bankruptey is a thing settled if the war drags on. Since the best part of the Chinese continent is already with us in friendly terms, we are not fighting with the whole of China. Our enemy is only the Kuomingtung government, a miserable puppet of the west. If Chiang Kai-shek wishes a long war, we are quite ready for it. Five years? Ten years? Twenty years? As long as he desires, my friend. Now one year has passed since the first bullet was exchanged between China and Japan; but with a fresh mind as if it sees that the war has just begun, we are now looking the event in the face. After the fall of Hankow, the Kuomingtung government will retire to a remote place of her country; but until the western countries change their attitude towards China, we will keep up fighting with fists or wisdom.

The Japanese poverty is widely advertised in the west, though I do not know how it was started. Japan is poor beyond doubt, - well, according to the measure you wish to apply to. But I thing that the Japanese poverty is a fabricated story as much as richness of China. There is no country in the world like Japan, where money is equally divided among the people. Supposing that we are poor, I will say that we are trained to stand the pain of poverty. Japan is very strong in adversity.

But you will be surprised to know that the postal saving of people comes up now to five thousand million yen, responding to the government's propaganda of economy. For going on, surmounting every difficulty that the war brings in, we are saving every cent and even making good use of waste scraps. Since the war began, we grew spiritually strong and true ten times more than before. There is nothing hard to accomplish to a young man. Yes, Japan is the land of young men. According to nature's law, the old has to retire while the young advances. Behold, the sun is arising, be gone all the sickly bats and dirty vermins! Cursed be one's intrigue and empty pride that sin against nature's rule and justice.

China could very well avoid the war, of course, if Chiang Kai-shek was more sensible with insight. Listening to an irresponsible third party of the west a long way off, thinking too highly of his own strength, he turned at last his own country, as she is today, into a ruined desert to which fifty years would not be enough for recovery. He never happened to think for a moment that the friendship of western countries was but a trick of their monetary interest itself in his country. And it is too late now for Chiang to reproach them for the faithlessness of their words of promise.

For a long time we had been watching with doubt at Chiang's program, the consolidation of the country, because the Chinese history had no period when the country was unified in the real meaning, and the subjugation of various war-lords under his flag was nothing. Until all the people took an oath of co-operation with him, we thought, his program was no more than a table talk. Being hasty and thoughtless, Chiang began to popularize the anti-Japanese movement among the students who were pigmy politicians in some meaning because he deemed it to be a method for the speedy realisation of his program; but he never thought that he was erring from the Oriental ethics that preached on one's friendship with the neighbours. Seeing that his propagation had too great effect on his young followers, he had no way to keep in check their wild jingoism, and them finally made his country roll down along the slope of destruction. Chiang is a living example who sold his country to the west for nothing, and smashed his skin with the crime of westernisation. Dear Rabindranath, what will you say about this Chiang Kai-shek?

Dear poet, today we have to turn our deaf ears towards a lesson of freedom that may come from America, because the people there already ceased to practice it. The ledgerbook diplomacy of England is too well known through the world. I am old enough to know from experience that no more worse than others. Though I admit that Japan is today ruled by militarism, natural to the actual condition of the country, I am glad that enough freedom of speaking and acting is allowed to one like myself.

Japan is fairly liberal in spite of the war time. So I can say without fear to be locked up that those service-crazy people are drunken, and that a thing in the world, great and ture, because of its connection with the future, only comes from one who hates to be a common human unit, stepping aside so that he can unite himself with Eternity. I believe that such a one, who withdraws into a snail's shell for the quest of life's hopeful future, will be in the end a true patriot, worthy of his own nation. Therefore I am able to disgrace the name of poet, and to try to live up to the words of Browning who made the Grammmarian exclain:

"Leave now for dogs and apeas! Man has Forever".

Yours very sincerely,

Yone Noguchi.

"Uttarayan,"

Santimiketan, Bengal.

Sepember 1, 1938.

Dear Noguchi,

I am profundly surprised by the letter that you have written to me: neither its temper nor its contents harmonise with the spirit of Japan which I learnt to admire in your writings and came to love through my personal contacts with you. It is sad to think that the passion of collective militarism may on occasion helplessly overwhelm even the creative artist, that genuine intellectual power should be led to offer its dignity and truth to be sacrificed at the shrine of the dark gods of war.

You seem to agree with me in your condemnation of the massacre of Ethiopia by Fascrist Italy but you would reserve the murderous attack on Chinese millions for judgment under a different category. But surely judgments are based on principle, and no amount of special pleading can changethe fact that in launching a ravening war on Chinese himanity, with all the deadly methods learnt from the West, Japan is infringing every moral principle on which civilisation is based. You claim that Japan's situation was unique, forgetting that military situations are always unique, and that pious war-lords, convinced of peculiarly individual justification fcr their atrocities have never failed to arrange for special alliances with divinity for anihilation and torture on a large scale.

Humanity, in spite of its many failures, has believed in a fundamental moral structure of society. When you speak, therefore, of "the inevitable means, terrible it is though, for establishing a new great world in the Asiatic continent" - signifying, I suppose, the bombing on Chinese women and children and the desecration of ancient temples and Universities as a means of saving China for Asia-you are ascribing to humanity a way of life which is not even inevitable among the animals and would certainly not apply to the

East, in spite of her occasional aberrations. You are building your conception of an Asia which would be raised on a tower of skulls. I have, as you rightly point out, believed in the message of Asia, but I never dreamt that this message could be identified with deeds which brought exaltation to the heart of Tamer Lane at his terrible efficiency in manslaughter.

When I protested against "Westernisation" in my lectures in Japan, I contrasted the rapacious Imperialism which some of the Nations of Europe were cultivating with the ideal of perfection preached by Buddha and Christ, with the great heritages of culture and good neighbourliness that went to the making of Asiatic and other civilisations.

I felt it to be my duty to warn the land of Bushido, of great Art and traditions of noble heroism, that this phase of scientific savagery which victimised Western humanity and had led their helpless masses to a moral cannibalism was never to be imitated by a virile people who had entered upon a glorious renascence and had every promise of a creative future before them. The doctrine of "Asia for Asia" which you enunciate in your letter, as an instrument of political blackmail, has all the virtues of the lessor Europe which I repudiate and nothing of the larger humanity that makes us one across the barriers of political labels and divisions. I was amused to read the recent statement of a Tokyo politician that the military alliance of Japan with Italy and Germany was made for "highly spiritual and moral reasons" and "had no materialistic considerations behind them".

Quite so, what is not amusing is that artists and thinkers should echo such remarkable sentiments that translate military swagger into spiritual bravado. In the West, even in the critical days of war-madness, there is never any dearth of great spirits who can raise their voice above the din of battle, and defy their own war-mongers in the name of humanity. Such men have suffered, but never betrayed the conscience of their peoples which they represented. Asia will not be westernised if she can learn from such men: I still believe that there are such souls in Japan though we do not hear of them in those newspapers that are compelled at the cost of their extinction to reproduce thier military master's voice.

"The betrayal of intellectuals" of which the great French writer spoke after the European war, is a dangerous symptom of our Age. You speak of the savings of the poor people of Japan, their silent sacrifice and suffering and take pride in betraying that this pathetic sacrifice is being exploited for gun running and invasion of a neighbour's hearth and home, that human wealth of greatness is pillaged for inhuman purposes. Propaganda, I know, has been reduced to a fine art, and it is almost impossible for peoples in non-democratic countries to resist hourly doses of poison, but one had imagined that at least the men of intellect and imagination would themselves retain their gift of independent judgment.

Evidently such is not always the case ; behind sophisticated arguments seem to lie a mentality of perverted nationalism which makes the "intellectuals" of today to blustering about their "ideologies" dragooning their own "masses" into paths of dissolution. I have known your people and I hate to believe that they could deliberately participate in the organised drugging of Chinese men and women by opium and heroin, but they do not know; in the meanwhile, representatives of Japanese culture in China are busy practising their craft on the multititudes caught in the grip of an organisation of a wholesale human pollution. Proofs of such forcible drugging in Manchukuo and China have been adduced by unimpeachable authorities. But from Japan there has come no protest, not even from her poets.

Holding such opinions as many of your intellectuals do, I am not surprised that they are left "free" by your Government to express themselves. I hope they enjoy their freedom. Retiring from such freedom into "a snail's shell" in order to savour the bliss of meditation "on life's hopeful future", appears to me to be an unnecessary act, even though you advice Japanese artists to do so by way of though you advice Japanese artists to do so by way of change. I cannot accept such separation between an artist's function and his moral conscience. The luxury of enjoying special favouritism by virtue of identity with a Government which is engaged in demolition, in its neighbourhood, of all salient bases of life, and of escaping, at the same time, from any direct responsibility by a philosophy of escapism, seems to me to be another authentic symptom of the modern intellectual's betrayal of humanity.

Unfortunately the rest of the world is almost cowardly in any adequate expression of its judgment owing to ugly possibilities that it may be hatching for its own future and those who are bent upon doing mischief are left alone to defile their history and blacken their reputation for all time to come. But such impunity in the long run bodisaster, like unconsciousness of disease in its painless progress of ravage.

I speak with utter sorrow for your people; your letter has hurt me to the depths of my being. I know that one day the disillusionment of your people will be complete, and through laborious centuries they will have to clear the debris of their civilisation wrought to ruin by their own war-lords run amok. The will realise that the aggressive was on China is insignificant as compared to the destruction of the inner spirit of chivalry of Japan which is proceeding with a ferocious severity. China is unconquerable, her civilisation, under the dauntless leadership of Chiang Kai-Shek, is dis-playing marvellous resources ; the desperate loyalty of her peoples, united as never before, is creating a new age for that land.

Caught unprepared by a gigantic machinery of war, hurled upon her peoples, China is holding her own no temporary defeats can ever crush her fully aroused spirit. Faced by the borrowed science of Japanese militarism which is crudely western in character, China's stand reveals an inherently superior moral stature. And today I understand more than ever before the meaning of the enthusiasm with which the big-hearted Japanese thinker Okakura assured me that China is great.

You do not realise that you are glorifying your neighbour at your own cost. But these are considerations on another plane: the sorrow remains that Japan, in the words of Madame Chiang Kai-Shek which you must have read in the spectator, is creating so many ghosts. Ghosts of immemorial works of Chinese art, of irreplaceable Chinese institutions, of great peace-loving communities drugged, tortured, and destroyed. "Who will lay the ghosts?" she asks. Japanese and Chinese people, let us hope, will join hands together, in True Asian humanity will be reborn. Poets will raise their song and be unashamed, one believes, to declare their faith again in a human destiny which cannot admit of a scientific mass production of fratricide.

Yours sincerely,

Rabindranath Tagore.

P.S. - I find that you have already released your letter to the Press; I take it that you want me to publish my answer in the same manner.

41, Sakurayama,

Nakano, Tokyo.

Oct. 2nd, 1988.

Dear Tagore,

Your eloquent letter, dated Sept. 1st. was duely received. I am glad that the letter inspired me to write you once more.

No one in Japan denies the greatness of China, - I mean the Chinese people. China of the olden times was great with philosophy, literature and art, - particularly in the T'ang dynasty. Under Chinese influence Japan started to build up her own civilisation. But I do not know why we should not oppose to the misguided government of China for the old debt we owe her people. And nobody in Japan ever dreams that we can conquer China. What Japan is doing in China, it is only, as I alreay said, to correct the mistaken idea of Chiang Kai-shek; on this object Japan in staking her all. If Chiang Kai-shek; on this object Japan is staking her hands for the future of both the countries, China and Japan, the war will be stopped to once.

I am glad that you still admire Kakuzo Okakura with enthusiasm as a thinker. If he lives to-day, I believe that he will say the same thing as I do. Betraying your trust, many Chinese soldiers in the front surrender to our Japanese force, and join with us in the cry, "Down with Chiang Kai-shek!" Where is Chinese loyality to him?

Having no proper organ of expression, Japanese opinion is published only seldom in the west; and real fact is always hidden and often comouflaged by cleverness of the Chinese who are a born propagandist. They are strong in foreign languages, and their tongues never fail. While the Japanese are always reticent, evern when situation demands their explanation. From the experiences of many centuries, the Chinese have cultivated an art of speaking for they had been put under such a condition that divided their country to various antagonistic divisions; and being always encroached by the western countries, they depended on diplomacy to turn a thing to their advantage. Admitting that China completely defeated Japan in foreign publicity, it is sad that she often goes too far and plays trickery.

For one instance I will call your attention to the reproduced picture from a Chinese paper on page 247 of the Modern Review for last August, as a living specimen of "Japanese Atrocities in China: Execution of a Chinese Civilians." So awful pictures they are - awful enough to make ten thousand enemies of Japan in a foreign country. But the pictures are nothing but a Chinese invention, simple and plain, because the people in the scenes are all Chinese, slaughterers and all. Besides any one with commonsense would know, if he stops for a moment that it is impossible to take such a picture as these at the front. Really I cannot understand how your friend-editor of the modern Review happened to published them.

It is one's right to weave a dream at the distance, and to create an object of sympathy at the expense of China. Believe me that I am second to none in understanding the Chinese masses who are patient and dilligent, clinging to the ground. But it seems that you are not acquainted with the China of corruption and bribery, and of war lords who put money in a foreign bank when their country is at stake. So long as the country is controlled by such polluted people, the Chinese have only a little chance to create a new age in their land. They have to learn first of all the meaning of honesty and sacrifice before dreaming it. But for this new age in Asia, Japan is engaging in the war, hoping to obtain a good result and mutual benefit that follow the swords. We must have a neighbouring country, strong and true, which is glad to co-operate with us in our work of recons-tructing Asia in the new way. That is only what we expect from China.

Japan's militarism is a tremendous affair no doubt. But if you condemn Japan, because of it, you are failing to notice that Chiang's China is a far more great military country than Japan. China is now mobilizing seven or eight million soldiers armed with European weapons. From cowardice or being ignorant of the reason why they had to fight, the Chinese soldiers are so unspirited in the front. But for this unavailability you cannot foregive Chiang's militarism, if your denial is absolute and true. For the last twenty years Chiang had been trying to arm his country under the western advisers; and these western advisers were mostly from Italy and Germany, the countries of which you are so impatient. And it should be attributed to their advice that he started war ; though it is too late to blame the countries that formally provided him with military knowledge, it is never too late for him to know that the western countries are not worthy of trust.

There is no country in the world that comes to rescue the other at her own expense. If you are a real sympathizer of China, you should come along with your program with she had to do, not passing idly with your condemnation of Japan's militarism. And if you have to condemn militarism, that condemnation should be equally divided between China and Japan.

It is true that when two quarrel, both are in the wrong. And when fighting is over, both the parties will be put perhaps in the mental situation of one who is crying over spilt milk. War is situation of one who is crying over spilt milk. War is atrocious, - particularly when it is performed in a gigantic way as in China today. I hope that you will let me apply your accusation of Japanese atrocity to China, just as it is. Seeing no atrocity in China, you are speaking about her as an innocent country. I expected something impartial from a poet.

I have to think (sic) you that you called my attention to the "Modern intellectual's betrayal of humanity," whatever it be. One can talk any amount of idealism, apart from in reality, if he wishes, and take the pleasure of one belonging to no country. But sharing patriotism equally with the others, we are trying to acquit the duty of talk Heaven when immediate matter of the earth is well arranged.

Supposing that we accept your advice to become a van-guard of humanity according to your prescription, and supposing that we leave China to her own will, and save ourselves from being a "betrayal of the intellectuals," who will promise us with the safety of Japanese spirit that we cultivated with pairs of thousand years, under the threat of communism across a fence? We don't want to barter our home land for an empty name of intellectuals. No, you musn't talk nonsense! God forbid!

Admitting, that militarism is criminal, I think that, if your humanity makes life a mutilated mud-fish, its crime would never be smaller than the other. I spent my whole life admiring beauty and truth, with one hope to lift life to a dignity, more vigorous and noble; from this reason, I face in madness, with three wild eyes, promised me with a forthcoming peace. And also at Elephanta Island; near Bombay, I learned from the Three-headed Siva a lesson of destruction as inevitable truth of life. Then I wrote:

"Thy slaughter's sword is never so unkind as it appears.

Creation is great, but destroying is still greater,

Because up from the ashes new Wcnder take its flight."

But if you command me to obey the meekness of humanity under all the circumstances, you are forgetting what your old Hindu philosophy taught you. I say this not only for my purpose, because such reflection is important for any country.

I wonder who reported to you that we are killing innocent people and bombing on their unprotected towns. Far from it, we are trying to do our best for helping them, because we have so much to depend on them for co-operation in the future, and because Bushido command us to limit purnishment to a thing which only deserves it. It was an apt measure of our Japanese soldiers that the famous cave temples of the 5th century in North China were saved from savage repacity of the dereated Shinese (sic) soldiers in fight. Except madame chiang with frustrated brain, no one has seen the "ghosts of Chinese institutions and art, destroyed". And if those institutions and art, admitting that they are immemorial and irreplacable, had been ever destroyed it is but the crazy work of Chinese soldiers, because they want to leave a desert to Japan. You ought to know better since you are acquainted with so many Japanese, whether or not we are acquainted with so many Japanese, whether or not we are qualified to do anything barbarous.

I believe that you are versed in Bushido. In olden time soldiery was lifted in Japan to a status equally high as that of art and morality. I have no doubt that our soldiers will not betray and tradition. If there is difference in Japanese militarism from that of the west, it is because the former is not without moral element. Who only sees its destroying power is blind to its other power in preservation. Its human aspect is never known in the foreign countries, because they shut their eyes toit. Japan is still an unknown existence in the west.Having so many things to displease you, Japanese militarism has still something that will please you if you come toknow more about it. It is a excusable existence for the present condition of Japan. But I will leave the full explanation of it to some later occasion.

Believe me that I am never a eulogist of Japanese militarism, because I have many differences with it. But I can not help accepting as Japanese what Japan is doing now under the circumstances, because I see no other way to show our minds to china. Of course when China stops fighting, and we receive her friendly hands, neither grudge nor ill feeling will remain in our minds. Perhaps with some sense of repentence, we will then proceed together on the great work of reconstructing the new world in Asia.

I often draw in my mind a possible man-who can talk from a high domain and act as a peace-maker. You might write General Chiang, I hope, and tell him about the follishness of fighting in the presence of a great work that is waiting. And I am sorry that against the high-pitches nature of your letter, mine is low-toned and faltering, because as a Japanese subject I belong to one of the responsible parties of the conflict.

Finally one word more. What I fear most is the present atmosphere in India that tends to wilfully blacken Japan to alienate her from your country. I have so many friends there, whose beautiful nature does not harmonise with it. My last experiences in your country taught me how to love and respect her. Besides there are in Japan so many admirers of your countrymen with your noble self as the first.

Yours sincerely,

Yone Noguchi.

"Uttarayana",

Santiniketan, Bengal.

October, 1938.

Dear Noguchi,

I thank you for taking the trouble to writer to me again. I have also read with interest your letter addressed to the Editor, *Amrita Bazar Patrika*, and published in that journal. It makes the meaning of your letter to me more clear.

The following is the text of the letter referred to:

"Dear Editor,

Dr. Tagore's reply to my letter was a disappointment, to use his words, hurted me to the depths of my being. Now I am conscious that language is an ineffective instrument to carry one's real meaning. When I wanted an impartial criticism he gave me something of prejudiced bravado under the beautiful name of humanity. Just for a handful of dream, and for an intellectual's ribbon to stick in his coat, he has lost a high office to correct the mistaken idea of reality.

"It seems to us that when Dr. Tagore called the doctrine of "Asia for Asia" a political blackmail, he relinquished his patriotism to boast quiescence of a spiritual vagabond, and wilfully supporting the Chinese side, is encouraging Soviet Russia, not to mention the other western countries. I meant my letter to him to be a plea for the understanding of Japan's view-point which, in spite of its many failures, is honest.

I wonder whether it is a poet's privilege to give one whipping before listening to him words. When I dwelled on the saving of the people of Japan at the present time of conflict, he denounced it as their government's exploitation "for gun running and invasion of a neighbour's hearth and home." But when he does not use the same language towards his friend China his partiality is something moustrous. And I wonder where is his former heart which made us Japanese love him said lonour him. But still we are patient, believing that he will come to senses and take a neutral dignity fitting to a prophet who does not depart from fair judgment.

"Living in a country far from your country, I do not know where Dr. Tagore's reply appeared in print. Believing that you are known to his letter, I hope that you will see way to print this letter of mine in your esteemed paper.

Yours sincerely

Yone Noguchi."

I am flattered that you still consider it worthwhile to take such pains to convert me to your point of view, and I am really sorry that I am unable to come to my senses, as yu have been pleased to wish it. It seems to me that it is futile for either of us to try to convince the other since your faith in the infallible right of Japan to bully other Asiatic nations into line with your Government's policy is not shared by me, and my faith that patriotism which claims the right to bring to the altar of its country who sacrifice of other people's rights and happiness will endanger rather than strengthen the foundation of any great civilisation, is sneered at by you as the "quiescence of a spiritual vagabond".

If you can convince the Chinese that your armies are bombing their cities and rendering their woman and children homeless beggars - those of them that are not transformed into "multilated mud-fish", to borrow one of your own phrases -, if you can convince these victims that they are only being subjected to a benevolent treatment which will in the end "save" their nation, it will no longer be necessary for you to convince us of your country's noble intentions. Your righteous indignation against the "polluted people" who are burning their own cities and art treasures (and presumably bombing their own citizens) to malign your soldiers, reminds me of Napoleon's noble wrath when he marched into a deserted Moscow and watched its palaces in flames.

I should have expected from you who are a poet at least that much of imagination to feel, to what inhuman despair a people must be reduced to willingly burn their own handiwork of years', indeed centuries', labour. And even as a good nationalist, do you seriously believe that the mountain of bleeding corpses and the wilderness of bombed and burnt cities that is every day widening between your two countries, is making it easier for your two peoples to streatch your hands ina clasp of ever-lasting good will ?

You complain that while the Chinese, being "dishonest", are spreading their malicious propaganda, you people, being "honest", are reticent. Do you not know, my friend, that there is no propaganda like good and noble deeds and that if such deeds by yours, you need fear no "trickery" of your victims? Nor need you fear the bogey of communism if there is no exploitation of the poor among your own people and the workers feel that they are justly treated.

I must thank you for explaining to me the meaning of our Indian philosophy and of pointing out that the proper interpretation of Kali and Shiva must compel our approval of Japan's "dance of death" in China. I wish you had drawn a moral from a religion more familiar to you and appealed to the Buddha for your justification. But I forget that your priests and artists have already made sure of that, for I saw in a recent issue of "The Osaka Mainichi and The Tokyo Nichi Nichi" (16th September, 1988) a picture of a new colossal image of Buddha erected to bless the massacre of your neighbours.

You must forgive me if you words sound bitter. Believe me, it is sorrow and shame, not anger that prompt me to write to you. I suffer intensely not only because the reports of Chinese suffering batter against my heart, but because I can no longer point out with pride the example of a great Japan. It is true that there are no better standards prevalent anywhere else and that the so-called civilized peoples of the West are proving equally barbarous and even less "worthy of trust." If you refer me to them, I have nothing to say. What I should have liked is to be able to refer them to you. I shall say nothing ofmy own people, for it is vain to boast until one has succeeded in sustaining one's principles to the end.

I am quite conscious of the honour you do me in asking me to act as a peace-maker. Were it in any way possible for me to bring you two peoples together and see you freed from this death-struggle and pledged to the great common "work of reconstructing the new world in Asia", I would regard the sacrifice of my life in the cause a proud privilege. But I have no power save that of moral persuasion, which you have so eloquently ridiculed. You who want me to be impartial, how can you expect me to appeal to Chiang Kai-Shek to give up resisting until the aggressors have first given up their aggression? Do you know that last week when I received a pressing invitation from an old friend of mine in Japan to visit your country, I actually thought for a moment, follish idealist as I am, that your people may really need my services to minister to the bleeding heart of Asia and to help extract from its riddled body the bullets of hatred? I wrote to my friend:

"Though the present state of my health is hardly favourable for any strain of a long foreign journey, I shoudl seriously consider your proposal if proper opportunity is given me to carry out my own mission while there, which is to do my best to establish a civilised relationship of national amity between two great peoples of Asia who are entangled in a desolating mutual destruction. But as I am doubtful whether the military authorities of Japan, which seem bent upon devastating China in order to gain their object, will allow me the freedom to take my own course, I shall never forgive myself if I am tempted for any reason whatever to pay a friendly visit to Japan just at this unfortunate moment and thus cause a grave misunderstanding. You know I have a genuine love for the Japanese people and it is sure to hurt me too painfully to go and watch crowds of them being transported by their rulers to a neighbouring land to perpetrate acts of inhumanity which will brand their name with a lasting stain in the history of Man."

After the letter was despatched came the news of the fall of Canton and Hankow. The cripple, shorn of his power to strike, may collapse, but to ask him to forget the memory of his mutilation as easily as you want me to, I must expect him to be an angel.

Wishing you people whom I love, not success, but remorse,

Yours sincerely,

Rabindranath Tagore.

4

Tagore as Preceptor

If one individual is to be singled out for representing the values and traditions of India from the ancient times to the modern age, it cannot be any one other than Rabindranath Tagore (1861-1941). He was the one person who incorporated the wisdom of the past, reflected in the spiritual and intellectual attainments of the Vedas and the Upanishads: Yet, he was never so immersed in India's seemingly other-worldly heritage, underlined in the philosophical concept of the world being an illusion (maya), as to negate rationalism. To use a cliché, he combined the best of both worlds.

Tagore scored in this respect over his other great contemporary, Mahatma Gandhi, for the Mahatma placed a far greater emphasis on the spirit of renunciation marking a rejection of the Western industrial civilisation. To a large extent, it is this attitude extolling the 'simple living, high thinking' outlook that is still favored in India, even if it is not infrequently identified with hypocrisy.

Tagore set his face against such a rule of thumb approach to life if only because his horizon was much wider than Gandhi's. He had no time for Gandhi's rejection of European machines and preference for primitive Indian ones like the 'charkha', or the spinning wheel. "If a man is stunted by big machines", Tagore wrote, "the danger of being stunted by small machines must not be lost sight of. The charkha in its proper place can do no harm... but where... it is in the wrong place, then the thread can only be spun at the cost of a great deal of the mind itself. The man is no less valuable than the cotton thread."

Poet, thinker, playwright, novelist, writer of short stories, dance dramas and songs, painter and educationist - Tagore's versatility was matched only by his genius. Truly, he was Gurudev, the epitome of the preceptor idealized in Indian myths and folklore. Not surprisingly, Gandhi bestowed the title on Tagore - an honor that befits him even today - just as Tagore called Gandhi the Mahatma, recognizing the sterling qualities of a saint in the politician, who is embroiled in the heat and dust of quotidian battles.

It was left to Nehru to say that although Tagore and Gandhi were "entirely different from each other, and yet both of them (were) typical of India, both in the long line of India's great men". If Tagore's legacy remains as relevant today as it was in his time, the reason is that he cherished certain ideals that have come to distinguish India in the present-day world. Hence, perhaps, the statues, busts and university chairs named after him which dot the world.

The first and foremost concept of Indian nationhood that he lauded was its inclusiveness. He recounts in one of his poems how the streams of Aryans, non-Aryans, Sakas, Huns, Pathans, Mughals et al have merged to give India its distinctive identity. It is not impossible that he developed this concept from a study of his own family, which he regarded as a product of the "confluence of three cultures, Hindu, Mohammedan and British".

It is this ideal of an integrated and vibrant multicultural society, a rainbow nation, which India holds up today as the only valid model which can ensure the survival and advancement of all. Otherwise, the so-called civilisational clashes between ethnic, religious and linguistic groups will tear the world apart. It is perhaps just as well that the great man died before India itself fell prey in 1947 to one such murderous conflict based on religion. And, then, the broken nation saw another divisive conflict in 1971 based on language and sub-nationalism, which led to the creation of Bangladesh.

Tagore would probably have been even more mortified by the second rupture because he came from that part of the subcontinent - East Bengal. In his time, he witnessed the colonial rulers partition Bengal in 1905, a traumatic upheaval for his Sonar Bangla. Fittingly, it is his song of love and reverence for the land where he was born (*Amar Sonar Bangla*) which is now the national anthem of Bangladesh.

Tagore recognized the seeds of the conflicts that tore apart India in Gandhi's use of religious symbols, both Hindu and Muslim as in the concept of Ram Rajya and the exhortation in favor of the Caliphate. He was as opposed to Gandhi's love for "small machines", with their numbing effect on the mind, as to his idealisation of religious emblems, which can exert an equally stifling impact on the largely illiterate masses. "I blamed Mahatmaji", Tagore wrote, "for exploiting (the) irrational force of credulity in our people." While Gandhi defended the Hindu idols, as the English clergyman and admirer of India C.F. Andrews recalled, "believing the masses (to be) incapable of raising themselves immediately to abstract ideals", Tagore could not "bear to see the people eternally treated as a child".

Many will see Tagore's depiction of the crafty politician mouthing nationalistic slogans to mobilize the credulous in his novel Gharey Bairey as a mirror image of the present political scene, just as his prescient vision that a revolution devours its own children, as in Char Adhyay, will be appreciated today although it was written in the context of the much-lionized anti-British revolutionaries and anarchists of his time. Tagore wasn't without his critics at home and abroad.

Even while accepting the Nobel Prize for Literature in 1913, he referred to the "calumnies and insults" he had received from his countrymen. The West, too, lost its interest soon enough. Graham Greene thought in 1937 "I cannot believe that anyone but Mr Yeats can still take his (Tagore's) poems very seriously". And Yeats himself had come to the conclusion by then that Tagore wrote "sentimental rubbish".

Notwithstanding these ups and downs, as in the life of all individuals, big and small, Tagore's thinking had a stamp of modernity which can act as guideposts for India and the world - just as his song, "*Ekla Chalo Re*" (walk alone), inspired Gandhi during the communal violence of 1946-47. And nowhere is Tagore's modern outlook more evident than in his paintings, with their remarkable stark originality, quite in contrast to the mellifluous nature of his verse. Perhaps more than any other aspect of his vast artistic output, it is in his paintings that apparently depict his real self - "I am by nature a savage" - that Tagore will live for generations.

It is Rabindranath's sincere conviction that the Hindu religion can stand against the onslaught of Western civilisation, religion, and culture, on condition that it rids itself of its dogmatism and superstition. The Aryan faith, in its unsullied purity, can give unity to the chaotic channels pouring in floods into India from Western sources. But they will overwhelm the Indian faith, if it does not in the meantime look about itself, and with an unsparing hand cut off the weedy outgrowths. We must free ourselves from all the exhausted traditions, spent forces, and obsolete watch- words which still possess us.

A spiritual religion like that of Rabindranath Tagore, which has for its ideal a right heart and a saintly character, which has for its principle love of God and service of man, can make no truce with idle rites and ceremonies, blind dogmas and superstitions, snobbery and pharisaism, orthodoxy of a priestly caste, pride and prejudice of position and authority, selfishness of classes and exclusiveness of nations. The soul of India has to be delivered from these besetting sins, and people like Rabindranath Tagore help in the process.

Among the evils which are poisoning the very springs of national life, the first and foremost is the caste system. Rabindranath is not oblivious to the purposes which it served, to the value of the principles on which it was framed. When the Aryans first came to India they had to encounter the previous inhabitants of the country. As the Aryans were dominated by the spiritual impulse, they did not adopt the lazy device of either extirpating the native peoples or reducing them to slavery, but organised a social system based on the recognition of spiritual unity as well as racial differences.

The caste system when instituted was a social unity in which the different peoples could live together in mutual harmony while enjoying the freedom to maintain their differences. The social organisation of India was based on the principle of reconciliation and not discord. "It is not the case in Europe that all classes do their respective, legitimate functions, and thus try by their collective efforts to maintain the social organisation; on the contrary, they are mutually antagonistic: every class is always on the alert to prevent others from growing stronger. Thus the social harmony is destroyed.... India has tried to reconcile things that are mutually alien to each other.. She set limits to and fenced off all the rival conflicting forces of society, and thus made the social organism one, and capable of doing its complex functions."

About the class of Brahmins, it is his opinion that every good society should have a section corresponding to it. In the Indian social organisation, which is a work of art, the Brahmins are at the top, and are the recognised leaders of society. Though India passed through several vicissitudes in her political fortunes, the society has not been much shaken, as her ideals and traditions were long preserved by this class. The Brahmins are the trustees of tradition and the conservers of the religious spirit.

The Brahmins, according to the ideal, count poverty a privilege, consider learning their calling, and pursue the ideals of spirit with self-sacrifice and in a disinterested manner. Scorn of wealth and the pursuit of spirituality, reckless of praise or blame, are their characteristic features. Division of labour is now recognised to be a valid principle not only in economics but in other matters also, social organisation included. If we cannot make our clothes or our shoes for ourselves, if specially trained men can do these things much better than we can for ourselves, why should we not have a class set apart for artistic production and spiritual discovery?

Members of this class are to discover and bring home to the community the joy of art and spiritual beauty. Automatically this class happens to be considered higher than the others, for while the tradesman and the merchant contribute to the physical needs, the members of this class are the purveyors of spiritual health and joy to the community. These are the leaders of society, regulating the things in which the community ought to take pleasure, exerting great moral influence on them.

Those who are in the thick of the strife of the world have not the time to think of the welfare of the whole community, or to contemplate the higher things of life. But this is not to defend the present degraded and degenerated Brahmin class. These have done, besides much good, much evil in the name of God. As they have lost their old self-sacrifice and spirituality they have no claim to the respect and regard of the other classes. It is because they drilled the other classes into submission, and decreed their inferiority, that they fell in esteem and prestige.

They crippled the minds of the Sudras, and today the insult has come back their minds are being crippled. "When the Sudra joined his palms in submission to the brahmanical decree of inferiority, on that very day was dug the pit for the fall of the Brahmins." They want the powers and prestige of the old Brahmin class, but they do not possess their ideals and spiritual strength which would win respect. Hence the bathos. But there is no question that the hierarchy of values incorporated in the caste system of India is right. The highest place is given to the philosopher who finds his life work in search for truth, artistic creation, and moral endeavour.

While the work of the philosopher is the recognised aim of society, the political stability and economic basis of it are also secured. Preserving peace and political order is the function of the warrior community. Classes for trading and agricultural interests are also included. It is an aristocratic organisation, where every function has a definite value assigned to it, and the scale of values depends not upon the amount of wealth, but on the development of the soul. Rise in the social scale is determined not by increase in wealth, but by ascent of spirit. We ought not to abandon this judgment of values.

The Western civilisation, which is a civilisation of the rich, measures status by bank balances. With such a material aim and basis, selfishness and competition increase. But the Indian system has no ideas of propertied respectability. The caste system aims at universal brotherhood and love. Freedom is its basis and freedom its end. Man is looked upon as an end in himself, and not a mere creature of the moment, whom we can use for our purposes and then throw off.

He is an eternal being whose purpose and destiny are to express his free spirit in actions of the world. The modern class system of the West is material in its outlook, while the caste system is spiritual. Realising that the material display of modern life conceals within it flimsiness of faith, and cannot satisfy the deeper needs of man, we have to take a lesson from the caste system, and build a spiritual civilisation on love and brotherhood, freedom and fellowship. This does not mean that we are holding a brief for the caste system as it prevails in India at the present day. We are aware that we have come to a time when that institution requires modification.

The rigid and exclusive caste system has served its purpose and must vanish. Rabindranath writes: "It has largely contributed to the freedom from narrowness and intolerance which distinguishes the Hindu religion, and has enabled races with widely different cultures and even antagonistic social and religious usages and ideals to settle down peaceably side by side.... But this very absence of struggle, developing into a ready acquiescence in any position assigned by the social system, has crushed individual manhood, and has accustomed us for centuries not only to submit to every form of domination, but sometimes actually to venerate the power that holds us down....

The regeneration of the Indian people, to my mind, directly and perhaps solely depends upon the removal of this condition." The institution of caste served a purpose till not long ago, but to-day it is a positive hindrance to the spiritual faith within and progress outside. The caste system failed to recognise the flow of life, the mobility of mind, and the mutability of characteristics.

It failed to realise "that in human beings differences are not like the physical barriers of mountains, fixed for ever, they are fluid with life's flow, and they are changing their courses and their shapes and volume." The soul of the caste system has departed, and what India is now worshipping with awe and veneration is a dead corpse. The vast social mechanism created by man is now crushing the soul. Independent thinking and individuality are suppressed.

The individual is caught in the wheels of the machine, and the machine will have to give up its nature, for man to regain life and soul. If like the child Amal in the Post Office we cripple our minds and narrow our freedom by confining it to our closed prisons and taking the directions of our traditional doctors, the Shastras, we shall not recover from our illusions. As the child longs to be out, mind craves for freedom. But we have to break open the gates and pull down the walls of our closed house, for the air and light of God to pour in and enlighten us.

Rabindranath does not view the social problems of the time from the narrow economic or utilitarian point of view. He brings his spiritual vision to bear on the social problems, and lifts them up to a higher idealist plane. His attitude to them is determined, not by the accident of birth, habit, or training, but by the spiritual vision, the one central principle to which he devotes his whole life.

The present social unrest would be at an end if people adopted the right attitude to life, and developed reverence for the divine in man.

The materialist view of life makes us afraid of poverty, and in nations of spiritual vision, poverty is not the cause of social discontent. India is very poor, but centuries of spiritual discipline have given the Indian peoples so much restraint and self-suppression that though the problem of poverty is most intense in India, social unrest and struggle are greater in the West. When a great famine invades the country, or death - dealing plague stalks through the land, the Indian people submit to it in meek resignation.

In suffering and distress they beg and pray, mope and pine, and at worst, weep and die in silence, handing over their souls to God. We do not hear of strikes and riots, breaking windows and throwing bombs, mass movements and demonstrations of starving women and children. Their calm acceptance of pain and silent submission to suffering are the wonder of the world. Their patience of spirit dimly suggests the Cross of Calvary, the immortal reproach of divine virtue and wisdom against the blows of evil and circumstance. A materialist view of life is the root cause of social discontent, and the remedy for the social unrest is a spiritual one.

Professor L. P. Jacks observes: "It is not the poorest nations which reveal the maximum of social discontent. It is the richest. And the prime cause does not lie in the sense of inequality between individuals who have more and individuals who have less: that no doubt is a cause, but secondary. The root evil is that a community which makes wealth its object, and pursues it on the terms laid down by the economic machine, is living under conditions which satisfy nobody and against which all men are by the higher human nature born rebels." The troubles of the Western nations are due to the predominance of the economic motive. Nations have for their ideal economic efficiency. The greatest output is the prime consideration.

Man becomes but a cogwheel in the great machine. At the altar of this machine, human victims are sacrificed. Men, women, and children, and values of spirit are given the go-by. At the present day we find that the people are highly sensitive to all this loss, but with the best will in the world they are not able to get rid of the troubles of industrialism. It is because they consider them economic problems and devise economic remedies. But so long as we are moving within the charmed circle of economics, we cannot cure these ills. In condemning them as evils, it is not our economic side that asserts itself, but our human nature.

We then occupy a higher standpoint; for the economic policy requires them and so must justify them. The solution lies in the steadfast occupancy of the higher, human, or spiritual point of view. India has had this spiritual ideal, and unless she preserves it there is no chance for her. India cannot regain her former prestige and glory by merely tinkering here and there with the social system, or getting a few more seats on the councils, or by the substitution of manufactures for cottage industries. If India becomes free in soul and preserves her spiritual individuality, then all other things shall be added unto her.

"Then in India, province will join province, race will join race, knowledge will be linked with knowledge, endeavour with endeavour: then the present chapter of Indian history will end, and she will emerge in the larger history of the world."

Educated Indians of the present; day are not quite in sympathy with Rabindranath's ideal of preserving the national identity of India, and feel that India's salvation lies in the imitation of the West. That way lies madness. In their eagerness to save their skins, they forget it will ultimately be more profitable to save their souls. If the educated classes do not realise it, it is only the sign of how far the disease has gone, and the case is so much the worse. It is impossible to believe, unless one acquainted with the inspiration of ancient India sees for oneself, the extent to which modern India has succumbed, body and soul, to the materialist influence.

These Indians pride themselves that they are practical. What a price it costs to be practical to-day! Their soul is the price they pay. There is no use in acquiring the externals and the outward forms of a political civilisation and losing the soul. Imitation, according to Rabindranath Tagore, is "like dressing our skeleton with another man's skin, giving rise to eternal feuds between the skin and the bones at every movement."

If the political salvation of India is to be attained at the expense of her soul, we had better preserve the soul and lose the earthly kingdom. India then will vindicate spirit. And if she is doomed to disappear, then will she die with dignity, with the colours of spirit flying. "But let us stand firm and suffer with strength for the True, for the Good, for the Eternal in man, for Thy kingdom which is in the union of hearts, for the freedom which is of the soul."

From this it should not be inferred that Rabindranath has no sympathy with things non-Indian. He is quite sure that the civilisation of the West is as much a creation of the spirit as any other civilisation. Only its soul cannot be grafted on the Indian soul. Radical reformers seem to think that it is an easy process, as they imagine that India is some recent throw-up from the bottom of the sea, due to a caprice of the earth, with a clean waxen surface ready to receive any impression from the outside.

But India is an ancient land with established traditions, honoured throughout recorded history for her spiritual civilisation, for her dignity of soul, for her intense piety, for her valour and chivalry, tolerance and hospitality, and love and peace. All these qualities have become part and parcel of the mentality of the Indian. It is not possible for him to give up what is in his blood and bone. He can only take in the outer and lose the inner. It is easier to acquire the vices of an alien civilisation than to get its virtues. As a matter of fact, contact with the West has disturbed the simple religion and life of the Indian.

His intense belief in God, his sense of the strength of holiness and sacrifice, are slowly giving way to materialism and worship of money. The passion for things unseen is being replaced by the fierce eagerness to grow rich. The brows intended to look up to heaven are kissing the dust. The heart to be filled with God is set upon comfort and display. The joy of life and creativeness is yielding to the fever of acquisition and possession.

A long purse and a happy home are looked upon as the ultimate destiny of man. People of a country which never spurned poverty are growing afraid to be poor. People who knew how to die for a cause with cheerfulness and calm are growing pale by the fear of death, and loving life even at the sacrifice of their souls. Life is ceasing to be life and is becoming mere existence. It is ceasing to be human and is becoming animal.

Men are living for pleasure and not for anything else. Their minds are becoming stunted down, from the shortage of intellectual material. Their souls are shrinking, from the famine of spirit. The materialist influence has been steadily growing, and eating subtly into the very substance of the Indian soul. If Rabindranath is against the political subjection of India, it is not due to any selfish motive. He is afraid of the Western spirit, which is slowly subduing the soul of India and impoverishing her life and spirit.

As an instance of how much the present outlook of the Indian is shaped by the West, Rabindranath mentions the fact that the modern Indian looks to Government for aid in everything. Though hordes of invaders deluged the country, the people of India were little affected by these, as they were administering their own affairs in many spheres. All matters connected with education and sanitation, agriculture and industry were under the control of the people. Government was only a nominal head suspended over the people, and not an organic part of it.

So when Government changed hands people did not mind it. But to - day everything is to be granted by Government. Prayers and petitions, memorials and resolutions, pious protests and impotent indignations are the talk of the day. If now Government should change, chaos would prevail. The State which was only a symbol of unity has become the whole body now.

This idea that everything should be done by the State is completely materialist, and we have unconsciously adopted it. Judged by the greatest test of the vitality of a nation, namely its capacity for self-sacrifice, it must be said that India is becoming denationalised and devitalised. Those who want us to go the whole length in the imitation of the West are dupes of a delusion.

Rabindranath feels that there is a great difference between the spiritual ideal for which India stands, and the material ideal with which it is in conflict. Through the acceptance of the civilisation of the East, which is religious and not secular, it is easy for us to enter the kingdom of God.

Though not exclusively, still mainly, the emphasis in the East is on life and not possession, intuition and not intellect, religion and not science, freedom arid not direction. It is because India represents this ideal that Rabindranath is proud to be a son of India. "I shall be born in India again and again; with all her poverty, misery, and wretchedness I love India best."

Blessed is my birth because I was born in the country; blessed is my life, mother, because I have loved thee.

I do not know if thou hast wealth and riches to be a queen. I know this much that my limbs are cooled as soon as I stand in thy shade.

I know not in what grove blossom flowers that madden the soul with such scents. I know not the sky where the moon rises with such sweet smiles.

My eyes were ^first opened in thy light, and they will be closed finally upon that very light.

We see that Rabindranath has no sympathy with those who, with a light heart, ridicule everything that is old and established and view the past of India as one unbroken period of inertia and darkness. Nor has he much in common with those who in an easy and care- less mood accept with veneration everything old and established, and reject with equal vehemence the new and the untried.

But when the educated Indians, carried away by the spirit of innovation, look down upon their more cautious brethren with contempt and ridicule, and view them as the enemies of progress, and when this spirit goes beyond bounds and becomes militant and aggressive, Rabindranath feels it his duty to counsel caution and calm, steadiness and self-examination. He asks them to pause for a moment and reflect on the consequences of what they propose to do.

But he is not a conservative who wishes to perpetuate mischievous forms simply because they are picturesque. To him progress and reform consist in conserving the ancient ideals and building upon them. Preserving the soul of the Indian type, we may adopt whatever is good and noble in the West. Rabindranath demands a synthetic integration of the old and the new, the East and the West. "It is idle mendicancy to discard our own and beg for the foreign," while at the same time" it is the abjectness of poverty to dwarf ourselves by rejecting the foreign."

Rabindranath remarks that " taking shelter in the dead is death itself, and only taking all the risk of life to the fullest extent is living" India has preserved her vitality because, whenever she came into contact with alien civilisations, she absorbed whatever was great in them without surrendering the fundamentals of her own type.

Whatever we adopt from others we have to adapt ourselves to our needs and to our life. India has her own self-identity, her life and soul. She can grow strong and vigorous not by the mere accumulation of Western forms and modes, but by the assimilation of them all. She should affix the stamp of her genius to whatever she lays her hands upon and accepts, otherwise her work will not be a creation, but a mere repetition. The process of assimilative synthesis has been the characteristic of India from the beginning of her history.

When first the original Aryans settled at the foot of the Himalayas, the Dravidian civilisation was indented upon to a large extent. "Let none; however, imagine that non-Aryans have contributed nothing of value to Indian life. The ancient Dravidians were not indeed deficient in civilisation. Contact with them made the Hindu civilisation varied in aspect and deeper in spirit.

The Dravidian was no theologian, but an expert in imagination, music, and construction. He excelled in fine art. The pure spiritual knowledge of the Aryans, mingling with the Dravidian's emotional nature and power of aesthetic creation, formed a marvellous compound, which is neither entirely Aryan nor entirely non-Aryan, but Hindu."

When later Buddhism became merged in Hinduism, it is the same process. Hinduism has synthesised all the foreign influences which invader after invader has brought to her from outside, and moulded them to its own ideals. India had always welcomed foreign influence. Hinduism has been ever old and ever new. It has been both creative and constructive. The secret of the strength of Hinduism lies in its power of assimilation.

"Doubt not the nation's capacity for self-help: know for certain that the time has come. Remember how India has ever kept alive her power of binding together. She has ever established some sort of harmony amidst all kinds of difficulties and conflicts, and hence she has survived till now. I have full faith in that India. Even now that India is slowly building up a marvellous reconciliation of the old order with the new. May each of us consciously join in that work, may we be never misled by dulness or revolt into resisting it."

If Indian nationality is to be a live spirit and not a dead imitation, then India must build up from within. Her hope lies within herself. The basis and foundation of the great India lies in the recovery of her soul and the regaining of a fresh self-confidence in her own national life. If India recovers her strength of soul and grip of spirituality, which is the secret spring of life, then no power on earth can stand against her newly acquired energy of spirit.

If the soul is diseased, then it will inevitably bend in decay and death, however much we might try to prevent it by external means; but if the soul is healthy it will live down disaster, retrieve ruin, and reassert itself in spite of all external opposition. Nothing has power over it. Nothing can stand against the uprush of spirit. The soul of a nation with ideals of spirit cannot be overcome. If this faith possesses the souls of men enduringly, India will "emerge one day."

The Upanishad says: "This self is not to be gained by the weak." This recovery of soul is a hard task. We may have anxious times to go through. For it, it may be, we may have to "give up our father and mother, wife and children." To us, with our materialist outlook, the heights to which we may have to mount may seem giddy and dreadful. We may fall the first climbers are certain to but such falls are needed for the rise of India.

However threatening the idea may appear, it is not impossible. For the spirit of India is not yet dead, though it may have gone to sleep. Her heart has been beating slower and slower, but it has not come to a stop. The flame of spiritual life is kept burning, though dim, all these years of stress and strain. It is this spiritual self-possession, won through ages of mysticism that has made the Indian civilisation survive the onslaughts of the outside world.

Heaven does not send such men 'as Rabin- dranath Tagore to undeserving nations. Their presence is a standing proof of the fact that the ideas for which India stands are not eclipsed, and her song not silenced. Great ideas still move her, and are the inspiration of her life and the breath of her poetry.

Rabindranath has full faith in the great future of India, and with the burning faith which animates the prophet he speaks out: "Is it impossible to utilise the supreme ideas of the Panchayagnya in forming a daily tie between our whole country and every member of our community? Cannot every one of us daily offer one piece or even a handful of rice in the name of our fatherland?

Cannot Hinduism bind every one of us, every day of our life, with the direct bond of devotion to India, to Bharatavarsha, the haunt of our Gods, the hermitage of our ancient

Rishis, the nourishing mother of our forefathers? Cannot our relation with our benign fatherland be brought home to every one of us as a particular personal tie? "Rabindranath, with the devouring flame of his patriotism, calls upon his countrymen to strive to create a devotion to the mother country, a sense of pride in its glory, and a passion for its progress.

5

Krishna Chandra Bhattacharyya and Contemporary Philosophy in India

In the 19th century, India was not marked by any noteworthy philosophical achievements, but the period was one of great social and religious reform movements. The newly founded universities introduced Indian intellectuals to Western thought, particularly to the empiricistic, utilitarian, and agnostic philosophies in England, and John Stuart Mill, Jeremy Bentham, and Herbert Spencer had become the most influential thinkers in the Indian universities by the end of the century.

These Western-oriented ideas served to generate a secular and rational point of view and stimulated social and religious movements, most noteworthy among them being the Brahmo (Brahma) Samaj movement founded by Rammohan Ray. Toward the later decades of the century, the great saint Ramakrishna Paramahamsa of Calcutta renewed interest in mysticism, and many young rationalists and skeptics were converted into the faith exemplified in his person.

Ramakrishna taught, among other things, an essential diversity of religious paths leading to the same goal, and this teaching was given an intellectual form by Swami Vivekananda, his famed disciple. The first Indian graduate school in philosophy was founded in the University of Calcutta during the first decades of the 20th century, and the first incumbent of the chair of philosophy was Sir Brajendranath Seal, a versatile scholar in many branches of learning, both scientific and humanistic.

Seal's major published work is The Positive Sciences of the Ancient Hindus, which, besides being a work on the history of science, shows interrelations among the ancient Hindu philosophical concepts and their scientific theories. Soon, however, the German philosophers Kant and Hegel came to be the most studied philosophers in the Indian universities. The ancient systems of philosophy came to be interpreted in the light of German idealism. The Hegelian notion of Absolute Spirit found a resonance in the age-old Vedanta notion of Brahman.

The most eminent Indian Hegelian scholar is Hiralal Haldar, who was concerned with the problem of the relation of the human personality with the Absolute, as is evidenced by his book Neo-Hegelianism. The most eminent Kantian scholar is K.C. Bhattacharyya. Among those who deserve mention for their original contributions to philosophical thinking are Sri Aurobindo (died 1950), Mahatma Gandhi (died 1948), Rabindranath Tagore (died 1941), Sir Muhammed Iqbal (died 1938), K.C. Bhattacharyya (died 1949), and Sarvepalli Radhakrishnan (died 1975).

Of these, Sri Aurobindo was first a political activist and then a yogin, Tagore and Iqbal poets, Gandhi a political and social leader, and only Radhakrishnan and Bhattacharyya university professors. This fact throws some light on the state of Indian philosophy in this century. In his major work, The Life Divine, Sri Aurobindo starts from the fact of human aspiration for a kingdom of heaven on earth and proceeds to give a theoretical framework in which such an aspiration would be not a figment of imagination but a drive in nature, working through man toward a higher stage of perfection. Both the denial of the materialist and that of the ascetic are rejected as being one-sided.

The gulf between unconscious matter and fully self-conscious spirit is sought to be bridged by exhibiting them as two poles of a series in which spirit continuously manifests itself. The Vedantic concept of a transcendent and all-inclusive Brahman is sought to be harmonized with a theory of emergent evolution. Illusionism is totally rejected. The purpose of man is to go beyond his present form of consciousness.

Yoga is interpreted as a technique not for personal liberation but for cooperating with the cosmic evolutionary urge that is destined to take mankind ahead from the present mental stage to a higher, supramental stage of consciousness. A theory of history, in accordance with this point of view, is worked out in his The Human Cycle. Rabindranath Tagore's philosophical thinking is no less based on the Upanisads, but his interpretation of the Upanisads is closer to Vaisnava theism and the Bhakti cults than to traditional monism.

He characterized the absolute as supreme person and placed love higher than knowledge. In his Religion of Man, Tagore sought to give a philosophy of man in which human nature is characterized by a concept of surplus energy that finds expression in creative art. In his lectures on Nationalism, Tagore placed the concept of society above that of the modern nation-state. Mahatma Gandhi preferred to say that the truth is God rather than God is the truth, because the former proposition expresses a belief that evens the atheists share.

The belief in the presence of an all-pervading spirit in the universe led Gandhi to a strict formulation of the ethics of Non-violence (ahimsa). But he gave this age-old ethical principle a wealth of meaning so that ahimsa for him became at once a potent means of collective struggle against social and economic injustice, the basis of a decentralized economy and decentralized power structure, and the guiding principle of one's individual life in relation both to nature and to other persons.

The unity of existence, which he called the truth, can be realized through the practice of ahimsa, which requires reducing oneself to zero and reaching the furthest limit of humility. Influenced by the British philosopher J.M.E. McTaggart's form of

Hegelian idealism and the French philosopher Henri Bergson's philosophy of change, Muhammed Iqbal conceived reality as creative and essentially spiritual, consisting of egos. "The truth, however, is that matter is spirit," he wrote,

Citaz: In space-time reference. The unity called man is body when we look at it as acting in regard to what we call external world; it is mind or soul when we look at it as acting in regard to the ultimate aim and ideal of such acting.

Citaz: Influenced by British Neo-Hegelianism in his interpretation of the Vedantic tradition, Sarvepalli Radhakrishnan was primarily an interpreter of Indian thought to the Western world. He defended a realistic interpretation of the concept of maya-thereby playing down its illusionistic connotation, .a theory of intuition as the means of knowing reality, and a theory of emergent evolution of spirit (not unlike Sri Aurobindo, but without his doctrine of supermind) in nature and history.

The most original among modern Indian thinkers, however, is K.C. Bhattacharyya, who rejected the conception of philosophy as a construction of a worldview and undertook a phenomenological description of the various grades of subjectivity: (1) the bodily, (2) the psychic, and (3) the spiritual. With regard to (1), he distinguished between the objective body and the felt body and regarded the latter as the most primitive level of the subjective sense of freedom from the objective world.

The stage (2) includes the range of mental life from image to free thought. In introspection, the level (2) is transcended, but various levels of introspection are distinguished, all leading to greater freedom from objectivity. It would seem, however, that for Bhattacharyya absolute freedom from objectivity was a spiritual demand. According to his theory of value, value is not an adjective of the object but a feeling absolute, of which the object evaluated appears as an adjective, and his logic of alternation is a modern working out of the Jaina theories of anekanta (non-absolutism) and syadvada (doctrine of "may be").

Among later philosophers, N.V. Banerjee (1901-81) and Kalidas Bhattacharyya (1911-84), the son of K.C. Bhattacharyya, have made important contributions. In Language, Meaning and Persons (1963), Banerjee examines the development of personhood from a stage of individualized bondage to liberation in a collective identity, a life-with-others. This liberation, according to Banerjee, also entails an awareness of time and freedom from spatialized objects.

In his earlier writings such as Object, Content and Relation (1951) and Alternative Standpoints in Philosophy (1953), Bhattacharyya developed his father's idea of theoretically undecidable alternatives in philosophy. In the later works Philosophy, Logic and Language (1965) and Presuppositions of Science and Philosophy (1974), he developed the concept of metaphysics as a science of the nonempirical a priori essences that are initially discerned as the structure of the empirical but are subsequently recognized as autonomous entities.

The method of metaphysics for him is reflection, phenomenological and transcendental. Kalidas Bhattacharyya was concerned with the nature and function of philosophical reflection and its relation of unreflective experience. What reflection brings to light, he held, is present in pre-reflective experience, but only as undistinguished and fused, in a state of objective implicitness. The essences as such are not real but demand realisation in pure reflective consciousness.

At the same time, he emphasized the limitations of any doctrine positing the constitution of nature in consciousness. Such a doctrine, he insisted, cannot be carried out in details. Among those who apply the phenomenological method and concepts to understanding the traditional Indian philosophies, D. Sinha, R.K. Sinari, and J.N. Mohanty are especially noteworthy. Others who interpret the Indian philosophies by means of the methods and concepts of analytical philosophy include B.K. Matilal and G. Misra.

In the field of philosophy of logic, P.K. Sen has worked on the paradoxes of confirmation and the concept of quantification, and Sibajiban on the liar paradox and on epistemic logic. Sibajiban and Matilal have made important contributions toward rendering the concepts of Navya-Nyaya logic into the language of modern logic. In ethics and social philosophy, notable work has been done by Abu Sayyid Ayub, Daya Krishna, Rajendra Prasad, and D.P. Chattopadhyaya.

6

OUTLOOK TOWARDS WOMEN: INFLUENCE OF INDIAN RENAISSANCE

WOMEN: STRIDE TOWARD FREEDOM

This unit is developed for seventh and eighth grade classes. The unit's focus will be on the rise of women's movements beginning in the late seventeen and eighteen hundreds. The thinkers of the age of reason questioned the established political and religious authority and stressed the importance of reason, equality, liberty, and women in the workplace as well as the political arena. Included in the unit are lesson plans, activities for students, a suggested bibliography and reading list, for the students and teachers alike.

The different women's organisations such as Women's Bureau, Women's ORT, Women's Equal Rights Amendment, and the amendment that gave women the right to vote, also Women's Relief Corps and various others will be considered. The more contemporary women's movements have had an impact on several levels of society in the United States. Women's groups have changed many people's views about male and female roles. The changes have affected their roles in the workplace and the family, and the way women live their lives.

Through their vote, women's groups have influenced election results and government. They have also been instrumental in influencing legislation. The most notable single change in women's lives was their growing participation in the paid labor force. In the United States, the percentage of employed women surveyed over a fifty year period rose from 28 per cent to 57 per cent. This contemporary women's movement contributed to an increasing acceptance of careers for all women, including mothers with young children.

Such changes were incorporated with a growing expectation that women would combine employment with their roles as wives and mothers. The road for equality for women has been an arduous one. They have had to fight their way through legislatures and congressional obstacles, face ridicule and indifference. Without the resources of money and political power women found their way blocked, and only through determination and perseverance did they make impressive achievements.

The struggle for equal rights in not only a part of the past, but has continued throughout the entire fabric of American history. There is still a long road ahead and many obstacles to overcome. Women must band together and continue. For more than a century women have tried to achieve full citizenship, the right to take part in the political and social life of their time and to stand on equal human dignity with men in their relationship.

Many will not claim that these goals have been fully achieved. The women's movement has come far enough for them to look back and see where they started, and how they reached their present status. The alterations in the status of women arose from the efforts of a small but very active group of feminists. These feminist groups were the recipients of the forces that transformed the country in a comparatively short space of time from a small, undeveloped country into one with wealth, industrialisation, and international responsibilities.

Women played various roles in the transformation, not as inventors, generals, business leaders, presidents, but as homemakers, producers, reformers, and eventually as citizens. Women were deprived of a vital step toward achieving human dignity, and the recognition that they too were endowed with the faculty of reason, the power of judgement, and the capacity for social responsibility. Over the past 150 years, women in the United States and around the world have organized political movements in order to obtain the same social, economic, and political rights that men have traditionally enjoyed.

These feminist movements have sought to change the laws to prevent discrimination against women and to provide them with equal opportunities in all aspects of life, including education, employment, and representation in the government. Women's struggle for equal rights is not just a part of the past. It is a cord that runs through the entire fabric of our history. From early settlements throughout our nation's development, its political changes, its wars, its industrial growth, and labor movements women have fought for their rights, and the rights of others. Women had to fight, fight, and fight.

When the Plymouth Colony of 1620 established itself it was one of families, who brought with them the traditions of their English backgrounds. In the colonial society, women had no standing in the eyes of the law. They did not have the right to own or inherit property. They could not vote or hold any office in government. Married women, under English common law, could not sign contracts, have their own money, or sue for divorce. Women had no political or legal rights and were without political representation. Women often could not speak out, their husbands spoke for them.

In addition to bearing and caring for the children, some women worked long hours in the field, raising food for their families. They tended the cattle. They spun the wool that they later used to make clothing and bedding. They made the soap, the candles and many of the medicines. Some women shared with their husbands in such occupations as retailing, printmaking, shipbuilding, innkeeping, ferry boat operations, and prison management. They acted as nurses for their communities, and even some as teachers.

Women were rarely found in such esteemed professions as law and medicine, although no formal education was required for either profession until the end of the eighteenth century. Women who were able to work outside the home were the exceptions, not the rule. Indian and black women fared even worse than their white sisters in the early days of American History. The Indian woman was considered inferior, and an enemy, and the black woman was a slave.

About one-third of the slaves forcibly brought to America were women and they had no rights at all. They did field labor on the plantations, performed household duties, raised children, and were often married to slaves. Marriage did not prevent slave women from being separated from their husbands and children. During the colonial revolution men and women worked together to bring about a new nation. Women generally did not venture onto the battlefields but there were exceptions to be found among nurses, cooks, and aides.

Women in these positions received half of the pay that men did. In some instances women took over the duties or combat replacing wounded soldiers. During the seventeen and eighteen hundreds women were employed in various fields, such as Marguerite Hastner of New York, a silversmith, and Ann Franklin, a newspaper editor in Rhode Island, Mary Salmon of Boston ran a blacksmith shop, Mary Wilson of Norfolk, Virginia was a shoe maker, Mary Katherine Goddard was a printer in Baltimore and she was authorized by the Continental Congress to print the first copy of the Declaration of Independence with the names of the signers attached, and Anna Zenger, wife of John Peter Zenger continued to publish her husband's newspaper while he was in jail for publishing an article opposing the New York Colonial government in 1735.

Women such as Abigail Adams, Martha Curtis Washington, and Mercy Otis Warren gave valuable counsel to their husbands. "The Daughters of Liberty" banded together to protest taxes on teas and imported fabrics. They also protested about the English laws under which they were forced to live. Many women acted as spies for the revolutionaries aiding in victories against the British soldiers. Women's mobility began when they took over men's roles.

The home in Colonial America was the place where the family labored to feed, house and clothe themselves. A new established government brought industrialisation, growth of cities, with factories, mercantile establishments and a group of working class people. Men began to compete in the marketplace so they could earn money to purchase the products and merchandise that were previously produced at their homes by their wives. The roles of the wives then changed.

They were to maintain their homes, set an example of virtue and religious piety and raise their children to be morally upright and industrious and become productive members of their society. Many young, poor and unmarried women from the farms or newly immigrated from Europe went to work in textile mills in New England. The south was largely agricultural but in the industrialized south, women whether poor farmer's wives or mistresses of plantations with the slaves were also expected to be virtuous, religious and devoted to the care of their families.

The Civil War brought new responsibilities for women, for some, opportunities as well. While the men fought, women became heads of households, farms, business managers, and income earners. There was a shortage of nurses; women in both the south and north rendered their services. At first there was prejudice against women but they were needed and they rallied to the cause with thousands volunteering to assist on the battlefields and in care of the wounded, including working in the operating rooms.

Although women were discriminated against they continued to struggle, work, and take on difficult roles. As women took on more and more responsibilities and discovered that they could function they began to look at their roles and status and they wanted change. In ancient societies the lives of most women centered around their households. For example, in the Greek city of Athens, women raised children and managed the spinning, weaving and cooking in the household.

Wealthy women surpervised slaves in these tasks, but they also did some of the work themselves. Respectable Athenian women seldom left their homes. Only men could purchase goods, or engage in soldering, lawmaking, and public speaking. The societies of ancient Egypt and of the Greek city of Sparta provided a rare contrast. Both Egyptian and Spartan women could own property and engage in business. In ancient Rome, women's primary role was to manage household affairs.

Women could not hold public office. Men dominated as head of the household. But the Romans developed a system of government based on the authority and leadership of a noble class that included not only statesmen and military leaders, but also the married women of leading Roman families. The Roman matron Cornelia, achieved fame and respect for her managerial skill, patriotism, and good works. In time, such upper-class women, gained greater control over their property and over marriage decisions. However, even these women could not vote or hold public office.

During the middles ages, women's lives continued much as before, like the Roman matrons, medieval noblewomen managed large households and supervised servants, oversaw gardens, attended to clothing and the household furnishings. Many other women worked as cooks, servants, or worked in the pastures and fields of large estates. Two new roles for women did appear in the middle Ages, the nun and the woman active in trade, either as an artist or as a merchant. Convents flourished during the early middle Ages.

They offered primarily upper-class women an alternative to marriage and provided education, spiritual development, and control over extensive land. Women found increasing opportunities for independence as artisans and merchants. From the Renaissance to the eighteen hundreds, fundamental changes in religious and political outlook took root, as leading thinkers began to emphasize the rights of the individual. The Renaissance was a period of great cultural and intellectual activity that spread throughout Europe.

The most significant intellectual movement was humanism, which stressed the importance of human beings and their nature and place in the universe. Some humanists questioned certain traditional ideas about women, and favored better education and a more responsible family role for women. The Reformation, the religious movement that gave rise to Protestantism, also encouraged reassessment of women's roles. Protestant leaders permitted ministers to marry and began to picture marriage as a mutual relationship of spiritually equal partners.

Husbands had less control over the lives of their wives. Protestants also began to view marriage and divorce as matters of individual choice rather than as a fulfillment of obligations to such authorities as parents and the church. The Age of Reason was another period of great intellectual activity and change. In Europe, in the seventeen hundreds, during this era, educated women participated in intellectual and political debates. In Paris for instance, gatherings called salons promoted conversation and discussion among learned men and women.

The salons widened these fortunate women's view of society and their possible roles in it. Women's roles as workers also expanded during this Age of Reason. In Western Europe and the American colonies, women worked as innkeepers, landowners, midwives, printers, servants, teachers and textile workers. But rural occupations continued to employ the largest group of female and male workers. Rural women toiled as laborers on large farms and in their own small gardens and cottages.

Both urban and rural women engaged in knitting, sewing, and other home industries that made crucial contributions to household income. The forces of change that made several developments during the late seventeen and eighteen hundreds set the stage for the rise of women's movements. Those thinkers of that Age of Reason questioned established political and religious authority and stressed the importance of reason, equality and liberty.

This new intellectual atmosphere helped to justify women's rights to full citizenship. On the eve of the French Revolution, the Marquis de Condorcet spoke in favor of women's right to vote. The British author Mary Wollstonecraft argued for women's rights and equality with men. The spread of industrialisation during the eighteen hundreds also had an effect on the woman's place in society. The Industrial Revolution moved not only women's work, but also men's and children's as well, out of the home and into the factories.

Factory jobs offered middle-class women the opportunity to earn wages. But, if a woman was married, her husband legally controlled her earnings. Industrialisation had a different effect on the middle-class women in small towns and cities. With this new separation of work and home life, these women lost a sense of useful involvement in productive work. They became regarded as "ladies" whose place was in the home, while their husbands provided the family income. Many of these women turned to such pursuits as needlework and craftwork and to religious and charitable activities as well.

There is no end in the list of things that women began to do. They took part in strikes. In 1877, men, women and children took part in the railroad strike in Pittsburgh. The strike began because the railroad announced that worker's wages were to be cut by ten per cent. These workers already were not earning enough to meet their financial obligations. National Guard soldiers were sent in to quell the strike but it continued and spread rapidly.

The most important part of the disturbance was the active role taken by women. They developed methods, techniques, and strategies to deal with scabs, a name for workers that the companies brought in to do the work. Because of this railroad cars and their contents were burned, including property along the railroad tracks. The guard troops were no match for the people. The people met them with sticks, stones and bullets alike. Women played an important part in the workers' wars.

In the coalfields of the east, miners' wives developed a special technique in order to deal with "scabs", workers who were called in by the mining companies to dig coal, when the miners went on strike. The scabs would take mule-carts down the mine with them to bring the coal up in. But crowds of women, armed with mops, metal dishpans and washtubs, would run down the hillside toward them, screaming, shouting, and banging their dishpans, thereby setting the mules to flight afraid of the noise and racket they made.

The law usually took the side of the employers, but both employers and law enforcement officers came to dread the pots and pans raids and their leaders. Early one morning, at one dawn raid at Arnot in Pennsylvania, an Irish woman in her nightgown hurriedly bundled up and was pushed into action by her husband who was on strike. When the local sheriff told her not to frighten the mules, she decided not to let him get away with it. She took up the old tin pan and she hit him in the head with it, and she yelled, "To hell with you and the mules!"

He fell over and dropped into a creek. Then the mules began to rebel against the scabbers. They bucked and kicked the scab drivers and started off for the barn. This woman was Mary Harris Jones, the Irish widow who had watched the roundhouse burn in Pittsburgh in eighteen seventy-seven. Known everywhere as "Mother Jones", she spent her life traveling through the mining areas urging workers to join a union and to strike for better pay and treatment. It was Mother Jones who sent the miner's wives at Arnot careering downhill after the scabs, and led the miners themselves to victory.

The union Mother Jones worked for was the United Mine Workers of America. A young trade union, it was soon to become one of the most powerful protectors of worker's rights in the whole United States. More and more workers were realizing that they would have to fight hard to win concessions from their bosses and that union organisation was essential. The metal workers of the western states now had their own union too, so did the railway workers, the tailors, printers, carpenters, dockers and many others.

Most employers, and many of the other people in authority, hated and feared the unions that forced them to pay workers more. They did all they could to harass unions that forced them to pay workers more. Mother Jones was a pioneer. But soon, women all over the states were following her into trade unions. Taking the militancy of the coalfield wives a stage further, they set up their own trade union league. Some male unionists doubted how well women could fight in the workers' war, they received a hard lesson, very similar to the one taught to the Arnot sheriff.

Women were on the move and fighting for equality. But it wasn't always a forward move. Let's backtrack for a moment to eighteen forty, when abolitionists in London, England decided to hold a world conference on the importance on antislavery. People came from all over the world to attend this meeting, among them two American abolitionists, Lucretia Mott and Elizabeth Cady Stanton.

They had made the long transatlantic trip in order to speak out against the evils of slavery, rampant here in America. Mott and Stanton were forced to take seats in the balcony and were told to sit quietly. These women were fighting for the rights of slaves, citizens who had less than they did, and this is the treatment they received. Of course this was an era when almost everyone believed that women should not play any active role in society. Mott and Stanton had the courage to disagree. They returned home determined to make changes.

One of the most important incidents in the history of women took place in the summer of 1848, in upstate New York. It was the

Seneca Falls Convention, the official beginning of the women's movement in the United States. At that time, women had few rights. They were routinely denied admission to colleges and to the trades and professions. Most found work in four areas: teaching, sewing, factory jobs, or domestic service. Their wages, if married, belonged to their husbands. Indeed, a wife herself was then considered as her husbands' personal property.

On July 19, 1848, the organizers of that convention; Elizabeth Cady Stanton, Lucretia Mott, Martha Coffin Wright, Jane Hunt, and Mary Ann Mclintock, stood before 300 people and presented a Declaration of Rights and Sentiments. That document, modeled after the Declaration of Independence, declared that all men and women are created equal. It demanded equal access to all means of employment and the ministry, and it insisted that women had "the duty to secure themselves their sacred right to franchise," or suffrage (the right to vote).

Elizabeth Cady Stanton, Susan B. Anthony, and Lucy Stone quickly became the movement's undisputed leaders. They and their followers tirelessly petitioned the nation's state legislatures for women's suffrage and for the reform of property and child custody laws. Many of them worked simultaneously as abolitionists to end slavery. Many male abolitionists also supported their female colleagues' new demands. As far as women were concerned, there was plenty for Mott and Stanton to change. Since the beginning of American history, women had only limited rights.

Although they were citizens, they were second-class citizens compared to men. As previously stated, they could not vote most university positions were closed to them. If they were married, they could not own property, control whatever money they might earn, even though they earned it, they could not bring cases to court, they were unable to sue for divorce, and even when that changed, they rarely received the right to keep their children. In their daily lives, women were expected to spend their time on home, children and church.

After Mott and Stanton returned from London in 1840, they began organizing the women's rights movement. Their primary goal was to gain women equal rights with men. Among the early women's rights leaders were famous abolitionists, such as Frederick Douglass and William Lloyd Garrison. As the Abolition Movement raised questions about the status and rights of individuals, women began to look at their own position and to speak out.

In 1848 Mott, Stanton, and others held a women's rights convention at Seneca Falls, New York. Stanton lived in Seneca Falls with her husband and their seven children. Women and some men traveled many miles by horse and wagon to meet at this small town. Sojourner Truth, a well-known abolitionist, took part in the fight. There the delegates approved a "Declaration of Sentiments" based on the American Declaration of Independence. They resolved that women should no longer be "satisfied with their present position."

The Seneca Falls meeting was important for two reasons. First, it was the first women's rights convention. Second, the declaration summed up women's many complaints in one program for action.

The Seneca Falls Declaration, like the Declaration of Independence, first attacked the treatment of women that made the document necessary. Whereas the colonists blamed the British, the women at Seneca Falls blamed men. Then, also like the Declaration of Independence, the Seneca Falls Declaration listed specific complaints. The feminists listed many "injuries" that man had done to women in trying to establish "an absolute tyranny" over them. Here are some of them:

He has never permitted her to exercise her inalienable right to the elective franchise.

He has taken from her all right in property, even to the wages she earns.

He has monopolized the profitable employments.

He has denied her the facilities for obtaining a thorough education.

He has tried in every way he could to destroy her confidence in her own powers, to lessen her self-respect, and to make her willing to lead a dependent and abject life.

Although the women's rights movement made few gains at first, many individual women were able to achieve success. Even before the Seneca Falls meeting, educator Mary Lyon had established Mount Holyoke, the first women's college in the United States. Several women writers gained wide audiences. They included Louisa May Alcott, who wrote Little Women, and Harriet Beecher Stowe, author of Uncle Tom's Cabin. Against all odds, a few women were able to succeed in fields usually closed to them.

For instance, many people were against Elizabeth Blackwell's effort to become the first American woman physician. Maria Mitchell, an astronomer, was the first woman, and the only one for one hundred years, to be elected to the American Academy of Arts and Sciences. More important than such individual successes were changes that affected thousands of women. One change was education. Beginning in the eighteen sixties, several new state universities accepted both women and men. These were called coeducational schools. In 1870, only about twenty per cent of college students were women.

Before women's movements emerged, women began to form many kinds of groups based upon common interests. After the French Revolution, various women's political clubs took shape in both France and Great Britain. In the United States, women formed temperance societies. In the United States and Britain, two major types of women's movements gradually developed; (1) social or domestic women's movements, and (2) equal rights feminist groups. Women's social movements carried out religious charitable and social activities. Equal rights feminists primarily worked to remove educational and political barriers to women and to change women's roles.

Before our American Civil War, many American women's movements were of the benevolent social type. These included societies to promote temperance, to aid poor women and orphans, and to send missionaries to the Indians. Women also formed similar religious and charitable associations in Britain before eighteen sixty and in other Western countries during the late eighteen hundreds.

Few groups were centered on gaining equal rights for women. But such groups had a clear goal to improve women's situation through such reforms as better education for girls, support for women's property rights, and voting rights for women.

Women's educational opportunities gradually expanded throughout the eighteen hundreds. In 1821, American teacher Emma Willard founded the Troy Female Seminary in Troy, New York. Willard's school was one of the first institutions to offer girls a high school education. In 1833, Oberlin Collegiate Institute opened as the first coeducational college in the United States. Women's efforts to secure legal rights, particularly property rights, also brought reform.

In America, many states enacted property laws during the 1840's and 1850's. Such laws allowed married women to make contracts, to own property, to control their own earnings, and to have joint custody of their children. In 1848, a New York law gave married women the right to retain control of their own real estate and personal property. The new laws, especially aided widowed, deserted, and mistreated wives. Similar legislation passed in Britain and other Western countries during the middle and late 1800's.

Also in 1848, Lucretia Mott and Elizabeth Cady Stanton convention in Seneca Falls prompted other women's conventions. National ones met almost every year from 1850 until the onset of the Civil War in 1861. The delegates' discussions regarding the rights of women would lead to the afore-mentioned laws and reforms. The issue of suffrage also became increasingly important to women during the 1800's. In the United States, the cause of women suffrage was championed by two key organisations; the National Woman Suffrage Association, and the American Woman Suffrage Association.

Stanton and women's rights leader Susan B. Anthony led the NWSA, founded in 1869. The more radical organisation of the two, the NWSA demanded equal education, equal employment opportunities, and voting rights for women immediately. Women's rights leader Lucy Stone, her husband, Henry Blackwell, and other reformers formed the AWSA, also in 1869. The more moderate AWSA supported gradual advances, such as suffrage for women.

In 1890, the two organisations joined to form the National American Woman Suffrage Association (NAWSA). Suffragists held conventions, waged state-by-state campaigns, and distributed literature to win support for their cause. New methods of campaigning used by British women suffragists-especially parades and outdoor speeches spurred the drive for suffrage. Support from both social and equal rights women's movements proved necessary to the final suffrage victory.

Women's social movements, temperance organisations, missionary societies, and progressive reformers realized that they needed the vote to reach their goals. Suffrage movements also arose in other Western countries during the 1800's. In 1893, New Zealand became the first nation to grant women full voting rights. Australia gave women the right to vote in federal election in 1902. Swedish women with property could vote in city elections in 1862. Sweden granted women full suffrage in 1921. In Britain, the suffrage movement began in in the 1860's, though women did not win full voting rights until 1928.

While mankind has been slow to grant women full recognition, her influence on the course of human progress has been great. The thread of women's influence stands out in the unraveling of all recorded history. Women have exerted greater and more influence on the course of history than any of the so called "great women" of the ages. Women were vital factors in all the great movements of mankind.

The pilgrim women who endured the hardships of the first winter in New England provided death-defying proof of the courage and endurance of women. The American West could not have been settled without the skill and bravery of the pioneer women who labored and improvised to make homes in the wilderness, and even took up arms to fight beside their men when hostile adversaries attacked.

Beginning with the Industrial Revolution in the 1760's, women began taking their place in industrial life. Constantly increasing numbers of women have entered into activities that were once exclusively the domain of men. Today, there are no fields of enterprise which women have not entered, and where the best of them have not made outstanding success. It is true that many of them have found serious conflicts between a career and the fundamental desires for love and marriage.

Women have also found that their participation in trades and professions has been marked by unfairness in wage rates or salaries, and in the same vein opportunities to advance themselves. But many of these difficulties have been overcome by women in the democracies, and there is confidence among women that their remaining goals are attainable. From the first offering, women's entrance into the arts and sciences was marked by outstanding contributions to the knowledge and culture of humanity.

These contributions were made in such field as science, medicine, government, nursing, welfare, education, literature, journalism, sculpture, architecture, engineering, drama, international relations, labor organisation, and aviation. Women have become governors of states, been elected to Congress, as well as having been appointed to diplomatic posts. In social advancement, women have been particularly active. The number of outstanding women social workers is large, and constantly increasing.

One of the greatest social workers was Jane Addams, founder of Hull-House, the famous international settlement house in Chicago. Miss Addams inspired other leaders in social welfare, such as Florence Kelley, who became the first factory inspector in Illinois, and Julia Lathrop, the first chief of the Children's Bureau of the United States Department of Labor. In the field of welfare, Florence Nightingale, pioneer nurse, and Clara Barton, founder and first president of the American Red Cross, are deserving of special recognition.

Leaders in the movement to improve woman's lot included Sarah Margaret Fuller, one of the most learned women of the 1800's; Lucretia Coffin Mott, a minister in the Society of Friends and promoter of many social and domestic reforms; Elizabeth Cady Stanton, one of the earliest women lawyers and founder of the suffragist movement.

In the field of education, many women rose above the ranks of their sister teachers. Anna Garlin Spencer, instructor in leading American universities during the early 1900's, first brought to public attention the need for women's participation in broad cultural activities. The Russell Sage Foundation for the improvement of social and living conditions was founded by a woman, Margaret Olivia Slocum. Mary Van Kleeck, a director of the foundation, conducted valuable studies on industry and the problems of employees. Edith Abott and Sophonisba Breckenridge founded the first school of social service administration at the University of Chicago.

In the sciences, women have met their greatest test of their ability to demonstrate equality with men. During the 1890's Dr. M. Carey Thomas, later president of Bryn Mawr College, asked to attend a class at Johns Hopkins University School of medicine in Baltimore. No woman had ever before been permitted to attend the lectures, and Dr. Thomas was granted her request only on condition that she sits behind a screen. Today the "screen" has disappeared, and women have not only witnessed and studied new discoveries of science, but many of them have also made discoveries of their own.

When Madam Marie Curie and her husband announced the discovery of radium in 1898, the woman scientist won immediate fame. She was awarded the Nobel Prize in 1903 and again in 1911 for her studies in chemistry and physics. Annie J. Cannon, winner of the Draper Medal for her work in Astrophysics at the National

Academy of Sciences, won recognition as one of the world's leading astronomers. She and her feminine associates at Harvard University discovered nearly five thousand new stars in a period of forty years. Florence Rena Sabin became one of the world's outstanding scientists in the study of blood and blood diseases.

The work of Lise Meitner in atomic physics played an important part in the development of the atomic bomb. Other women who rank high in the annals of science include Katherine Burr Blodgett and Alice Hamilton. Women have regularly been given research fellowships or scholarships such as are offered men in almost every field of science. Often women have had to work hard in order to pay for the scientific study they wanted. But today there are few research laboratories which do not employ large numbers of women workers.

In the arts, women have shown the greatest variety of natural gifts. Because of the feeling for personal and concrete matters, women have accomplished the most in literature. Such novelists as Jane Austen, Charlotte and Emily Bronte, Pearl Buck, Edith Wharton, and Virginia Woolf rank with the great male authors. Women make up more than half of the successful writers of fiction in contemporary literature.

Agatha Christie and Mary Roberts Rinehart won fame for their mystery and detective stories. Such authors as Sara Orne Jewett and Katherine Ann Porter wrote outstanding short stories. Women have ranked especially high in writing books for children and young people. Louisa May Alcott, Frances Hidgson Burnett, Selma Lagerlof, Beatrix Potter wrote books that many generations of children have cherished.

They have been many good women poets, from Sappho in ancient times to Edna St Vincent Millay, Marianne Moore and Edith Sitwell. Women seem to have been less successful playwrights, although many popular plays have come from women authors. However, there have been many famous and successful actresses, such as Sarah Siddons, Eleanor Duse, Sara Bernhardt Ethel

Barrymore and Helen Hayes. In music, there have been outstanding instrumentalists, and a few composers, but the women singers rank among the leading artists in the field.

Marian Anderson, Maria Callas and Lotte Lehman are among the opera singers who have achieved greatness. Great dancers and choreography include Agnes De Mille, Martha Graham and Ruth St. Dennis.

There have also been many talented women artists, such as painters Mary Cassatt and Georgia O'Keefe, and sculptor Malvine Hoffman. Last but not least, many women have also made outstanding records in the field of sports. Althea Gibson, Alice Marble, and Helen Willis won many prizes for tennis. In golf, "Patty" Berg and Mildred "Babe Didricksen set many course records. Florence Chadwick and Gertrude Ederle excelled in swimming, and Tenley Albright and Barbara Ann Scott were outstanding as figure-skaters.

Objectives:

1. To make students aware of the women's struggle for equality and justice.
2. To increase students written and oral communication and to develop reading comprehension and interpretive evaluation skills.
3. To build pride and self-esteem within themselves especially the females.
4. An important objective is to develop a goal for yourself.
   a. Set a goal that you would like to accomplish.
   b. Select and describe your first step.
   c. Devise the major steps based upon your ability and skills.
   d. Discover where to obtain helpful and or necessary information.
   e. Select places and individuals who could possibly assist in your achievement.

HISTORY OF SOCIAL RELATIONS IN INDIA

No aspect of Indian history has excited more controversy than India's history of social relations. Western indologists and Western-influenced Indian intellectuals have seized upon caste divisions, untouchability, religious obscurantism, and practices of dowry and sati as distinctive evidence of India's perennial backwardness. For many Indologists, these social ills have literally come to define India - and have become almost the exclusive focus of their writings on India.

During the colonial period, it served the interests of the British (and their European cohorts) to exaggerate the democratic character of their own societies while diminishing any socially redeeming features of society in India (and other colonized nations). Social divisions and inequities were a convenient tool in the arsenal of the colonizers. On the one hand, tremendous tactical gains could be achieved by playing off one community against the other.

On the other hand, there were also enormous psychological benefits in creating the impression that India was a land rife with uniquely abhorrent social practices that only an enlightened foreigner could attempt to reform. India's social ills were discussed with a contemptuous cynicism and often with a willful intent to instill a sense of deep shame and inferiority. Strong elements of such colonial imagery continue to dominate the landscape of Western Indology.

A liberal, dynamic West embracing universal human values is posed against an obdurate and unchanging East clinging to odious social values and customs. It is little wonder, therefore, that India's intellectuals have been unable to either fully understand the historic dynamics and context which gave life to these social practices or find effective solutions for their cure. Many historians and social activists appear to have tacitly accepted the notion that caste divisions in society are a uniquely Indian feature and that Indian society has been largely unchanged since the writing of the

Manusmriti which provides formal sanction to such social inequities.

But caste-like divisions are neither uniquely Indian nor has Indian society been as socially stagnant as commonly believed. In all non-egalitarian societies where wealth and political power were unequally distributed, some form of social inequity appeared and often meant hereditary privileges for the elite and legally (or socially) sanctioned discrimination against those considered lower down in the social hierarchy. In fact, caste-like divisions are to be found in the history of most nations - whether in the American continent, or in Africa, Europe or elsewhere in Asia.

In some societies, caste-like divisions were relatively simple, in others more complex. For instance, in Eastern Africa some agricultural societies were divided between land-owning and landless tribes (or clans) that eventually took on caste-like characteristics. Priests and warriors enjoyed special privileges in the 15th C. Aztec society of Mexico as did the Samurais (warrior nobles) and priests of medieval Japan. Notions of purity and defilement were also quite similar in Japanese society and members of society who carried out "unclean" tasks were treated as social outcasts - just as in India.

Amongst the most stratified of the ancient civilisations was the Roman Civilisation where in addition to state-sanctioned slavery, there were all manner of caste-like inequities coded into law. Even in the Christian era, European feudalism provided all manner of hereditary privileges for the knights and landed barons (somewhat akin to India's Rajputs and Thakurs) and amongst the royalty, arranged marriages and dowry was just as common as in India.

Discrimination against the artisans was also commonplace throughout Europe and as late as the 19th century - artisans in Germany had to go through a separate court system to seek legal redress. They were not permitted to appeal to courts that dealt with the affairs of the nobility and the landed gentry. (For instance, Beethoven wrote numerous letters to German judicial authorities pleading that he not be treated as a second-class citizen - that as Germany's pre-eminent composer he deserved better treatment.)

A common pattern that seems to emerge from a study of several such ancient and medieval societies is that priests and warriors typically formed an elite class in most medieval societies and social privileges varied according to social rank; in settled agriculture based societies, this was usually closely related to ownership of land. For instance, we find no evidence of caste-like discrimination in societies where land was collectively owned and jointly cultivated, or where goods and services were exchanged within the village on the basis of barter, and there was no premium assigned to any particular type of work.

All services and all forms of human labor were valued equally. Such village communes may have once existed throughout India and some appear to have survived until quite recently - especially in the hills, (such as in parts of Himachal and the North East, including Assam and Tripura), but also in Orissa and parts of Central India. In such societies, we also see little evidence of gender discrimination.

In India, caste and gender discrimination appear to become more pronounced with the advent of hereditary and authoritarian ruling dynasties, a powerful state bureaucracy, the growth of selective property rights, and the domination of Brahmins over the rural poor in *agrahara* villages. But this process was neither linear nor always irreversible. As old ruling dynasties were overthrown, previously existing caste equations and caste hierarchies were also challenged and modified.

In many parts of India this process may have taken several centuries to crystallize and caste rigidity may be a much more recent phenomenon than has been commonly portrayed. The impression that caste divisions were always strictly enforced, or that there were no challenges to caste rigidity does not seem to square with a dispassionate examination of the Indian historical record. It should also be emphasized that caste-distinctions were not the only way, or even the most egregious way in which social inequities manifested themselves in older societies.

In ancient Greece and Rome, the institution of slavery was at least as cruel a practice, if not worse. (It is therefore quite ironic how the slave-owning Greek states are revered by Western intellectuals as the world's first "democratic" societies but ancient India is denigrated for its incomprehensible social ills.) Levels and degree of caste discrimination in India have varied with time and there has been both upward and downward mobility of castes and social groups.

Going by the strictures outlined in the *Manusmriti,* one might conclude that caste distinctions were set in stone, rigidly enforced and the possibilities of caste mobility completely circumscribed. But a closer examination of the historical record suggests otherwise. Already in the Upanishadic period there were tensions between Brahmins and Kshatriyas, and there are explicit parables in the Upanishadic texts illustrating how an enlightened Kshatriya was able to exceed a Brahmin in spiritual wisdom and philosophical knowledge.

In the *Mahabharatha*, there are references to a Brahmin warrior suggesting that caste categories were not entirely inflexible. There is also criticism of parasitism amongst Brahmins in some of the texts from the Upanishadic period, and social commentators emphasized how those who reneged on their social obligations were undeserving of their caste privileges. This is an important point because it suggests that there was an implied social contract that involved both privileges and social obligations.

The monarch might have enjoyed immense power and prestige, and exacted numerous rights over the common people, but also had the obligation to defend the people - to protect them from invaders, to dispense justice in an unprejudiced manner and assist in the development and preservation of irrigation facilities and roads. Failure to meet such expectations could and did lead to revolts, and dynasties rose and fell within a matter of few generations.

CHALLENGES TO BRAHMINICAL HEGEMONY AND CASTE-RIGIDITY

In the Upanishads, there is also recognition that conceptions of god could be quite varied, that Brahminical rituals were not essential to spiritual release, and that individuals might choose different deities or methods of worship. This ecumenical outlook facilitated the growth of alternative viewpoints not only in the realm of religious practice but also on norms of how society ought to be structured.

Social challenges to absolute monarchical rule and the immense power of the priestly class probably led to a crescendo during the Buddhist period when Brahmin hegemony received challenges from several quarters - from radical atheists such as the *Lokayatas,* from Jain agnostics, and heterodox Hindus and Buddhists who wanted to reconstruct society on a less discriminatory and more humane basis. Although it would be wrong to romanticize the Buddhists as being completely against caste distinctions {since there is evidence that they accepted caste distinctions in society outside their *sanghas* (communes)}, Buddhists along with other social critics undoubtedly played a powerful role in ensuring that caste was not the sole or even the dominant factor in shaping Indian society of that period.

This is borne out by how so many ruling clans arose from a non-Kshatriya (and also non-Brahmin) background. The Nandas, the Mauryas, the Kalingas and the Guptas are just some of the more illustrious of India's ruling dynasties that did not arise from a Kshatriya background. (Of course, once some of these clans established themselves as ruling dynasties, they took on the Kshatriya mantle, and over time, the radical changes that accompanied their ascent to power gave way to social conservatism and a decaying of the radical currents that had contributed to their rise to power).

It is also worth noting that the classical four varna division of Hindu society (as described in the *Manusmriti)* does not appear to have had much practical significance if one were to go by the accounts of the Greek chronicler, Megasthenes. In his accounts of Mauryan India Megasthenes appears to list a seven fold social order in which he differentiates between the priest and the philosopher (who he ranked much above the priest, and who could have been a Brahmin, Jain or Buddhist) and also gives special attention to court bureaucrats such as record keepers, tax collectors and judicial officials.

He also ascribed to the peasantry a higher status than might be inferred from the *Manusmriti* and noted with amazement how the peasantry was left unharmed during battles. According to Megasthenes, philosophers - whether Brahmins or Jain/Buddhist monks also had obligations in terms of offering advice to the ruler in matters of public policy, agriculture, health and culture. Repeated failure to provide sound counsel could lead to a loss of privileges - even exile or death. Thus, although many Brahmins may have held on to their privileges by being shameless sycophants - others made significant contributions in the realm of science, philosophy and culture.

Social mobility was possible since learning was not an exclusive preserve of the Brahmins and both the Buddhist and Jain sanghas admitted people from different social backgrounds and also admitted women. (Jyotsna Kamat points to a Karnataka inscription from 1187 A.D. that suggests that Jain nuns enjoyed the same amount of freedom as their male counterparts.) The more advanced *sanghas* enforced a separate quorum for women to ensure that a largely male gathering may not take decisions that did not meet with the approval of the women members of the *sangha*.

Over time, it appears that the *sanghas* degenerated, losing their intellectual vitality and egalitarian spirit allowing the Brahmins to gradually consolidate their power and influence in the Gangetic plain. But even as late as the 6th-7th C, Gupta-period inscriptions describing land grants in Bengal appear to corroborate Megasthenes' view of how Indian society was structured. Social rank of senior court administrators (who may have risen from different caste backgrounds) invariably exceeded the rank of ordinary village priests.

(In Orissa, Rajasthan and parts of Central and Southern India, this pattern prevailed till even later. Moreover, as society headed towards caste-ossification, it was the court administrators who after acquiring hereditary caste status, became the most privileged agents in society. In some instances, these administrative castes simply merged with other privileged castes such as Brahmin or Kshatriya, or else they were treated as equivalent and the historic distinctions between then became blurred or obscured.)

In a sampling of Gupta period land grant decrees, it is intriguing that caste identities are omitted more often than explicitly included. Had caste been as important or dominant a social category, one might expect otherwise. Some of the most important figures appear to be officials involved in tax collection and land measurement. Various ranks of officials are mentioned without any explicit mention of their caste. Villagers are also frequently named without reference to their cast.

Only occasionally, there are references to villagers who are also mentioned as being Brahmins. Some of the land grant records indicate that before land grants were made, certain categories of villagers - perhaps those considered more important - were consulted by the higher officials. Although Brahmins are mentioned in the list of those consulted, there are equal references to other categories of villagers such as *kutumbins* and *mahattaras* who may have been village officials or important landholders in the village. {Vishwa Mohan Jha describes the *kutumbins* and *mahattaras* as *varna/jati* nuetral categories (i.e. caste-independent categories) that included Brahmins and non-Brahmins alike.}

Other references point to consultative committees that included the chief artisan, the chief scribe, the merchant and the guild-president of the town. It also appears that administrative changes led to the creation of new posts, the merger or elimination of older posts, and changes in ranks of various officials over time. An examination of the land grant decrees over a space of three centuries (5th-7th C Bengal) points to such changes and others - such as changes in procedures, or changes in the constitution of consultative committees, perhaps to reflect changing political alliances or changes in the economic status of different groups of townspeople and villagers.

In a land allotment plate from Paschimbagh (Bengal) Brahmins are mentioned as tax payers, and the status of ordinary Brahmins does not seem at all exceptional. For instance, it points to a teacher or a Vedic scholar as being entitled to 10 *patakas* of land, but other Brahmins were entitled to only 2 *patakas* - a share less than that of a *Kayastha* (record-keeper) or *Vaidya* (medical practitioner). Carpenters, smiths and artisans were also put far above other service communities in terms of their share of land.

The Paschimbagh inscription also describes the grant of plots of land to florists, potters, carpenters, masons, blacksmiths and sweepers for serving a *matha (*monastery*)* indicating that when land was granted for a temple or monastery, priests were not the exclusive beneficiaries of land grants. (Two Bhaumakara charters from Talcher/Dhenkanal in Orissa similiarly refer to donations of land for a Buddhist temple, and allocations for its maintenance.)

A study of land grants from 12th C Rajasthan (Pali) and Karnataka (Kalikatti) suggests that land grants had limited life tenure even when initially decreed to be for life or for perpetuity. Beneficiaries of land grants were subject to transfers, and grants to a particular beneficiary were transferred to another beneficiary five or ten years later. It also appears that the beneficiaries were selected based on administrative rank rather than any particular caste-affiliation.

It is also not at all apparent that administrative rank was limited by birth. In Orissa, there is explicit evidence to the contrary. Ordinary peasants were able to rise up in the ranks of the military, and it is likely that a similar situation prevailed in the administrative ranks. Mayadhar Mansinha suggests that a combination of factors such as training, merit and personal determination played a role, (in addition to social standing and political connections) in determining rank and promotions. In Karnataka, there is evidence that some of the chief administrators were women.

BRAHMINICAL ASCENDANCE

Nevertheless, the seeds for a more privileged role for the Brahmins were also being sown through the process of land grants to Brahmins. In some instances, thousands of Brahmins were granted rights to hitherto uncultivated land. In other cases, Brahmins were appointed as the local representatives of the state authorities in what are described as *agrahara* villages where Brahmins presided over small peasants, who in Bihar were mostly landless sharecoppers or bonded labourers.

These *agrahara* villages were typically small villages and sattelites of bigger villages that included members of several castes and bigger land-holders. In Bihar, such *agrahara* villages proliferated and it is quite likely that in such *agraharas* oppressive social relations and some of the most egregious patterns of caste-centred discrimination and exploitation may have developed.

(While early Gupta period records indicate the existence of rural consultative councils that mediated between the rulers and the artisans and peasants, it seems that such consultative councils became less important or were phased out with the growth of the *agraharas*. Thereafter, the Brahmins became the sole intermediaries between the village and the state, and over time, this may have enabled the

Brahmins to exercise social and political hegemony over other inhabitants of the village. It also appears that the greatest incidence of the practice of untouchability occurs in conjunction with the growth in the power and authority of the Brahmins in such villages.)

But these developments took time to spread elsewhere in India, first spreading to Bengal and eastern UP, and very gradually elsewhere in India. However, this pattern was not necessarily replicated in identical form throughout India and some parts of India virtually escaped this trend. In *agrahara* villages in other parts of India, Brahmins did take on the role of local administrators and tax collectors, but the status of the small peasantry was not always as miserable as in Bihar. The degree of exploitation and oppression appears to be related to the extent of alienation from land-ownership.

For example, evidence for Brahmin domination in Kalikatti, Southern Karnataka emerges after the 13th C. when villagers were instructed to pay taxes to the Brahmin assignees, leading to constant tensions and disputes, but without dramatic changes in the overall status of the tax-paying villagers.

Although Brahminisation was an important factor in leading to caste ossification, it was not necessarily the sole or even the most important factor in the mix. The impact of the Islamic invasions, colonisation by the British and ecological changes played an equally crucial if not decisive role in many instances.

For instance, in Orissa, the ossification of the bureaucracy and its conversion into a group of privileged and exclusive castes appears to take place after the 14th-15th C. when we begin to see a general decline in its overseas trade due to the silting up of its rivers. At the same time, we see the growth of Brahminical hegemony in the realm of religion and military defeats at the hands of the Mughal armies led by Raja Man Singh of Jaipur. All these factors may have played a role in destroying the vibrancy of Oriya society and encouraging caste conservatism.

IMPACT OF THE ISLAMIC INVASIONS

Unfortunately, many social historians have studiously ignored the effect of such external factors in the shaping of social relations in India. But we know that the Islamic invasions led to monumental changes in the political and cultural life of the sub-continent and especially so in the Gangetic plain - so it would be exceedingly odd if the invasions had no impact on the social structure of Indian society.

While some social analysts have tried to analyze Hindu society during the period of Islamic rule as though it had been untouched by the Islamic invasions and left to stagnate in a cocoon of its own making, others have succumbed to illusory simplifications such as Islam was an egalitarian faith whereas Hinduism had caste divisions. Because Islam first arose in those parts of the world where settled agriculture was not possible - i.e. in the desert sands of the Arabian Peninsula - social divisions had not yet emerged in quite the same way that they had in long settled agricultural societies like India.

For the warring nomadic tribes of the desert, Islam may have been a tool for the upward mobility of clans that may have earlier survived on petty thievery and by raiding the wealth of settled urban societies (and later for those who joined the ranks of the military in the Islalmic states), the upward mobility of some came at the expense of enormous human rights violations against others. In the hands of expansionist conquerors, Islam became more an instrument of devastation and terror rather than a vehicle for social equality or social justice.

Taken in its entirety, the period of Islamic rule in India cannot be seen as furthering social equity or social harmony in the subcontinent. As a faith-based ideological system Islam could at best guarantee equality before "God" - i.e. equality after death. However, a closer study of the Quran dispels even such notions, for even amongst believers, there is gender discrimination and rank based on the "quality" and "type" of service provided to the Islamic cause. In any case, on earth, the plight of Muslim converts depended more on social realities, on political equations - than on the abstract and remote promise of equality offered by Islam.

During times of heavy political and economic oppression, the only option for the poor was complete and total submission to the will of "God" which in effect meant sacrificing all their autonomy in favor of the clergy, (who rarely challenged political authority), and more often than not, were largely beholden to the rulers who chose to support and promote them. When the clergy did resist political authority, it often tended towards social conservatism and reaction rather than social progress.

By and large, social inequities widened with the onset of Islamic rule in the sub-continent. Land revenue records clearly indicate that with few exceptions (as in Kashmir and Bengal for a time), Islamic rulers taxed the peasantry at significantly higher rates. If the average rate of taxation during the pre-Islamic period varied between 10% to a maximum of 20% - averaging around 15-16%, it had increased to 33% or even more under the Mughals. (Note that even the Manusmriti limited the tax rate on the peasantry to one-sixth - about 16%)

While all Islamic rulers may not have insisted on the discriminating *jaziya,* many of the earlier invaders insisted upon it, and more than one court chronicler of the Delhi Sultanate describes the violent means taken to suppress peasant rebellions and extract the high taxes from the crushed peasantry. Urban revolts were also not uncommon and the Arab chronicler Ibn Batuta mentions how such rebellions were suppressed with great cruelty.

Punishment for those who rebelled could mean loss of adults (particularly young women) and children to slavery, massacres or forced evacuations of entire villages and small towns, pillage and destruction of places of learning, of temples and other symbols of cultural identification, and denial of job opportunities in the courts.

In the early centuries of Islamic rule, the distrust of the locals was so intense that virtually all the important administrative positions were kept in the hands of foreigners.

(Romila Thapar has pointed out that prior to the Islamic invasions; Hindu rulers also invaded or pillaged the temples of their rivals, especially since these temples were repositories of great wealth. She has also indicated that the management of some of these rich temples was extremely corrupt. Plunder of temple wealth was definitely a factor in the destruction of such temples during raids and attacks by Islamic invaders and conquerors. However, during the Islamic invasions, this practice accelerated both in frequency and intensity.

It should also be noted that not all temples were storehouses of great wealth or under the management of corrupt Brahminical trusts. The majority of temples had considerable cultural significance for the local populations and many were built and maintained by non-Brahminical cults. For instance, in Bundelkhand, Rajasthan, Madhya Pradesh and Orissa, there are a sizable number of surviving temples that not only escaped the path of the Islamic invaders, but were obviously left untouched in local battles between rival Hindu kings.

There are even scattered remains from the Gupta period. But in the Gangetic plain, virtually nothing from the region's pre-Islamic past has survived. Clearly, there were important political dimensions to the destruction of Northern India's cultural wealth. One might speculate that the political subjugation of a reluctant and possibly even hostile population required the physical elimination of cultural symbols that instilled pride and self-confidence, and thus threatened the authority of the alien rulers.

In any case, the smashing of facial features, genitalia and breasts on sculpted figures has no parallel to earlier practices. There is also little evidence that those defeated in battle were killed or enslaved on the scale of what happened during the Islamic invasions.)

For instance, the Afghanistan region (which once had a sizeable Hindu and Buddhist population) acquired the reputation of being a land where Hindus were slaughtered and hence took the name Hindu-Kush, and references to wanton destruction occur with boastful regularity in the records of the triumphant conquerors. However, in the Gangetic plain the Hindu population was essential in maintaining the tax base for the rulers and therefore, it was only necessary to break the autonomy of the Hindu population and crush their resistance to higher taxation.

This was largely achieved through the almost complete destruction of older centres of culture and learning, burning of libraries such as in Nalanda and Vikramshila, the widespread conversion of Buddhists to Islam, and violent acts of reprisal against those who resisted. One of the most deleterious effects of the Islamic invasions on social relations in India was the practice of slavery, which was introduced on a scale hitherto unseen in the subcontinent. Unlike the societies of the East, slavery appears to have played an important role almost throughout the history of the Western world and the Quran has passages that endorse the practice of slavery.

During the Islamic period, in sub-Saharan Africa, slaves labored in the salt mines and copper mines and served as a vital link in the trans-Saharan trade routes acting as porters where camels and donkeys could not go. Scott Levi (Univ. of Wisconsin) points to judicial documents of medieval Samarqand (and other Central Asian sources) that disclose the presence there of many thousands of Indian slaves throughout the medieval period.

A number of Indian sources make it clear that, from the early Ghaznavid raids to the Mughal period, hundreds of thousands (if not millions over the centuries) of men, women and children were marched over to the slave markets in Iran and Central Asia, i.e. beyond the northwest frontier of India, and out of the reach of their familial support systems.

(Although state sanctioned slavery came to an end with the dawn of the Christian era in Europe, a slave-owning replica of ancient Rome arose in the American South, and slaves were employed throughout the Caribbean and South America. The Portuguese were notorious for their slave-markets in India. Even as slavery was banned in Europe, the European trading companies made huge profits from the slave trade. Slavery was not a practice confined to the Islamic parts of the world.)

The practice of slavery probably led to the growth in the custom of *Jauhar* and *Sati* amongst the military castes. Prior to the Islamic invasions, there are very few records to indicate that such practices were widely followed. But the onslaught of the Islamic invaders had led to a complete breakdown in the implementation of war ethics.

Whereas in earlier wars, it was required of both sides to protect the peasantry, to leave women, children and the elderly at peace, and there were injunctions against the enslavement of prisoners or of harming those who surrendered in battle - the invaders had few if any compunctions in unleashing all manner of torments on the defeated population. In such an environment, it is not surprising that for the proud Rajput societies, the act of *jauhar,* or mass suicide was a more honorable option.

(It should be noted that such acts of mass or individual suicide are not unknown elsewhere in the world. Sometimes these acts were voluntary (as was usually emphasized in the Indian tradition), at other times they were entirely coerced. Amongst the Vikings, it was customary for a warrior's young concubines to join the funeral pyres of dead Viking warriors.

In ancient Nubia (upper Sudan and Lower Egypt) there are records of mass suicide upon the death of a warrior king and Nubian burials of warriors indicate practices quite similiar to *Jauhar / Sati.* There are also parallels in the Japanese tradition of *Harakiri* '(suicide for honour) or *Sepukku* amongst the *Samurai* - warrior nobles of Japan. Voluntary suicide of widows (although rare) also took place in China during the reign of the Qing dynasty. There are also records of the Celts and the Romans practicing human sacrifice.

Amongst the Aztecs of the 15th C, the custom of human sacrifice of the defeated does not appear to have any voluntary character, and was seen as a legitimate rite in the celebration of a victory in war. Western feminist indologists who see the practice of Sati as a unique form of gender oppression peculiar to India might note that in the Christian world, the scourge of witch-burning was a far more dangerous threat to the lives of women. The mere charge of being a "witch" could lead to public hanging, and the Salem-witch trials in America were part of a long chain of witch-burnings that took place throughout Christian Europe and carried over into New England)

Nevertheless, Islamic rule in India did not prevail entirely without benefits for specific social classes who chose to collaborate with the invaders. Trading communities probably benefited from the installation of Islamic rulers whose policies of lower taxes on trade, and state support of local traders and financiers was in their interest. Scott Levi suggests that from the end of the thirteenth century, and throughout much of the Delhi Sultanate period, the Muslim nobility were dependent upon heavily capitalized indigenous banking firms (identified in the Tarikh-i Firuz Shahi as *'Sahs'* and *'Multanis'*).

These domestic financiers loaned seeds and other necessary inputs to peasants and village-artisans and manufacturers (such as textile weavers) in return for a share of the produce. The rest they bought in cash and a part of that cash was then recovered by the state treasuries through taxation. It should also be noted that, (by and large), Islamic rulers born and raised in India relied less on violence and sheer terror, but sought alliances with sections of the local population, especially with those amongst the Hindu elite who were willing to collaborate. Although some of these alliances were coerced, others led to tangible material benefits for the royal collaborators.

Alliances were forged through marriage, or simply from political convenience. Military alliances with Hindu rulers were crucial in maintaining the power of many Islamic rulers. After Akbar, the Mughals relied heavily on the Jaipur and Bikaner Rajputs, who in return were given rights to a share of the taxes extracted from the Gangetic plain. And although Hindus were numerically discriminated in jobs at the courts, by skillfully playing off different caste communities against one another, the Mughals were able to win over a section of the Hindus in maintaining their position of political preeminence.

Hence, it would be wrong to see the many centuries of Islamic rule in India purely from the prism of religious antagonisms. But it would be equally wrong to see the long period of rule by Islamic-identified rulers (even those that were born in India) as entirely benevolent or benign, or no different from the rule of earlier Hindu kings. Since most were heavier taxers, the distance between the ruling elites and the peasant and artisan masses tended to widen and there were other aspects of Islamic rule (particularly during the rule of the more oppressive Sultanates) that limited social mobility.

For many of the Islamic rulers, the Brahmin dominated *agraharas* were highly suited to efficient tax collection and the might of the Sultanates came down very heavily on social challenges that weakened the ability of the state to collect taxes. The fear of enslavement and the denial of equal access to job opportunities in the Sultanate courts led to Hindu society becoming extremely inward-looking in large parts of the plains. With opportunities for jobs in the administrative ranks shrinking, caste loyalties were in all likelihood strengthened not weakened.

Thus, rather than shake up the caste system as some might expect, Islamic rule (by foreign invaders who distrusted the locals) may have actually helped in its crystallisation. Neither is there any evidence that Islamic rule helped end the practice of untouchability.

(In fact, the problems of untouchability and caste-discrimination are especially notable in states like UP and Bihar where Islamic rule held complete sway for five centuries. In Sindh and Western

Punjab, where almost the entire population was converted to Islam, it is important to observe that janitorial workers were never converted, and to this date remain a highly oppressed and discriminated group.

There is also evidence that Muslims developed their own versions of caste. Romila Thapar points out how foreign-origin Muslims such as Syeds, Sheiks and Ashrafs kept themselves consciously apart from Muslims who came from artisan and peasant backgrounds. Language was another divider. In Bijapur district, the elite Muslims spoke Urdu whereas the ordinary Muslims spoke Kannada. Zarina Bhatty in an essay on "Social stratification among Muslims" describes caste differentiation amongst Ashraf and non-Ashraf Muslims and notions of impurity that closely parallel caste cleavages and attitudes in Hindu society. Sandra Mackey in the *Caste/Class System in Iran* describes patterns of social differentiation remarkably similiar to India's.)

Over time, Islamic rule in India created a much stronger and more unified elite, which made it more difficult for the ordinary masses to resist regressive social changes, particularly in the realm of philosophical choice, religious pluralism, regional and local autonomy in matters of religion, gender equity, freedom of sexual expression and sexual orientation. For instance, prior to the arrival of Islam, women enjoyed greater freedom of movement and dress. 11th C chronicler of Indian life, *Al-Biruni* expresses puzzlement at how the Hindu men (of Punjab) took the advice of the women "in all consultations and emergencies". But in a matter of few centuries, Islamic notions of gender separation and sexual prudery had infected Hindu households as well. A weaker version of the *Purdah* system and a more conservative dress code became the custom even in Hindu homes, especially so amongst those of the trading community that had frequent contacts with Muslims.

Although in sime passages, the Quran states that their ought to be no compulsion in matters of religion, in other passages, the Quran leaves no doubt that force and coercion are acceptable in furthering Islamic practice. Consequently, the practice of Islam conformed more to the passages advicating force and coercion. In Mali, the Tunisian chronicler Ibn Batuta noted that children who were neglectful in learning the Quran were put in chains until they had it memorized.

Regarding India, he commented how newly converted peasants had a very lackadaisical attitude towards attending regular prayers and how the Imams had to cane non-attendees to force attendance. He also describes how he personally led a battle against the reluctance of women to cover their breasts in the Maldives. In the Indian tradition, moral codes concerning dress were more in keeping with the natural environment. Clothes were light and simple, consistent with the generally hot climate.

And in matters of religion, there was greater diversity, and much more personal choice. It was often up to the devotee to visit a temple at a time of his or her choosing. Which deity to worship involved an element of local choice and different *jatis* might worship different deities. Local versions of the epics such as the *Ramayana* and the *Krishna-Leela* were popularized and recent research points to hundreds of different versions in circulation. Unlike in Islam, pilgrimages were undertaken under less pressure and with greater individual volition. *Al-Biruni* also noted how the Hindus were remarkably flexible and willing to change customs and traditions they no longer felt to be relevant or essential.

(Although notions of *Dharma* played an important role in determining the boundaries for social conduct, these varied with time and were also adapted to suit the individual needs and preferences of different regions and localities.)

PLURALISM IN INDIAN HISTORY

In religions that paid tremendous stress on "revealed truth" (such as Christianity or Islam) there have always been strong tendencies towards dogmatic rigidity. But even at the peak of their influence, India's Brahmins were never quite able to impose any comparable sort of rigid uniformity in the practice of Hinduism on a national (let alone, international) scale. In some localities, the lower castes did without the Brahmins entirely while elsewhere, especially in the South, or in Central India and Orissa - Brahmins often felt obliged to give due deference to dissenting and heterodox cults, and incorporated their belief systems into mainstream Hinduism.

T.K Venkatasubramaniam describes how in Tamil Nadu, Brahmins begin to play an important role in politics and society only after the 7th C., when the Pallavas began to challenge the authority of the previous ruling clans such as the Chera, Chola and Pandya. Because the Pallavas did not rise from an aristocratic background, they used the Brahmins to validate their right to rule through a combination of persuasion and coercion.

At that time, Tamil Nadu was a hotbed of a variety of non-Brahminical traditions, (such as Buddhist, Jain and many others) - hence, a synthesis of these different traditions took place between the 7th and the 11th centuries. Vajrayana Buddhism, Shaivite Tantrism and Hata-Yoga were amongst the trends that became integrated. The Bhakti tradition in which the devotee is held in a higher status than the Brahmin had it's impact as did the ideals of the Siddhis whose supreme ideal was freedom, perfect health and immortality - all to be gained on this earth through magic and yoga.

The Kalamukas, Pasupatas and Kapalikas were popular practitioners of Yogic and Tantric cults - the latter helped assimilate the ecstatic tribal cults of earlier times. This was also the period when the androgyne forms of the Hindu gods (the *Ardhanarishwara*) became popularized.

The existence of these numerous cults was partly an expression of the struggle for social equality and freedom from exploitation, but for some, it was also a means for accessing greater social privileges. The Brahmins of Tamil Nadu (along with the rulers) attempted to manage these social tensions through co-option, philosophical accommodation and synthesis.

In Andhra, folk religions played a powerful role in mediating Brahminical influences, and a vibrant example of the deep penetration of folk influences in popular religion is to be seen in the sculpted array of folkloric panels in the temple of Srisailam (sponsored by the Vijayanagar rulers in the 14th-15th C.). In neighbouring Karnataka, the Bhakti ideal and Jain influences put their stamp on prevailing religious practices.

Religion in India thus developed in a much more organic fashion than is commonly realized, and it was never completely divorced from popular inputs. Both male and female deities drew followers, and while goddesses were sometimes displayed in demonic warrior roles, gods were sometimes displayed with feminine qualities. In the Yogini temples, all the deities were women and although today, there are only a handful of surviving Yogini temples, (mostly in Orissa and Madhya Pradesh) it is not unlikely that many more may have been in existence.

In the 8th-10th C Pratihara era temples, men and women were sculpted in identical heights and proportions - perhaps implying that male domination had not yet fully come to pass. Tantric ideas on sexual liberation found their way into the grand temples not only of Khajuraho and Konarak but also in temples in Rajasthan, the Jabalpur and Raipur regions, in Telengana and elsewhere in the South. Unlike Islam where entry into mosques was curtailed for women, and separate *zenana* areas were constructed, restraints on the entry of women in temples were not commonplace. Contrary to the suppression of female sexuality in the Semitic religious streams, temple architecture from the 11th-13th C appears to revel in the eroticism of both genders - and there are even displays of same-gender interaction.

In this relatively liberal atmosphere, philosophy continued to flourish and while some tendencies drifted towards religious idealism, others emphasized the rational and worldly. The slow but steady record of scientific progress up to the 12th-13th C points to the toleration that atheist, agnostic and rational currents may have enjoyed in Indian society in contrast to the violence meted out towards "heretics" and disbelievers in medieval Europe and the Middle East.

Religion in India developed in a relatively secular atmosphere where all manner of religious variations coexisted with the abstract and all-inclusive monotheism articulated in the Upanishads and later emulated in the various Bhakti streams of worship. At the grassroots level, these relatively more liberal tendencies had their impact on the practice of Islam as well. Sufism, the worship of *pirs* (saints), the practice of the *Urs* were attempts at forging some sort of a compromise.

(Romila Thapar points to peasant and artisan Muslims of Bijapur who continued to celebrate Hindu festivals. To this day, Muslim peasants of Northern Karnataka celebrate Islamic festivals with folk dances that have Hindu origins - quite unlike the orthodox practice of these festivals where singing and dancing might be frowned upon. Such hybrid Muslim communities exist elsewhere in India too.)

But in the Madrasahs, (with few exceptions) conservatism and orthodoxy were the norm; attempts at providing a secular education never really took off, and over time this had a distinctly illiberal effect on how social relations matured in the sub-continent.

THE SIKH RENAISSANCE

Just prior to British rule, Mughal rule had virtually collapsed and power had gone into the hands of Sikh rulers in the North and the Maratha kings in much of Central and Southern India. The Sikhs had been at the forefront of powerful social reforms as they fought against the intolerable burden of high taxes imposed by the Mughals. Gender equality received particular attention from the early Sikh Gurus as did caste discrimination. During the time of Guru Gobind Singh - women not only participated as warriors but they also led some of the battles, and 40% of the spiritual leadership came from the ranks of women.

However once the Sikhs became rulers, the egalitarian currents in the Sikh tradition became successively dissipated. Upper caste converts to Sikhism retained their caste identification, and *Gurudwaras* became divided between those for the upper and lower castes. Nevertheless, the peasantry did win some concessions and the *Gurudwaras* institutionalized charitable practices on a scale unmatched in previous eras. Overall, the century that preceded colonisation was a period of growing social ferment in India, but as British colonial rule tightened, it was to put a great damper on the pace of social reforms.

THE BRITISH COLONIAL ERA

Although some versions of Indian history ascribe to the early colonial administrators a penchant for social reform, it should be noted that the colonial "reformers" were at best aligning themselves with active indigenous reform currents. They were not usually the initiators or great crusaders for social reform as is frequently portrayed.

In any case, after 1857, the cynical strategy of divide and conquer not only impacted relations between Hindus and Muslims, but also aggravated caste tensions. But even independently of conscious attempts by British administrators to inflame caste tensions, the ruination of the Indian economy alone led to a disastrous degradation in social relations.

The Zamindari system particularly disenfranchised the peasantry whose status dropped dramatically in comparison to those castes who were able to find a foothold in the new administration, or find some employment in the new colonial cities. The enormous burden of high taxes led to unprecedented levels of indebtedness and the privileging of the money-lending castes. The economic devastation caused by the Mahalwari system of taxation in the Awadh region led to higher levels of gender discrimination, and an increase in coercion in matters related to dowry. Differential access to modern education and jobs in the colonial administration increased the distance between the favored castes - and the Indian masses.

(The favored castes naturally included Brahmins, Kshatriyas and Banias, but also other important administrative castes such as Kayasthas. Large land owning castes such as Mehtas and Reddis were also favored, as were Marathas, Jatts and other castes who had risen during the decline of Mughal rule.)

It was also the British who resurrected the *Manusmriti* and used it to frame the "Hindu Civil Code". Prior to colonisation, the *Manusmriti* was nothing more than an obscure text, long-forgotten and rarely used to determine what was acceptable social practice. The *Manusmriti* came in very handy in social control. Because the numerical presence of the Britishers in India was not substantial, the Britishers had to rule largely by proxy. It was important that their agents did not face resistance or rebellion, even in the social realm. Owing to its repressive and highly divisive character, the *Manusmriti* helped in preventing both individual and collective resistance to local authorities, who were typically upper caste and often Brahmin. That the *Manusmriti* represented an archaic and outdated social code didn't matter. It fit in very well with the British colonial project.

It was also convenient in providing ideological cover for repressive legal steps the British wanted to take anyway. For instance it didn't hurt that the *Manusmriti* advocated laws that legitimized gender discrimination or attacked same-gender relationships. Such attitudes were then equally prevalent in Europe and it made it easier to disenfranchise women in matters of inheritance or introduce legal injunctions against same-gender sexual relations (as was the case in Britain during the 18th C.).

CHANGES IN CASTE EQUATIONS

Historians who have attempted to draw a straight line between the *Manusmriti* and post-independence India are clearly unfamiliar with those patterns of Indian history that contradict such a linear view. While some of the social evils of modern India may have ancient roots, many others have a fairly recent history. And even those that may have ancient precedence were modulated and modified as a result of numerous struggles for social equality that have taken place throughout Indian history.

For example, after independence one could find temples built in the late 18th or 19th century that restricted entry to dalits and menstruating women. But it is not at all clear if such strictures were widespread prior to colonisation. Research indicates that during the Pratihara period, caste categories were relatively flexible and popular temples were constructed by those considered low-caste. Temple construction was often a way of gaining social respect and upward mobility.

Restrictions on temple entry most likely reached a peak during the British period partly because only the upper castes had the means to build temples, and also because the control of existing temples passed into the hands of trusts who were hand-picked by the British, and were given free license (possibly even encouraged) to promote discriminatory practices. The iron hand of the colonial state made it much more difficult to challenge such reactionary tendencies.

Economic factors were also crucial in determining caste rank and caste relationships. In periods of intense economic exploitation, caste discrimination intensified, and the reverse took place in periods of economic expansion. For instance, most historians are in agreement that the Gupta period was a period of rising prosperity and also a period of increasing social mobility. Improvements in agricultural productivity led to concomitant improvements in the social rank of the cultivators.

Similiarly, (though much later) there is evidence for the rise in status of the *telis* - cooking oil manufacturers and traders whose earlier low caste status did not fit with their growing economic importance, and were thus granted a higher caste rank. Besides, all through Indian history, phony lineages for non-Kshatriya rulers were constructed to create the aura of continuity and legitimacy. Hence, the mere existence of a document like the Manusmriti should not cause serious social scientists to jump to broad conclusions without greater scrutiny and dispassionate analysis of the Indian historical record.

It is also important not to judge an older society by modern standards. Social relations cannot be entirely separated from how productive activities are carried out and what the level of available technology makes socially possible. In today's world, the widespread availability of printed matter, of computers and other means to store and develop knowledge systems makes the older systems of learning and skill-preservation largely redundant. But in older times, the artisans' guild system helped in the development and preservation of specialized knowledge and perfection of important manufacturing skills.

In India, artisans' guilds were closely correlated to *jati* or caste. It was not only the Brahmins and upper castes who favored hereditary continuity, but skilled carpenters, weavers, metalworkers, painters and numerous categories of other artisans also saw certain benefits in maintaining their *jati* identities. While the artisan castes often fought for greater social equality - the complete breakdown of caste identities was never a serious option except for those at the very bottom of the caste totem pole.

The caste system survived not just because it was enforced by the legal writ of an elite class, but as much because it served a social purpose in an era in which it was difficult if not impossible to organize the educational and productive activities of society in a more flexible and democratic way.

OTHER FORMS OF SOCIAL DISCRIMINATION

In addition, societies that may not have overtly practised a caste system (such as Europe in the Christian era) may have yet prevented egalitarian social interaction and free social mobility through other means. The virtual annihilation and isolation of

Native American communities by Christian invaders and immigrants is a striking and tragic example of systematic social exclusion.

While slavery in America was a thoroughly cruel and demeaning practice, the abolition of slavery did not end injustices against African Americans or other non-European immigrants. For instance, until the passing of the civil rights act - discrimination against African Americans and other nationalities such as Chinese, Indian and Mexican were enshrined in law. Inter-racial marriages were banned in many states and the mere charge of taking an interest in a Caucasian woman could lead to the lynching of Afro-American men in the South.

Early Chinese and Indian immigrants were paid substantially less than the prevailing wages, were not allowed to bring wives and family members into the country, and prevented from owning property. Even workers guilds and trade unions discriminated against non-European immigrant workers.

(The evidence from the richest of the world's capitalist countries suggests that both overt and covert forms of social inequality continue to this day. For instance, many elected Presidents in the US (including Clinton, Bush and Reagan) can trace their lineage to the British royal family, implying that the old ruling classes continue to enjoy special access to power. In Britain, hereditary privileges are enshrined in the constitution for the monarchy, as well as other members of the nobility. The House of Lords is another vestige of the old system that privileges certain elites. The 'old-boys' network, exclusive college sororities and fraternities are another way in which the elite are usually able to arrange privileged and differential access to jobs and business opportunities.

At the other end of the social spectrum, African Americans in the US remain a highly discriminated group. Although comprising less than 10% of the US population, they make up almost fifty per cent of prisoners on death row and a similarly high percentage of jail inmates. Numerous studies have pointed to highly discriminatory practices in how African Americans are arrested (much more frequently), charged (with much lower thresholds of incriminating evidence) and sentenced (to much longer prison terms) relative to Caucasian Americans. In California, there are more African Americans in jails than in universities. The unemployment rate amongst African Americans in some US cities is as high as 50 % whereas the average rate of unemployment is less than 5% in the country as a whole.)

DISCRIMINATION IN THE MODERN WORLD

While in India, caste continues to be an important category leading to grave social inequities, national origin and race have become important factors in how inequality is propagated in much of the modern world. Racial and national discrimination was at the core of how colonial rulers justified their exploitation of the colonies. The colonial system was unique in how human exploitation reached a level of intensity unseen in human history and enabled the creation of exploitative patterns across vast oceans and geographical territories. The legacy of this economic devastation lives on in how negative social practices from older eras continue to survive not only in India but in much of Africa and other colonized nations.

The legacy of colonialism also shows up in how there is no equal work for equal pay across nations. Even accounting for differences in purchasing power, the income and ability to consume for a doctor, engineer, skilled industrial worker or service worker in the US, Europe or Japan is often five to ten times greater than say in India or Bangladesh or Kenya or Indonesia.

While it is undeniable that the task of democratisation of Indian society is incomplete, that caste and gender discrimination continue to cause grave harm, that Adivasis and Dalits still face all manner of trials and tribulations, and that all such social inequities need to be fought with continued vigour - India's social evils cannot be analyzed or eliminated in isolation of other necessary changes. It is important that the process of how social relations become shaped in a certain way be better understood. While battles for social equality need widespread support, their ultimate success may be determined as much by how India's economy develops.

All through human history, property-less class have suffered social discrimination of one kind or another. Economic disparities remain a serious contributor to social inequities today. Any social system that is based on unequal access to economic assets - (whether they be land, raw materials, industrial or commercial wealth) will inevitably lead to some form of social discrimination and inequity. Victims of older forms of discrimination will either continue to be victimized, or simply become victims of new forms of discrimination.

For that reason, the challenge for countries like India is not only to fight against all instances of social discrimination, but to also struggle for greater economic equality - not only within India, but also in terms of India's equality with the rest of the world.

Sri Rama Krishna Paramahamsa "If you must be mad, be it not for the things of the world. Be mad with the love of God." Sri Ramakrishna Paramahamsa (February 18, 1836 - August 16, 1886), was born as Gadadhar Chattopadhyay in the village of Kamarpukur, in the Hooghly district of West Bengal, into a very poor but pious, orthodox brahmin family. His parents were Khudiram Chattopâdhyâya and Chandramani Devî. According to traditional accounts, Ramakrishna's parents experienced supernatural incidents, visions before his birth.

His father Khudiram had a dream in Gaya in which Lord Gadadhara (a form of god Vishnu), said that he would be born as his son. Chandramani Devi is said to have had a vision of light entering her womb from Shiva's temple. Ramakrishna was a popular figure in the village, with a natural gift for fine arts. Though he attended a village school with some regularity for 12 years, he later rejected the traditional schooling saying that he was not interested in a "bread-winning education".

Kamarpukur, being a transit-point in well-established pilgrimage routes to Puri, brought him into contact with renunciates and holy men. He became well-versed in the Puranas, the Ramayana, the Mahabharata, and the Bhagavata Purana, hearing them from wandering monks and the Kathaks-a class of men in ancient India who preached and sang the Pura?as. He could read and write in Bengali. Ramakrishna describes his first spiritual ecstasy at the age of six: while walking along the paddy fields, a flock of white cranes flying against a backdrop of dark thunder clouds caught his vision.

He reportedly became so absorbed by this scene that he lost outward consciousness and experienced indescribable joy in that state. Ramakrishna reportedly had experiences of similar nature a few other times in his childhood-while worshipping the goddess Vishalakshi, and portraying god Shiva in a drama during Shivaratri festival. From his tenth or eleventh year on, the trances became common, and by the final years of his life, Ramakrishna's samadhi periods occurred almost daily.

Ramakrishna's father died in 1843, after which time family responsibilities fell on his elder brother Ramkumar. This loss drew him closer to his mother, and he spent his time in household activities and daily worship of the household deities and became more involved in contemplative activities such as reading the sacred epics. When Ramakrishna was in his teens, the family's financial position worsened. Ramkumar started a Sanskrit school in Calcutta and also served as a priest.

Ramakrishna moved to Calcutta in 1852 with Ramkumar to assist in the priestly work. Priest at Dakshineswar Kali Temple In 1855 Ramkumar was appointed as the priest of Dakshineswar Kali Temple, built by Rani Rashmoni-a rich woman of Calcutta who belonged to the kaivarta community. Ramakrishna, along with his nephew Hriday, became assistants to Ramkumar, with Ramakrishna given the task of decorating the deity. When Ramkumar died in 1856, Ramakrishna took his place as the priest of the Kali temple.

The name Ramakrishna is said to have been given him by Mathur Babu, the son-in-law of Rani Rashmoni. After Ramkumar's death Ramakrishna became more contemplative. He began to look upon the image of the goddess Kali as his mother and the mother of the universe. He became seized by a desire to have a darshana (vision) of Kali-a direct realisation of her reality-and believed the stone image to be living and breathing and taking food out of his hand.

Dakshineswar Kali Temple and Bhavatarini Kali, the deity that Ramakrishna worshipped At times he would weep bitterly and cry out loudly while worshipping, and would not be comforted, because he could not see his mother Kali as perfectly as he wished. People became divided in their opinions-some held Ramakrishna to be mad, and some took him to be a great lover of God.

One day, brought to the point of suicide by this longing, he had the experience of goddess Kali as the universal Mother, which he described as "... houses, doors, temples and everything else vanished altogether; as if there was nothing anywhere! And what I saw was an infinite shoreless sea of light; a sea that was consciousness. However, far and in whatever direction I looked, I saw shining waves, one after another, coming towards me."

MARRIAGE

Rumors spread to Kamarpukur that Ramakrishna had become unstable as a result of his spiritual exercises at Dakshineswar. Ramakrishna's mother and his elder brother Rameshwar decided to get Ramakrishna married, thinking that marriage would be a good steadying influence upon him-by forcing him to accept responsibility and to keep his attention on normal affairs rather than being obsessed with his spiritual practices and visions. Far from objecting to the marriage, Ramakrishna mentioned that they could find the bride at the house of Ramchandra Mukherjee in Jayrambati, three miles to the north-west of Kamarpukur.

The five-year-old bride, Saradamani Mukhopadhyaya was found and the marriage was duly solemnised in 1859. Ramakrishna was 23 at this point, but the age difference was typical for 19th century rural Bengal. They later spent three months together in Kamarpukur. Sarada Devi was fourteen while Ramakrishna was thirty-two. Ramakrishna became a very influential figure in Sarada's life, and she became a strong follower of his teachings. Their marriage is now seen in India, to be one of the most spiritual and perfect unions between a man and a woman.. After the marriage, Sarada stayed at Jayrambati and joined Ramakrishna in Dakshineswar at the age of 18.

RELIGIOUS PRACTICES AND TEACHERS

Many of his religious views were based on traditional Hindu thought and practice. Ramakrishna's personal and religious views focused on living a traditional life, with Hindu gods at the center. It was very much a philosophy of godly worship and dependence. He believed that everything in life-caste, wealth, family, and personal achievement-was already determined by the gods. He believed that every religion was welcome, and that worshiping a god in any way was better than not worshiping one at all. He became very known for his views on religious tolerance and was seen as a saintly figure to many because of them. His views of tolerance were also passed on through the Ramakrishna Mission and his followers.

BHAIRAVI BRAHMANI AND TANTRA

In 1861, Bhairavi Brahmani, an orange-robed, middle-aged female ascetic, appeared at Dakshineshwar. She carried with her the Raghuvir Shila, a stone icon representing Ram and all Vaishnava deities. She was thoroughly conversant with the texts of Gaudiya Vaishnavism and practiced Tantra. According to the Bhairavi, Ramakrishna was experiencing phenomena that accompany mahabhava-the supreme attitude of loving devotion towards the divine and quoting from the bhakti shastras, she said that other religious figures like Radha and Chaitanya had similar experiences.

The Bhairavi initiated Ramakrishna into Tantra. Under her guidance, he went through a full course of sixty four major tantric sadhanas which were completed in 1863. Ramakrishna took the attitude of a son towards the Bhairavi. The Bhairavi on the other hand looked upon Ramakrishna as an avatara, or incarnation of the divine, and was the first person to openly declare that Ramakrishna was an avatara. The Bhairavi also taught Ramakrishna the kumari-puja, a form of ritual in which the Virgin Goddess is worshiped symbolically in the form of a young girl. Under the tutelage of the Bhairavi, Ramakrishna also became an adept at Kundalini Yoga.

VAISHNAVA BHAKTI

The Vaishnava Bhakti traditions speak of five different moods, referred to as bhavas-different attitudes that a devotee can take up to express his love for God. They are: santa, the serene attitude; dasya, the attitude of a servant; sakhya, the attitude of a friend; vatsalya, the attitude of a mother toward her child; and madhura, the attitude of a woman towards her lover. At some point in the period between his vision of Kali and his marriage, Ramakrishna practiced dasya bhava. He started worshiping Rama in the attitude of Hanuman, the monkey-god, who is considered to be the ideal devotee and servant of Rama. According to Ramakrishna, towards the end of this sadhana, he had a vision of Sita, the consort of Rama, merging into his body.

In 1864, Ramakrishna practiced vatsalya bhava under a Vaishnava guru Jatadhari. During this period, he worshipped a metal image of Ramlala (Rama as a child) in the attitude of a mother. According to Ramakrishna, he could feel the presence of child Rama as a living God in the metal image. Ramakrishna later engaged in the practice of madhura bhava- the attitude of the Gopis and Radha towards Krishna.

According to Ramakrishna, towards the end of this sadhana, he attained savikalpa samadhi-vision and union with Krishna. Ramakrishna visited Nadia, the home of Chaitanya and Nityananda, the 15th-century founders of Bengali Gaudiya Vaishnava bhakti. According to Ramakrishna, he had an intense vision of two young boys merging into his body. Earlier, after his vision of Kali, he is said to have cultivated the Santa bhava-the passive "peaceful" attitude - towards Kali.

In 1865, Ramakrishna was initiated into sanyasa by Tota Puri, an itinerant monk who trained Ramakrishna in Advaita Vedanta, the Hindu philosophy which emphasizes non-dualism. Totapuri first guided Ramakrishna through the rites of sanyasa-renunciation of all ties to the world. Then he instructed him in the teaching of advaita-that "Brahman alone is real, and the world is illusory; I have no separate existence; I am that Brahman alone." Under the guidance of Totapuri, Ramakrishna reportedly experienced nirvikalpa samadhi, which is considered to be the highest state in spiritual realisation.

ISLAM AND CHRISTIANITY

In 1866, Govinda Roy, a Hindu guru who practiced Sufism, initiated Ramakrishna into Islam. Ramakrishna said that he "devoutly repeated the name of Allah, wore a cloth like the Arab Moslems, said their prayer five times daily, and felt disinclined even to see images of the Hindu gods and goddesses, much less worship them-for the Hindu way of thinking had disappeared altogether from my mind. According to Ramakrishna, after three days of practice he had a vision of a "radiant personage with grave countenance and white beard resembling the Prophet and merging with his body".

At the end of 1873 he started the practice of Christianity, when his devotee Shambu Charan Mallik read the Bible to him. Ramakrishna said that for several days he was filled with Christian thoughts and no longer thought of going to the Kali temple. According to Ramakrishna, one day when he saw the picture of Madonna and Child Jesus, he felt that the figures became alive and had a vision in which Jesus merged with his body.

ARRIVAL OF FOLLOWERS

In 1875, Ramakrishna met the influential Brahmo Samaj leader Keshab Chandra Sen. Keshab had accepted Christianity, and had separated from the Adi Brahmo Samaj. Formerly, Keshab had rejected idolatry, but under the influence of Ramakrishna he accepted Hindu polytheism and established the "New Dispensation" (Nava Vidhan) religious movement, based on Ramakrishna's principles- "Worship of God as Mother", "All religions as true" and "Assimilation of Hindu polytheism into Brahmoism".

Keshab also publicized Ramakrishna's teachings in the journals of New Dispensation over a period of several years, which was instrumental in bringing Ramakrishna to the attention of a wider audience, especially the Bhadralok (English-educated classes of Bengal) and the Europeans residing in India. Following Keshab, other Brahmos such as Vijaykrishna Goswami started to admire Ramakrishna, propagate his ideals and reorient their socio-religious outlook. Many prominent people of Calcutta- Pratap Chandra Mazumdar, Shivanath Shastri and Trailokyanath Sanyal- began visiting him during this time (1871-1885).

Mazumdar wrote the first English biography of Ramakrishna, entitled The Hindu Saint in the Theistic Quarterly Review (1879), which played a vital role in introducing Ramakrishna to Westerners like the German indologist Max Müller. Newspapers reported that Ramakrishna was spreading "Love" and "Devotion" among the educated classes of Calcutta and that he had succeeded in reforming the character of some youths whose morals had been corrupt.

Ramakrishna also had interactions with Debendranath Tagore, the father of Rabindranath Tagore, and Ishwar Chandra Vidyasagar, a renowned social worker. He had also met Swami Dayananda. Ramakrishna is considered as one of the main contributors to the Bengali Renaissance. Among the Europeans who were influenced by Ramakrishna was Principal Dr. W.W. Hastie of the Scottish Church College, Calcutta.

In the course of explaining the word trance in the poem The Excursion by William Wordsworth, Hastie told his students that if they wanted to know its "real meaning", they should go to "Ramakrishna of Dakshineswar." This prompted some of his students, including Narendranath Dutta (later Swami Vivekananda), to visit Ramakrishna.

DEVOTEES AND DISCIPLES

Most of Ramakrishna's prominent disciples came between 1879-1885, and were influenced by his style of preaching and instructing.

His chief disciples consisted of:

- Grihastas or The householders-Mahendranath Gupta, Girish Chandra Ghosh, Akshay Kumar Sen and others.
- Monastic disciples who renounced their family and became the earliest monks of the Ramakrishna order-Narendranath Dutta (Swami Vivekananda), Rakhal Chandra Ghosh (Swami Brahmananda), Kaliprasad Chandra (Swami Abhedananda), Taraknath Ghoshal (Swami Shivananda), Sashibhushan Chakravarty (Swami Ramakrishnananda), Saratchandra Chakravarty (Swami Saradananda) and others.
- A small group of women disciples including Gauri Ma and Yogin Ma. A few of them were initiated into sanyasa through mantra deeksha. Among the women, Ramakrishna emphasized service to other women rather than tapasya (practice of austerities). Gauri-ma founded the Saradesvari Ashrama at Barrackpur, which was dedicated to the education and uplift of women.

As his name spread, an ever-shifting crowd of all classes and castes visited Ramakrishna.

SARADA DEVI

At the age of eighteen Sarada Devi joined Ramakrishna at Dakshineswar. By the time his bride joined him, Ramakrishna had already embraced the monastic life of a sanyasin; as a result, the marriage was never consummated. As a priest Ramakrishna performed the ritual ceremony-the Shodashi Puja-where Sarada Devi was made to sit in the seat of goddess Kali, and worshiped as the Divine mother.

Ramakrishna regarded Sarada as the Divine Mother in person, addressing her as the Holy Mother, and it was by this name that she was known to Ramakrishna's disciples. Sarada Devi outlived Ramakrishna by 34 years and played an important role in the nascent religious movement. In the beginning of 1885 Ramakrishna suffered from clergyman's throat, which gradually developed into throat cancer. He was moved to Shyampukur near Calcutta, where some of the best physicians of the time, including Dr. Mahendralal Sarkar, were engaged.

When his condition aggravated he was relocated to a large garden house at Cossipore on December 11, 1885. Ramakrishna asked Vivekananda to look after the welfare of the disciples, saying, "keep my boys together" and asked him to "teach them". Ramakrishna also asked other monastic disciples to look upon Vivekananda as their leader. Ramakrishna's condition gradually worsened and he expired in the early morning hours of August 16, 1886 at the Cossipore garden house.

According to his disciples, this was mahasamadhi. After the death of their master, the monastic disciples lead by Vivekananda formed a fellowship at a half-ruined house at Baranagar near the river Ganga, with the financial assistance of the householder disciples. This became the first Math or monastery of the disciples who constituted the first Ramakrishna Order.

Ramakrishna's teachings were imparted in rustic Bengali, using stories and parables. These teachings made a powerful impact on Calcutta's intellectuals, despite the fact that his preachings were far removed from issues of modernism or national independence. His spiritual movement indirectly aided nationalism, as it rejected caste distinctions and religious prejudices. Ramakrishna looked upon the world as Maya and he explained that avidya maya represents dark forces of creation (e.g. sensual desire, evil passions, greed, lust and cruelty), which keep people on lower planes of consciousness. These forces are responsible for human entrapment in the cycle of birth and death, and they must be fought and vanquished.

Vidya maya, on the other hand, represents higher forces of creation (e.g. spiritual virtues, enlightening qualities, kindness, purity, love, and devotion), which elevate human beings to the higher planes of consciousness. Ramakrishna practised several religions, including Islam and Christianity, and recognized that in spite of the differences, all religions are valid and true and they lead to the same ultimate goal-God.

Ramakrishna's proclaimed that jatra jiv tatra Shiv (wherever there is a living being, there is Shiva) which stemmed from his Advaitic perception of Reality. His teaching, "Jive daya noy, Shiv gyane jiv seba" (not kindness to living beings, but serving the living being as Shiva Himself) is considered as the inspiration for the philanthropic work carried out by his chief disciple Vivekananda.

Several organisations have been established in the name of Ramakrishna. The Ramakrishna Math and Mission is one of the main organisations founded by Swami Vivekananda in 1897. The Mission conducts extensive work in health care, disaster relief, rural management, tribal welfare, elementary and higher education. The movement is considered as one of the revitalisation movements of India.

Other organisations include the Ramakrishna Vedanta Society founded by Swami Abhedananda in 1923, the Ramakrishna Vivekananda Mission formed by Swami Nityananda in 1976, and the Sri Sarada Math and Ramakrishna Sarada Mission founded in 1959 as a sister organisation by the Ramakrishna Math and Mission.

Ramakrishna was born during a period of social upheaval in Bengal in particular and India in general. During Ramakrishna's time, Hinduism faced a significant intellectual challenge from Westerners and Indians alike. The Hindu practice of Idol worship came under attack especially in Bengal, and many had denounced Hinduism and embraced Christianity or atheism. Ramakrishna and his movement, the Ramakrishna Mission, played a leading role in the modern revival of Hinduism in India, and on modern Indian history.

His life and teachings were an important part of the renaissance that Bengal, and later India, experienced in the 19th century. Many great thinkers including Max Müller, Mahatma Gandhi, Jawaharlal Nehru, Sri Aurobindo, and Leo Tolstoy have acknowledged Ramakrishna's contribution to humanity. Ramakrishna's influence is also seen in the works of artists such as Franz Dvorak (1862-1927) and Philip Glass.

7

VIOLENCE OR NON-VIOLENCE: INTERPRETATIONS BY RABINDRA NATH TAGORE AND MAHATMA GANDHI

REVIEW OF RABINDRANATH TAGORE: THE HOME AND THE WORLD

Tagore's enormous celebrity among Germany's 'intellectual elite' is one of the cultural scandals occurring with ever greater intensity again and again - a typical sign of the total cultural dissolution facing this 'intellectual elite'. For such celebrity indicates the complete loss of the old ability to distinguish between the genuine article and the fake. Tagore himself is - as imaginative writer and as thinker - a wholly insignificant figure. His creative powers are non-existent; his characters pale stereotypes; his stories threadbare and uninteresting; and his sensibility is meagre, insubstantial.

He survives by stirring scraps of the Upanishads and the *Bhagavada Gita* into his works amid the sluggish flow of his own tediousness - and because the contemporary German reader's instinct has become so unsure that he can no longer recognise the difference between the text and quotations. As a result these scanty leftovers from Indian philosophy do not annihilate the unworthy material which frames them; on the contrary, they give it an esoteric sanction of profundity and of wisdom from afar.

That is not surprising. When Germany's educated public is accommodating itself more and more to intellectual substitutes, when it is incapable of grasping the difference between Spangler and classical philosophy, between Ewers and Hoffmann or Poe and so forth, how is it to perceive this difference in the far remoter world of India? Tagore is the Indian Frenssen, whom he faintly recalls in his unctuous tediousness, although his creative powers even fall short of Frenssen.

All the same, his great success has some significance as a symptom of the German mentality today. A possible response to this sharp rejection of Tagore is to invoke an international fame (or rather, fame in Britain). The English bourgeoisie has reasons of its own for rewarding Mr. Tagore with fame and riches (the Nobel Prize): it is repaying its intellectual agent in the struggle against the Indian freedom movement. For Britain, therefore, the scraps of 'wisdom' from ancient India, the doctrine of total acquiescence and of the wickedness of violence - only, of course, when it relates to the freedom movement - have a very concrete and palpable meaning. The greater Tagore's fame and authority, the more effectively his pamphlet can combat the freedom struggle in his native country.

For a pamphlet - and one resorting to the lowest tools of libel - is what Tagore's novel is, in spite of its tediousness and want of spirit. These libels seem all the more repugnant to the unprejudiced reader the more they are steeped in unctuous 'wisdom' and the more slyly Mr. Tagore attempts to conceal his impotent hatred of the Indian freedom fighters in a 'profound' philosophy of the 'universally human'.

The intellectual conflict in the novel is concerned with the question of the use of violence. The author portrays the beginnings of the national movement: the struggle to boycott British goods, to squeeze them out of the Indian market and to replace them with native products. And Mr. Tagore broaches the weighty question: is the use of violence in this struggle morally admissible? The hypothesis is that India is an oppressed, enslaved country, yet Mr. Tagore shows no interest in this question. He is, after all, a philosopher, a moralist only concerned with the 'eternal truths'.

Let the British come to terms as they wish and in their own way with the damage done to their souls through their use of violence: *Mr. Tagore's task is to save the Indians spiritually and to protect their souls* from the dangers posed by the violence, deceit etc. with which they are waging their struggle for freedom. He writes: "Men who die for the truth are immortal; and if a whole people dies for the truth it will achieve immortality in the history of mankind.'

This stance represents nothing less than the ideology of the eternal subjection of India. But Tagore's attitude is even more blatantly manifest in the manner in which he shapes this demand in the action and the characters of his novel. The movement which he depicts is a romantic movement for intellectuals. It strongly reminds us - without taking the analogy too far, since the social circumstances are entirely different - of such movements as the Carbonari in Italy and indeed, in certain aspects (particularly the psychological aspects), the Narodniks in Russia. Romantic Utopianism, ideological exaggeration and the crusading spirit are an essential part of all these movements.

But this is only the starting point for Mr. Tagore's libellous pamphlet. He turns this crusading romanticism, whose *typical representatives* were without question motivated by the purest idealism and self-sacrifice, into a life of adventure and crime. His hero, a minor Indian noble who advocates the current doctrine, is destroyed both inwardly and outwardly by the rapacious excesses of such a 'patriotic' criminal band. His home is destroyed. He himself falls in a battle that was sparked off by the unscrupulousness of the 'patriots'.

He himself is supposed, according to Mr. Tagore, to be by no means hostile to the national movement; on the contrary, he even wants to promote the nation's industry. He experiments with native inventions - provided, though, that he does not pay for them. He gives shelter to the patriots' leader, a contemptible caricature of Gandhi! But when the affair becomes too hot for him, he protects everybody afflicted by the violence of the 'patriots' with his own instruments of power and with those of the British police.

This propagandistic, demagogically one-sided stance renders the novel completely worthless from the artistic angle. The hero's adversary is not a real adversary but a base adventurer, who, for instance, when he wheedles a large sum of money out of the hero's wife for national ends and talks her into theft, does not hand the money over to the national movement but feasts on the sight of the gleaming pieces of gold. No wonder the men and women whom he has led astray turn away from him in disgust the moment they see through him.

But Tagore's creative powers do not even stretch to a decent pamphlet. He lacks the imagination even to calumniate convincingly and effectively, as Dostoyevsky, say, partly succeeded in doing in his counter-revolutionary novel 'Possessed'. The 'spiritual' aspect of his story, separated from the nuggets of Indian wisdom with which it is tricked out, is a petty bourgeois yarn of the shoddiest kind. Ultimately it boils down to the 'problem' of the standing of the 'man of the house': how the wife of a 'good and honest' man is seduced by a romantic adventurer, but then sees through him and returns to her husband in remorse.

This brief sample will suffice to give an impression of the 'great man' whom German intellectuals have treated like a prophet. To rebut such totally dismissive criticism, of course, his admirers will point to his other, 'more universal' writings. In our view, however, the significance of an intellectual trend is evident precisely from what it can say about the most burning contemporary questions if it presumes to point the way in an age of confusion. Indeed the value or worthlessness of a theory or outlook (and of those who proclaim it) is evident precisely from what it has to say to the people of that age in their sufferings and their strivings.

It is difficult to assess wisdom 'in itself' in the vacuum of pure theory (and within the walls of an elegant salon). But it will reveal itself the moment that it comes out with the claim to act as men's guide. Mr. Tagore has come out with that claim in this novel. As we noted, his 'wisdom' was put at the intellectual service of the British police. Is it necessary, therefore, to pay any closer attention to the residue of this 'wisdom'?

THE HOME AND THE WORLD

The Home and the World 1916 is a 1916 novel by Rabindranath Tagore. The book illustrates the battle Tagore had with himself, between the ideas of Western culture and revolution against the Western culture. These two ideas are portrayed in two of the main characters, Nikhil, who is rational and opposes violence, and Sandip, who will let nothing stand in his way from reaching his goals.

These two opposing ideals are very important in understanding the history of this region and its contemporary problems. There is much controversy over whether or not Tagore was attempting represent Gandhi in Sandip but many argue that Tagore would not even venture to personify Sandip as Gandhi because Tagore was a large admirer of Gandhi and Gandhi was anti-violence while Sandip would use violence in any respect to get what he wanted. The book shows "the clash between new and old, realism and idealism, the means and the end, good and evil" (p xxiv) within India and southern Asia.

POLITICAL MOVEMENT

The novel's setting is in early 20th century India. The story line coincides with the National Independence Movement taking place in the country at the time, which was sparked by the Indian National Congress. There were various national and regional campaigns of both militant and non-violent ideas which all had the common goal of ending British colonial rule. Militant nationalism had a strong showing in the early part of the 20th century, especially during the World War I period.

Some examples of this movement are the Indo-German Pact and Ghadar Conspiracy, unfortunately both of these failed. The latter stages of the movement saw a transition to non-violent forms of resistance led by Mohandas Gandhi. India remained a British colony until 1947, when Pakistan (August 14) and India (August 15) gained their freedom. On January 26, 1950, India adopted a constitution and became its own republic.

At the time of Indian Independence, the Muslim dominated North West and eastern parts of the country were separated to form West Pakistan and East Pakistan (which later became Bangladesh). Particularly important to the novel is an understanding of the Swadeshi movement, as a part of the Indian Nationalist Movement. The Swadeshi Movement started in response to the Partition of Bengal by Lord Curzon which occurred in 1905. The Swadeshi movement was a successful resistance policy against the British colonisation. Indian citizens were encouraged to boycott British goods in order to foster Indian identity and independence. This movement was important in fostering the "the new spirit in India," and separating India from Britain, which was largely thought to be responsible for the subsequent widespread poverty.

TRADITIONAL INDIAN HOUSEHOLD

Family structures in traditional India consist of not only the nuclear family but also grandparents, parents-in-law, and unmarried sister-in-laws as well. Though the joint-family is linked to ancient India, it's still prevalent in modern day India. Traditionally, baby boys were preferable to baby girls since boys were able to earn money and support the family. Girls on the other hand, were expensive to raise.

They didn't bring home the bread and the girl's marriage dowry required a hefty amount of money and other luxury goods such as valuable jewelries and saris. Once girls were married off to the other families, they would have to address their new parents-in-law as "father" and "mother". As home maker of the family, the wife's duty was to supervise the household and take care of the children; she also had to try hard to please her new in-laws.

The Home and the World tells us not only the personal struggles of the three main characters, but also little details of the family structure and how traditional Indian households were like. In the book, Bimala starts off as a traditional, obedient house wife who is faithful to her husband and even forces herself to be respectful towards her nagging sister-in-law. "I would cautiously and silently get up and take the dust of my husband's feet without waking him, how at such moments I could feel the vermilion mark upon my forehead shining out like the morning star".

However as she falls "in love" with Sandip, she slowly weens away from her traditional housewife role. She becomes more daring, more confidently brushes off her sister-in-law's criticisms, and crosses outside the women's quarter of the house, and easily converses with another man, Sandip, who is not her husband. Through her dilemma, the readers are able to learn about the traditional ways of the Indian household through Bimala's change from the good house wife to an independent, more modern woman.

The novel is set in early 20th century India in the estate of the Bengali zamindar Nikhil. He marries Bimala, a woman who is both of a lower status and of a darker complexion, which is contradictory to his family traditions. Their love is idyllic and both are dedicated to one another until the appearance of his friend and radical revolutionist, Sandip.

Sandip, a passionate and active man, is a contradiction to the peace-loving and somewhat passive Nikhil. His charismatic speech, support of the Swadeshi movement, and a renewed appreciation of everything Indian while denying everything British garnered support from local natives across the province. After hearing Sandip speaks at a rally, Bimala insists that Sandip visit Nikhil's estate.

While visiting, Sandip's influential nature easily attracts the innocent and unsuspecting Bimala, and she suggests he make his headquarters at their house. Once empowered by the inside world, knowing only her husband and home, she becomes engaged with the outside world, taking part in the Swadeshi movement by working with Sandip. As the novel develops, Bimala is drawn to Sandip's passion and the attraction between the two becomes inevitable, producing a love triangle. She begins to question her marriage with Nikhil and finds in Sandip what she has always sought after in a man: zeal, ambition, and a hint of danger.

She begins to help Sandip by stealing money from Nikhil's treasury, convinced that if it is not equally his money as well as hers, then it belongs to the country. While Bimala claims her national duty as motivation, her true intentions lie in pleasing Sandip. Nikhil subsequently discovers their actions, but grants Bimala freedom to grow and choose what she wants in her life (as their marriage was arranged when she was a young girl). Meanwhile, Bimala experiences love for the first time, which ultimately helps her understand that it is indeed her husband Nikhil who really loves her.

The novel ends with a riot, resulting in Sandip fleeing the city. Nikhil is mortally wounded in the head. Amulya, a young follower of Sandip's movement who considered Bimala as his sister and whom Bimala thinks of as her son (since she has no children) dies by a bullet through his heart.

MAJOR EVENTS

THE RALLY

Near the beginning of the novel, Nikhil brings his wife Bimala to a political rally in an attempt to get her to join the outside world and get in touch better with "reality." Though Bimala had heard of Sandip before this time, and developed a somewhat negative opinion of him, this was the first time she heard Sandip speak.

This event not only changes her opinion of Sandip, but affects her entire outlook on her life both at home and in the outside world.

"I was no longer the lady of the Rajah's house, but the sole representative of Bengal's womanhood," Bimala says. "I returned home that evening radiant with a new pride and joy." After returning home, Bimala asks her husband to invite Sandip to their home for dinner, setting the plot of the novel in motion.

BIMALA'S REALISATION

Towards the end of the book Sandip convinces Bimala to steal from her husband, Nikhil. While in the act of stealing 6000 rupees, she comes to a realisation of the terrible crime she is committing, "I could not think of my house as separate from my country: I had robbed my house, I had robbed my country. For this sin my house had ceased to be mine, my country also was estranged from me".

This represents a character turning point for Bimala: While in the act of thieving, she realizes that Sandip is not only corrupting and robbing the nation, but encouraging her and others to do the same. Ultimately, she ends up giving the money to Sandip and receives unceasing praise from both Sandip and Amulya for her newly recognized sin.

However, Bimala realizes that she has made a mistake by stealing the money from Nikhil and attempts to have Amulya pawn off some of her jewelry in order to replace the money. Amulya attempts to give the box back, but Sandip steals it and gives it back himself. This event allows both Amulya and Bimala to see that Sandip is concerned only with himself, thus allowing them to break free from part of his web. It is during this time that Bimala realizes her power over Sandip by being able to easily make him jealous.

CHARACTERS

NIKHIL – HUSBAND OF BIMALA

Nikhil is seen and described as an educated and gentle man. The reader can see that as the story is told from his point of view. His words flow more poetically, as if possessing a higher proficiency of language. He is from an aristocratic family of landlords, and his family prides themselves in beautiful women. However, Nikhil is different in that he married not only a poor woman, but also one who was not particularly attractive. Nikhil loves his wife very much as he likes to buy her European style dresses and other modern gifts. He also tries to educate her about the outside world and bring her away from the traditional female life in India.

However, due to his gentle and soft nature, he cannot do anything but watch and standby as he sees a relationship unfolding between his wife and his old friend, Sandip. He is also unpopular in the town because he has not joined them stating, "I am not running amuck crying *Bande Mataram*." In light of this, the police also suspect him of harboring some "hidden protest." In reality, Nikhil considers himself to be more aware of his country's role in a broader sense, and refuses to take part in Swadeshi. He claims that "'[He] is willing...to serve [his] country; but [his] worship he reserves for Right which is far greater than [his] country.'

"In traditional texts Nikhil's full name reads as Nikhilesh. Its literal translation is "Lord of the Universe" with Nikhil being literally translated to '"whole" and insinuating harmony, wisdom, and awareness.

BIMALA – WIFE OF NIKHIL

Bimala is described as not very pretty and from a much more humble background than Nikhil. She loves her husband dearly, and enjoys being completely devoted to him. At the beginning of the novel, she seems to be confined to the traditional female role, and has no thoughts of entering the real world, even with persuasion from her husband. Her feelings make a rapid change with the occurrence of the Swadeshi movement. "My sight and my mind, my hopes and my desires, became red with the passion of this new age". When she meets Sandip, her new ideals are fueled by his zealous nature and a fiery, shameless side of her emerges.

As time goes on she becomes more interested and involved in the Swadeshi movement; it is at this time that she starts to develop romantic feelings for Sandip. Literally translated Bimala means "without mal or blemish" and it is often used to mean clean, pure, and immaculate. Oftentimes the name is shortened to Bimal. Although Bimala is married to Nikhil and their marriage was arranged since she was a little girl, Nikhil believes that Bimala is free to make her own decisions to her life. "I was married into a Rajah's house. When I was a child, I was quite familiar with the description of the Prince of the fairy story".

Therefore, Bimala is very dedicated to her husband, her marriage, and most importantly, her family values. However, Nikhil sometimes questions her view of him, basically that of a traditional woman. She cannot stand her husband's idleness, and unwillingness to participate in more "patriotic" endeavors. "Bimala has no patience with patience. She loves to find in men the turbulent, the angry, the unjust. Her respect must have its element of fear." Bimala was not raised the way her husband was raised: well and educated. However, she understands the social differences between her and her husband.

"My husband's grandmother and mother were both renowned for their beauty… [o]nly the auspicious marks with which I was endowed gained me an entry into this family – otherwise, I had no claim to be here".

SANDIP

Sandip is the third major character in the novel, completing the love triangle. He is a guest in the home of Nikhil and Bimala and his revolutionary ideas and speeches have a significant impact on Bimala. He is very vocal in his anti-imperialistic views and is a skilled orator. Sandip represents characteristics that are directly opposite to those Nikhil possesses, thus drawing Bimala to Sandip. Bimala gets caught up in the ideas that Sandip presents as well as the man himself. Her seemingly increasing patriotism causes her to spend more and more time with Sandip, thereby solidifying the love triangle conflict.

Where her husband is reserved and proper, Sandip is impassioned and stirs the emotions not only of Bimala, but the people of Bengal. He spreads the notion of "Swadeshi", or using goods made locally and boycotting British goods. However, his character is far from the ideal patriot. His motivations are selfish at times, prompted by the need to better him socially. He fools people with his mask of goodness, something that Nikhil sees through at the beginnings of Sandip's relationship with his wife. "I have been noticing for some time that there is a gross cupidity about Sandip.

His fleshly feelings make him harbor delusions about his religion and impel him into a tyrannical attitude in his patriotism. His nature is coarse, and so he glorifies his selfish lusts under high-sounding names".

At one point he convinces Bimala to steal from her house and her husband for the "cause". Sandip's presence in the novel concludes with him fleeing while his speeches and ideas result in communal riots. Sandip's full name is Sandip Babu. His first name is translated to "with dipa (light fire flame)". According to the notes in the novel this is used to describe him as "inflaming, exciting, arousing".

Sandip's last name "Babu" originated as an aristocratic title however has come to describe Bengali's educated in the west, or comparable settings. The British used "Babu" as a patronizing term however, its usage as an honorific title still survives in India today.

BARA RANI (BIMALA'S SISTER-IN-LAW)

Bimala and her sister-in-law's relationship is strained at best. Bimala's sister-in-law causes a lot of tension in the household. Bara Rani also uses Nikhil to get the material items that she desires. Bimala constantly complains about her to Nikhil. Bara Rani taunts Bimala for her mingling with Sandip Babu.

AMULYA

Bimala considers Amulya to be her adoptive son, whom she met from the Swadeshi Movement. When first they meet, Bimala asks him to acquire money for their cause. He lists wild schemes and plans, to which Bimala replies "you must not be childish". After pondering their situation, Amulya resolves to murder the cashier for the money. Tagore uses him to symbolize the raw emotion and passion, yet lack of sympathy for others often emcompassed by group or riot mentality.

Tagore also characterizes Amulya as the typical idealistic youth when Amulya rationalizes the murder with a phrase from the *Bhagavada Gita* stating "Who kills the body kills naught!" Amulya is used as a parallel to Sandip, comparing follower to leader.

When Bimala shows such sympathy by calling him "little brother", he is caught off guard, suggesting that the youth is even more impressionable with emotions than Sandip's ideals. Amulya struggles, as any youth, between completing the goals of the movement and developing strong relationships on an individual level, such as with Bimala; this is made extremely difficult by Sandip's powerful influence. Amulya frequently accepts Sandip's motives by rationalizing the necessary actions. In a sense, he can be considered a pawn used by Bimala and Sandip in their strategic power struggle, particularly when Bimala requests he sell her jewels.

IMPORTANT THEMES

NATIONALISM

While the entire novel centers around the Swadeshi movement, the author of the novel is not advocating it but rather warning his audience of the dangers of such a movement. Tagore knows that it is possible for even a seemingly peaceful movement to turn quickly into aggressive nationalism. Such a change would do the country more harm than good. The character named Sandip is the vivacious and ardent leader of Swadeshi. He knows that his movement has the potential to turn ugly. He fervently believes however that freedom must be achieved no matter the cost.

On page 123-4, Sandip cites a story from the Bhagavad Gita in support of his own path. The story tells of the Hindu Lord Krishna advising Arjuna to perform his duty as a warrior regardless of the result. Sandip's use of the Hindu epic poetry to support his movement illustrates the tendency of individuals to use religion as a basis for nationalism.

The use of excerpts from the Indian epic poem was indicative of the blending tradition elements of Indian culture with the ideals and goals of modern Indian Independence movement. As both have the potential to yield individuals claiming an unshakable fervor for their cause, this can be a rather dangerous combination, a fact clearly acknowledged by the novel's author.

Nationalism is also expressed through the rejection of foreign goods, which was a part of the Swadeshi movement. Sandip was strongly against the sale of foreign goods as Bimala stated that "Sandip laid it down that all foreign articles, together with the demon of foreign influence, must be driven out of our territory". Nikhil on the other hand felt the opposite. He stated that in terms of banishing foreign goods from his Suskar market that he "could not do it" and he refused to "tyrannize". Bimala even pleaded with her husband to "order them to be cleared out!" She also stated that banishing foreign goods "would not be tyranny for selfish gain, but for the sake of the country".

TRADITION VERSUS MODERNISM

As the title suggests, a major theme is the relationship of the home with the outside world. Nikhil enjoys the modern, western goods and clothing and lavishes Bimala with them. However, Bimala, in the Hindu tradition, never goes outside of the house complex. Her world is a clash of western and traditional Indian life. She enjoys the modern things that Nikhil brings to her, but when

Sandip comes and speaks of nationalism with such fire, she sees these things as a threat to her way of life.

Bimala's struggle is with identity. She is part of the country, but only knows the home and her home is a mix of cultures. She is torn between supporting the ideal of a country that she knows she should love, or working toward ensuring that her home, her whole world, is free from strife and supporting her husband like a traditional Indian woman should. Bimala is forced to try to understand how her traditional life can mix with a modern world and not be undermined.

This theme ties in with the nationalism theme because it is another way that Tagore is warning against the possibility that nationalism can do more harm than good.

SANDIP VS. NIKHIL

Nikhil and Sandip have extremely different views for the growth of the nation. Nikhil believes in a nation that is peaceful, demonstrates the equality of individuals, and respects social harmony.

Nikhil demonstrates these beliefs in him marrying Bimala, an "unattractive" woman because of her skin color. In the novel, Nikhil talks about disliking an intense patriotism nation, "Use force? But for what? Can force prevail against Truth?" On the other hand, Sandip has contrasting views for the growth of the nation believing in power and force, "My country does not become mine simply because it is the country of my birth. It becomes mine on the day when I am able to win it by force".

The contradicting views of Nikhil and Sandip set up the story and construct an interesting dilemma for Bimala. Unfortunately for Nikhil, he has already tried to show Bimala the outside world, and stir some sort of emotion within her since the beginning of the novel, and failed. Sandip possesses great oratory skill that wins Bimala over simply because of his passion and ferocity, something that her husband may lack.

ILLUSIONS

The constant forming of illusions in the novel grows to be a major recurring theme. Sandip tends to create illusions that almost always have negative affects on his followers and on the nation of Bengal. He builds an illusion of his beliefs that sucks the people of Bengal into a sort of cult. His illusion is complete sovereignty, free of all other worlds, and an endless supply of wealth and self enjoyment. This illusion, as many are, is a fake and a lie. It ultimately sells these people a front row ticket to watch their nation fall into complete chaos and civil war among people with different beliefs. He constructs an illusion for Bimala to believe, saying she is the future, women are the future, and they are the chosen path to salvation. Bimala builds an illusion that she is to blame for this war, it is solely her doing.

That she has done all wrong and no right. She refuses to accept that she too was a victim of Bande Mataram. "I now fear nothing-neither myself, nor anybody else. I have passed through fire. What was inflammable has been burnt to ashes; what is left is deathless. I have dedicated myself to the feet of him, who has received all my sin into the depths of his own pain." The biggest illusion of all of is his mask of caring and passion, while he hides his own selfishness and desire for the world.

TRUTH

In more than one way, this novel is a comparison of different views of truth. Which reality is truer is up to the reader's interpretation. Nikhil maintains an idealistic view of the world while Sandip takes a radical, nature-worshiping view. He feels Nikhil's view of the world is inferior to the real, raw world in which he lives as a radical leader. Bimala as well must compare truths. Through her interactions with Sandip, she is introduced to the truth of "sakti" (female power), yet her life with Nikhil is centered on the truth of conjugality.

Each of these instances is a comparison of truth as being something simply objective to being something with a more spiritual or moral dimension. While the story ends in tragedy, both views of truth are important players in the story's outcome and it is left to the reader to ponder with which he or she agrees or disagrees.

LOVE/UNION

From page one of the novel, the love and union between Nikhil and Bimala is illustrated as something sacred. Nikhil proved throughout the story that he was undeniably devoted to his wife. He proved this first by marrying a woman who hailed a poor family, along with accepting her darker skin. He made great effort to not only educate her, but also for her to understand her place in the world and not just her place in the captivity of their house. He shows his love by giving her freedom. Bimala also adores her husband, but in a less material manner.

This is demonstrated in Bimala's daily ritual of "taking the dust", an Indian ritual of reverence not usually performed by a wife to her husband. Due to Bimala's extreme devotion to Nikhil, in the beginning of the novel, the union between the two of them is seen as one that cannot be broken. However as, the story progresses, Bimala is slowly overcome by her feelings for Sandip.

She eventually realizes that she has found in Sandip what she longed for in Nikhil, fierce ambition and even violent defense of ones ideals. Her deep desire for Sandip led her to completely break her scared union with Nikhil, going as far as to steal money from her household funds. Sandip shows his love for Bimala through idolisation. This idolisation comes about due to her freedom though.

The tale clearly presents the theme of love and union time and time again, going from Nikhil and Bimala's marriage, through the love triangle created by Sandip, and once again returning to Bimala's love for Nikhil at the very end. This story tests the boundaries of the union of marriage. It stretches and twists it to the point where a 9 year marriage is nearly destroyed simply because of a raw temptation.

In addition to the idea of romantic love, there is a sense of love of owns country depicted throughout the novel. Questions such as, is it best to love ones country through action, perhaps even violence, or by passive tolerance are posed in the arguments of Nikhil and Sandip. While love and worship seem parallel in marriage, Nikhil believes these feelings cannot apply to ones country. "To worship my country as a god is to bring a curse upon it".

THE ROLE OF WOMEN

Throughout the novel as stated earlier a strong sense of devotion is seen in the relationship between Bimala and Nikhil. It is key to notice that an indirect evaluation of the role of women is seen in this novel also, in a very subtle manner. In the society described, Bimala, like most women, blindly worships her husband. This can be seen when, Bimala is described, "taking the dust of my husband's feet without waking him," and when she is caught doing this act of kindness, her reaction is, "That had nothing to do with merit. It was a woman's heart, which must worship in order to love."

This seen shows the average woman in this society who believes love will happen and worship is a given in a marriage. She blindly respects her husband without understanding or having a grasp of who he is. Another one of the many scenes that alludes to a woman's place in this society is when Nikhil and Sandip Babu argue and Bimala is asked her opinion, which she finds unusual, in addition to "Never before had I [Bimala] had an opportunity of being present at a discussion between my husband and his men friends".

These lines shows how there are a strong disconnect and there is no place, usually, for a woman in real world conversations. To further prove this, in Nikhil's story, the role of a woman is seen clearly,"Up till now Bimala was my home-made Bimala, the product of the confined space and the daily routine of small duties". The indirect references and descriptions are quite frequent throughout the novel and clearly allow the reader to get a sense of what women were subject to and their overall role in the society.

RELIGION VERSUS NATIONALISM

One major theme in the novel is the importance of religion and on the other hand nationalism. In this novel, religion can be seen as the more "spiritual view" while nationalism can be seen more as the "worldly view." Nikhil's main perspective in life is by the moral and intangible while Sandip is more concerned about the tangible things, which to him is reality.

Sandip believes that this outlook on life, living in a way where one may follow his or her passions and seek immediate gratification, is what gives strength and portrays reality, which is linked to his strong belief in nationalism.

From Sandip's point of view, "when reality has to meet the unreal, deception is its principal weapon; for its enemies always try to shame Reality by calling it gross, and so it needs must hide itself, or else put on some disguise" (Tagore 55).

To Sandip, reality consists of being "gross," "true," "flesh," "passion," "hunger, unashamed and cruel" (Tagore 55). On the other hand, Nikhi's view is more concerned with controlling one's passions and living life in a moral way. He believes that it is, "a part of human nature to try and rise superior to itself," rather than living recklessly by acting on instinct and fleshly desires (Tagore 57). Nikhil argues that a person must learn to control their passions and "recognize the truth of restraint" and that "by pressing what we want to see right into our eyes we only injure them: we do not see". All these moral precepts tie in with his faith.

Nikhil also speaks from a more religious perspective when he speaks of how "all at once my heart was full with the thought that my Eternal Love was steadfastly waiting for me through the ages, behind the veil of material things". This shows that Nikhil does not live morally just for the sake of trying to be good but that it is grounded in his religious views. Sandip reiterates the fact that in their country, they have both "religion and also our nationalism" and that "the result is that both of them suffer".

FILM, TV OR THEATRICAL ADAPTATIONS

Ghare Baire was first released at the Cannes Film Festival in France on May 22, 1984, under the direction of Satyajit Ray. It was also nominated for the Golden Palm award, one of the highest awards received at the Cannes Film Festival. It was later released in the United States on June 21, 1985. The scriptwriters were Satyajit Ray (writer) and Rabindranath Tagore (novel).

Sandip was played by Soumitra Chatterjee, Nikhilesh was played by Victor Banerjee and Bimala was played by Swatilekha Chatterjee. At the beginning of the movie a woman tells the story of the events in her life and how they changed her perspective on the world. She recalls how her husband challenged traditions by providing her with education and letting her, a married woman, out of seclusion. Her husband's friend is a leader in the rebellion against the British when they come to visit and the movie takes off from there.

HISTORICAL CONTEXT

The story of The Home and the World takes place in 1916 in the Bangladesh Region. From the period of 1858 to 1947, the British Empire ruled 8 major provinces throughout the region of India. These regions include Pakistan, Bangladesh, Singapore, and Burma. Drawn to region for trading purposes, the British soon had set up an expansive empire most noteworthy the East India Trading Company.

Not only was it one of the biggest trading powers in the world, it also allowed Britain to enlarge its already huge Navy. The majority of the local people in India did not like being under Colonial Rule resulting in many rebellions. These uprising became known as the Indian Independence Movement. This movement included a variety of political parties, ideas, and movements that all strived to end British rule. Perhaps the greatest influence on the people of India came from the ideas and beliefs of Mohandas Gandhi who stressed that non violence was the ultimate tool to opposing foreign rule.

GANDHI'S NON-VIOLENT REVOLUTION

Mohandas Karamchand Gandhi was born on October 2, 1869 at Porbandar in western India. His father was prime minister of the very small state, and his mother was a religious Vaishnavite. At the age of 13 Mohandas was married to a girl his own age and began an active sex life. In his autobiography he admitted that as a boy he secretly ate meat with his friends so that they could become strong like the English.

After some local education it was decided that he should go to England to study law. He gained his mother's permission by promising to refrain from wine, women, and meat, but he defied his caste's regulations which forbade travel to England. He joined the Inner Temple law college in London. In searching for a vegetarian restaurant he discovered its philosophy in Henry Salt's A *Plea for Vegetarianism* and became convinced.

He organized a vegetarian club and met people with theosophical and altruistic interests. He discovered the *Bhagavada Gita* in Edwin Arnold's poetic translation, *The Song Celestial*, and offered his limited knowledge of Sanskrit to others. This Hindu scripture and the Sermon on the Mount later became his bibles and spiritual guidebooks. He memorized the *Gita* during his daily tooth brushing and often recited its original Sanskrit at his prayer meetings.

GANDHI'S EXPERIMENTS IN SOUTH AFRICA

By the time Gandhi returned to India in 1891, his mother had died. He was not successful at breaking into the legal profession because of his shyness. So he took the opportunity of representing an Indian firm in Natal, South Africa for a year. South Africa, which was notorious for racial discrimination, gave Gandhi the insults which awakened his social conscience. He refused to remove his turban in court; he was thrown out of a first-class railway compartment; he was beaten for refusing to move to the footboard of a stage-coach for the sake of a European passenger; and he was pushed and kicked off a footpath by a policeman.

As a lawyer Gandhi did his best to discover the facts and get the parties to accept arbitration and compromise in order to settle out of court. After solving a difficult case in this way he was elated and commented, "I had learned to find out the better side of human nature and to enter men's hearts. I realized that the true function of a lawyer was to unite parties riven asunder." He also insisted on receiving the truth from his clients; if he found out that they had lied, he dropped their cases. He believed that the lawyer's duty is to help the court discover the truth, not to try to prove the guilty innocent.

At the end of the year during a farewell party before he was to sail for India, Gandhi noticed in the newspaper that a bill was being proposed that would deprive Indians of the vote. His friends urged him to stay and lead the fight for their rights in South Africa. He founded the Natal Indian Congress in 1894, and their efforts were given considerable notice by the press. While he was visiting India, Gandhi wrote a green pamphlet entitled *The Grievances of the British Indians in South Africa*.

When he returned from fetching his family from India in January 1897, the South Africans tried to stop him from landing by bribing and threatening the ship-owner Dada Abdulla Sheth; but Dada Abdulla was Gandhi's client, and finally after a long quarantine period Gandhi was allowed to disembark. The waiting mob recognized Gandhi, and some whites began to hit his face and body until the Police Superintendent's wife came to his rescue. The mob threatened to Iynch him, but Gandhi escaped in a disguise and remained in protective police custody for a few days.

Later he refused to prosecute anyone, holding to the principle of self-restraint in regard to a personal wrong; besides, it had been the community leaders and the Natal government who caused the problem. Gandhi felt it was his duty to support the British during the Boer War; so he organized and led an Indian Ambulance Corps to nurse the wounded on the battlefield. Even this effort was somewhat delayed by race prejudice; but when three hundred free Indians and eight hundred indentured servants volunteered, the whites were impressed.

Gandhi was given a medal for his service in the Boer War. In 1902 he traveled in India, and with Gokhale's support his resolution for the Indians in South Africa was passed by the Indian Congress in Calcutta. Gandhi served the Indian community in Johannesburg, and during the plague of 1904 he got Indian money sterilized so that they could get nursing services. He was instrumental in publishing *Indian Opinion* weekly in English, Gujarati, Hindi, and Tamil from the hundred-acre Phoenix Farm community he founded.

Attracted to the simple agricultural life, Gandhi was influenced by John Ruskin's *Unto This Last*, which he translated into Gujarati. He readily agreed with Ruskin's idea that the good of the individual is contained in the good of all; but the value of labor in tilling the soil or in handicrafts was a revelation to Gandhi. He recruited another Indian ambulance unit during the Zulu Rebellion and was made a sergeant major. Gandhi experimented with celibacy during his thirties, and in 1906 he took the Brahmacharya vow for the rest of his life.

That year Gandhi led a delegation to London and met with the Secretary of State for India, John Morley, to present the case for Indians' rights in South Africa. Gandhi also met with Winston Churchill, who promised to help. His first use of civil disobedience on a mass scale began in September 1906 when the Transvaal government wanted to register the entire Indian population and passed what the Indians called the "Black Act." In response they held a mass meeting in the Imperial Theatre of Johannesburg; some were so angry at the humiliating ordinance that they threatened a violent response if put to the test.

However, with Gandhi's advice they all decided as a group to refuse to comply with the registration provisions. Gandhi suggested that they take a pledge in the name of God; even though they were Hindus and Muslims, they all believed in one and the same God. Every one of the nearly three thousand Indians present took the solemn pledge. Gandhi decided to call this technique of refusing to submit to injustice *Satyagraha*, which means literally "holding to the truth." One week after the pledge, Asiatic women were excused from having to register.

When the Transvaal government finally put the Asiatic Registration Act into effect in 1907, only 511 out of 13,000 Indians registered. Gandhi and several other Indians were arrested. He was given two months without hard labor, and he spent the time reading. During his life Gandhi would spend a total of 249 days in South African jails and 2,089 days in Indian jails. Gandhi declared to his followers that a *satyagrahi* must be fearless and always trust his opponent, "for an implicit trust in human nature is the very essence of his creed." *Satyagraha* thus by its honest purity appeals to the best in the adversary and exposes the true situation for all to see.

It uncovers concealed motives and reveals the truth.
It puts the best possible interpretation
on the opponent's intentions and thereby
gives him another chance to discard baser impulses.
If he fails to do so,
his victims see more clearly and feel more intensely,
while outsiders realize who is wrong.

On February 3, 1908 General Jan Christiaan Smuts promised Gandhi that he would repeal the Transvaal Asiatic Registration Act if they would accept the compromise and register. Gandhi explained the agreement to a meeting, and a majority agreed to register. However, Gandhi's former client Mir Alam Khan accused him of selling out to General Smuts and swore he would kill any man who gave his fingerprints. A week later Gandhi went to register, and the tall Mir Alam knocked him out. Gandhi was kicked and beat by Mir Alam and his companions until he was rescued by passing Europeans. Gandhi was taken to the home of Baptist minister Joseph Doke, where he gave his fingerprints and recovered from his injuries.

General Smuts then introduced a bill to validate the voluntary certificates but not to repeal the Black Act. So on August 16, 1908 three thousand Indians gathered outside the Hamida Mosque in Johannesburg to hear Gandhi make a speech before they burned about two thousand registration certificates. Mir Alam apologized to Gandhi, and they shook hands. Some Chinese burned their certificates too. Two days later the government started deporting new Asiatic immigrants for not knowing a European language. On October 7 Gandhi was arrested for not having his certificate and for refusing to be fingerprinted. He asked for the maximum punishment and was sentenced to a fine or two months hard labor; he chose the latter.

While reading in jail, Gandhi discovered Thoreau's "Civil Disobedience." He was already familiar with the works of Tolstoy and was "overwhelmed" by *The Kingdom of God is Within You* as he "began to realize more and more the infinite possibilities of universal love."4 Gandhi distinguished *Satyagraha* from "passive resistance," which had been used by religious Non-conformists and suffragettes in England and sometimes inflicted injuries and damage.

In *Satyagraha in South Africa* Gandhi wrote that passive resistance had been used along with the use of arms; but *Satyagraha* is the negation of brute force and avoids any injury to the opponent while being willing to suffer in one's own person. As other examples of *Satyagraha* he gave Jesus Christ, the early Christians, and the Russian Doukhobors cited by Tolstoy.

The protest movement for Indian rights in South Africa continued to grow; at one point out of the 13,000 Indians in the province 2,500 were in jail, while 6,000 had fled Transvaal. In being civil to the opponents during the disobedience, Gandhi developed the use of *ahimsa,* which means "non-hurting" and is usually translated "Non-violence." Gandhi followed the precept, "Hate the sin and not the sinner." Since we are all one spiritually, to hurt or attack another person is to attack oneself.

Though we may attack an unjust system, we must always love the persons involved. Thus *ahimsa* became his method in the search for truth. People said that Gandhi was a saint who was losing himself in politics, but he considered himself a politician trying his hardest to be a saint. Gandhi was sent to London again in 1909, but he felt that suffering in jail did more good than spending money in England seeing politicians and journalists. After meeting extremists who insisted that India could never win its independence without violence, on his return voyage Gandhi wrote the dialog *Hind Swaraj*, which means "Indian Self-Rule."

Based on the conversations he had in London, in this diatribe against the corruption of Western civilisation Gandhi suggested that India could gain its independence by Non-violent means and self-reliance. He rejected brute force and its oppression and declared that soul force or love is what keeps people together in peace and harmony. History ignores the peaceful qualities but notices the interruptions and violations which disrupt civilisation. He concluded the dialog by declaring that his life was henceforth dedicated to attaining Indian self-rule.

Aided by a donation of 1500 pounds and the 1,100-acre farm bought and built by architect Hermann Kallenbach, Gandhi named this ashram Tolstoy Farm. He exchanged a few letters with the Great Russian novelist before he died and continued to write and edit the journal *Indian Opinion* in order to elucidate the principles and practice of *Satyagraha.*

Three issues brought the quest for Indian rights in South Africa to a crisis-there was a three-pound annual tax on former indentured servants; Asian immigration was banned; and in March 1913 a law went into effect invalidating all but Christian marriages. When Gandhi explained the new law to his wife Kasturbai, she and others crossing the border into Transvaal in protest were arrested on September 15, 1913. Gandhi could not figure out how to feed the striking miners that gathered around him at Newcastle; so after warning them about the horrors of European-run jails, at the end of October he led them from Natal into Transvaal so that they could be "safely deposited in jail."

He was followed by 2,037 men, 127 women, and 57 children. After they crossed the border, they were not arrested. Gandhi was arrested and paid bail to return to his army; he was arrested again and released and arrested once more, all within four days. The pilgrims headed toward Tolstoy Farm but were deported back to the Newcastle mines, where they were imprisoned. Gandhi was sentenced to three months' hard labor, but the strikes and demonstrations went on with about 50,000 indentured laborers on strike and thousands of free Indians in prison.

The Christian missionary Charles F. Andrews donated all his money to the movement. Gandhi and the other leaders were released and announced another march. However, Gandhi refused to take advantage of a railway strike by white employees and called off the march in spite of Smuts' broken pledge in 1908. Gandhi explained, "Forgiveness is the ornament of the brave."5 After six months of negotiation the issues were finally resolved by Smuts and Gandhi at the end of June in 1914, and the Indian Relief Act went into effect in July.

All marriages regardless of religion were valid; the tax on indentured laborers was canceled including arrears; and Indians were allowed to move more freely. General Smuts expressed his respect for Gandhi and his gentle but powerful methods, which had made him realize which laws had to be repealed. Gandhi summarized in *Indian Opinion* the power of the *Satyagraha* method and prophesied how it could transform modern civilisation.

It is a force which, if it became universal,
would revolutionize social ideals and do away with despotisms
and the ever-growing militarism
under which the nations of the West are groaning
and are being almost crushed to death,
and which fairly promises to overwhelm
even the nations of the East.

NON-VIOLENT CAMPAIGN FOR INDIAN INDEPENDENCE

Meanwhile India was still suffering under British colonial rule. Gandhi arrived in England during the first week of the World War, and again he supported the British by raising and leading an ambulance corps; but he became ill and returned to India in January 1915. The great poet Rabindranath Tagore gave Gandhi the title "Mahatma," meaning "Great Soul," and in May 1915 Gandhi founded the Satyagraha Ashram for his family and co-workers near the textile city of Ahmedabad in Gujarat. When a family of untouchables asked to live in the ashram, Gandhi admitted them. Orthodox Hindus believed this polluted them.

Funds ran out, and Gandhi was ready to live in the untouchable slums if necessary; but an anonymous benefactor donated enough money to last a year. To help change people's attitudes about these unfortunate pariahs, Gandhi renamed them "Harijans" or "Children of God." Later he called his weekly magazine *Harijan* also. In a speech at the opening of Benares University on February 6, 1916 Gandhi said he was ashamed to be speaking in English but questioned whether the anarchists' use of assassination and bomb-throwing was honorable.

Yet he agreed that Indians must take power into their hands to gain self-government. Actually Gandhi had not planned to say these things but did so after he was interrupted by the opposition of Theosophist Annie Besant. Gandhi began wearing home-spun *khadi* in order to encourage self-sufficient village industries and thus help alleviate poverty in India. In April 1917 Gandhi went to Bihar to learn how suffering indigo workers in Champaran were being exploited by exorbitant fees of landlords. He was arrested and ordered to leave; but as he insisted on staying, he was put in jail.

However, the officials soon realized that the Mahatma was the only one who could control the crowds. Assistants helped by carefully documenting the grievances of several thousand peasants, and reforms were won again by civil disobedience. The textile workers of Ahmedabad were also economically oppressed. Gandhi suggested a strike; when the workers were weakening in their resolve, he went on a fast to encourage them to continue the strike. Gandhi explained that he did not fast to coerce the opponent but to strengthen or reform those who loved him. He did not believe in fasting for higher wages, but he fasted so that the workers would accept the system of arbitration to resolve the conflict, which they did.

In the spring of 1918 Gandhi was persuaded by the British to help raise soldiers for a final victory effort in the war. Charlie Andrews criticized Gandhi for recruiting Indians to fight for the British. Gandhi spoke to large audiences but gained hardly any recruits. He was experimenting with a limited raw-food diet and became sick. Even after the war the Rowlatt Act continued the strict laws against sedition. Despite India's cooperation with Britain during the war, they did not receive Dominion Status, and civil liberties were being curtailed.

Guided by a dream or inner experience, Gandhi decided to call for a one-day *hartal* or general strike on all economic activity. Many signed the *Satyagraha* pledge, and Gandhi suggested making "a continuous and persistent effort to return good for evil." Before that day in Old Delhi, Gurka troops opened fire on a march and killed five Hindus and four Muslims. On April 6, 1919 all Indians stopped working. Gandhi spoke and said that machine-guns would no longer afflict them. Two days later he was arrested trying to go to Delhi.

News of his arrest led to civil disobedience. Gandhi was allowed to return to Ahmedabad, which he found under martial law because mill workers had killed a British officer, burned government buildings, extorted money, captured weapons, plundered shops, and attacked private houses. Gandhi realized that now he must protest the behavior of his own people, and he announced a penitential fast for three days, calling off the campaign and declaring he had made a "Himalayan miscalculation."

In an infamous incident at Amritsar on April 13, 1919 Brigadier General Reginald Dyer, reacted to the killing of three Englishmen by an Indian mob by prohibiting public meetings and then ordering his soldiers to fire into the crowd at an outdoor gathering, killing 379 and wounding 1,137 with only 1,650 bullets. The Hunter Report quoted Dyer's own report that he was less concerned with dispersing the crowd and more intent on "producing a sufficient moral effect from a military point of view."

General Drake-Brockman of Delhi also made the statement, "Force is the only thing that an Asiatic has any respect for." The Hunter Report concluded that the moral effect was quite opposite from the one intended; General Dyer was censured and later relieved of his command.

Gandhi was given editorial control over two weeklies without advertisements-*Young India* in English and *Navajivan* in Gujarati and later Hindi. More than seven thousand delegates attended the Amritsar Congress the last week of 1919. Gandhi agreed to support the Muslim Khilafat movement without requiring them to stop slaughtering cows. Instead of civil disobedience, he proposed a nation-wide campaign of Non-violent noncooperation with the British government. For the peasant this meant not paying taxes and not buying liquor because the government gained revenue from its sale. Gandhi wrote to the Viceroy, returning his war medals.

In October 1920 at the annual Indian Congress 14,000 delegates enthusiastically agreed on noncooperation with the British and to end untouchability. Gandhi promised that noncooperation would bring about self-government in one year. At the beginning of 1921 Motilal Nehru, D. R. Das, Vallabhbhai Patel, and thousands of others abandoned their law practices and British courts as students, teachers, and professionals went into the villages to teach literacy and noncooperation.

Gandhi traveled throughout India addressing mass meetings, and imported fabrics were burned. He urged people to spin and weave their own cloth while boycotting British products, and he designed a Congress flag with a spinning wheel in the center. When the Prince of Wales (Edward VIII) visited Bombay in November 1921, protests degenerated into mob violence with looting. Some policemen were beaten to death; in three days of riots 58 Bombay citizens were killed, and four hundred were injured. Gandhi went on a fast to end the violence.

In December the arrests began. By the time Congress met in the last week of 1921 there were 20,000 in jail. Some nationalist patriots urged rebellion. Although Gandhi believed that cowardice is worse than violence, he still believed that Non-violent action is better than both. Six thousand delegates approved Gandhi's resolution for civil disobedience of all government laws, especially those banning public meetings.

Gandhi planned a massive Non-violent campaign in Bardoli, a county of 87,000; but news of how an Indian mob had murdered 23 constables by burning their police station reached him on February 8, 1922, the day it was to begin. Although this incident occurred 800 miles from Bardoli, he once again canceled the campaign, this time before it had started; instead, he fasted for five days in penance. Yet the British Viceroy ordered Gandhi's arrest, and on March 10, 1922 Gandhi was given his only judicial trial by the British. He made no apology for his noncooperation, which he admitted was legally seditious. To Justice Robert Broomfield he said,

> I do not ask for mercy.
>
> I do not plead any extenuating act.

I am here, therefore, to invite and cheerfully submit to
the highest penalty that can be inflicted upon me
for what in law is a deliberate crime
and what appears to me to be the highest duty of a citizen.

He explained, "In my opinion, non-cooperation with evil is as much a duty as is cooperation with good." Broomfield sentenced him to six years and hoped the government would reduce the term. Gandhi was in fact released after 22 months after he had an appendectomy.

Perhaps the greatest block to Indian unity and self government was the religious conflict between Hindus and Muslims. In 1924 an anti-Muslim book led to riots and the murder of its author. After 36 Hindus were killed at Kohat, Gandhi fasted for three weeks. He pleaded for unity in diversity, religious tolerance, and love for one another. After he approved of killing stray dogs, Gandhi was accused of abandoning *ahimsà*. He was blamed for killing a maimed calf that was suffering from an incurable disease at his ashram; but he considered that action non-violent because the unselfish purpose was to relieve the pain of the calf.

During the late 1920s Gandhi wrote *An Autobiography*, which he subtitled "The Story of My Experiments with Truth." This book is quite candid and humble in the way he examined his faults and his efforts to overcome them. In the preface he indicated that his goal was spiritual liberation *(moksha)*. In his speeches he pointed out his five-point program on the fingers of his hand: equality for untouchables, spinning, no alcohol or opium, Hindu-Muslim friendship, and equality for women. They were all connected to the wrist, which stood for Non-violence.

Finally in 1928 he announced a *Satyagraha* campaign in Bardoli against a 22% increase in British-imposed taxes. Refusing to pay taxes, the people had their possessions confiscated, and some were driven off their land; but they remained non-violent. It lasted several months, and hundreds were arrested. Finally the government gave in and agreed to cancel the tax increase, release all prisoners, and return confiscated land and property; the peasants agreed to pay their taxes at the previous rate.

The Indian Congress wanted self-government and considered war for independence. Gandhi naturally refused to support a war but declared that if India was not free under Dominion Status by the end of 1929, then he would demand independence. Consequently on January 26, 1930 he asked people to celebrate Independence Day, and he proclaimed a manifesto that India must sever its connection with Britain and attain complete independence.

Gandhi announced an eleven-point programme that included reducing land revenue by fifty per cent, abolishing the salt tax, prohibiting alcohol, passing a tariff to protect against foreign cloth, enacting a coastal reservation bill to help Indian shipping, revaluating the rupee, reducing military expenditures by at least fifty per cent, reducing salaries of civil servants by half, releasing all political prisoners except for murder, abolishing or controlling the Criminal Investigation Department that was targeting Congress, and issuing firearms for self-defense under popular control.

Then on March 2, 1930 Gandhi wrote a long letter to Viceroy Irwin informing him that civil disobedience would begin on March 11. He noted how ruinously expensive was the British military administration that was exploiting them. Even the salt from the sea was taxed. He believed that nothing but organized non-violence could stop the organized violence of the British government. Civil disobedience would begin with a few people from his Satyagraha Ashram, but others might choose to join.

Gandhi explained, "My ambition is no less than to convert the British people through Non-violence, and thus make them see the wrong they have done to India. I do not seek to harm your people." Gandhi decided to disobey the Salt Laws, which forbade Indians from making their own salt, because this British monopoly especially struck at the poor.

Beginning with 78 members of his ashram, Gandhi led a 240-mile march to the sea that took 24 days. Thousands had gathered at the start, and several thousand joined them on the march. First Gandhi and then others all along the seacoast gathered some salt water in pans to dry it. In Bombay the Congress had pans on the roof; 60,000 people assembled, and hundreds were arrested. At Karachi, where 50,000 watched the salt being made, the crowd was so thick that the police could make no arrests.

The jails were filled with at least 60,000 offenders. Amazingly enough there was practically no violence at all; the people did not want Gandhi to cancel the movement. Gandhi was arrested before he could invade the Dharasana Salt Works, but the poet Sarojini Naidu led 2,500 volunteers and warned them not to resist the blows of the police. According to an eye-witness account by the United Press reporter Webb Miller, they continued to march in hour after hour and were beaten down with steel-shod lathis by the 400 police; but they did not try to fight back, and the injured were dragged away by women. The poet Tagore declared that Europe had lost her moral prestige in Asia. Soon more than 100,000 Indians were in prison, including almost all the leaders.

Gandhi was called to meet with Viceroy Irwin eight times. Lord Irwin wanted the civil disobedience ended, but Gandhi demanded an inquiry into the police brutality. Finally on March 5, 1931 they signed the Delhi Pact that treated India as an equal with England and provided for constitutional issues to be discussed at a Round Table Conference in London. Civil disobedience was called off; prisoners were released; and salt manufacture was permitted on the coast.

Gandhi traveled to London, where he met Charlie Chaplin, George Bernard Shaw, and Maria Montessori among others. Not having seen a movie, Gandhi did not know who Chaplin was; but his criticisms of modern civilisation may have influenced his film *Modern Times*. Gandhi spoke for a half hour on radio to the United States about a non-violent way better than brute force to fight for freedom that is more consistent with human dignity. He appealed to the conscience of the world to rescue his people, who were dying in order to regain liberty. In discussing relations with the British he said he did not want isolated independence but voluntary interdependence based on love.

However, the British Labour Party had been replaced by a coalition led by Ramsay MacDonald, and they used the Indian minorities' problems to divide the Indian Congress. In his final speech at the Conference on November 30, 1931 Gandhi said he still wanted complete independence and warned, "Today you have to fight the school of terrorists which is there with your disciplined and organized terrorism, because you will be blind to the facts or the writing on the wall."

Back in India at the beginning of 1932, communication with the Viceroy broke down over the threat of civil disobedience, and Gandhi was arrested. As during the salt campaign, the old Regulation XXV of 1827 was used to detain him indefinitely without a trial. While in the Yeravda jail Gandhi fasted on behalf of the Harijans because they had been given a separate electorate. It was to be a "fast unto death" unless he could awaken the Hindu conscience. On September 21, 1932 millions of Indians fasted with him for 24 hours. Three days later the Yeravda Pact was signed, and it was ratified the next day.

After an overwhelming vote in favor of it, Hindu temples were opened to untouchables for the first time. Gandhi replaced *Young India* with the weekly *Harijan*. Still concerned about the Harijans, he fasted for three weeks in May 1933; British officials, afraid he might die, released him from prison. In August 1933 he was arrested again and was sentenced to one year. On the seventh day of his fast he was released unconditionally in a very precarious condition. After he recovered, Gandhi went on a speaking tour and raised money for the Harijans (untouchables), traveling more than 12,000 miles.

In May 1934 the All-India Congress endorsed Gandhi's proposal to call off the civil disobedience campaign except for specific grievances. By the time the Second World War was approaching, Gandhi had been confirmed in his pacifist principles. He pointed out how Abyssinia could have used Non-violence against Mussolini, and he recommended it to the Czechs and China. He suggested, "If it is brave, as it is, to die to a man fighting against odds, it is braver still to refuse to fight and yet to refuse to yield to the usurper."

As early as 1938 he exhorted the Jews to stand up for their rights and die if necessary as martyrs so that a degrading manhunt could be turned into calm and determined stand. Gandhi even recommended the British use non-violent methods to fight Hitler; no longer could he support any kind of war or killing. On December 24, 1938 he wrote,

> How can Non-violence combat aerial warfare,
>
> seeing that there are no personal contacts?
>
> The reply to this is that behind the death-dealing bomb
>
> there is the human hand that releases it,
>
> and behind that still is the human heart
>
> that sets the hand in motion.
>
> And at the back of the policy of terrorism
>
> is the assumption that terrorism if applied in a sufficient measure
>
> will produce the desired result,
>
> namely, bend the adversary to the tyrant's will.
>
> But supposing a people make up their mind
>
> that they will never do the tyrant's will,
>
> nor retaliate with the tyrant's own methods,
>
> the tyrant will not find it worth his while
>
> to go on with this terrorism.

He even wrote an open letter to Hitler himself, asking him not to go to war. In April 1939 Gandhi prophesied that before the war ended, the democracies would have adopted the tactics of the Fascists and Nazis, including conscription and methods of force to compel and exact obedience.

Calling for mass *Satyagraha* in defiance of the ban on propaganda against the war, Gandhi promised Congress he would stay out of jail; but his disciple Vinoba Bhave was arrested in October 1940, and about 15,000 were in prison by May 1941. The next year Gandhi wrote, "Supposing that the women and the children of Europe became fired with the love of humanity, they would take the men by storm and reduce militarism to nothingness in an incredibly short time."

He suggested ways to resist the Japanese Non-violently, though he also said that if India had a national government, it should ally itself with the United Nations against the Fascist powers. He criticized the Japanese for attacking China and predicted that their ambition would fail and might prevent the "world federation and brotherhood without which there can be no hope for humanity."

Gandhi was concerned that the British presence would invite the Japanese to invade India. So on July 14, 1942 the Congress Working Committee adopted the famous "Quit India" resolution, and on August 7 the massive Non-violent struggle began under the leadership of Gandhi. Two days later he and the other leaders were arrested, and Congress was declared illegal. The paper *Harijan* was put under a ban and was not allowed to publish again until 1946. Thus for three and a half years we have little or no writing from Gandhi.

While he was detained at the Aga Khan palace, he complained that the government was spreading rumors that he was encouraging violent activities. He announced a three-week fast to seek justice from God because the government had denied him justice. Although the Viceroy warned him that he would consider a fast by

Gandhi "political blackmail" and would let him die, Gandhi disagreed and began fasting on February 10, 1943. If he had not taken some lime juice with his water, he probably would have died. Gandhi's release from prison on May 5, 1944 has been called the end of the Gandhian era.

When the war ended, Gandhi hoped for a real peace based on freedom and equality for all races and nations. He contrasted Non-violence to the horrible violence of the atomic bomb, and he called the use of this weapon on Japan cowardice. In his last years he became more of a socialist, because he believed that inequality breeds violence while equality produces Non-violence.

He went on a pilgrimage to Noakhali to help the poor. Independence for India was now imminent, but the Muslim leader Jinnah was holding out for the creation of a separate state of Pakistan. In a last-ditch effort to salvage Indian unity, on April 1, 1947 Gandhi proposed that Jinnah and his Muslim League control the new government; but this was considered impractical as partition became inevitable. Two weeks later the last viceroy Mountbatten and Gandhi did get Jinnah to sign with them the following statement:

We denounce for all time the use of force to achieve political ends,

and we call upon all the communities of India,

to whatever persuasion they may belong,

not only to refrain from all acts of violence and disorder,

but also to avoid both in speech and writing,

any word which might be construed as an incitement of such acts.

Gandhi prayed for unity and tolerance, and he even read from the *Qur'an* at his prayer meetings. Hindus attacked him because they thought he was partial to Muslims; but Muslims demanded he let them have Pakistan.

Gandhi went to Calcutta to calm the Hindu-Muslim strife and violence, and on August 15, 1947, the long-awaited Independence Day for India, he fasted and prayed there instead of going to the ceremonies at Delhi. On the first of September he fasted again, and he only broke it three days later after municipal officials assured him that there had been no violence for 24 hours. The princely state of Kashmir was invaded by Muslim tribesmen and Pakistani troops.

The Hindu maharajah asked to join the Indian Union and said he intended to appoint the Muslim Sheikh Abdulla prime minister, whose National Conference party also appealed to India to repel the invaders. On October 29, 1947 India announced the accession of Kashmir and sent in troops. Gandhi was criticized for approving this action; but he believed it was justified in these circumstances because not to stand one's ground to defend oneself against an aggressor would be cowardice.

Although he may not help one retaliate, Gandhi believed that he must not let a coward find shelter behind the guise of Non-violence. His last fast began on January 13, 1948, and on the third day the Indian cabinet followed Gandhi's advice and agreed to pay the forty million pounds from united India's assets that they had withheld from Pakistan because of Kashmir. Gandhi's kidneys were not functioning well, and on January 18 Congress got the Hindus, Muslims, Sikhs, Christians, Jews, and other religious groups to sign a peace agreement; on that day he ended his fast.

Although this religious hatred saddened Gandhi, India had gained her independence, accomplishing the greatest Non-violent revolution in the history of the world. Finally Gandhi was assassinated by a small Hindu conspiracy on January 30, 1948 at a prayer meeting; with his last breath the Mahatma chanted the name of God.

SOUL FORCE AND NON-VIOLENCE

Albert Einstein considered Gandhi to be the most enlightened statesman of the age and declared,

Gandhi had demonstrated that a powerful human following
can be assembled not only through the cunning game
of the usual political maneuvers and trickeries
but through the cogent example
of a morally superior conduct of life.

Einstein also predicted, "The problem of bringing peace to the world on a supranational basis will be solved only by employing Gandhi's method on a large scale." The *Encyclopedia Britannica* summarizes Gandhi's significance with the statement, "He was the catalyst if not the initiator of three of the major revolutions of the 20th century: the revolutions against colonialism, racism, and violence."

What was his philosophy of Non-violent soul-force, and what instructions did he give in the use of these methods? *Satyagraha* means literally holding on to the truth. The Hindu understanding of *Sat* is more than conceptual truth but means also being, existence, and reality; ultimately we realize that our spiritual beingness is the essence of truth as a reality greater than any concept of the mind. Thus the term "soul-force" conveys the idea of employing our spiritual energies.

For Gandhi this truth or spiritual reality is the goal, and the means to the goal must be as pure and loving as possible. He noted that we may always control the means but never the ends. Thus the means must be as good as the goal. *Ahimsa* therefore is the way of acting without hurting anyone or inflicting oneself against another spiritual being. We may hate an injustice for the harm that it brings to people, but we must always love all the people involved out of respect for human dignity.

Satyagraha attempts to awaken an awareness of the truth about the injustice in the perpetrators, and by *ahimsa* this is done without hurting them. Since humans are subject to error and we cannot be sure we are judging accurately, we must refrain from punishing.

Thus *ahimsa* is an essential safeguard in the quest for truth and justice. Gandhi explained that *Satyagraha* is not a method of the weak, like passive resistance, but it is a tool for the strong that excludes the use of violence in any shape or form. *Satyagraha* is insisting on the truth and can be offered in relation to one's family, rulers, fellow citizens, or even the whole world. Gandhi elucidated three necessary conditions for its success:

1. The *satyagrahi* should not have any hatred in his heart against the opponent.
2. The issue must be true and substantial.
3. The *satyagrahi* must be prepared to suffer till the end for his cause.

Gandhi emphasized self-suffering rather than inflicting suffering on others. By undergoing suffering to reveal the injustice the *satyagrahi* strives to reach the consciences of people. *Satyagraha* does not try to coerce anyone but rather to convert by persuasion, to reach the reason through the heart. *Satyagraha* appeals to intelligent public opinion for reform. In the political field the struggle on behalf of the people leads to the challenging of unjust governments or laws by means of noncooperation or civil disobedience.

When petitions and other remedies fail, then a *satyagrahi* may break an unjust law and willingly suffer the penalty in order to call attention to the injustice. However, one does not hide or try to escape from the law like a criminal, rather one openly and civilly disobeys the law as a protest, fully expecting to be punished. In *Hind Swaraj* Gandhi wrote, "It is contrary to our manhood if we obey laws repugnant to our conscience."

By eliminating violence *Satyagraha* gives the opponent the same rights and liberties. *Satyagraha* requires self-discipline, self-control, and self-purification, and *satyagrahis* must always make the distinction between the evil and the evil-doer. They must overcome evil with good, hatred with love, anger with patience, falsehood with truth, and violence with *ahimsa*. This takes a perfect person for complete success, and therefore training and education are essential to even make it workable.

Gandhi emphasized that every child should know about the soul, truth, love, and the powers latent in the soul. Both men and women and even children may participate, and it demands the courage that comes from spiritual strength and the power of love. Surely it takes more courage to face the weapons of death without fighting than it does to fight and kill. From his experience Gandhi believed that those who wished to serve their country through *Satyagraha* should observe chastity, adopt poverty, follow truth, and cultivate fearlessness.

It is through fearlessness that we can have the courage to renounce all harmful weapons, filling and surrounding ourselves with the spiritual protection of a loving and peaceful consciousness. Gandhi listed detailed rules to guide the *satyagrahi*. One should harbor no anger but suffer the anger of the opponent, putting up with assaults without retaliating but not submitting out of fear of punishment nor to any order given in anger.

One should not resist arrest by a person in authority nor resist confiscation of property; but if one is the trustee for the property of another, one may refuse to surrender it. One should not swear or curse or insult the opponent nor join cries that are contrary to the spirit of Non-violence. Civil resisters may not salute the Union Jack (a flag), but they should not insult it nor officials. If officials are being assaulted, one should protect them by risking one's life. In prison one should behave with decorum and observe discipline that is not contrary to self-respect; one should not consider oneself superior to other prisoners nor observe any distinction.

One should not fast to gain conveniences. Gandhi believed that civil resisters who have chosen to join the corps should obey all orders of the leader. One should trust the care of dependents to God. One should not cause communal quarrels; but in the event of a disagreement should support the party clearly in the right.

Noncooperation is a comprehensive policy used by people when they can no longer in good conscience participates in or support a government that has become oppressive, unjust, and violent.

Although *satyagrahis* do not attack the wrong-doer, it is their responsibility not to promote or support the wrong actions. Thus noncooperators withdraw from government positions, renounce government programs and services, and refuse to pay taxes to the offending government. While challenging the power of the state in this way noncooperators have the opportunity to learn greater self-reliance.

Gandhi held that noncooperation with an unjust government was not only an inherent right but as much a duty as is cooperation with a just government. Most of the time Gandhi and his followers were involved in constructive programs, and he considered these the most important part of Non-violent action. For Gandhi they included Hindu-Muslim friendship or communal unity, removing untouchability or racial discrimination, abstaining from alcohol and drugs, practicing spinning, weaving, and other village industries, sanitation, schooling and adult education, uplift of women, education in hygiene and health, cultivating one's language, working for economic equality, forming labor unions, helping the poor, rural people and lepers, and improving the education and lives of students.

Ahimsa or Non-violence is absolutely essential to Gandhi's civil disobedience. *Satyagrahis* are expected to give their lives in efforts to quell violence if it erupts. Gandhi interpreted *ahimsa* broadly as refraining from anything at all harmful. This principle can be hurt by every evil thought, by undue haste, by lying, by hatred, by wishing ill to anybody, or by our holding on to what the world needs. Thus even greed and avarice can violate *ahimsa*. Non-violence has a great spiritual power, but the slightest use of violence can taint a just cause.

The strength is not physical but comes from the spiritual will. Non-violence implies self-purification, and the spiritual power the

Non-violent person has is always greater than one would have by using violence. The end of violence is always defeat, but Non-violence is endless and is never defeated. The following is Gandhi's summary of the implications of Non-violence:

1. Non-violence is the law of the human race and is infinitely greater than and superior to brute force.
2. In the last resort it does not avail to those who do not possess a living faith in the God of Love.
3. Non-violence affords the fullest protection to one's self-respect and sense of honor, but not always to possession of land or movable property, though its habitual practice does prove a better bulwark than the possession of armed men to defend them. Non-violence, in the very nature of things, is of no assistance in the defense of ill-gotten gains and immoral acts.
4. Individuals or nations who would practice Non-violence must be prepared to sacrifice (nations to the last man) their all except honor. It is, therefore, inconsistent with the possession of other people's countries, i.e., modern imperialism, which is frankly based on force for its defense.
5. Non-violence is a power which can be wielded equally by all-children, young men and women or grown-up people, provided they have a living faith in the God of Love and have therefore equal love for all mankind. When Non-violence is accepted as the law of life it must pervade the whole being and not be applied to isolated acts.
6. It is a profound error to suppose that while the law is good enough for individuals it is not for masses of mankind.

Gandhi's struggle was so overwhelming and significant, because he challenged the institutional violence of the modern state. He not only recommended refusing military service but also refusing to pay taxes to a militarized state. In addition to citizens' not cooperating with an evil government, a neutral country also has the obligation to refuse to support or assist a military state or aggressor.

Gandhi suggested a Non-violent army that could engage in constructive activities, lessen tensions, and sacrifice their lives to calm mobs and end riots. He described the qualifications for such a peace brigade in 1938. One must have a living faith in non-violence and the courage to die without anger, fear, or retaliation. The peace messenger must have equal respect for all religions.

This work for peace is done locally alone or in groups. Peace messengers will cultivate contacts with people through personal service. One must have integrity and be strictly impartial. Peace brigades should be aware of brooding conflicts and anticipate conflicts before they break out into conflagrations. Volunteers can be drawn from various walks of life. A distinctive dress would enable the brigade to be recognized without difficulty. The cost of training and equipping such a peace brigade or even an army of *satyagrahis* would be insignificant compared to the huge expenses of the modern military establishment.

Gandhi envisioned a Non-violent state which would protect itself by not cooperating with any aggressor. He was concerned that the democracies would adopt the forceful methods of the Fascists; but true democracy must ultimately be Non-violent, for violence is an obvious restriction of liberty. He observed that the science of war leads to dictatorship, but the science of Non-violence leads to democracy.

In 1946 Gandhi asserted that a true democracy will not rely on an army. It is a poor democracy that depends on military assistance because military force interferes with the free growth of the mind and smothers the soul. Gandhi criticized America for its treatment of the Negro. He observed that armaments are used for greedy exploitation and that the competition and desire for material possessions and the great power's imperialistic designs are the biggest blocks to world peace.

Also they must shed their fear of destruction; then by disarmament peace can be attained. Gandhi warned that if the mad arms race continued, it would result in unprecedented slaughter. If a victor remains, the victory will be a living death for that nation. The only escape from this impending doom is by boldly and unconditionally accepting Non-violence with all its glorious implications.

His concept of *sarvodaya* urged us to go beyond family and country to consider the good of all, and he recommended a world governing body which would recognize the equal independence of each nation. He believed that religion means being friendly to one's opponents because being friendly to friends is just business. Gandhi said that the golden way is to be friends with the world and regard the whole human family as one.

8

THE REVOLUTIONARY MOVEMENT: TAGORE AND AUROBINDO

INDIA'S RENAISSANCE 1881-1905

Viceroy Curzon's division of the large province of Bengal was announced in July 1905. Eastern Bengal and Assam would have 18 million Muslims and 12 million Hindus. Western Bengal would have 42 million Hindus to 9 million Muslims, but those speaking Bengali were outnumbered by the Biharis and Oriyas.

The secret motivation of Lord Curzon seems to have been to divide the Bengali movement that he considered seditious. This technique of divide and rule increased the conflicts between Hindus and Muslims in Bengal. The plan was approved by the Secretary of State without consulting the Parliament.

The Bengal Legislative Council strongly denounced the plan on July 8, and the Indian press in Bengal and other provinces condemned the proposal. Curzon won over Dacca nawab Salimullah with a low-interest loan and with the prospect of Dacca becoming the new capital. The weekly *Sanjivani* in Calcutta suggested a boycott of British goods on July 13, and a public meeting at Bagerhat adopted it three days later. The boycott idea spread as two thousand public meetings were organized in the cities and in hundreds of villages. In the town of Barisal students and even teachers went to school barefoot and were threatened with expulsion.

During the Durga Puja national festival in Bengal on September 28 about 50,000 people gathered in the Kali temple at Kalighat despite a heavy rain. They vowed not to purchase or use foreign articles or to employ foreigners. The two Chief Secretaries of Bengal and Eastern Bengal and Assam issued circulars ordering teachers to discipline protesting students. The partition of Bengal went into effect on October 16.

On that day after bathing in the sacred Ganga River more than 50,000 people attended a meeting to lay a foundation for Federation Hall in Calcutta. At a meeting in the house of ailing Ananda-mohan Bose 70,000 rupees were collected for the Swadeshi movement. An Anti-Circular Society was formed on November 4.

The movement began with verbal protests in meetings, the newspapers, petitions, and conferences before most turned to the more coercive tactic of the boycott. Bengal was the richest market in India for Manchester cotton goods, and they also wanted to revive their indigenous *(swadeshi)* textile industry. Mill owners in Bombay and Ahmadabad quickly increased their production and their profits. Societies *(Samitis)* formed in Bengal to promote the boycott campaign.

Brahmins and priests honored the boycott, and washer-men vowed not to wash foreign cloth. Shops selling foreign goods were picketed, and altercations led to police beating protesters with *lathis* (bamboo sticks). Those advocating the boycott were expelled from schools and colleges, imprisoned, fined, and flogged. The Government used its influence on local landlords (zamindars). Processions and meetings were banned, and newspapers were censored.

Finally leaders were detained without trials. The boycott developed a four-fold program that included not using English cloth and other products, not using English speech, resigning Government offices, and socially boycotting persons who purchase foreign articles. When Lord Curzon refused to receive a deputation from Congress in 1905, they sent Gokhale and Lajpat Rai to England.

The Congress met at Benares in December 1905, and 758 delegates elected Gokhale president.

The Moderates complained that the boycott methods of passive resistance were impractical or even injurious by denying themselves educational opportunities. Yet for the first time Gokhale mentioned "self-government within the empire" as their goal and denounced the partition of Bengal. He spoke of *swadeshi* as a profound and passionate movement that calls people to serve the Motherland. The Moderate Congress condemned the Government repression and justified the boycott as a "last protest." They repeated their demands for reform of the legislative councils.

The Extremists held a conference and formed a new National Party. As soon as he heard of the Bengal National College, Aurobindo Ghose left his teaching position at Baroda and went to Calcutta to be its principal. The National Council of Education was founded in March 1906 with thirteen distinguished members, and only Aurobindo had been involved in the anti-partition agitation.

The Bengali weekly *Jugantar (New Age)* began publishing that month, and within a few months its circulation was over 7,000. The English daily *Bande Mataram* started in August. They advocated fighting violence with violence because they believed that injustice must be opposed to win independence. Viceroy Curzon had appointed Bamfylde Fuller to govern the province of East Bengal and Assam. He alienated Hindus by favoring the Muslim majority. He sent Gurkhas to Barisal, and they took supplies from shops without paying for them.

During the provincial conference at Barisal on April 14-15, 1906 the cry of "Bande Mataram" was forbidden in the streets. Aurobindo and Surendranath Banerji led protesting marchers that were beaten with *lathis*. Magistrate Emerson fined Surendranath 400 rupees. A deputation of 36 Muslims led by Aga Khan met with Viceroy Minto on October 1 to ask for concessions. Minto decided to allow the Muslims special representation on government bodies according to their status and influence rather than by their numbers.

His new policy accepted Hindus and Muslims as separate nations and gave Muslims special favor on legislative councils.

The issue was settled at Simla by the Viceroy's secretary Dunlop Smith and Archbold, the principal of the Aligarh College. Future Prime Minister Ramsey MacDonald noted that this agreement sowed discord between the Hindu and Muslim communities by favoring the latter, and historians have seen this as the beginning of a policy that would lead to the separate nation of Pakistan.

In 1906 the nationalist Extremists were encouraged by Japan's victory over Russia, and Congress Moderates pointed to the Liberal Party's win in the English election. Gokhale met with John Morley five times in 1906. During the Congress at Calcutta in December 1906 the 81-year-old Parsi Dadabhai Naoroji was accepted as a compromise president while 1,663 delegates and some 20,000 visitors attended.

The most noted part of his speech was stating that *swaraj* (self-government) is the goal of India. The Extremists were able to get a series of resolutions passed in favor of the boycott, *swadeshi*, and national education. After Nawab Salimullah of Dacca convened a meeting of the Central Muhammadan Association, the All-India Muslim League was founded on December 30, 1906.

Their main purposes were to promote Muslim loyalty to the British Government and to protect and advance the rights of Muslims in India. They were concerned that a representative government would be unfair to them as a minority, and they believed that competitive examinations deprived Muslims of Government jobs. The way they saw of avoiding Hindu rule was by supporting the British. Muslims in East Bengal supported the partition, and Hindu-Muslim riots broke out.

The Red Pamphlet *(Lal Ishtahar)* accused Hindus of taking money from Muslims and urged Muslims to boycott Hindus. When Salimullah of Dacca came to Comilla on March 4, 1907, Muslims began attacking Hindus and looted their shops for four days as the riots spread to Jamalpur and other places. An investigation by C. J. O'Donnell, a Member of Parliament, later showed that public proclamations assured Muslims they would not be punished for oppressing Hindus.

The Muslim League met at Karachi in December 1907, and a British branch of the Muslim League opened in London in 1908. That year the Muslim League announced its opposition to the Hindu movement to unsettle the partition of Bengal. At their annual meeting at Amritsar the Muslim League overwhelmingly supported the separate electorate for Muslims.

In April 1907 Aurobindo wrote seven articles on "Passive Resistance" in *Bande Mataram*. He argued that organized political strength was needed for national self-development. Aurobindo wrote that "political freedom is the life-breath of a nation" and was needed to bring about moral, social, and educational reforms as well as industrial expansion. He argued their popular authority would rival the "despotic foreign bureaucracy."

The National Congress had recognized the boycott and the national programs for *swadeshi* and education, and arbitration could be passed at the next session. The New Party and Bengal had accepted passive resistance or what Aurobindo also called "defensive resistance." This must be organized, and the only effective way to remove foreign tyranny is to establish a democracy under a free constitution to control the executive and judiciary as well as the legislative branch of government.

Only when the people become responsible can a government be a protector, instead of an oppressor. Aurobindo advised that, as long as the oppressive government was still legal and respected life, liberty, and property, there was still time for using peaceful resistance. He believed that using defensive resistance for self-development was the last chance to avoid extremist methods. He noted that aggressive resistance tries to harm the Government while defensive or passive resistance exerts the same pressure by abstaining from helping the Government. The British could not rule and exploit India without the assistance of the Indians.

Aurobindo suggested they extend self-development to every aspect of national life, not only to Swadeshi and national education but also to national defense, arbitration courts, sanitation, insurance against famine, etc. To avoid indoctrination they refused to send their boys to Government schools. By extending their self-development they would universalize their defensive resistance, boycotting the courts and the bureaucracy.

All these methods are legal. If the administration persistently refuses, then he recommended refusing to pay taxes as "the strongest and final form of passive resistance." He noted that British justice has shown its contempt for life by giving European murderers leniency. He anticipated the British reaction of enacting coercive laws, and he said the passive resisters must be willing to suffer by disobeying unjust laws and orders.

Aurobindo also recommended the social boycott against Indians who refused to honor the boycotts of salt, sugar, and cloth. He believed that passive resistance was a method by which they could meet disturbers of the peace with self-contained divine power. He concluded that the sooner they put this into practice, the sooner they would gain national liberation.

BRITISH REPRESSION 1907-10

The Extremist militant nationalists led by Tilak, Lajpat Ral, B. G. Khaparde, B. C. Pal, and Aurobindo challenged the Moderates in the Indian National Congress who relied on petitions and verbal persuasion to seek colonial self-government. In April 1907 a provincial Congress at Surat excluded the propositions of boycott and national education from the program. Conflicts between the Moderates and Extremists during the Reception Committee meeting at Nagpur led to shifting the December Congress also to Surat, where the Moderate Pherozeshah Mehta was influential.

Tilak tried to meet with the leaders to arrange a compromise that would affirm the status quo of the 1906 resolutions; but when he was ignored, the Extremists disrupted the proceedings. The Moderates held a separate convention, and in April 1908 at Allahabad their Convention Committee drafted a new Constitution for the Indian National Congress. The first article declared that their goal was to become self-governing within the British Empire by using constitutional means, and the second article required every delegate to accept these goals in writing.

Thus they excluded the Extremists. Attendance at the annual Congress meetings declined with only 243 delegates attending in 1909, only 202 in 1912, and 349 in 1913. The 4th Earl of Minto, whose great-grandfather had been governor-general of India (1807-13), was a sportsman (jockey) who had been governor-general of Canada for six years. He was appointed viceroy by the Conservative Party, but the newly elected Liberals chose John Morley as secretary of state for India.

When Lt. Governor Fuller advocated disaffiliating two high schools from the University of Calcutta and refused to back down, Viceroy Minto accepted his resignation. While Indian editors were being censored and arrested, Anglo-Indian newspapers such as the *Civil and Military Gazette* of Lahore were publishing virulent propaganda and false reports about revolutionary activities.

During a public meeting at Rawalpindi on April 24, 1907 the former schoolteacher Ajit Singh strongly criticized the increased land assessment and proposed that peasants stop cultivating until it was reduced. When a public inquiry was postponed, a crowd began attacking the houses of Europeans. Sixty people were arrested, and five were convicted of riot and arson and were sentenced to imprisonment for three to seven years.

Three others, who were not at the riot, were kept in jail through the hot summer. The *Civil and Military Gazette* warned of trouble in May during the 50th anniversary of the Mutiny. People were urged to withhold payments to the Government. Lala Lajpat Rai and Ajit Singh were feared as the most eloquent speakers, and Viceroy Minto's Executive Council had them deported to Mandalay, Burma on May 9.

Many people were arrested for seditious speeches, articles, or books. In July 1907 *Jugantar* editor Bhupendra Nath Dutta was tried by Chief Presidency Magistrate Kingsford for publishing the articles "Free from Fear" and "Big Stick Medicine." He did not deny the charges and said he considered it his duty. He was sentenced to a year of hard time in prison, and in September the printer of *Jugantar* was sentenced to two years. Yet *Jugantar* continued publishing.

Aurobindo and Satish Mukherjee of the Dawn Society believed that the surest way to arouse the people was to get the Government to repress the Indian nationalists. Aurobindo was also charged with sedition. Bipin Chandra Pal refused to testify that Aurobindo was the editor of *Bande Mataram*, and Aurobindo was acquitted for lack of evidence; but Pal was sentenced to six months in prison.

Magistrate Kingsford ordered the boy Sushil Sen who shouted "Bande Mataram" silenced. When the boy hit Sergeant Huey, Kingsford had him flogged. After each of the 15 strokes Sushil Sen cried "Bande Mataram." Kavyavisharad composed the famous song "Make me forget my mother by flogging! Am I such an unworthy son of the Mother?" *Bande Mataram* continued to be published but as a weekly.

Aurobindo's *Bhawani Mandir* (Temple of the Holy Mother) was also banned along with *Vartaman Rananiti* (The Technique of Modern Fighting) and *Mukti Kon Pathe* (Which Way Freedom?) which he and his brother Barindra Ghose published. The latter contained articles from *Jugantar* calling for an armed uprising. Also during the summer of 1907 the editor, printer, and publisher of *Sandhya* were prosecuted.

Editor Brahmabandhab said he was carrying out his God-appointed mission for *swaraj*, and he accurately prophesied his own death during the trial. In February 1908 the printer of *Sandhya* was sentenced to two years. A Hindu holy man advised Aurobindo to empty his mind in order to receive inspiration. Speaking at Bombay in January 1908, Aurobindo suggested that Indians go beyond the nationalism that would replace one political oppression with another by realizing their great heritage of spiritual nationalism.

The first repressive law issued on May 11, 1907 severely restricted public meetings by requiring advance written notice so that police could attend. Rashbehari Ghosh predicted that the Seditious Meetings Act would lead to secret sedition and secret societies planning violent responses. The Newspapers Act of 1908 authorized the District Magistrate to stop publication and confiscate presses that printed any incitement to violence. *Bande Mataram*, *Sandhya*, and *Jugantar* were immediately shut down. Secret leaflets and booklets then advocated violent actions against the foreign tyrants.

The Jugantar group prepared bombs in the Manicktola garden house of the Ghose family, and in a secret trial they condemned Magistrate Kingsford. On April 30, 1908 the teenagers Khudiram Basu and Profulla Chaki threw a bomb at a coach they thought was his, but it killed instead the wife and daughter of a Kennedy.

When Profulla was about to be arrested, he shot himself. Khudiram went to the gallows in the Muzaffarpur jail saying "Bande Mataram." Lt. Governor Andrew Fraser survived more than one attempt on his life. These events led to passing the Explosive Substances Act on June 8, 1908. The latter mandated the penalty of transportation for fourteen years for just possessing bomb materials. The British called the revolutionaries "terrorists."

On May 2, 1908 police raided the Manicktola garden and found rifles, revolvers, dynamite, and "objectionable" literature that included a bomb formula. Aurobindo had moved on April 28, but they arrested eighteen people. Barindra Ghose took responsibility and disclosed many names. Aurobindo was arrested on May 5.

Some of the arrested were discharged, but eventually 34 were indicted in what was called the Aligarh Conspiracy. During the trial a revolver was smuggled into jail that enabled Kanailal Dutt and Satyen Bose to kill Naren Gosain for being an informer. Kanai and Satyen refused to appeal and were hanged. On January 24, 1909 Biren Datta Gupta killed Samsul Alam, the Deputy Superintendent of Police, in the Calcutta High Court, and on February 10 Charu Basin murdered the prosecutor Ashutosh Biswas outside the Aligarh courthouse.

Neither assassin defended himself, nor were both hanged. Four men were sentenced to transportation for life, and ten received sentences from five to seven years. Again Aurobindo was acquitted. The defense lawyer Chitta Ranjan Das called him "the poet of patriotism, the prophet of nationalism, and the lover of humanity." The *Jugantar* published an editorial calling for people to take up the revolutionary program, and it was banned again.

Also in 1908 Tilak was prosecuted for seditious writings in *Kesari*, and he spoke for 21 hours in his defense. The jury found him guilty by a 7-2 vote, and he was sentenced on July 22 to transportation for six years and a fine of 1,000 rupees. He handled the injustice philosophically, saying, "It may be the will of the Providence that the cause I represent may prosper more by my sufferings than by my remaining free." Students and mill-workers in Bombay had already gone on strike after Tilak's arrest.

On July 23 workers at nine mills went on strike for six days to protest his six-year sentence. The next day seventy mills stopped work, and on July 25 another 76 mills went on strike. After some police were injured, the military fired on the demonstrators, killing and wounding many. In December 1908 the Criminal Law Amendment Act allowed a special court of three judges without a jury to accept evidence not valid under ordinary law, and their decision was final.

In what was called the Samitis Act the Government could declare unlawful any association it considered inimical to peace and order, and attending their meetings could be punished with imprisonment. The popular Anushilan Samiti, which had 116 branches and more than 8,400 members, was declared unlawful in January 1909. Aswini Kumar Dutt was influenced by Vivekananda and emphasized the virtues of truth, love, and purity. He and eight others were deported in December 1908 without even knowing the charges against them under an 1818 regulation aimed at plundering warlords.

In May 1909 Morley reported to Minto that 150 members of Parliament had written to Prime Minister Asquith protesting the deportations; but they were not released until February 1910. Madan Lal Dhingra assassinated Secretary of State William Curzon Wyllie at the Imperial Institute in London on July 1, 1909 and was hanged. The Morley-Minto reforms added more Indians to the legislative councils; but the Indian Councils Act of 1909 was designed to put mostly Muslims and those loyal to the Government on the legislative councils, and they had little power.

In December the Indian National Congress passed resolutions criticizing the reforms for unjustly giving one religion excessive representation, for arbitrarily restricting candidates for election, for distrusting the educated class, and for keeping the Councils ineffective. Mohandas Gandhi went to London on behalf of Indians in South Africa in 1909, but he felt that suffering in jail did more good than spending money in England seeing politicians and journalists.

After meeting Extremists who insisted that India could never win its independence without violence, on his return voyage to South Africa he wrote the dialog *Hind Swaraj* (Indian Self-Rule). Based on the conversations he had in London, in this diatribe against the corruption of Western civilisation Gandhi suggested that India could gain its independence by Non-violent means and self-reliance.

He rejected brute force and its oppression and declared that soul force or love is what keeps people together in peace and harmony. History ignores the peaceful qualities but notices the interruptions and violations which disrupt civilisation. He concluded the dialog by declaring that his life was henceforth dedicated to attaining Indian self-rule. Gandhi's *Hind Swaraj* was published in Gujarati and English and was republished in 1921 and 1938.

Aurobindo practiced yoga and was transformed by his spiritual experience while he was in jail for a year. He said that in meditation he felt the presence of Vivekananda and heard his voice. When he was released in May 1909, most of the revolutionary leaders were either in prison or exile. He began the *Karmayogin* in English and the *Dharma* in Bengali. In "An Open Letter to my Countrymen" on July 31 he explained the boycott as refusing to cooperate with the Government in the economic exploitation of their country.

He argued that other foreign nations should not be boycotted because India needed to export as well as import. Aurobindo combined patriotic nationalism with religious fervor by calling it a religion to realize God in the nation. He considered God the leader of the movement for the redemption of their Motherland. He advocated armed revolution, but some of the revolutionaries engaged in robberies to raise money for weapons. The robberies (dacoities) led to three big conspiracy cases of Howrah, Khulna, and Dacca in 1910, and many people received long prison sentences.

Aurobindo went to Chandernagore, where the French helped them smuggle arms. He believed he was guided by God to go to the French colony at Pondicherry, where he became a spiritual recluse for the rest of his life. The Indian Press Act of 1910 required owners of printing presses and newspapers to deposit security of up to 5,000 rupees, which could be forfeited for publishing any objectionable material that included criticizing the Government. If the security was forfeited, the next security was heavier, and a third offense meant that the printing press could be forfeited.

The Post Office and Customs could detain packages with objectionable material. The Moderate leader Gokhale supported these measures to control political violence. Over the next decade the Press Act of 1910 penalized more than 350 presses, 300 newspapers, required £40,000 in securities, and proscribed more than 500 publications.

The security requirement prevented 130 newspapers from starting. Yet the Anglo-Indian press and its provocative writings were immune from these restrictions. Morley complained that the sentences were outrageous, monstrous, and indefensible. He warned Minto that "excess of severity is not the path to order," but to the bomb.

INDIA IN AN IMPERIAL WAR 1911-18

In November 1910 Charles Hardinge replaced Minto as viceroy; his grandfather had also been governor-general of India. Lord Crewe became secretary of state for India. Hardinge wanted a conciliatory policy to prepare for the visit of King George V to India the next year. He ordered that no political prosecutions were to be initiated without his consent and that any pending prosecution that was not going to secure a conviction was to be withdrawn.

On the first day of 1911 at Allahabad sixty Hindus met with forty Muslims, and Gokhale urged Hindus to understand Muslim fears. In June 1911 John Jenkins gave Hardinge the idea to restructure the partition of Bengal by 1) moving the capital from Calcutta to Delhi, 2) creating a United Bengal as a Presidency, 3) making Bihar and Orissa a Lieutenant-Governorship with a capital at Patna, and 4) restoring Assam as a Chief Commissionership. Crewe indicated his support in August, and the Cabinet and India Council approved the proposals in November.

At his coronation on December 11, George V announced that ending the Bengal partition was his gift to India. The changes were put into effect by proclamations in March 1912, and the Act of Parliament was approved by the King in June. Assam got its legislative council in November, and the Central Provinces got one a year later.

Most Indians were glad that the partition of Bengal had been undone, but many Muslims considered it a betrayal. However, in March 1913 the Muslim League adopted the Congress goal of self-government under the British and sought to attain it by promoting national unity and cooperation. The Indian National Congress responded by electing the distinguished Muslim Syed Muhammad as president for their annual session at Karachi in December.

Soon after King George V visited the new capital, a bomb was thrown on December 23, 1912 at the elephant carrying Viceroy Hardinge, who was seriously wounded; but only the servant holding the umbrella was killed. Four men were executed, and two others were sentenced to seven years. The Moderate Gokhale gave the assurance that he and his party would not oppose the Viceroy on anything.

The 1913 Indian Criminal Law Amendment Act made conspiracy a criminal offense. The Defence of India Act empowered special tribunals to ignore the Code of Criminal Procedures to inflict sentences of death, transportation for life, and imprisonment for violating rules or orders in the Act without any appeal. Any civil or military authority could order a person to remain in an area, abstain from acts, search and seize possessions, and arrest anyone suspected of planning something.

This Act negated the previous rule of law and was used to bring nine conspiracy cases involving 175 people, of whom 18 were executed, 58 were transported for life, and 58 others were imprisoned. Because of torture by police, many people were convicted based on confessions they later recanted. In Bengal about eight hundred people were interned without any trial at all.

About 30,000 Indians, mostly peasants from the Punjab, had emigrated to America. Lala Hardayal fled India and went to France and then San Francisco. In November 1913 he founded the Yugantar Ashram and the weekly *Ghadar (Rebellion)*, publishing it in Urdu, Marathi, Gurumukhi, Hindi, and English. They reported on the crimes perpetrated by the British in India and highlighted biographies of Indian patriots and fighters for freedom in other countries.

Circulation increased quickly, and distribution became worldwide. After Hardayal criticized US immigration policy that excluded Orientals and spoke for the Syndicalist Party, he was arrested on March 24, 1914 to be deported; but probably because of the sympathetic Secretary of State William Jennings Bryan he was given bail. Hardayal fled to Geneva, Switzerland, where he edited a paper called *Bande Mataram*.

In 1914 Gurdit Singh, a Sikh businessman in Singapore, chartered the Japanese steamer *Kongamata Maru* to take 376 Sikhs to Canada, but in July the Canadian immigration department sent them back to India. Britain declared war on Germany on August 4, 1914, and Japan joined their alliance with France and Russia. When Turkey joined the Central Powers of Germany and Austria in October, most of the troops the British sent to Mesopotamia, Palestine, and Egypt were Indian.

The ruling chiefs of India declared their loyalty to Britain, and many Indians were sent to fight in France also. Recruiting for the Indian army jumped from 15,000 men a year to 300,000 by 1918. According to Edwin Montagu's speech in November 1918, India sent 1,215,338 men overseas and suffered 101,439 casualties. The Government of India bore these enormous expenses and even contributed an extra £100 million for the British Empire's war, increasing India's national debt by thirty per cent. India supplied 1,874 miles of railway track, 6,000 vehicles, 237 locomotives, 883 steamers and barges, and ten million cubic feet of timber.

In India, a country larger than Europe, the British garrison was reduced to 15,000 men. Some Muslims in Afghanistan took the side of Turkey, but Amir Habibulla of Afghanistan remained loyal. Indian troops were sent to the mouth of the Euphrates River to protect the oil tanks and pipelines of the Anglo-Persian Oil Company, and they captured Basra in November 1914. They advanced toward Baghdad, but the Turks stopped General Townshend's forces at Kut-el-Amara.

After a five-month siege he and his 10,000 men surrendered. Another 12,000 Indian troops arrived at Basra, but they could not move up river because they lacked transportation. Bad leadership and disease caused 23,000 casualties. Later Lloyd George appointed the Mesopotamia Commission that reported negligent planning, especially by the Viceroy, the aged Commander-in-Chief Beaufort Duff in India, the Director of Medical Services, and General John Nixon, the commander in Mesopotamia. Secretary of State Austen Chamberlain resigned and was replaced by his critic Edwin Montagu.

Some revolutionaries and politicians considered England's necessity India's opportunity. About sixty Indian revolutionaries from the Ghadar party sailed from San Francisco to fight in India, and a hundred joined on the way; they were detained at Hong Kong, and a hundred were interned. Several thousand people came back to India; 400 were kept in jail, and 2,500 were restricted to their villages in the Punjab.

Sikhs were especially suspected, and on September 29, 1914 police massacred eighteen Sikhs from the *Kongamata Maru* who wanted to go to Calcutta and refused to get on a train to the Punjab. In February 1915 fifteen Muslims from Lahore, Peshawar, and Kohat joined the Mujahidins in Kabul. That same month the Muslim battalion of Fifth Light Infantry, believing they were being sent to fight Turks, mutinied at Singapore, killing eight officers, nine soldiers, and seventeen civilians.

About three hundred mutineers dispersed into the jungle, and forty mutineers were executed in public. A few revolutionaries tried to work with the Germans to foment a rebellion against the British in India; but efforts to smuggle arms from the United States failed, and many were arrested or killed. The day after the US declared war in April 1917, seventeen Indians were arrested in San

Francisco. Ram Chandra had given names, and on the last day of the trial he was murdered by another defendant, who was shot dead by a marshal.

Eventually more than a hundred defendants were either convicted, became Government witnesses, or fled the country. A few revolutionaries continued using violence, and the number of political murders since 1907 reached 64 by 1917. In that decade there were 112 robberies, twelve bombings, and three attempts to wreck trains. The secret Abhinava Bharata operated in Maharashtra, and many colleges had branches.

Annie Besant went to England in 1914 and raised support for the cause of India. She bought a daily newspaper in Madras and renamed it *New India* on July 14; her coverage of the war helped increased the circulation to ten thousand by November. Besant published a series of articles on the history of the Indian National Congress in *Commonweal* and as the book *How India Wrought for Freedom*. She invited 237 members of the All-India Congress Committee and the All-India Muslim League to a closed conference December 25 on strategy for attaining home rule.

Three days later the Congress postponed action on a Home Rule League until a report could be made. Tilak was released from prison after six years in June 1914, and at a provincial conference in Puna the following May he condemned violence and proposed supporting the British. Annie Besant consulted with him, and he said that prominent nationalists were serving in municipal and legislative councils.

They agreed to work for self-government under the British. Gokhale and Pherozeshah Mehta still objected to admitting the Extremists, but they both died in 1915. Tilak and the Conference of Nationalists met twice in 1915 and established the Indian Home Rule League. Besant proposed amending the Congress constitution, and Tilak came back in December 1915, receiving a great ovation by the 2,259 delegates at Bombay.

In July 1916 Tilak was ordered to furnish a personal bond of 20,000 rupees. The Bombay High Court set aside his order; but Besant lost her appeal on a second levy of 10,000 rupees for *New India* and the weekly *Commonweal*. So she sold her two presses and suspended publication, but three days later *New India* re-appeared under a new editor. After waiting for approval from the Congress, Besant decided to go ahead with another Home Rule League in September 1916.

She decreed September 14 as Home Rule Day and at the first celebration said that she used the term Home Rule because she wanted self-government for India within the British Empire. Branches were quickly formed in the major cities, and she made extensive speaking tours, as did Tilak. He covered Maharashtra and the Central Provinces while she went to the rest of India. In December 1916 at Lakhnau (Lucknow) the Indian National Congress and the Muslim League united to demand reforms for self-government within the empire. Congress adopted the following goals:

1. The Council of the Secretary of State shall be abolished.
2. Half of the Governor-General's Executive Council shall be Indians elected by the Imperial Legislative Council.
3. Four-fifths of the Imperial Legislative Council shall be elected, one-third of these by Muslims.
4. The Government of India shall not interfere in local affairs.
5. The Imperial Legislative Council shall control the Government of India except in military and foreign affairs.
6. Four-fifths of the Provincial Legislative Councils shall be elected by the people with specified numbers of Muslims in each province.
7. Provincial Legislative Councils shall control their governments.
8. Three-fourths of any community may block a bill.
9. Executive officers in India shall have no judicial powers.

This Congress was extraordinary for its religious quality and the participation of women. The Home Rule resolution was passed unanimously. Gandhi proposed that the Lakhnau Pact be translated into the Indian languages, and by the end of 1917 a million people had signed the petitions. Besant also worked for the woman suffrage resolution passed by Congress, and in May 1917 she was elected the first president of the Women's Indian Association.

She protested Government Order 599 that prevented students and teachers from attending unapproved political lectures and conferences. The governments of Bombay, the Central Provinces, and Bihar banned Besant from entering while the governments of the Punjab and Delhi prohibited Tilak and B. C. Pal. On June 15 the Government of Madras ordered Besant interned with her secretary George Arundale and philanthropist B. P. Wadia, who joined her at Ootacamund. Newspapers publicized their informal detention that lasted 94 days.

The retired judge Subrahmaniya Aiyar and two thousand people declared that they would stand by the Home Rule League if it was declared illegal. President Woodrow Wilson of the United States proclaimed that the war was "to make the world safe for democracy" and "to give the right of self-determination to the people in choosing their own government." Aiyar wrote to Wilson that autonomy for India would result in ten million more volunteers for the war. American newspapers publicized this, and labor supported home rule for India as in Canada and Australia.

On August 14 a Madras committee approved of using passive resistance, and six days later Secretary of State Montagu announced that responsible government was the new goal of British policy in India. The British removed the racial bar from giving Indians royal commissions in the army, and Besant and her associates were released from detention. In response the Congress and the Muslim League set aside passive resistance and sent an All-India deputation to Viceroy Chelmsford and visiting Montagu.

Tilak nominated Besant as president for the 1917 Congress, and by the end of the year his League had 14,000 members. Besant spoke eloquently to the 4,967 delegates about how the war could not end until England realized that autocracy must perish in India. They demanded home rule because freedom is the birthright of every nation and because her resources were not being used for her greatest needs.

Money was being spent on the army instead of education. India was no longer begging for boons but was standing up for rights. However, Montagu met with the Moderates who had seceded from the Congress, and they formed the National Liberal Federation. The report signed by Montagu and Viceroy Chelmsford in April 1918 was published in July and proved to be a disappointment even to the Moderates.

The Montagu-Chelmsford Report recommended giving more popular control to local bodies, but the Government of India was to remain completely responsible to the Parliament. Congress held a special session at Bombay on August 29; but even though they were not very far apart, the Moderates declined to rejoin the Congress. In their annual meeting in December at Delhi the Congress resolved to send a deputation to England to ask the Parliament to let their representatives attend the Peace Conference, and they demanded responsible government in India.

The Congress named Tilak, Gandhi, and Hasan Imam to attend the Peace Conference. The membership of Tilak's Home Rule League had grown to more than 33,000, but the British War Cabinet would not even let Tilak go to England. After the Bolsheviks took over Russia and withdrew from the war, the Turks invaded Central Asia, Azerbaijan, and Persia. In April 1918 the Viceroy called a conference at Delhi and asked India to redouble its war efforts. Khaparde said Indians would mobilize enthusiastically if the British Parliament would promise them responsible self-government within a reasonable period, but he was not allowed to present his resolution.

Tilak was not invited as he had been declared out of order at the Bombay War Conference. Mohandas Gandhi told the Viceroy that he and others would help the British Empire in their time of need if self-government would come more quickly. Meanwhile the Government was inflicting much pressure on Indian men in order to meet their recruiting goals. Most of the Indians fought for the money as mercenaries. In the second half of 1918 India suffered severely from the world-wide influenza epidemic. Official figures estimated that six million people died, but others said it was closer to sixteen million.

Mohandas Gandhi arrived in England during the first week of the Great War, and again he supported the British by raising and leading an ambulance corps; but he became ill and returned to India in January 1915. The great poet Rabindranath Tagore called Gandhi "Mahatma," meaning "Great Soul," and in May 1915 Gandhi founded the Satyagraha Ashram for his family and co-workers near the textile city of Ahmadabad in Gujarat. When a family of untouchables asked to live in the ashram, Gandhi admitted them. Orthodox Hindus believed this polluted them. Funds ran out, and Gandhi was ready to live in the untouchable slums if necessary; but an anonymous benefactor donated enough money to last a year.

To help change people's attitudes about these unfortunate pariahs, Gandhi renamed them "Harijans" or "Children of God," and he later called his weekly magazine *Harijan*. In a speech at the opening of Benares Hindu University on February 6, 1916 Gandhi said he was ashamed to be speaking in English, and he commented on the jewelry worn by the dignitaries on the stage. The Theosophist Annie Besant was one of the most popular orators of her era, and she liked to speak last.

However, Gandhi had been late and spoke after her. She interrupted his discussion of anarchism, and this dispute caused the princes to leave the stage. Yet Gandhi agreed that Indians must take power into their hands to gain self-government. Gandhi began wearing home-spun *khadi* in order to encourage self-sufficient village industries and thus help alleviate poverty in India. In April 1917 Gandhi went to Bihar to learn how suffering indigo workers in Champaran were being exploited by exorbitant fees of landlords. He was arrested and ordered to leave; but as he insisted on staying, he was put in jail.

However, the officials soon realized that the Mahatma was the only one who could control the crowds. Assistants helped by carefully documenting the grievances of 20,000 tenants, and a government commission unanimously accepted the tenants' complaints as valid. Rents were reduced, and the planters had to compensate the tenants. The Government abolished the growing of indigo, and most planters sold their factories and left the district.

Gandhi had developed his methods of Non-violent action for social change in South Africa, where Indians suffered discrimination. He was especially aware of how the indenture system was used to recruit Indian laborers in British colonies. When the Government refused to introduce a bill to abolish this in the Central Legislative Council, he announced he would start a Non-violent campaign if the system were not abolished by July 31, 1917. The Government averted that by deciding to end the system.

Gandhi also used *Satyagraha* (truth power) in Kaira in 1918. Peasants were suffering from a famine but still had to pay taxes. Petitions and prayers had failed. After Sirdar Vallabhbhai Patel and others helped educate them, the peasants pledged to forfeit their lands rather than pay the assessments; Bombay merchants supported the campaign. Gandhi advised the farmers to remove their crops from the attached fields, and they were arrested for doing so. Eventually the authorities suspended the taxes for the poor peasants.

The textile workers of Ahmadabad were also economically oppressed. Gandhi suggested arbitration; but it fell apart when some workers went on strike. After examining the issues, Gandhi believed they deserved a 35% increase in pay. The mill-owners would not go beyond 20% and declared a lock-out on February 22, 1918.

When the workers became hungry and were weakening in their pledges, Gandhi went on a fast to strengthen their resolve to continue the strike. He explained that he did not fast to coerce the opponent but to strengthen or reform those who loved him. He did not believe in fasting for higher wages, but he fasted so that the workers would accept the system of arbitration to resolve the conflict. After four days the mill-owners accepted the arbitrator's award of a 35% increase.

In the spring of 1918 Gandhi was persuaded by the British to help raise soldiers for a final victory effort in the war. Charlie Andrews criticized Gandhi for recruiting Indians to fight for the British. Gandhi spoke to large audiences but gained hardly any recruits. He was experimenting with a limited raw-food diet and became sick.

BESANT, KRISHNAMURTI, AND BHAGAVAN DAS

After Henry Olcott died in 1907, Annie Besant was elected president of the Theosophical Society (TS). She was re-elected every seven years until her death in 1933. She and the clairvoyant Charles Leadbeater had founded the Central Hindu College (CHC) in Benares where boys lived like monks and received a spiritual education that included modern science. Leadbeater had been accused of teaching boys to masturbate as a sexual release; this created a scandal, but he was never formally charged. In 1909 he discovered Jiddu Krishnamurti and his brother Nityananda at a private beach in Adyar.

Leadbeater said that Krishnamurti had an extraordinary aura, and he and Besant began educating him to be the vehicle for the coming Messiah (Maitreya) or World Teacher. Their father Narayaniah allowed the Theosophists to adopt the two boys, but later he brought a suit trying to reclaim them. Leadbeater and Besant wrote a book about the past lives of Krishnamurti, whose soul they called by the star name Alcyone.

In 1909 they published *At the Feet of the Master*, claiming that it was written down by 13-year-old Krishnamurti from the instructions of his master Kuthumi while preparing him for initiation. The master on the inner planes teaches the pupil using the Theosophical paradigm. The four qualifications for the spiritual path are discrimination, desirelessness, good conduct, and love. You should avoid the selfish aims of wealth and power by working for evolution to help others.

Your religion or nationality does not matter because they are all one. Discrimination helps you choose right and avoid wrong. The soul is divine and master of the physical, astral, and mental bodies. Thus you must not let the body's animal desires hinder you from doing good. The body is like your horse that you should care for and treat well. The astral body may lead you astray by emotions such as anger, jealousy, greed, envy, and depression. The mental body is susceptible to pride and ambition, but by meditating you may turn away from worldly things.

You must always be gentle, kind, reasonable, and accommodating. Knowers are able to feed the souls of the poor. God is wisdom and love. You must distinguish truth from falsehood, think for yourself, be honest, and help others. Freedom comes from not being bound by selfish desires. Avoid gossip, cruelty to people or animals, and superstition. Six points of good conduct are self-control of thoughts and actions, tolerance, cheerfulness, concentration, and confidence in your inner master.

Love is the most important qualification and means doing no harm and serving God by helping others. Besant founded the Order of the Star and began publishing the monthly *Herald of the Star* in January 1912. The deification of Krishnamurti caused 25 people on the staff at CHC to resign in April 1913, including Bhagavan Das, George Arundale, and E. A. Wodehouse.

That month Judge Bakewell decided the custody battle with the mixed verdict that the boys were to be turned over to their father, who was charged with the legal expenses for having brought unproved charges. However, the boys were in England, and by the time the appeals were decided they had passed the legal age of 18 in Indian law. They chose to remain with Besant. Arundale became Krishnamurti's tutor, and the Order of the Star grew to 12,000 members.

Besant claimed that she was guided by Rishi Agastya, a legendary saint whom she called the Regent of India, to work for home rule in India. She began publishing the weekly *Commonweal* on January 2, 1914. The Irish Home Rule movement persuaded her that the world needed a federation of self-governing nations. She consulted with the Moderate Gokhale and soon became involved in Indian politics, as described above.

Meanwhile Krishnamurti failed the entrance exams for Oxford and Cambridge despite preparation by several tutors. He and Nityananda attended a private school in Kent, where other students hazed them and called them "black monkeys." During her internment in 1917 Besant was elected president of the Indian National Congress, but her long speech was not well received, especially her intention that she would break the tradition by continuing as the leader for a year until the next Congress.

After the Conservatives returned to power in England, she visited the ailing Gandhi and tried to persuade him to limit his civil disobedience tactics and in March 1919 she issued a statement that she could no longer support Gandhi's movement. She became even more unpopular in India when she justified the use of British force against rioting demonstrators. In 1920 she published the pamphlet "Gandhian Non-Cooperation, or Shall India Commit Suicide?" Nityananda died in 1925, and this deeply affected his brother, who gradually began to awaken and think for himself.

Krishnamurti never really felt comfortable in being heralded as the vehicle for the World Teacher, and on December 28, 1929 he renounced the claim and disbanded the Order of the Star, saying that truth cannot be approach by any path, religion, or sect. Although Krishnamurti was born on May 12, 1895, he later claimed that he had no memory of his life before 1929. Bhagavan Das (1869-1959) was an expert in Sanskrit and a philosopher who became a Theosophist.

He and Annie Besant founded the Central Hindu College that later became Benares Hindu University. He also founded a national university called Kashi Vidya Peeth and was headmaster. Das wrote about thirty books. He was expelled from Agrawal Samaj for letting his son violate caste rules by going to England to study law. Bhagavan Das completed his third edition of *The Science of the Emotions* in 1924. This comprehensive analysis of human emotions draws on Indian philosophy and classics as well as recent work by western psychology and psychoanalysis.

The positive emotions of love and joy expand the self while the negative hatred and sadness diminish one. Das differentiated the feelings expressed toward perceived superiors, equals, and inferiors. He philosophically suggested that the altruism of love and helping produce more happiness than egotism and harming. He discussed the virtues of wisdom, courage, self-control, justice, love, faith, and hope while warning against the seven deadly sins of lust, anger, greed, pride, jealousy, hate, and fear as well as other vices and negative emotions.

He observed that by self-restraint emotions that are felt but not acted upon may be sublimated into higher expressions. Das discussed Tolstoy's theory of art, and he noted that Beethoven's anger at his cook was expressed in his music. From the spiritual perspective of Indian philosophy he emphasized the importance of detachment *(vairagya)* for transcendence.

Bhagavan Das also published *The Science of Peace* in 1904 and his commentary on the ancient *Laws of Manu* in *The Science of Social Organisation* in 1910. His ecumenical compilation of *The Essential Unity of All Religions* was first published in 1932 and was enlarged in 1939. This comparative study of all the major religions organizes their teachings into the three ways of knowledge, devotion, and works.

AUROBINDO'S SPIRITUAL EVOLUTION

After his spiritual transformation while he was in jail for a year during the Aligarh conspiracy case, Sri Aurobindo went to the French colony at Pondicherry in southern India on April 4, 1910. During his years as a young revolutionary he believed that India needed strong action to liberate itself from the emasculation, stagnation, poverty, economic dependence, and alien rule of the British Government.

He had advocated independence for India since 1907 and was an early leader of the Extremists. Now he answered a spiritual calling and believed that an evolutionary process was in motion that would lead to India's liberation from British domination. He devoted himself to the spiritual disciplines of yoga and meditation and wrote extensively. For a few years he wrote letters to the revolutionaries. He had come to believe that armed insurrection was no longer needed and could be dropped without harming the nationalist cause.

On August 15, 1914 Aurobindo began publishing the monthly *Arya* with the financial help of Paul and Mira Richard. The Richards left in 1915, but Mira came back in 1920 and eventually became known as the Divine Mother. They founded the Aurobindo Ashram in 1926, and Aurobindo recognized her as having the same spiritual consciousness as himself.

They kept the Ashram free of political connections or action. Aurobindo gave talks in the evenings until November 24, 1926 when he experienced the descent of a higher consciousness. He did not resume his talks until 1938. From 1914 for seven years Aurobindo wrote many articles in *Arya* that were later collected and published as books.

The Ideal of Human Unity was published in 1919, *War and Self-determination* in 1920, *The Life Divine* in 1939 and 1940, and *The Human Cycle* in 1949. That the independence of India was achieved on his birthday on August 15, 1947 he took to be a confirmation of his spiritual influence.

In *The Ideal of Human Unity* Aurobindo examined the political evolution toward the human unity he considered inevitable. He acknowledged that fundamental equality is necessary to make human differences inoffensive. The social aggregates of the family, clan, class, and nation developed, but the freedom of the human individual exceeds them and will not tolerate too much coercion.

He noted that humanity seems to be moving toward the socialist ideal. The energy of individuals is what drives social progress, and he considered the state more mechanistic than organic because of its tendency to perpetuate the status quo. Although socialism may be beneficial, human freedom will not let it interfere unnecessarily with individual growth. The human spirit must subordinate the mechanical to its true development.

The natural evolution of nations, especially in Europe, has made them indestructible; but empires are more artificial and perish because they lack psychological unity. As the Roman Empire was falling, European nations gradually evolved into durable entities by means of unifying languages, feudalism, monarchy, and the Church.

Powerful nations, such as England and France, have become imperialistic, but he noted they are losing their desire to replace Islamic culture in Africa or Hinduism in India. Aurobindo concluded that an empire was unlikely to be able to conquer the entire world because people will naturally resist that. He wrote, "War can only be abolished if national armies are abolished." He recognized that this is very difficult and that humanity has not yet learned how to do this.

He noted that most governments have become or are becoming democratic; but they are not real democracies because they are dominated by the propertied class. An international council would also likely be governed by a few great empires. In the second part of *The Ideal of Human Unity* Aurobindo explained how human unity could be attained. The three main factors in social evolution are individuals, communities, and all humanity.

The aim of Nature is to develop all three to fulfill their capacities. Freedom is as necessary as law, and unity is not complete without diversity. Life demands diversity, but human reason often prefers uniformity. By liberty we can obey the law of our being and grow into self-fulfillment in harmony with our environment. Humans should be allowed to form their groups by locality, race, culture, and economics without violent interference from powerful nations.

The drive toward economic and social centralisation is causing democracy to develop into socialism. A world state could be formed based on centralized uniformity, or a world union could be founded as a free and intelligent federation. The Great War caused many European monarchies to fall, and Aurobindo predicted that Europe would become as universally republican as the two Americas. Yet the modern parliamentary democracies are instruments of the aristocrats and the middle class, and modern people want minorities protected from majorities.

Wars are caused by national egoism in the name of patriotism. Aurobindo warned that the new League of Nations would fail because the war had accentuated force, and the commercially driven nations would eventually come into conflict again over the control of markets and wealth. He noted that the bourgeois democracies were developing "stupendous military organisation." Even democracies would subordinate liberty to the efficient life of the community in socialism.

The common consent of conflicting national egoisms is not likely to preserve peace. A great nation is likely to take risks to enhance its power. The world authority must have the psychological assent of all humanity that force can be used to restrain nations, and this can only be done by achieving total disarmament. The international authority must be in command of the remaining military force to police the nations; otherwise it will not be effective, and war will result. To do this the world state must have the legislative, executive, and judicial powers of government.

To transcend the commercial interests a stronger spiritual motive must subordinate the economic and political motives. Modern war has become "the bastard offspring of wealth-hunger and commercialism with political ambition as its putative father." As long as commercial rivalries are not prevented, covert wars will continue. Capital and labor will be in chronic conflict, and strong nations will crush the weak.

Thus the world state will tend to centralize all control including economic, social, and cultural under one international authority, especially as socialism comes into existence. Conditions that interfere with the common good of humanity will not be tolerated, but otherwise nations will be allowed to pursue their own ideals. Eventually the world may even adopt a common language, perhaps Esperanto. Aurobindo believed that the world state would lead to uniformity and mechanical regulation in a socialist system, but he preferred "healthy freedom" with diversity in the oneness.

Aurobindo suggested that a free union could be attained by confederation that could eliminate war and settle differences in peaceful ways. International relations and mutual aid could be regulated while protecting the internal freedom of each unit. He traced the idea of internationalism back to the 18th century. He noted that modern science is naturally international because scientific facts and truths are universal. A world federation of democratic people could be formed to give international courts and police the authority to resolve conflicts.

For Aurobindo the essential motivating factor that could make this work is what he called "the religion of humanity." When people realize that all humans are sacred "regardless of all distinctions of race, creed, color, nationality, status, political or social advancement," then all can be protected from violence. This faith in humanity is concerned about its earthly future and would abolish legalized torture, slavery, and oppression while encouraging philanthropy and charity. He believed that egoism of the individual, class, and nation is the enemy of real religion.

The practice of oneness will result in the fulfillment of liberty, equality, and fraternity. The last has been lacking, but the religion of humanity may spiritualize by the inner law of human life which is love. Thus the psychological factor is the most important aspect of human unity. He warned that humans must choose to cooperate, or they face a lingering suicide. A world federation that protects liberty allows the healthy progress of the human race.

A world federation is most likely to resolve conflicts while preserving the freedom of national life; but a centralized world state would eventually stagnate or suffer revolution or reform until it was transformed into a system that affirms freedom. The religion of humanity has no dogma or outward rite, but the oneness respects the freedom of all people. Aurobindo published *War and Self-Determination* in 1920. War and violent revolution can be eliminated by removing the inner causes of war. He exposed the illusions that people thought would end wars.

Some had argued that increasing commerce would eliminate war, but the Great War showed that militarism has increased with commercialism. Others thought that increasing democracy would stop the wars of greedy kings and martial nobles, but the history of ancient Greece and modern democracies demolished that illusion too. In the 19th century Europeans hoped that the concert of Europe, the balance of powers, and arbitration courts would prevent wars; but they only reduced them for a while.

Some thought that modern science and technology would make war too deadly to consider, and a book on the "Great Illusion" hoping that the realisation that wars do not bring commercial advantages was quickly refuted by the Great War. War became industrialized and a titanic struggle leading to military and economic exhaustion with the aid of famine. The final illusion was that war could end war. Aurobindo argued that only when people realize their oneness will they stop killing each other. True self-determination comes from knowing the infinite God within.

The democracy of ancient Greece was based on slavery, violence, and the subjection of women, and modern democracy is a plutocratic system in which the bourgeoisie dominate the workers. Aurobindo proclaimed that women must be regarded as free individuals. In oneness people will respect the self-expression of others. Aurobindo criticized the League of Nations as the tool of the five dominant powers to force their will on others.

In a post-script chapter to *The Ideal of Human Unity*, written in 1950, Aurobindo noted that the United Nations Organisation was formed as a consequence of the Second World War, but like the League of Nations, it was also an oligarchy dominated by the five winning powers, especially with the veto device in the Security Council. The "so-called Communism of Bolshevist Russia" had become autocratic and a police state. Its ideological conflict with the capitalist nations led by the United States has become a cold war because of the awesome new weapons both sides feared to use.

He noted that America was so attached to individualism and capitalism that it was likely to resist the trend toward democratic socialism. He warned that a powerful nation with strong allies might try to dominate the world using their military superiority. *The Human Cycle* by Aurobindo was based on a series of articles on "The Psychology of Social Development." He analyzed social evolution from the ancient times to the age of individualism and reason. His spiritual experience helped him to see beauty and goodness that he called "suprarational."

He prophesied that the suprarational Spirit is the ultimate law of life and that only a spiritual transformation can lift people beyond the limits of materialism. He described the needed transformation from the mental to the spiritual order of life that would be accomplished in individuals. A large number of individuals must be influenced by those leading the spiritual awakening for it to take effect in the community.

Aurobindo believed that the three main aspects of the spiritual age are God, freedom, and unity. Freedom comes from the Spirit within and enables one to consciously master the lower nature. The healthiest condition for humans is the largest possible freedom. The spiritual age will be manifest when the common people realize and are moved by the truths of the Spirit. Truth is what we create within us.

This spiritual evolution is the goal of humanity, and Aurobindo based his ethics on what advances or hinders such evolution. By expressing their inner freedom human individuals grow in consciousness. The spiritual affects every aspect of life from the intellectual and ethical and aesthetic to the physical. The crude emotions, egoism, and desires of our vital nature need to be refined and transformed by the light of the soul in the heart.

Aurobindo described his philosophy of spiritual evolution in *The Life Divine*. He agreed with the ancient *Upanishads* that Spirit is also in matter and that it has been evolving life into its highest forms, the humans. Now God through freedom is evolving the human consciousness from the mental to the spiritual. Humans experience God or the spiritual as *satchitananda*, which means truth *(sat)*, consciousness *(chit)*, and bliss *(ananda)*. Every soul is divine, and those humans who transcend the mental to the spiritual become superhuman.

By practicing integral yoga that includes love, wisdom, and action as well as psychological liberation an individual learns how to integrate one's life with the oneness of all. Aurobindo described ignorance as being unaware of this spiritual beingness and failing to integrate oneself internally and externally with life. As more individuals manifest this spiritual consciousness, society and culture will be transformed by their cooperation. Those who experience this superconsciousness he called gnostics or knowers, and by living divine love they will influence others to cooperate with the spiritual integration that does what is best for everyone.

TAGORE'S SPIRITUAL EXPRESSIONS

Rabindranath Tagore was born on May 7, 1861 into a wealthy family in Calcutta. His grandfather Dwarakanath became rich trading with the British East Indies Company, and he bought several estates. His son Debendranath Tagore managed those estates and was a scholar, a reformer, and co-founder of Brahmo Samaj. Rabindranath was the youngest of Debendranath's fourteen children, and his mother died when he was a child. He was taught at home and was exposed to Sanskrit and English literature. He began writing poetry when he was eight.

When Rabi was fourteen, he perpetrated a hoax by publishing in the Bengali journal *Bharati* some love poems about Krishna and Radha he wrote, claiming they were by Bhanusimha from the 17th century. He acted in a Moliere play at age sixteen and wrote his first play in 1881 about the legendary Valmiki, who turned from being a robber to compose the epic *Ramayana*. Rabindranath visited England 1878-80, but he quit studying law at University College in London after only a year.

Tagore was very close to his sister-in-law Kadambari, who committed suicide in 1884, the year after he married a ten-year-old girl. Rabindranath had five children, but his wife and most of his children died young. While the death rate was falling in England, it was climbing in Bengal. He began managing his father's estates at Shelidah in 1890, and he allowed village headmen and a local court to settle disputes with him as the final court of appeal. He disliked regimented schools and educated his own children at home.

Even though he had criticized early marriages, he arranged for his two oldest daughters to marry men they had never met at the ages of 14 and 10. This made it easier for him to start a school at Shantiniketan in 1901 for his son Rathindranath and four other boys. Tagore wanted to combine the best aspects of East and West in education, and three of the five teachers were Christians.

Tagore wrote most of his short stories in the early 1890s. In his eighty years he would write volumes of poetry, short stories, a few novels, plays, essays, letters, and autobiographies. He made more than two thousand paintings and drawings and composed even more songs, including national anthems for India and Bengal. He once said that his art was for Europe, but his songs were for his own country. One of his songs began, "You think you are strong enough to break the bonds that destiny has tied?"

Gandhi's favorite included the line, "If no one answers to your call, walk alone, walk alone." On Partition Day in Calcutta on October 16, 1905 Rabindranath Tagore began the Rakhibandhan tradition of tying a thread around the wrist of another Bengali as a symbol of friendship. Thousands of people did this on the banks of the Ganges and then marched through the streets singing.

During this Swadeshi movement Tagore founded a Benevolent Society for the 65,000 people in his 125 villages. His father could borrow money at 8% interest, and so he could charge them 12%, which was much lower than what loan-sharks charged. When he received the Nobel Prize for Literature in 1913, he donated the 110,000 rupees to the Shantiniketan School, which invested it in the Agricultural Bank, giving the tenants more capital.

Tagore criticized the Hindu-Muslim riots and the bombing of British officials. He warned that if India's unity was based on animosity toward the British, this would find new targets after the British left. In July 1908 he lectured on East and West and suggested India needed an inner harmony between the two.

Tagore's most famous play, *The Post Office*, was written in 1911. A doctor tells a very sick boy that he must not go outside. So he talks to people through a window and sees a new post office. His receiving a letter from the King just before he goes to sleep implies the mystical symbolism of death. After Tagore translated his *Gitanjali (Song Offerings)* into English and met the poet William Butler Yeats in 1912, he became the first Asian to win a Nobel Prize.

In 1914 Tagore was depressed and wrote his most famous novel, *The Home and the World (Ghare Baire)*. The autobiographical Nikhil is an idealistic zamindar who is disgusted by the terrorism and religious zealotry of the Swadeshi movement. The novel ends nihilistically with his being wounded in a communal riot between Hindus and Muslims. When Gandhi left South Africa, Charlie Andrews brought him and his followers to Tagore. Although Annie Besant may have been the first to call Gandhi a "Mahatma," Tagore made the name popular.

Tagore also hosted British officials at Shantiniketan, and in 1915 he was dubbed a knight, which he renounced four years later after the Amritsar massacre. In 1916 Tagore traveled to Japan and the United States, warning about militaristic nationalism, commercialism, and technology. His lectures were published in the books *Nationalism* and *Personality*. In the latter he affirmed his belief in a spiritual world that is not separate from this world in which "we are living in God."

Human love, the greatness of the good and heroic martyrdom personally expresses the ineffable beauty of nature. He fought against the education which teaches that "a country is greater than the ideals of humanity."

He visited Europe in 1919 and signed "La déclaration pour l'independence de l'esprit" with Romain Rolland, Albert Einstein, and others. At Shantiniketan he started three departments in fine arts, music, and Indology as the nucleus for an international university he called Visva-Bharati.

On March 2, 1921 Tagore wrote to Charlie Andrews from Chicago commending Gandhi's Non-violent campaign.

> We, in India, have to show the world what is that truth
>
> which not only makes disarmament possible
>
> but turns it into strength.
>
> The truth that moral force
>
> is a higher power than brute force
>
> will be proved by the people who are unarmed.

Life, in its higher development, has thrown off
its tremendous burden of armor
and a prodigious quantity of flesh,
till man has become the conqueror of the brute world.

The day is sure to come when the frail man of spirit, completely unhampered by airfleets and dreadnoughts, will prove that the meek are to inherit the earth. It is in the fitness of things that Mahatma Gandhi, frail in body and devoid of all material resources, should call up the immense power of the meek that has been waiting in the heart of the destitute and insulted humanity of India.

The destiny of India has chosen for its ally the power of soul, and not that of muscle. And she is to raise the history of man from the muddy level of physical conflict to the higher moral altitude.

Tagore wrote to Andrews again in May from Stockholm that when people love their own countries, this causes hatred and suspicion of other nations. Only the country that loves God more than herself can claim to be loved by all people. With its deep spiritual traditions Tagore hoped that India could be that country.

In 1924 Tagore visited China and called for the great streams of idealism to show that moral power through heroic sacrifice can demonstrate their wealth and strength. He doubted that any nation could be great while being materialistic. Yet loving material things will not be harmful if they bring soul into them. To the teachers he said that he was building an institution based on the spiritual unity of all races.

He prophesied that when the races become closer, new truths will be revealed. He referred to a preacher who seemed to be a failure during the height of the Roman Empire; but despite his crucifixion he lives forever as a symbol. Tagore noted that in his own time martyrs were going to prison for a deathless future.

On February 3, 1922 Tagore published a warning in the Bengali press that violence was latent in the non-cooperation movement. Two days later a mob killed the police at Chauri Chaura, causing Gandhi to cancel the campaign. Although Tagore often criticized the specific tactics of Gandhi, such as burning foreign cloth, he agreed with his philosophy and strategy of Non-violence. In 1924 he wrote that Gandhi's new political warfare has a spiritual character, and only those with the courage to accept suffering can wage this spiritual war.

If an entire nation could be trained not to fear death, armaments would lose their power. Only when people accept this idea will freedom become permanent. Jesus Christ had faith in this vision, but people may not be ready yet to act on such a message. Tagore objected to Gandhi's mandate that all patriotic Indians should spend several hours every day spinning, and in September 1925 he published his essay, "The Cult of the Charka."

Tagore's lectures at Oxford in May 1930 were published as *The Religion of Man*. His ideas on religion are very similar to those of Aurobindo. Humans may have a relationship with the divine principle of unity, and his religion was being true to that spiritual unity. Tagore emphasized the eternal divinity in humanity. Truth does not come from an individual mind but from the universal Spirit that comprehends the individuals. Humans are always struggling for freedom. Greed does not satisfy, and true joy comes from surrendering our individual self to the universal Self. Civilisation progresses as individuals seek ideal perfection. Tagore said,

> We must realize not only the reasoning mind,
> but also the creative imagination,
> the love and wisdom that belong to the Supreme Person,
> whose Spirit is over us all,
> love for whom comprehends love for all creatures
> and exceeds in depth and strength all other loves,
> leading to difficult endeavors and martyrdoms
> that have no other gain
> than the fulfillment of this love itself.

Evolution is progressing toward the revelation of its own truth as the eternal realizes itself in history by overcoming obstructions. As an animal the human depends on Nature, but as a sovereign one builds one's world and rules it. In detachment humans realize a deeper relationship with the universe. Being responsible to the community enhances the freedom of social relationship and collective power.

In the freedom of consciousness one realizes unity with a greater being, and with active love one may dedicate one's life to the eternal progress of truth. Joy comes from the love that realizes ourselves in others. Love testifies to the greater whole. True freedom leads to a broader path of self-realisation. Each age reveals its personality as a dreamer. The mind is involved in the economy of the human organism, but union with the Spirit transcends the mind. Tagore recognized Zarathushtra as the first prophet to liberate religion from a tribal God to a universal Spirit and human ethics.

After Gandhi was arrested in May 1930, Tagore wrote that the English had lost their former moral prestige in Asia and were no longer the champions of fairness and high principles. Yet he still believed that the best minds of East and West could meet in honorable understanding. He and his friend Einstein understood Zionism, but in November 1930 Tagore wrote prophetically,

> The success of Zionism depends
>
> entirely upon Arab-Jewish cooperation.
>
> This can be obtained in Palestine only by means of
>
> a direct understanding between the Arabs and the Jews.
>
> If the Zionist leadership will insist on separating
>
> Jewish political and economic interests in Palestine
>
> from those of the Arabs,
>
> ugly eruptions will occur in the Holy Land.

Tagore supported the ideals of the League of Nations, but in 1931 he criticized its practice, saying that it was like "organizing a band of robbers into a police department." When Gandhi went on a fast to end untouchability in May 1933, Tagore wrote him a letter warning that his example could lead to noble souls leaving the world to the morally feeble. In 1936 Gandhi persuaded the businessman G. D. Birla to contribute 60,000 rupees to pay the debt for Tagore's college.

That year Tagore sent a message to the World Peace Congress at Brussels, emphasizing that peace must be built on the strength of the just, not on the weariness of the weak. To deserve peace they must pay its full price. "The strong must cease to be greedy, and the weak must learn to be bold."

Here are four inspiring songs from *Gitanjali:*

Life of my life, I shall ever try to keep my body pure,
knowing that thy living touch is upon all my limbs.
I shall ever try to keep all untruths out from my thoughts,
knowing that thou art that truth
which has kindled the light of reason in my mind.
I shall ever try to drive all evils away from my heart
and keep my love in flower,
knowing that thou hast thy seat
in the inmost shrine of my heart.
And it shall be my endeavour to reveal thee in my actions,
knowing it is thy power gives me strength to act.
If thou speakest not,
I will fill my heart with thy silence and endure it.
I will keep still and wait like the night with starry vigil
and its head bent low with patience.
The morning will surely come, the darkness will vanish,

and thy voice pour down in golden streams
breaking through the sky.
Then thy words will take wings in songs
from every one of my birds' nests,
and thy melodies will break forth in flowers
in all my forest groves.
Where the mind is without fear and the head is held high;
Where the knowledge is free;
Where the world has not been broken up into fragments
by narrow domestic walls;
Where words come out from the depth of truth;
Where tireless striving stretches its arms towards perfection;
Where the clear stream of reason has not lost its way
into the dreary desert sand of dead habit;
Where the mind is led forward by thee
into ever-widening thought and action-
Into that heaven of freedom, my Father,
let my country awake.
This is my prayer to thee, my lord-
strike, strike at the root of penury in my heart.
Give me the strength lightly to bear my joys and sorrows.
Give me the strength to make my love fruitful in service.
Give me the strength never to disown the poor
or bend my knees before insolent might.
Give me the strength to raise my mind
high above daily trifles.

And give me the strength to surrender my strength
to thy will with love.9

In 1916 Tagore published 325 epigrams in *Stray Birds*. Here are a few:

That I exist is a perpetual surprise which is life. (22)

Life finds its wealth by the claims of the world,
and its worth by the claims of love. (33)

He has made his weapons his gods.
When his weapons win, he is defeated himself. (45)

God finds himself by creating. (46)

Wrong cannot afford defeat, but Right can. (68)

Chastity is a wealth that comes from abundance of love. (73)

Every child comes with the messagethat God is not yet discouraged of man. (77)

The artist is the lover of Nature;
therefore he is her slave and her master. (85)

Power said to the world, "You are mine."
The world kept it prisoner on her throne.
Love said to the world, "I am thine."
The world gave it the freedom of her house. (93)

I carry in my world that flourishes
the worlds that have failed. (121)

If you shut your door to all errors,
truth will be shut out. (130)

They hated and killed, and men praised them.
But God in shame hastens to hide its memory
under the green grass. (186)

Life has become richer by the love that has been lost. (223)

Man is worse than an animal when he is an animal. (248)

God kisses the finite in his love and man the infinite. (302)

Man's history is waiting in patience
for the triumph of the insulted man. (316)

Fireflies had their origin in China and Japan, where Tagore wrote his thoughts on fans and pieces of silk. Here are three:

God seeks comrades and claims love,
the Devil seeks slaves and claims obedience.

Love remains a secret even when spoken,
for only a lover truly knows that he is loved.

I am able to love my God
because He gives me freedom to deny Him.

SRI AUROBINDO'S FIVE DREAMS: NATION-SOULS AND THE TRIPLE TRANSFORMATION

FIVE DREAMS

Sri Aurobindo was born on August 15, 1872 and on the same day in 1947 India achieved her freedom from British rule. On that occasion Sri Aurobindo wrote out a message to the new nation which was read out over the radio. This message outlined five dreams of Sri Aurobindo, in each of which India featured prominently. We find from a perusal of these dreams how significant a part India played in Sri Aurobindo's vision for the future of humanity and of the world.

The first of these dreams was the attainment of freedom for India. Sri Aurobindo announced this dream in the most profound sense, so that the newly acquired political freedom of India was acknowledged but the much that was left unaccomplished was also made clear. The scope of a national freedom for Sri Aurobindo was not merely freedom from colonial rule, but a true independence of the subjective life of the nation, a freedom within; and he linked this notion of freedom with the idea of national unity. He said that India was free but she was not united and he touched on a major source of disunity in the nation in Hindu-Muslim relations which manifested in the partition of the subcontinent into India and Pakistan.

The second dream announced by Sri Aurobindo was the rise of Asia in the comity of nations, so as to balance the Eurocentric inequality of the modern age and to regain the place of vital significance that she held in the pre-modern past. Sri Aurobindo shared his perception that this was beginning to happen and that India had an important role to play here. The third dream of Sri Aurobindo was world union – a global polity in which the security of the world was assured and a sense of harmony and concord developed among the peoples of the world.

The fourth dream was the spiritual gift of India to the world. Here he pointed to the fact that under present circumstances, with the various kinds of difficulties and cataclysms that mankind had created for itself and was forced to endure, increasing attention would turn to the spirituality of India, a process which had already substantially begun in his time. The fifth dream of Sri Aurobindo was humanity's rise to a new stage of being, a new kind of life or a new species which overcame the limitations of the present human constitution; and he placed this in the future.

Overall, Sri Aurobindo's five dreams announce a hopeful and optimistic vision for India and the future of the world. At the same time, this is not naïve optimism. We find him as one of the clearest observers and analysts of the difficulties and problems of modernity and yet, beyond these dangers, he holds out the light of optimism for the human future.

THE QUESTION OF UNITY

It is instructive for us to pay close attention to these five dreams of Sri Aurobindo today, so that we may assess where we stand with respect to them in our present time; and discover messages there which we may hold close to our hearts and turn into aspirations, and convert into will so as to fashion our national and international destiny. It is important to realize that to orient ourselves properly to Sri Aurobindo's dreams, it is necessary to divest ourselves of the inertia which treats them as prophecies written into some divine calendar. They are invitations to participation, dreams that seek our adherence to turn them into realities.

When we look at these dreams as a whole, we find that a major thread running through them all is the question of unity – national or subcontinental unity, continental unity and global unity. We may start by asking ourselves where we stand with respect to these unities in today's world. From the superficial point of view, we may say that we are more united today than ever before in history.

The world has shrunk today in our minds. We travel large distances very quickly, we enjoy routinely goods and services available at great distances; we mingle with people from cultures spread across the planet, working in multicultural projects of unheard of complexity. So when we contemplate these facts, it seems that a much greater global unity has developed since the time of Sri Aurobindo's announcement of his five dreams in 1947.

But when we contemplate more deeply the locus of unity which Sri Aurobindo intends in his five dreams, we realize that there is a big gulf separating us from his dreams of unity at a variety of levels. The unity we have achieved is only a materialistic unity – a unity driven by material and commercial forces. We seem to be closer to one another than before but that is because our subjectivity has been tailored into uniformity by the techno-commercial forces of the modern world.

Common lifestyles have become normalized across the world due to the determining regime of a world market. On the face of it, this is not apparent, since there seems to be so much choice we find ourselves faced with at every moment, we have even coined the term overchoice to describe this peculiarly contemporary phenomenon. But if we look closer at these choices, they turn out to be merely choices of consumption with cosmetic differences – flavors, tastes, hardly choices of alternate destiny arising from the human depths. We as a world humanity today lead lives in which everything is packaged into commodities – our work and leisure – so that every aspect of our time is conditioned and made demands on. This makes our subjectivity determined and dwarfed; we are left with little or no time, space or energy for a growth of consciousness in our lives. We have little creativity left outside of the constraining boundaries of this determination to express new dimensions of existence.

It is this common condition of servitude that constitutes our unity today. We are united in our bondage to the global world Market. Is this the unity Sri Aurobindo had in mind when he announced his five dreams?

COLONIALISM AND GLOBALISATION

Sri Aurobindo begins his address by saying: "August 15 is my own birthday and it is naturally gratifying to me that it should have assumed this vast significance. I take this coincidence not as a fortuitous accident, but as the sanction and seal of the divine force that guides my steps on the work with which I began life and the beginning of its full fruition." Let us contemplate this work with which as he says, he began his life, and the beginning of whose full fruition he observes on August 15, 1947.

The steps that he is referring to here take us back a hundred years to India's struggle for independence from colonial rule. India was occupied by the British at that time, but this was not a privilege granted only to India. Colonialism was an endemic condition that pervaded most of the non-western world, what is largely called today the developing nations. We may say that all of Asia was colonized, if not politically, then culturally and mentally. India was part of this condition of colonisation.

Colonisation meant racial and civilisational subjugation, economic exploitation, political domination, oppression of many kinds. Now, it is natural that sooner or later, an oppressed people would want freedom. And so, in India, there was a movement for freedom. But colonisation itself was an epiphenomenon, a symptom of a much larger ideological movement of European intellectual history that continues to work its way in the present. This is what took its roots in the 18th c. and is known as the European Enlightenment.

This term "Enlightenment," as we know it today, has a variety of connotations. It is a term used to describe, rather vaguely, the Buddha's spiritual attainment, for example. But it is more commonly a term which is used to describe a condition of freedom and expression of the mind as a common property of all humanity, an ideal which developed in 18th c. Europe. On the face of it, this sounds like a noble ideal and we would be hard put to see any connection between this and colonialism or to relate it to a study of what Sri Aurobindo meant by the term "unity" when he began his life in Indian politics.

The Enlightenment is an intellectual revolution in which the sense of the divinity of man as a rational being is brought to the front as the definition of humanity. It asserts the intuition of a world which can be understood by the mind in terms of laws. Historically, it arises as a reaction to the religious excesses of the Dark Ages with the revolutionary idea that human individuals do not need any intermediaries between themselves and God, because God is Reason and man possesses a faculty of reasoning.

The exercise of the Mind to arrive at the full "Reason" of the world and its expressions would constitute the godhood of man, since by knowing the laws by which the universe is run, he would be in possession of God's organ of Knowledge. He would thus be an equal of God. This would be the true freedom of the Mind, and this is what would constitute Enlightenment.

What this rational Enlightenment proposes thus, is nothing short of a seeking for omniscience. This becomes the entire project of Modernity, spawning a systematic development of rational knowledge, the birth of the modern Academy and its organisation of the world, a process continuing to this day. The utilisation of

Knowledge for expressing fully the potential of the world, for bettering the world we live in sounds like a most noble ideal, but what stamps it with defect is the Will to Power which it inevitably expresses.

This hinges on the question of the limits of human or rational knowledge but more so, on the misuse of the will which is natural to humankind. The Will to Power subjects the Will to Knowledge to its own desire to possess, exploit and enjoy the world and its resources and creatures. The essential experience of separateness endemic to humanity makes each individual person or group treat itself as the center of the universe and all "others" as either a threat or an element for assimilation, possession and enjoyment.

The goals of bettering the world slip easily into the goals of utilizing knowledge for accumulating more and more profit, developing huge machineries for creating more and more surplus for the accumulation of profit and expanding techniques for creating desire for the consumption of the surplus produced. Western man's religious life has also been exploited to make this possible. As analyzed by Max Weber, the guilt associated with Original Sin in Christianity has been displaced onto a "Protestant work ethic" so as to exploit labor for the accumulation of capital.

Similarly, as per thinkers like R.H. Toni, the Old Testament injunction to build perfection on earth has equally been grist to this mill. Thus, this capital accumulation has been a necessary accompaniment of the Enlightenment and, along with the need to convert the whole world to the civilisational ideology of the Enlightenment (what was known as "the white man's burden), it was as part of this drive for material and subjective exploitation that colonialism arose as a direct consequence of the Enlightenment.

Today, the world is no longer politically colonized, but the forces of capital accumulation and the society it produces is no less with us today in and as our era of globalisation.

NATION SOUL

Thus we can see how critical an understanding of this trajectory of modernity is to the notion of national independence.

When Sri Aurobindo entered the field of national politics, there were two kinds of approaches to colonialism. The parties who represented these two approaches were the Moderates and the Extremists. The moderate approach was not primarily interested in independence from colonial rule. It called for an end to oppressive policies.

It considered the injustices and evils of colonial rule to be what needed overcoming and sought to remedy this through pressing for constitutional change. In other words, its approach was an appeal to the conscience of the colonizer while accepting the superiority of its progressive drive and its right to rule over the nation. Thus, for the Moderates, what the British brought to India were the noble goals of the Enlightenment, which India sorely needed.

Humanism, Science and a rational organisation of life were seen by them as the great gifts of the west to India and what they pressed for was what they felt to be consonant with the "enlightened" goals of government, a removal of oppressive policies to become true benefactors of India. What Sri Aurobindo represented was another mode of thinking belonging politically to the group called the Extremists.

The Extremists held complete independence from the British to be their political goal and they justified this stand by claiming an alternate civilisational trajectory from that of the west. We find this line of argument consistently for example in the political writings of Sri Aurobindo which emerged in the journal of the Extremists, *Bande Mataram*. Here we find the call for national independence being issued in the name of a national law of becoming or "dharma."

The use of this term is related to the Gita's idea of a distinct law of being, *swabhava* and becoming, *swadharma* for each individual. Sri Aurobindo adapted this idea for the collective entity of the nation and thus asserted a psychic reality uniting the people of India. By this argument, it is not just to be free of oppression that India needed to be free, but for her people to express what lay latent in the depths of national self-becoming, the *swadharma* or *rashtra-dharma* of the nation. The idea of a national law of self-becoming was never articulated distinctly before this in India and is also an adaptation of the idea of the nation soul which was developed in late 18th c. Germany by thinkers like Johann Herder and G.W.F. Hegel. Looked at from a contemporary historical vantage, this idea of a nation soul is very controversial.

This is because we live in the wake of World War II, in which this idea was very drastically and dangerously abused. A national soul, as an ahistorical essence, gives rise easily to the idea of racism and radical cultural relativism. All nations, by this idea, would be seen as eternally distinct with its people making competitive claims on the earth. From this problem of relativism, also arises the question of hierarchy. How are these distinct entities to be ordered in relation to one another and the totality of the world? What is to be at the center and what at the periphery? It is clear that such ideas can easily be abused to justify Apartheid and racial or cultural expansionism.

These are also the kinds of problems that led to the second World War, whose disastrous effects brought humanity close to extinction and whose aftermath smoulders all around us. In occult terms, Sri Aurobindo and the Mother referred to the power behind this war as "the Lord of the Nations," which goes to show how the nation idea can be distorted into something very dangerous, with a possibility of falsehood which can abuse it hugely if one is not careful.

Apart from this, the idea of a nation soul can raise serious problems of an internal nature, if not properly understood. A nation tries to define its identity through the writing of its history. A variety of ideologies can become the bases for contested histories, each of which claim to give voice to the "true" soul of the nation. We see this all around us as a real problem of nationalism, a factor of fratricidal struggle, seeking to determine the destiny of the nation. In India, there are those, for example, who have built a history around the idea of a Hindu nation.

Equally ideological and contestational, may be the idea of a "secular nation." This, for example, was the entire idea behind

Nehru's work on Indian history, to show that the Indian people have accepted a wide variety of ideologies, religious and otherwise, with no priority given to any one. This allows him to posit a socialistic democracy as the form of polity suited to India's future.

All these ideas, based on the notion of an unchanging essence defining the nation, hold great dangers, which is why contemporary thinkers have chosen to discard this idea of a nation soul. But Sri Aurobindo and others who utilized this idea to speak of a national soul and law of national becoming, did not see this as the basis of a static racist or culturally essentialistic ideology but as an evolving entity with a cultural history moving towards universality.

Sri Aurobindo anticipated these dangers in the nation soul idea and made it very clear in his work on social and political philosophy, *The Human Cycle*, that the entry into a subjective age, one which opens itself to the subjectivity of a nation soul, is fraught with dangers. He writes here of true and false subjectivisms. But he does not discard the idea of a nation-soul. The truth of the nation soul, according to Sri Aurobindo, is the same as the truth of the individual soul as Sri Aurobindo develops it from the tradition of Indian spiritual philosophy.

That is, it is a self-concentration of the one Divine Being, one way of self-understanding of the One Being there is. In other words, nation souls are the same in essence, but different in form of perception and form of expression. This is what allows the soul, whether in an individual or a nation, to see itself as the same in all beings. It is the realisation of the One Being in many forms, arising from what Sri Aurobindo calls "the multiple self-concentration of the One." This is what forms the essence of the nation soul for Sri Aurobindo.

These nation souls are differentiated because the Divine Reality, which represents itself in all these souls, is the Infinite One. While being the Same, it is the aspect of its infinite possibilities which finds differentiated manifestation in the perception and expression of souls. This is what provides a radical uniqueness to each soul's expression, while basing it in Oneness. The realisation of such a subjective truth evades the dangers which arise from an essentialistic psychic ontology, a static monadology without any basis in unity.

Sri Aurobindo sees the espousal of such a radical essentialism without unity as a false subjectivism, which seeks to assert its "truth" against all others or dominate the others through a world ordering mythology in which it assumes the position of centrality. On the other hand, the realisation of a differentiation based on an expression of the Infinite One would move towards an acceptance of plurality based in the wonder of difference-in-unity, a Being-in-Becoming of the Infinite One. This Sri Aurobindo sees as a "true subjectivism."

THE FIVE DREAMS AND THE TRIPLE TRANSFORMATION

Such a "true subjectivism" is better understood in terms of cultural history, as a process of continuities and disjunctions. The evolving nation soul develops its forms through its cultural body. It makes its appearance as a self-identifying concept among the people of a region at a certain point in time and develops along certain lines of preserved preference due to cultural momentum, but is not restricted to them. To understand better the trajectory of evolution of a nation soul, we may compare its movements to those in the development of the individual soul.

Here we may see three major movements, which could be related to the idea of Triple Transformation introduced by Sri Aurobindo in *The Life Divine* and elsewhere. The first of these movements of history is the creation and proper unification of its instrumental body. This relates at once to the first of Sri Aurobindo's five dreams and the first of the three transformations which he sets up as the trajectory of human evolution in the individual. The first of the three transformations is the development of a nature body adapted to the use of the psychic being and the emergence of the psychic being as the controller and leader of this expressive nature.

Similarly, the first of Sri Aurobindo's dreams is the freedom and integration of the nation, the preparation and integration of the instrumentality for the use of the nation soul. Sri Aurobindo sees the *swadharma* of the Indian nation as one which seeks the realisation of the Divine in innumerable ways. Each constituent of the national body has its own approach to that Infinite One which attracts it and the nation soul is empowered in the fostering of cultural plurality and syntheses which allow all these myriad lines of seeking their full power of development.

The second movement in the evolution of the nation soul can be seen as its growth towards universality. This is also related to the second transformation in Sri Aurobindo's formulation of the triple transformation. This is the realisation of the Cosmic Consciousness, that which is all-inclusive and sees other forms of approaches as perspectives having differences which are related in a harmony based in an implied Oneness. For the nation soul, this means a growth in the power of relation with other ways of becoming, an expansion out of a narrow way of looking at reality.

Such an expansion takes delight in other ways of becoming and forms relations of commonalty, hybridity or syncretism, leading eventually to an inclusion of all other ways as part of one's own. However, such formulations would continue to respect other kinds of syntheses which may be developed by other ways of becoming. This provides the scope of the second and third dreams of Sri Aurobindo – the rise of Asia as a continental reality in which India plays its part, and the development of world union.

These movements are not temporally exclusive, that is they do not form phases of development which wait for completion before moving to the next. However, for the success of India's part in the rise to prominence of Asia and for its part in world union, it is important for the development of subjective unity based on an interchange of spiritual plurality in the nation. In fact, one may say that universality is part of the articulated essence of India's soul, in its espousal of "the world family," *basudhaiva kutumbakam*. To realize this, to make it concrete and manifest in the nature body that we call India, is part of its movement towards the goals of the second and third dreams of Sri Aurobindo.

Sri Aurobindo brings together the drift of these three dreams in his fourth dream – the gift of India's spirituality to the world. This, indeed, is how Sri Aurobindo sees India's *swadharma*. But this is not a static spirituality based on a monocultural reading of history – as for example in the idea of a Hindu nation. India's spirituality is not merely a repetition of its past, it consists in the lived adaptations of the present. This is what Sri Aurobindo makes very clear in his statement: "We belong not to the dawns of the past but to the noons of the future."

What may be seen as the third movement of the nation soul relates to the fifth of Sri Aurobindo's dreams. This is the most profound movement and is also identical with the third of the three transformations in Sri Aurobindo's yoga. This is the further journey of the soul out of its cosmic context into a transcendental dimension, from where it may create a new humanity or rather superhumanity.

This is the dream of a new species, where human souls, prepared through a cosmic unity, rise in consciousness to a higher level of being not yet manifest in the race, and from this vantage, can reformulate the expression of humanity. This goal, perhaps even in its beginnings, belongs to the future, as he says. For this, we need to have some sufficient realisation of the first four dreams and we are still very far from that.

THE ONE NATION AND THE TWO NATIONS

Now, the question to ask is what do these dreams have to do with us? The easiest answer is to say that these are predictions of an avatar and all we need to do is to wait for their achievement. Unfortunately, as the Mother says somewhere, Nature is in no hurry and predictions or not, these dreams will remain dreams were we not to participate in making them realities. So, let us consider these dreams in terms of their contemporary realisation.

Where these dreams today and what are is needed to move towards them? The first dream concerns itself with the unity of the nation, not merely political unity but cultural unity, a unity in cultural psychology. One may even say, that for Sri Aurobindo this psychological unity comes before political unity. Political unity can hardly be secure if there isn't a psychological unity among the peoples of the nation. As a nation, India has experienced various forms of cultural unity in the past.

Sri Aurobindo raises here one of the most difficult problems of unity we are faced with today – the Hindu-Muslim question and politically related to this, the India-Pakistan question. Sri Aurobindo says that the political division into India and Pakistan should not be treated as a settled fact. What he is saying here has its roots in cultural history in the debate between what is known as the one nation and the two nation theory?

The one nation theory is based on the idea that Hindus and Muslims in India share a cultural psychology, that in some way, Indian Islam has developed into a synthetic form which shares an acceptance in difference with Hindu forms and vice versa. The two nation theory implies that Hindus and Muslims in India live two completely different realities and are better parted into two nations.

The two nation theory has made its appearance in relatively modern times and represents a politicisation of religious identities, made to look like a historical fact. It is a rhetorical formulation. If we look back at India's past, we find many synthetic formulations which have tried to bring Hindu and Muslim spiritual forms into relation or unity with one another. These attempts have become part of the cultural history of the peoples of India, irrespective of religion.

Creative spiritual personalities have arisen in Indian history, such as the Chisti saints, Sufis like Kabir and Nanak, in modern times, personalities such as Rabindranath Tagore and Kazi Nazrul Islam or the spiritual genius of Sri Ramakrishna, who united in his own life the various spiritual experiences of different religious traditions. It could be said that India had been under Islamic hegemony for four or five hundred years, but during this period, there were also signal achievements of synthesis and harmony. A great flowering of hybrid Indian culture, transcending religious differences, developed during the Mughal period and the history of India would have been very different had Dara Shikoh, the eldest son and rightful heir of Shah Jehan assumed the throne of Mughal India.

The Mughal court was dominated by two Sufi denominations, the Chistis and the Naqshbandis. Of these, the Chistis created a synthetic spiritual culture through hybridisation with Vaishnavism. The Mughal emperors who were under the influence of the Chistis, eschewed orthodoxy and promoted spiritual dialog and synthesis. Unfortunately, the Naqsbandhis were more orthodox and lent their support to the *ulemas*. The regime of Aurangzeb established an Islamic orthodoxy which could be said to lay the seeds for the modern idea of the two nation theory.

If we study the periods and personalities who helped in the manifestation of a cultural closeness among Hindus and Muslims, we find an embracement of the spiritual history of India beyond all orthodox formations. This is what brings us into contact with the nation soul, a culture of pure self-discovery, experience and manifestation of the spirit, however it may come. This implies spirituality in a creative vein, not a clinging to forms and a policing of boundaries.

Spirituality stuck in the forms of the past is one thing, India has created many great forms of social practice leading to experiences of the spirit, but if these become exclusive or if they seek to erase the realities of other forms by co-optation, this leads only to internal strife and division, hardly the integration of the social body or the first step towards the manifestation of the nation soul as per Sri Aurobindo.

What we call Hinduism has created such a form which tends to define it today, a form of Puranic religion, habits and customs of life and worship, to give body to spiritual experiences. If we follow these forms with a spiritual aim, we may have high realisations of the spirit, as innumerable saints and yogis have affirmed. But let us not forget that these forms also have a historicity, they were created at a certain point in time and answer to certain social conditions. Can we dare to modify or break them? Can we dare to create new forms?

Do we have the power to create a new spirituality which will represent a greater cultural psychology of inclusion and realisation for the nation? This is the invitation of the first dream of Sri Aurobindo. It calls on the people of India attuned to its nation soul to allow the power of spirituality to become creative in them and embrace every form, all shades of realisation which have left their mark in the history of the nation. All this history belongs to us and is not to be thrown aside. What we need to protect ourselves from is not this or that spiritual form but all orthodoxy. What we need to embrace instead is a creative and all-embracing spirituality.

ASIA IS ONE

Sri Aurobindo's second dream concerns the rise of Asia. Today much is being said about Asia becoming a major player in the world market. India and China are often spoken of as holding the key to the economic future of the world. If this is the entire destiny of India and of Asia, as an economic giant in the drive for a new developing globalisation, then we have lost a great opportunity.

The Asia that Sri Aurobindo is speaking of is an Asia fertilized by powerful rivers of spirituality, many emanating from India – the Asia that received Buddhism and Hinduism and made its own forms of these, the Asia through which Islam spread not as an orthodoxy but as Sufi mysticism, the Asia in which Confucianism, Taoism and Shinto mingled their rivers with Buddhism in new creative forms through many regional histories. This eclectic spiritual continent called Asia is what Sri Aurobindo is referring to.

To approach this, we have to move our attention from the material and economic to the depths of the cultural and spiritual. Do we see any movements of this kind today? I don't see any. Here again, is where our aspirations come in, we have to make these dreams into realities. At the turn of the 19th/20th century, Sri Aurobindo started an anti-colonial revolutionary movement in Bengal with a few splinter groups who has already received some preparation towards revolutionary action, not by an Indian, but by a Japanese ideologue by name of Okakura Kakuzo. He had come from Japan to India in 1902 looking for a spiritual personality to take back so as to to re-enliven Japanese spiritual culture. The personality he wished to take back was Vivekananda.

This did not happen, since Vivekananda died that year, but Okakura also brought a message to India. This was the message of Pan-Asianism, which he expressed in his famous book, *The Ideals of the East*. Okakura began this book with the line "Asia is one" and in its very first page; he referred to an all-embracing "Advaita" as the very soul of Asia, a spirit of non-dual spirituality which flowed into the whole of the continent from India. It is this spirit which needs to be kindled in dynamic and living forms today. This rekindling is necessary if Asia of the ages is to rise again into the comity of nations and realize the dream of Sri Aurobindo. This is hardly the Asia which is today playing out a derivative role furthering the commercial vision of the European Enlightenment through neo-liberal globalisation.

THE RELIGION OF HUMANITY

Sri Aurobindo's third dream concerns world unity. Given the forces of globalisation weaving a single lifestyle across the world today, it would seem that this dream is close to fulfillment. But once again, this global reality is driven by forces of capital accumulation and economic inequality. Is this the confederation of nations which Sri Aurobindo had in mind? Or an international policy protecting the interests of all the peoples of the world? At the end of World War II, an organ was created for just such a purpose.

This was the United Nations. But the United Nations is a highly compromised entity today. It is merely a political tool for certain world powers. Here again, we must realize that for the world union Sri Aurobindo had in mind, external mechanisms like economics and politics are not enough. We must find creative powers to build a global unity which discovers the commonalty of all human beings. Ideologically, this was attempted in Europe through international movements such as Marxism and Socialism. Such ideologies are with us even today. Internationalism as an attempt to define and solve human problems irrespective of cultural differences, problems of human rights, democracy, equality, basic needs continue to be attempted, as variations of the ideals of the Enlightenment, but these solutions don't go deep enough in their dealings with the darkness that lurks in human hearts.

Sri Aurobindo presents instead the ideal of the religion of humanity. This 'religion of humanity' is very different from any sectarian religion, just as it is very different from an internationalist Socialism. It is based on the discovery of the soul. The ideal of psychic self-discovery equally enables the discovery of the soul in all individuals. There is a line in Sri Aurobindo's Synthesis of Yoga which opens up the kind of practice leading to such a goal. Here he says, "The realisation of oneness and the practice of oneness in difference is the whole of the yoga." This line returns us to the profound meaning of unity and difference in individual and national souls. It is a practice of this kind that constitutes the essence of realisation of the nation soul and of world unity.

A GRASS ROOTS SPIRITUALITY

Sri Aurobindo's fourth dream is that of India's spiritual gift to humanity. Sri Aurobindo points out that given the changing circumstances and anxieties of our times, people will turn more and more to spiritual solutions and look to India and her long history of spiritual experimentation for solutions. Here he warns that it would indeed be a pity if when the world most needs the benefit of India's spiritual gift, the citizens of modern India, attracted by the glittering trinkets of global materialism, would themselves devalue or cast away the riches of the soul. In the burgeoning mega-cities of contemporary India, how much value do we give to spiritual solutions?

Or has spirituality been reduced to a tool for stress-free and efficient business management? This is what contemporary thinkers such as Slavoj Zizek criticize when they talk of New Age Buddhism becoming the perfect and appropriate subjective counterpart of world capitalism. Yet, perhaps, beyond this easy co-optation, and under the surface of what seem to be comfortable neo-liberal lives, growing fears, anxieties and discontents stemming from nightmares of slippery terrorism, unpredictable financial collapse and/or ecological disaster also mark our age.

It is here that people are left to seek for personal solutions which the hubris and self-confidence of the Enlightenment cannot provide. Perhaps somewhere in the occult range of human species consciousness, a shadowy seeking for a new synthesis of yoga is beginning to raise its lonely tongue of aspiration. But even as this need grows around us, how many among us are in a position to offer the help that is necessary? For the spiritual gift of India to answer to the need of the hour, new leaders are necessary – not only at official or institutional levels but at the grass-roots.

Many times in India's past, such waves of spiritual adaptation and experimentation have spread through the country from among the masses. In recent history, the Sufi, Bhakti and Sant movements of the 16th c. are cases in point. But in our present times, when the light of tradition either burns dimly or has been transformed to the lurid glow of fundamentalism, a new inspiration is necessary to kindle the flames of post-secular world spirituality.

Sri Aurobindo has provided a spiritual vision which can sustain and transport us through our contemporary global condition. Thus, it is those who have been touched by the light of Sri Aurobindo and the Mother who carry a special responsibility, to make available viable spiritual solutions beyond an exotic traditionalism or a sectarian narrowness. This again, is something of India's future which needs to be built, a dream to be realized only through sincerity of practice. This too, is very far from being realized, unless enough individuals develop the will to accelerate and intensify its aspiration in their lives.

CITY STATES OF THE FUTURE

Sri Aurobindo's fifth dream, the transition of humanity (or at least a portion of it) to a new species, is still distant from us. But here, as in the case of his other dreams, it is Sri Aurobindo and the Mother who have left us their own examples towards this eventuality so that we may tune our aspirations towards it. Further, they have given us the beginnings of social formulations for preparing this transition, what Sri Aurobindo has termed "laboratories of the life divine." These include the communities founded by them, such as the Sri Aurobindo Ashram and Auroville.

To prepare ourselves for a change in consciousness leading to a new form of being and becoming, are we being told to gravitate to these places and swell their populations? There is much that we can learn from these places, but if we do not understand the forces with which they were constructed and the world forces they were put in dynamic relationship with, all we will see there are forms of shelter, locations of escape from the modern world.

Or if we turn to the practices of the inner life that form the habitus of these places, we may easily lose our connection with the demands of modernity. But it is not for this that these locations were established by their founders. These environments were established to be sites of selective assimilation and engagement with all the forces of the world, so as to have a world transforming potential. In some way, this kind of response to modernity has also been approximated by a number of other social experiments that arose during the period of India's national struggle for independence.

We may think of Rabindranath Tagore's Shantiniketan – Visvabharati, the educational center for the making of the Universal Man, Visva Manav, or even Gandhi's ashram at Sabarmati. These are all attempts at consolidating the inner life against the fragmenting sway of the global techno-commercial forces of modernity, the overwhelming flood which is occupying the world and fashioning human subjectivity today.

If humanity is to have a chance at opening up the possibility for Sri Aurobindo's fifth dream, it can only be through the creation of social conditions where the expressions of a collective spiritual life can take precedence over the ever-accelerating determinisms of production and consumption of a global world market. These are the sites of soul building, not ashrams in the sense of shelters but the autonomous intentional communities and city states of the future that we need to conceptualize and build collectively.

So long as the privileging of our national target remains economic success in the world market, this dream of the future will elude us. We have to think and act differently, as individuals and as collectives. Thus, to contemplate India's future, as extended in the vision of Sri Aurobindo, it is of paramount importance that we cease from a passive acquiescence to the forces of the world or treat Sr Aurobindo's dreams as inevitable prophecies. We must hold these dreams near to our hearts and make them our own. To sustain a dream in one's attention is the very essence of meditation.

The Mother makes this need of the hour very clear to us. She asks us never to forget that we are participating in the birth of a new world – to keep this idea in the forefront of our consciousness, to wake with it and go to sleep with it. The Mother says about the supramental manifestation that it may be achieved in a thousand years or it may be achieved in a few hundred years. It depends on human aspiration and practice.

The same can be said about Sri Aurobindo's dreams for the destiny of India. We are not called upon by Sri Aurobindo to be astrologers; we are called upon to be people of aspiration and will. Of course, it is not all in our hands, there are cosmic powers much greater than us as we are presently constituted that have a stake in the future. But unless we become active participants in the process, be able to interpret our times and intensify the movement towards the fulfillment of these dreams, they will remain deferred or even defeated.

Bibliography

Binodini: A Novel translated by Krishna Kripalani. New Delhi: Sahitya Akademi, 1959.

Crisis in Civilization: A Message on Completing His Eighty Years translated by Kshitis Roy and Krishna R. Kripalani. – Santiniketan: Santiniketan Press, 1941.

Essays on Rabindranath Tagore: In Honour of D.M. Gupta edited by T.R. Sharma. Ghaziabad: Vimal Prakashan, 1987.

Gitanjali (Song Offerings) with an Introduction by W. B. Yeats. London, 1913.

Glimpses of Bengal Life: Being Short Stories from the Bengali of Rabindranath Tagore translated by Rajani Ranjan Sen. Madras; Chittagong, 1913.

In Your Blossoming Flower-Garden: Rabindranath Tagore and Victoria Ocampo. Dyson, Ketaki Kushari. New Delhi: Sahitya Akademi, 1988.

Letters from Russia edited by Sasadhar Sinha. Calcutta: Visua-Bharati, 1960.

Mashi and Other Stories translated from the original Bengali by various writers. London: Macmillan, 1918.

My Reminiscences translated by Surendranath Tagore. New York: Macmillan, 1917.

Rabindranath Tagore: Prophet Against Totalitarianism. Rajendra Verma. London. 1964.

Rabindranath Tagore: The Myriad-Minded Man. Dutta, Krishna. London: Bloomsbury, 1995.

Rabindranath Tagore: Poet and Dramatist. Thompson, Edward John. London: Oxford University Press, 1948

Rabindranath Tagore: The Man and His Poetry. Roy, Basanta Koomar. New York, 1915.

Six Portraits of Rabindranath Tagore. Rothenstein, William. London, 1915.

Social Thinking of Rabindranath Tagore. Sasadhar, Sinha. London, 1962.

Song Offerings (Gitanjali) translated and Introduced by Joe Winter. London: Anvil, 2000.

Talks in China: Lectures Delivered in April and May, 1924. Calcutta: Visva-Bharati Book-Shop, 1925.

The Curse at Farewell translated by Edward Thompson. – London: Harrap, 1924.

The Cycle of Spring translated by Andrews and Nishikanta Sen. London: Macmillan, 1917.

The Home and the World translated by Surendranath Tagore, translation revised by Rabindranath Tagore. London: Macmillan, 1919.

The Hungry Stones and Other Stories translated from the original Bengali by various writers. London: Macmillan, 1916.

The Post Office: A Play translated by Devabrata Mukerjea. London: Macmillan, 1914.

The Religion of Man: Being the Hibbert Lectures for 1930. London: Allen & Unwin, 1931.

Wings of Death: The Last Poems of Rabindranath Tagore translated by Aurobindo Bose. London: Murray, 1960.

INDEX

J

M

N

O

P

Q

R

S

T

V